YOUR INCOME TAX

How to Save Money and Avoid Trouble

YOUR INCOME TAX

How to Save Money and Avoid Trouble

Joseph Newman — Directing Editor

U.S. NEWS & WORLD REPORT BOOKS

A division of U.S. News & World Report, Inc.

WASHINGTON, D.C.

Contents

Tables and Charts /9
Acknowledgments /10
1. Planning for Tax Savings /13
2. Are You Overpaying the Government? /29
3. Some ABCs of Income Tax /43
4. Don't Panic—It's Only Form 1040 /73
5. The Itemized Deductions /91
6. The Employe /121
7. The Executive /141
8. The Woman Who Works /165
9. The Outside Salesman /175
10. The Investor in Securities /181
11. The Home Owner and the Investor in Real Estate /197
12. The Art of Depreciation /221
13. The Businessman and the Professional Man /235
14. The Professional Corporation /259
15. The Farmer /273
16. The Retired Taxpayer /285
17. Tax Planning for Family Security /299
18. If You Are Audited . . . /311

Appendix

I—The Unallowables **/325**
II—Form 1040 **/335**
III—Federal Income Tax Rate Schedules **/338**
IV—Expense Account Records You Should Keep **/339**
V—Deductions for All Taxpayers **/341**
VI—Income Free of Tax **/343**
VII—Deductible Medical Expenses **/345**
VIII—Nondeductible Medical Expenses **/346**
IX—Deductions for the Outside Salesman **/347**
X—Employe's Business Deductions **/348**
XI—Expense Deductions for the Businessman and the Professional Man **/350**
XII—Deductions for the Farmer **/352**
XIII—Casualty Loss Deductions **/353**
Index **/355**

Tables
and
Charts

How Taxes Affect the Take-Home Pay of Working Wives /15
Who Files a Tax Return? /45
How to Calculate Your Income Tax /58-59
Computing the Capital Gains Tax /68
What Forms Do I Use? /78-79
Income Averaging: How to Do It /87
Average Deductions Claimed by Taxpayers /94
Deductions for an Office-at-Home /134
Apartments vs. Condominiums /208
Write-Off Percentages for Real Property /225

Acknowledgments

The editors of *U.S.News & World Report Books* have had the assistance of a number of economists, tax experts, and researchers in preparing the manuscript for *Your Income Tax—How to Save Money and Avoid Trouble*. They are particularly indebted to Sterling F. Green, former business news editor of the Associated Press, Washington, and now president of the Washington Forum, Inc., an information research service for institutional investors, for his work in connection with the research and the writing of the manuscript. A word of thanks also is due to Martin L. Kamerow, C.P.A., a senior partner in the firm of Harab, Kamerow & Serber, of Washington, D.C., for his help in gathering material, in securing the best available interpretations of new tax legislation, and in checking out the facts and figures in the text and the tables. Elizabeth Fagg Olds and Roslyn Grant edited the manuscript, rechecked the material, and saw it through the various stages of book production.

Form **1040**

US Department of the Treasury / Internal Revenue Service
Individual Income Tax Return

19___

1972, ending

For the year January 1–December 31, 1972, or other taxable year beginning...

First name and initial (if joint return, use first names and middle initials of both)

Last name

Your social security number (Husband's, if joint return)

Wife's number, if joint return

Present home address (number and street, including apartment number, or rural route)

Occu-pation

Years

City, town or post office, State and ZIP code

Wife's

Regular / 65 or over / Blind

Enter number of boxes checked

Filing Status—check only one:

1 ☐ Single

2 ☐ Married filing joint return (even if only one had income)

3 ☐ Married filing separately. If wife (husband) of your dependent children who lived with filing...

This is too difficult for a mathematician.
It takes a philosopher.

Albert Einstein, on completing his tax return

CHAPTER 1

Planning for Tax Savings

Taxes are probably the biggest item in your cost of living. With a good deal of help from inflation, they consume a rising portion of your income and erode your family's security.

If you are a salaried white collar employe, you probably spent 40 percent more for government last year than for food.

There is not much you can do about taxes except this: See that you don't pay any more than you are legally obliged to. This requires planning your personal finances—your everyday buying, saving, borrowing, giving, and investing—with the tax consequences always in mind.

This means learning enough about the federal income tax system so that you can take advantage of the scores of tax-saving opportunities that most taxpayers overlook each year.

It also means thinking in tax terms every day. Taxes should be a year-round concern, not just a once-a-year affliction. In computer jargon, this means you should crank a tax input into every decision about a mortgage, a doctor bill, a savings account, or a share of stock.

Yet the only time most taxpayers think of doing something about their taxes is once a year—the hours they spend actually grappling with Form

1040—or, more probably nowadays, when digging up the year's income and outgo records to deliver to a lawyer, accountant, or handy neighborhood tax service.

But when the April 15 deadline for filing the return draws near, it is too late to make any significant tax savings. You can, of course, pore over some hastily purchased newsstand "income tax guide." You can go to the tax booth in your supermarket or bank for a "quickie" tax preparation job. Or you can carry your receipts and canceled checks to a tax attorney or certified public accountant at the peak of his busy season. He will put the right numbers on the right lines and see that the arithmetic is correct. But the books actually were closed on your tax return back while you were singing Auld Lang Syne on New Year's Eve.

If you had talked to him in June or October, the tax professional might have spotted some opportunities for you. He might have suggested delaying some income until next year when taxes would be lower; taking some money from savings and putting it into a tax-exempt security; selling your money-losing shares of stock for a loss, to offset some taxable income; paying your church pledge and property tax in advance, so the deductions would ease the impact of a high-tax year.

Thinking of the tax consequences of every financial decision should be an all-year habit. It can become as automatic and natural as considering each family outlay in terms of its impact on the bank account.

Sometimes an advance peek into the tax consequences will complicate a seemingly easy family decision. Should your wife work? Why not? The family can use the extra money and the wife needs to break away from housework and the P.T.A.

But if the pay is important, look quite closely. A tidy little "second income" can dwindle, even vanish, when the tax take and the other added expenses of a working wife—like transportation, clothes, lunches, babysitter, and domestic help—are figured in.

The table following doesn't deal with the added outlays, just with the extra tax impact. It shows how much take-home pay is left to the wife when her income is added to her husband's on their federal and state income tax returns. On their joint return a big bite is taken from her income—one-third to one-half, and even more—because her pay is taxed at rates that start at the husband's top bracket and go up from there. Her Social Security is deducted too.

The disappointing result should not necessarily dissuade any wife from working; there are rewards other than the monetary ones. But the table should be consulted anyway, before the family makes plans to go to Europe on money that actually will wind up in the hands of the tax collector. The same considerations would hold if the wife were the major breadwinner and the husband's income secondary.

The table is useful, also, for a husband wondering whether to take a new job at higher pay. It shows how much he will really gain in spend-

How Taxes Affect the Take-Home Pay of Working Wives

Husband's tax- able income excluding wife's salary	Wife's Gross Salary					
	$2,000	$4,000	$6,000	$8,000	$10,000	$12,000
	Wife's Take-Home Pay After Taxes					
$ 8,000	$1,343	$2,686	$3,969	$5,252	$6,475	$7,698
12,000	1,283	2,566	3,789	5,012	6,155	7,298
16,000	1,223	2,446	3,589	4,732	5,795	6,858
20,000	1,143	2,286	3,349	4,412	5,415	6,418
24,000	1,063	2,126	3,129	4,132	5,075	6,018
32,000	943	1,886	2,769	3,652	4,475	5,298

Note: Includes 5 percent state tax (may vary from state to state); 5.85 percent Social Security tax; and federal income tax, computed at 1974 rates.

able income. If his taxable income is already upwards of $24,000, he will keep roughly half the pay increase.

The spoilers—inflation and taxes

Is tax planning worth all the trouble? It is, though many Americans do not realize how much tax they pay.

The average taxpayer is likely to think he has done rather well in the recent years of inflation if his pay has risen in step with living costs. He must think again. If his pay actually matched the price rises, he ends up a loser.

It works this way: If your pay rose from $10,000 in 1967 to $16,000 in 1975, your income just about matched the rise of 60 percent in the consumer price index. You had no more buying power, no more real income, than you started with. In fact you had less.

The pay increases pushed you up to higher tax rate brackets, increasing your overall rate of federal taxation. The tax rates themselves did not change; on the contrary, you got "tax relief" during this period—the personal exemptions were raised and the standard deduction was increased, for all taxpayers.

But an invisible tax process betrayed you. You had more dollars but less real income than you had eight years earlier. Experts have calculated that your 1975 income *actually came out substantially behind your 1967 income in real terms, after eight years of work, promotions, and pay increases.*

The invisible tax increase overtook you even while you climbed the income ladder; in the federal tax structure the tax rate brackets rise with bigger steps than the income brackets.

Over ten recent years your Social Security tax rose by 470 percent—from $174 in 1965 to $824.85 in 1975—and the total of your state and local income, sales, and property taxes moved to new high levels almost every year. Recently Congress has increased Social Security taxes by very large jumps— from a $468 maximum in 1972 to $631.80 in 1973, then to $772.20 in 1974, and on up to $824.85 in 1975. Those were the rates for employes; the maximums for self-employed persons went from $765 in 1972 to $960 in 1974 and then to $1,113.90 for 1975.

Here is another way to measure how the twin spoilers, taxes and inflation, have cheated you. If you had bought a city lot for $10,000 in 1967 and if you had found a buyer willing to pay $16,000 for it in 1975, you would have pocketed a $6,000 gain—in depreciated dollars. Actually you had no gain at all. The $16,000 would buy only what the $10,000 bought in 1967.

But you are taxed on the supposed gain of $6,000. You took a net loss on the transaction. The loss was the federal and state income tax you paid on your "profit," plus the local property tax you paid annually during your six years of ownership.

The gain was an illusion. The taxes were real.

The taxpayer finds it a tough game to beat when inflation hastens the tax erosion of the paycheck. He can hope that government policies will succeed in slowing the shrinkage of his income dollars. But he himself must learn how to hang on to more of the dollars.

This chapter mentions some of the basic strategies. It illustrates them, in briefest summary, with about eight examples of methods by which taxes can legally be avoided, reduced, or postponed. These are high spots and samples; later chapters provide further suggestions and the fuller details which can make these tax tools most useful.

First: Time your income and deductions to your own advantage.

Avoid having income bunch up in any year. An income bulge can lift you into a higher tax bracket. If this would be the effect of a substantial bonus, a large commission on a sale, or a fee for professional services, try to delay part of the payment until next year.

Postponing income sometimes can save you money even if you pay the same tax rate when your tax return ultimately is filed. This is because delaying the tax payment is the same as getting an interest-free loan from the government. As long as you have the money, it can be working for you in a savings account or other investment.

The delaying tactics should be followed whenever taxes are high and on their way down. Try to channel as much of your income as possible into the low-tax year.

If you itemize deductions, take the reverse tack with them. Crowd them into the high-tax year. If possible pay some or all of your property taxes before they are due; pay the church pledge ahead of time; catch up on waiting dental work.

But since Congress has increased the standard deduction, recheck whether you might now save more money by using it instead of itemizing. The standard deduction can be taken even if you had no deductible expense.

Or, if the standard deduction is fairly close to your total of itemized deductions, try "alternating": Pay in advance as many deductible expenses as possible, and in that year itemize. The next year, with fewer deductions, your total itemized deductions may fall below the amount allowed by the standard. This is the time to take the standard deduction. In the following year, back to itemizing. Some taxpayers save as much as $200 a year by this calculated switching.

The taxpayer who wants to do something about the timing of his income or deductions must plan ahead. Tax specialists usually advise taxpayers to review their tax outlook early in October. By then, they may know whether income will be higher or lower, whether investments will prove to be successful, and whether outlays should be hastened or slowed. Congress should have decided on any tax law changes. However, Congress no longer is dependable. It makes important tax changes, some retroactively, late in the year, sometimes deep in December. An October review is useful, but a constant year-round watch is better, with a late-year alert on Congress.

A newly liberalized device, income-averaging, can ease the tax pain of an unaccustomed jump in earnings. If your income is one-fifth higher than it averaged in the four preceding years and if the excess above one-fifth is more than $3,000, you can use the device profitably.

The excess income, called "averageable income," is taxed in effect as if it had been received in installments over five years. This lessens the impact of the one-year bulge.

A later chapter describes the case of the imaginary ballplayer, Joe Moore. He had a good year. His taxable income, usually about $14,000, shot up to $44,000. Without income averaging his tax would have been $14,060. "Averaging" made it $2,511 less.

Somewhat similar results can be obtained over a period of time by making an installment sale. You can take payments over two or more years and elect to pay your tax on the profit as the money comes in. If your income bulge was caused by the sale of a big item—a house, say, or an industrial tract—you can cushion the tax blow by taking 30 percent or less of the sale price in the year of sale and spreading the payments over at least two years.

If your profit is 25 percent on the deal, you pay tax each year on one-fourth of the payment you receive that year. The rest is a return on your investment, not taxed.

But heed what the tax specialists say: Income averaging may provide a better tax break than installment reporting of the tax.

There are other ways to defer income. An employe may be able to postpone some of his compensation by making an advance arrangement with his company that meets the rather strict income deferral rules of the Internal Revenue Service (IRS). Some of the payment could be scheduled for a future year or spread over several future years.

A self-employed individual has an even better opportunity to time income. An engineer, consultant, contractor, writer, or architect can fix the payment terms when he signs his contract. On a $120,000 job in 1972, an industrial designer might have specified payment over the next five years. If the payment were made all in the first year—assuming he was married and this was his only taxable income—the tax collector would have taken $52,060. With the fee spread over five years at $24,000 a year, the tax would be $28,300, or $23,760 less.

The designer had another choice; he could have used income averaging if he wanted to take the bulk of the income immediately. But the best tax bargain was to spread the income over several years.

Second: Take income in a form exempt from tax.

Fringe benefits are an obvious example. Tax-exempt bonds are another, for persons with more income. Company discounts to employes can be important tax savers.

Sometimes an employer is glad to give fringes instead of cash salary increases. He can deduct the cost to himself, give the employes a tax-free form of compensation, and promote employe goodwill. Usually fringes are tax bargains for the employe even when he contributes to part of the cost.

When an employe gets a health and hospital plan for which his company pays $15 a month, he is more than $15 ahead. Because of taxes he probably would have to earn at least $20 a month to have enough left to pay the $15 monthly premium.

Full-time use of a company car may be worth $1,500 to $2,000 a year. This is in effect tax-free income. If the employe had bought the car himself, he would have had to pay for it out of what the tax collector left him. A $50,000 life insurance policy may be worth $1,000 a year tax-free to the employe; as group insurance, it costs the employer much less, and the employer can deduct the amount as a business expense.

The higher your tax bracket, the more valuable the fringes become. To an upper-level employe in the 50 percent tax bracket, any fringe is worth twice its face value. He would have to earn $500 to pay for a free benefit which costs his employer $250.

You do not need management status to enjoy fringes, in most companies. Besides pensions, insurance, and health plans, there may be parking rights, discounts on the company's products, sick leave, clinic and infirmary service, sometimes the right to buy shares of stock at a bargain price.

An upper-middle-income taxpayer can get significant benefit from one of the most popular of all tax shelters: the tax-exempt bonds of state and municipal governments.

Their interest earnings sound low. But for a family with $20,000 taxable income, a municipal bond paying 6 percent is just as good an investment as a high-grade corporation bond paying 9 percent. Why? Because the federal tax collector would take about one-third of the earnings of the corporate bond. He gets none of the earnings from the municipals. (They usually are exempt from state taxes, too, in the state where issued.)

The higher your tax bracket, the more you save by buying municipals. A couple in the 50 percent bracket would have to find a corporate bond paying 12 percent to match the income from a 6 percent municipal; at the 60 percent tax rate, a 15 percent bond.

Third: Take income in a form on which the tax can be postponed.

Your employer's contributions to a pension, annuity, profit-sharing or other retirement plan are a tax break for you. You are not taxed on the money until it is paid out to you, usually upon your retirement. Then your tax rate presumably will be lower.

The funds piling up in the pension trust earn interest tax-free. If the employe wishes, he can take his retirement fund in a lump sum instead of monthly payments; in that case, part of it can be taxed at the lower rate provided for capital gains, as described in a later chapter, "The Retired Taxpayer."

Self-employed businessmen can set up their own retirement programs. Recently liberalized rules let them contribute up to 15 percent of their net income into a Treasury-approved plan and take deductions for the amount—up to $7,500 a year. Contributions up to $750 are permitted even if these exceed the 15 percent limit. The contributions earn income in the retirement fund, and this income is not taxed as it accumulates. These rules are amendments to the Keogh Act.

If you were in the 40 percent tax bracket and put $2,500 a year into such a plan, the tax deduction would cut your tax bill by $1,000. Your actual net outlay toward retirement therefore would be only $1,500, but your retirement fund would grow by $2,500 a year, plus its tax-sheltered earnings.

Incorporation provides even better tax-sheltered retirement benefits. If you, as a self-employed business or professional man, want to make larger tax-free contributions to your own retirement than the plans for self-employed individuals permit—and receive a much bigger pension upon retirement—you should consider incorporating.

Many proprietors of small businesses have done so, for exactly those reasons. They become employes of their own corporation; the corporation in turn makes tax-deductible contributions to their retirement funds up to 15 percent of income for profit-sharing plans, with no income limit for pensions. There are many other benefits in incorporation, and some drawbacks. They are described in two later chapters, "The Businessman and the Professional Man" and "The Professional Corporation."

Fourth: Take income when possible in a form that is taxed at lower rates.

Long-term capital gains—the profit made on the sale of securities, real estate, and some other kinds of property held for more than six months —are taxed at a rate never higher than half the ordinary income rate.

Sophisticated taxpayers therefore seek capital gains. Hence the preference of many stock market investors for "growth issues"; the investor is more interested in prospective price increases than in prospective dividends. He would pay much less tax on his profit from selling the stock than on his dividend income.

(But do not forget that Congress has decreed that the first $100 of dividend income is "excluded" from taxable income; that much is totally tax-free. If your dividend income is higher than that, you can turn over some of the stock to your wife or children. Each one gets a separate $100 exclusion. There have been proposals to close this minor loophole, but until that happens the "dividend exclusion" remains an aid to small investors.)

The capital gains rate is one of the charms of real estate investment for both big-scale investors and the ordinary taxpayer who sells a house, a farm, or a lot.

And if you are approaching retirement and thinking of selling your house and taking an apartment, consider waiting a bit. At age sixty-five or over you pay no tax on any gain arising from the first $20,000 of the price you get. If the house sells for $20,000 or less, your whole profit is tax-free.

If you face a loss in selling your house, you may do better to rent it before making the sale. A loss on the sale of a personal residence is not deductible; but if the house is rented before it is sold it becomes an income property; the government may let you deduct the loss by methods described in a later chapter.

Fifth: Know and use the legal deductions and exemptions.

If you earn money on your own, outside your regular job, you can set up your own tax-sheltered self-employment retirement plan. *You can take tax deductions currently for the amounts you invest in it,* up to the limits fixed by the Keogh Act. Even if you also participate in a company pension plan, the Keogh Act lets you contribute up to 15 percent of your self-employment income into an approved retirement fund for yourself, to a maximum of $7,500 a year.

If you use a car or any other property entirely for business, the $100 floor for a casualty or vandalism loss for personal property does not apply.

If you use a car 75 percent for business, and you suffer an uninsured loss of $200 from vandalism or accident, your loss deduction is $150. The business loss is wholly deductible—75 percent of $200, or $150. The 25 percent of the loss attributable to personal use, $50, is not deductible.

Your dependency exemptions are worth some advance planning. Sometimes you can gain an exemption by a single switch of family financing arrangements.

Take, for instance, the case of the George Walkers and their daughter Jill, nineteen, a student at the local college. Jill would qualify as a dependent except that her part-time job this year will pay her $1,900. George Walker, in his December checkup on the year's tax situation, realizes that the family is providing only about $1,850; to claim Jill as an exemption, the law says, the Walkers must provide more than half her support. This is what George did:

Knowing that Jill intended to buy some clothes for the holidays, he suggested that she put $100 into her savings account instead, to pay part of the cost of a planned ski trip in January. The Walkers bought her the clothes. Thus, Jill provided only $1,800 of her own support (because money saved is not counted as support), and the Walkers provided $1,950 (because clothing—like food, shelter, education and medical care—is a basic item of support).

By adding $100 to their support contribution, the Walkers gained a $750 tax exemption.

If you are buying a house, the costs of mortgage interest and real estate taxes will be so high that it is almost safe to say that you should itemize your deductions. Make sure you know them all.

Home buyers should remember to deduct not only the interest portion of their monthly mortgage payments but also any "points" they had to pay the lender to get the home loan. And if a penalty charge is made for paying off a mortgage ahead of schedule—or an auto loan or any other installment contract—that, too, is deductible.

If you use part of your house regularly as an office or work area, a portion of the upkeep and other costs of your home may be deductible as a business expense.

It is easier than it used to be to claim this office-at-home deduction. The IRS for years has held that an employe must show that the conditions of his job *require* him to provide space or facilities for work at home. The United States Tax Court has been overruling the IRS, taking a less stringent line. The court has allowed deductions if the employe proved that the office-at-home was "appropriate and helpful" in performing his work. Another court rejected the "appropriate and helpful" guideline, and IRS has given ground reluctantly. It will be wise to be cautious.

For the millions who "moonlight" at second jobs nowadays, it often is possible to establish the office-at-home deduction. If one room of a six-room dwelling is used exclusively for such income-producing work, for example, the taxpayer may deduct one-sixth of his outlays for depreciation, repairs, maintenance, utilities, and domestic help. If the room is available for family use half the day, he must halve the deduction; he could claim only one-twelfth of his household costs.

A doctor who has an office in his residence, or a lawyer who consults with clients in an office in his home, can claim a portion not only of the usual maintenance and operating costs but also of the landscaping, fencing, shrubbery and lawn upkeep.

Moving expense deductions have been liberalized for employes who are transferred to another city, or who go on their own to take new jobs. Self-employed persons also can now claim these deductions, which formerly were available only to employes. The deductions cover the actual, reasonable expenses of moving household goods and personal belongings, as well as the cost of transportation, meals, and lodging en route for the whole family.

Various expenses only indirectly connected with the actual move now are deductible—even house-hunting trips for the taxpayer and family after he has obtained the job, and temporary living costs for up to thirty days while waiting to occupy the new quarters.

With or without an office-at-home, the taxpayer who is required to spend money for business purposes on professional publications, an extra telephone extension, professional organization dues, equipment, instruments, typewriter, office machines, expenses for typing, duplicating, or copying can claim a deduction for business expenses.

The ownership of income-producing property can sometimes produce a loss for tax purposes while the taxpayer actually breaks even or produces a profit, even if the property is only a house that is rented. The rules for depreciation are a help.

For instance, Landlady Murphy rents a house for $4,800 a year. She spends $4,080 on taxes, upkeep, mortgage payments and operating costs. Her net cash proceeds are $720 for the year. But the factors of depreciation and mortgage interest give a tax loss of $80. She can use this loss to offset that much of her income from other sources.

The principle is the same, but magnified, in a big apartment project. Its profitability is helped along by the "rapid write-off" of depreciation, a device designed to encourage the building of rental housing. The owner has been permitted to deduct twice as much for depreciation at the outset as would be allowed under the usual "straight-line" method of deducting the same amount for each year—a welcome starting "bonus."

This write-off—plus the deduction for interest payments on the mortgage which largely financed the structure and the usual deductions for operation and upkeep cost—frequently results in zero profit, or a net loss, on the owner's tax return. But he may actually have tucked away a 9 or 10 percent gain for the year.

Taxpayers should consult the latest tax rules before claiming the "rapid write-off" of depreciation, however. The rules could be changed; the device has been under strong attack in Congress as a frequently-abused tax loophole.

The deductions available for charitable and medical outlays, state and local taxes, interest charges, and casualty losses fill many later pages of this book. Here are a few that are often overlooked:

• Using your automobile for business entitles you to deduct depreciation on the car. If one-third of your driving is for business, a third of the annual depreciation can be deducted.

• The IRS permits a flat mileage deduction for business travel. It has been 15 cents a mile for the first 15,000 miles and 10 cents a mile thereafter, but, before taking the flat allowance, check whether it has been increased. The Treasury raises the mileage rate periodically, as gasoline and other auto costs go up. If your car costs more to run than the flat mileage deduction—as many cars do—keep a record of the actual costs and claim them. If you use the flat mileage method, add turnpike and bridge tolls, as well as parking charges.

• Deductions for state gasoline taxes are not questioned if they conform to the tables provided by the IRS with your Form 1040. However, if your car burns more gas than the fifteen-miles-per-gallon average used by IRS, you can take a proportionately larger deduction.

• The state sales tax tables provided with Form 1040 do not necessarily limit your claim to deductions. The sales tax on any major purchase—a car, camper or boat for example—can be added to the amount shown on the table.

• The medical deduction is broader in certain respects than some suppose. Outlays that would not usually be deductible become so when a doctor certifies that they are needed—for instance, a swimming pool, home air conditioning, or an elevator; a trip to a warmer or drier climate (but not meals and lodging while there); a parent's trip to visit an ailing child, when a doctor said it would help the child. A woman claimed a wig as a medical expense after a disease caused her hair to fall out; she was supported by her doctor who said it was necessary for her mental health. The cost of birth control pills purchased by a woman for her personal use under a doctor's prescription is deductible. Men may deduct the cost of legal vasectomies to prevent conception. A woman who undergoes a legal abortion to end a pregnancy, at her own request, may deduct the total cost. Of course, these medical expenses are deductible only to the extent that they are not covered by insurance.

• It is wise to check before the year-end whether medical outlays already have reached the amount which will make a deduction possible, 3 percent of the adjusted gross income. If they have, that is the year to get all the family's waiting medical needs taken care of, along with dentures, dental work, eyeglasses or contact lenses, and hearing aids. All will be fully deductible. If you delay them until next year, the 3 percent limit must be reached again before any of them can be deducted.

• If you drive your car in the service of a church or charity, you can deduct either the actual costs or 7 cents a mile (after checking whether the 7-cent allowance has been increased).

• Not a big item, but worth remembering: Small cash contributions to charity will be accepted by IRS without proof, up to a reasonable amount. Some offices allow up to $70, others to $94.

• Your charitable contribution goes farther if it is an art object, rare coins, books or other articles which have increased in value. If you paid $200 for a rare book that is now worth $450 and if you sold the book, you would be taxed on the $250 gain. If you give it to a church instead, you escape the tax and get the full $450 as a deduction. The church can sell the book for the full $450 and keep the whole sum, tax free.

• The same kind of everybody-wins results are obtained by donating stocks which have risen in value.

Sixth: Divert income to someone who has a lower tax rate.

One way of doing this is hiring a son or daughter. It is easy if yours is a family business; IRS requires only that the child carry a regular workload and get the same pay and treatment as other employes. A taxpayer who employs typists, researchers, filing clerks or other helpers occasionally in income-producing activities may also adopt this method of keeping the money in the family while paring taxes. Father gets a deduction for the wages paid. The child, having relatively small earnings, pays tax at a low rate or no tax at all.

Outright giving-while-living is another tax-saving technique. You cannot give away part of your income without first paying tax on it. But you can give away *property that produces income,* such as securities or real estate, so that someone else is taxed on the income. You can place the property in the hands of a child, aged parent or other dependent whose income tax rate is low. You may have a gift tax to pay, but the rate is fairly low and the exemptions reasonably generous.

If you give property, of course, it is gone forever. You cannot legally control or reclaim it. There is another way, however, to divert income without forever losing control of the income-producing property. That is to create a trust—in effect, to "give birth to a new tax person" who pays a lower tax rate.

The real estate or securities are placed in custody of a legal trustee, often a bank trust officer. The income may be made payable to a child, to build up a fund for college education, or to an elderly parent or other beneficiary.

A time limit may be fixed for the trust's existence; it may not be less than ten years. The taxpayer who created the trust saves the tax on the income it generates. He loses control of the property only during the ten-year trusteeship. When the trust expires the property reverts to him.

Seventh: Learn which exclusions and credits you are legally entitled to take, and take them.

Taxpayers should make sure they know which types of income are not taxed. There are many—Social Security payments, workmen's compensation, and dividends on life insurance policies, for instance.

Watch, also, for the several tax-savers which can be subtracted from your gross income before you actually start figuring your tax bill. One of these is employes' moving expenses, newly liberalized. Another is sick pay, the payments you receive during absence from your job because of illness or accident. A third is the contribution of a self-employed person to his retirement plan. A fourth is very important—the business expenses of an employe. Costs of travel for your employer are subtracted in this way.

It is important to get these deductions in the right place on Form 1040. Any payments that a taxpayer can subtract from his gross income are more valuable to him than they would be if they were taken as itemized deductions; the reasons are set out in the chapter, "Some ABCs of Income Tax."

Tax-wise ears also prick up at mention of "tax credits." A credit is a super-deduction, one of the more agreeable things that happen to a taxpayer.

A deduction reduces the amount of income that is taxed; a credit is subtracted from the tax itself. So, if you are in the 30 percent tax bracket, a $100 deduction saves you $30. A $100 credit saves you $100.

The Retirement Income Credit is an example. It is a complicated device intended to help those retired taxpayers who do not receive Social Security benefits, or whose Social Security pensions are small. Because of its difficulty, many older taxpayers do not even try to compute it.

The maximum credit provided for 1971 was $343 for a retired couple, which does not sound impressive. But it means that an elderly couple may be relieved of tax on up to $2,286 of income. So the credit is worth learning about and using; any IRS office will help with the computation.

The old investment credit, renamed the Job Development Investment Credit, was restored by the 1969 tax law, despite opponents who called it a bonanza for big business. It may be that, but it also is a boon to small businessmen, including self-employed persons, retailers, repairmen, contractors, professional men and women, and many others.

The law permitted companies and individuals to subtract from the federal tax they otherwise would owe, 7 percent of the cost of new equipment, instruments, and machinery. Then, to fight recession, the credit was increased for 1975 and 1976 to 10 percent for all companies. It seemed possible that this rate might be extended in future years.

The investment credit became in effect a 10 percent federal subsidy of the cost of equipment and machinery.

It has been a boon to taxpayers as well as a spur to investment and a prop for business. But it must be considered an unreliable prop. When inflation gets too hot, Congress always considers repealing or reducing the investment credit to cool off the economy.

Eighth: Keep taxes in mind when you decide whether to be a sole proprietor, partnership, or corporation.

Thousands of doctors are switching from their sole practices or partnerships to the incorporated practice of medicine. Why? For one reason, in most cases: Corporate practice can provide important tax benefits, including tax-sheltered retirement plans far more generous than are available to them as self-employed professionals or partners.

This book devotes a chapter to the tax phenomenon of the professional corporation. It describes the arguments for and against, the legal requirements, and the tax procedures of corporate practice in terms that apply not only to doctors but also to architects, accountants, artists and artisans, dentists, economists, engineers, and all other professionals.

One example, summarized from the text, is illuminating: Dr. A, with a taxable income of $52,000, pays about $18,000 income tax. If he incorporates—and thus becomes an employe of his own corporation—the corporation can, for example, put $12,000 a year into a tax-sheltered retirement fund for him.

That would seem to mean a $12,000 cut in his current take-home pay, but it does not. The cut is roughly $6,000, because he saves the other $6,000 on his personal income tax (since only about half of the $12,000 would have been take-home pay if he had received it as salary; the tax collector would have got the rest). And the money he paid into the pension fund accumulates free of current taxation—which means that over a period of years it grows about twice as fast as if he had put it into an ordinary investment paying the same rate of interest.

Another chapter discusses the tax aspects of various forms of doing business—proprietorship, partnership, ordinary corporation, and the hybrids called small business corporations or Subchapter S corporations.

Each has distinct tax advantages. These alone should not govern a taxpayer's decision on how to manage his affairs or organize his business. Other factors frequently outweigh them.

But tax considerations are becoming more and more important for every American. They figure very prominently among the factors to be taken into account in the making of personal financial moves and major business decisions.

The most important of the potential tax savers mentioned in this chapter, like the others described in following chapters, do not just happen. They come about because the taxpayer has planned his financial affairs to *make* them happen.

The legal right of a taxpayer to decrease the amount of what otherwise would be his taxes, or altogether avoid them, by means which the law permits, cannot be doubted.

Justice George Sutherland, in Gregory vs. Helvering

CHAPTER 2

Are You
Overpaying
the
Government?

The income tax is a graduated tax. Taxpayers with lower income are taxed at a lower rate. On upper levels of income the tax rises to very high percentages.

A glimpse at the Tax Rate Schedules furnished with your Form 1040 shows high bracket rates up to 70 percent. The schedules indicate, for example, that a married man with $100,000 income is handing more than $45,000 of it over to the U.S. Treasury.

Actually, no $100,000-a-year executive pays that much income tax. Nor does anyone with an income of $200,000 give the government $110,980 of it—as the tax schedule indicates—plus 70 cents out of every additional dollar.

The taxes really paid by most people in the high-income groups may be half the amounts shown in the Tax Schedules. Or, quite possibly, less than half. This is because the seemingly straightforward theory of the graduated income tax—low rates for low incomes, higher rates on higher incomes, so that all Americans are taxed according to their ability to pay —is not a simple progression. It never has been. For one thing, the peak rates apply only to the topmost slice of any taxpayer's income.

More importantly, the income tax rate progression is overlaid by detours, beltways, freeways, and bypasses. These are the innumerable tax preferences, credits, exemptions, and deductions. Each represents a saving to some group of taxpayers. Usually the biggest savings go to the wealthiest taxpayers. One important reason is that a "capital gain"—profit from the sale of an asset such as stocks or real estate—is taxed at half, or less, of the regular tax rates. To get this preferred rate you must first have assets to sell.

Another tax shelter—probably the biggest and easiest of all—is the exemption from tax of the interest earned on state and municipal bonds. If your income consisted solely of such interest, you would pay no federal income tax at all even if your income were a million dollars a year.

Clearly, it takes affluence to buy your way into the comfortably tax-sheltered set. You must start by having the money to buy the stocks and bonds, real estate, oil holdings, works of art, rare stamps or coins, or whatever your shelter may be.

At the bottom of the income scale, the tax is zero. The 1969 tax law alone, by raising the income level at which taxation begins, added about 5 million families to the number who pay no tax because their incomes are below the poverty level.

But the tax burden remains heavy on the taxpayers in between. It hits especially those earning modest middle and upper-middle incomes—families, say, with $15,000 to $50,000 a year. They represent about one-fourth of all who pay income taxes, but they contribute about three-fifths of the total amount collected by the government.

In recent years, the middle-income taxpayer has been called the forgotten man of the federal tax system. Part of his problem, however, is self-neglect. Usually, he does not take all the deductions to which he is entitled. Frequently, he forgets to claim legitimate business expenses.

The Internal Revenue Service probably will catch any of his errors in arithmetic and either send him a bill for tax due or a refund for overpayment. If it notices that he has claimed a deduction not provided by the law, the process of examining his return and disallowing the deduction will start automatically. Or, if the taxpayer has failed to report some income of which the government was informed by the person who paid it, the IRS will question him and charge him for additional tax.

But if he fails to claim a deduction to which he is legally entitled, through oversight or ignorance, the IRS has no way to spot the omission or give credit for it. "Loopholes" exist for the little taxpayer as well as for the big one. But he must know enough about the tax rules to take advantage of them. Even if someone else prepares the tax return for him, no one else can make the family financial decisions that mean a tax saving or a tax squeeze.

Nobody else can do it

Fewer than half of all tax returns are prepared by the taxpayer himself. In many cases, professional guidance is advisable—for instance, when major investments or creation of tax-saving trusts are involved.

Some taxpayers simply need help with reading, writing, or arithmetic. Others are frightened by legal-sounding language and official-looking forms. The abolition of the simple punchcard Form 1040A in 1969 sent millions of low-income taxpayers seeking outside help. The restoration of a form almost as simple for 1972 and after, called the Short Form 1040A, was intended to lure the millions back to do-it-yourself tax return preparation. But the sheer bulk of the Form 1040 package, with its instructions and dozens of supplemental forms and schedules, is discouraging even to taxpayers of some sophistication.

The helper might be a family friend, a relative, the family lawyer, the low-price neighborhood tax service, or the high-priced professional.

The temptation is strong, if one has a trusted tax adviser, to hand him the whole distasteful job and be done with it, to pay him his fee, settle with the government on terms he prescribes and save time and temper ——but not necessarily money.

If you have been missing your tax-saving opportunities all year, you cannot make up for them in January by handing a tax adviser your year's accumulation of canceled checks and bills marked "paid."

A tax counselor, whether amateur or professional, is not a magician. He can do more or less for you depending on what you have done beforehand. He cannot be at your elbow all year to help you make the personal decisions that bear tax consequences. You must make these decisions yourself. And if you do not know the tax consequences—or don't know that tax consequences exist—you may be missing legitimate savings.

The sensible taxpayer must learn for himself at least the basic tax principles that affect his family budget. He should also gain the confidence to claim all the tax savings to which he is entitled.

Every tax professional meets a taxpayer now and then who does not claim a perfectly legitimate and substantial deduction because, he says, "I don't want the government investigating me." Many taxpayers pass up savings because they are not sure they understand the rules. "Don't get fancy and wind up in trouble," they tell themselves.

Others simply have not gained the habit of thinking in tax terms. This is true even of many wealthy taxpayers. In 1966, the Brookings Institution published a study of 957 high-income Americans conducted by University of Michigan researchers. It was titled "Economic Behavior of the Affluent."

The subjects of the survey were men who stood to save thousands of dollars a year, perhaps tens of thousands, by weighing the tax results of every financial decision they made. Surprisingly few of them did so. The study disclosed:

"Although they (the high-income men) are aware of many opportunities for reducing their taxes, most of these opportunities are regarded as involving more trouble than they are worth, and the only ones of which they frequently take advantage are those associated with capital gains, tax-exempt securities, and the making of gifts."

For everyone, the income tax exacts a toll not only of earnings but of time and patience. It is something we would rather not think about until we have to—once a year.

The burden is particularly annoying because it is a constantly shifting one. Congress changes the laws. The Treasury revises the regulations. The courts reverse the Treasury. Tax-avoidance loopholes are forever being discovered; by the time they become popular, the Treasury plugs them up. Then new ones are developed. It was once estimated that there are about 40,000 changes in the federal tax structure each year.

It is a real temptation to give Uncle Sam more than he asks, just to save time and sanity. You will do better, financially, if you resist that temptation by learning the basic tax consequences of your own earning, spending, borrowing and giving.

If you do, you will avoid most ordinary pitfalls. You will also know when it is time to call in an expert.

How it grew

The Internal Revenue Code is a tome of more than 1,000 pages.

It is a vast, complex lacework of interlocked laws. Its workings are explained and interpreted by U.S. Treasury Department regulations. These total another 3,000 pages for the income tax alone.

The Internal Revenue Service, which is the arm of the Treasury that administers and enforces the code, issues scores of different types of rulings every week describing how the tax laws apply to various situations.

And finally, decisions made at each level of the federal court system including the United States Tax Court fix the authority for what the law means and how it is applied, in the solving of conflicts between taxpayers and the government.

The English tariff system was the beginning of taxes in the United States. The colonies disliked a tariff imposed from without, and demonstrated their dislike by the Boston Tea Party. But they had their own tariffs and imposed duties even on imports from each other.

So the tariff was a going institution when the United States was born, and it became a federal monopoly at that moment.

A form of income tax also existed in colonial times. In 1646 Massachusetts had a tax on every laborer, artisan and tradesman. This was called a "faculty tax"; the amount varied from one trade to another according to the usual income in each calling, so it was indeed an income tax in principle.

But the Constitution of the newly independent nation said that no direct tax could be imposed unless the amount to be collected was apportioned among the states on the basis of population. Those who feared too much power in the central government thus planned to block any imposition of direct taxes by Congress. They succeeded, for generations. Direct taxation was simply not practical when poor states had to contribute as much tax revenue per citizen as rich states.

The pressure of the national crisis in the War of 1812 did cause a brief resort to direct taxes. They were used again in the Civil War; an income tax was imposed in 1861. It was a levy of 3 percent on all income over $800 a year. By 1865 it had risen to 5 percent on all incomes between $600 and $5,000 and 19 percent on the amount above $5,000.

This first trial of the income tax by the national government was a successful revenue-raiser. It had been conveniently assumed, during the emergency, that the income tax was an indirect tax and therefore constitutional. In 1872, with the emergency over, it was discontinued. But in 1894, when the government imposed the income tax again, the Supreme Court held that it was a direct tax which would have to be apportioned among the states according to population.

This was impossible. The income tax was canceled. The government got along with tariffs, liquor and tobacco taxes and other devices, but the financial strain increased. In 1909 a tax of 1 percent was imposed on income over $5,000 of every corporation doing busines for profit. This was declared legal on the grounds that it was a tax on the privilege of doing business, not a tax on income.

But a permanent solution came on February 25, 1913, when the Sixteenth Amendment to the Constitution was adopted. It provided:

"The Congress shall have the power to lay and collect taxes on incomes from whatever source derived, without apportionment among the several states, and without regard to any census or enumeration."

Congress quickly went to work on a law taxing all incomes. It was enacted October 3, 1913, and made retroactive to March 1; it has been altered, amended and developed continuously since then, but it is the same tax law that now produces 70 percent of the federal revenues.

From the day of its beginning, the income tax has been graduated, or "progressive." There was a normal tax of 1 percent on income above a "personal exemption"; the exemption then was $3,000 for single persons and $4,000 for couples. On top of that was a "surtax"; it began at $20,000; it was progressive, with rates ranging from 1 percent on incomes of $20,000 to $50,000 up to 6 percent on incomes over $500,000.

The principle was the same as in today's much steeper progression. The taxable income of the individual was divided into levels, or "brackets," and the rate of tax increased from one bracket to the next.

With World War I the income tax became not only higher but more complex and contradictory; the rates were lowered after 1918, but there never has been relief from the complexities. World War II brought soaring new rates and some novelties—a tax on excess profits of businesses, and a "defense tax"—actually, the addition of a percentage to the total of tax normally computed. A similar surcharge was reimposed for two years during the Vietnam War; something like it may return whenever the Treasury again becomes seriously strapped for revenue.

Perhaps the most important World War II innovation was the withholding system. The wartime rates were so toweringly high that meeting the April 15 tax bill became an almost insurmountable financial hurdle for millions of taxpayers. A merchant and former chairman of the Federal Reserve Bank of New York, Beardsley Ruml, proposed that the taxes be withheld at the source—that is, held out of the paycheck by the employer when he distributed wage payments—so that the tax would be paid in smaller, more frequent and relatively painless installments.

The "Ruml Plan" was tried out in 1943 with a six-month Victory Tax. It worked. At midyear general withholding went into effect, and employers became permanent collectors of a large portion of the nation's income tax; they were supplied with "withholding tables" telling them how much to withhold from each worker's pay.

The income tax has become such a potent force in the national economy that the White House and Congress cannot resist trying to manipulate it to achieve economic goals. In 1964 the greatest tax reduction in history gave citizens greater take-home pay and helped launch a prolonged economic boom. A few years later, the Vietnam War surtax was imposed not only to help finance the war but to repress inflation.

Presidents have pondered longingly the idea of asking Congress for the power to make small adjustments, up or down, in income taxes to offset the forces of inflation and recession. Some influential economists argue that such smaller and more frequent tax rate changes—more frequent, that is, than Congress has been willing to approve in the past—would help keep the economy on a more stable economic course.

Other factors also have helped bring tax policy to a fluid state. The tax law has been festooned over the years with exemptions, deductions, preferences, credits and allowances. Some were intended to insure fairness among different groups of taxpayers; many were designed to foster investment and economic expansion, such as the low capital gains rate and the investment credit; many others were meant to serve socially desirable ends such as home ownership and charitable giving.

A good many of the preferences have been abused. Many were converted into avenues of tax avoidance for the well-to-do; or they proved to be primarily subsidies to certain industries. As the late-1960s added serious inflation to the rising burden of state, local and federal taxes, public resentment was heightened by the disclosure that some persons with lofty incomes found ways to pay little or no income tax.

A so-called "taxpayers' revolt"—a purely vocal but massive wave of protest from press and public—influenced Congress to pass the Tax Reform Act of 1969; many revenue leaks were closed, but the reforms were coupled with amendments providing various degrees of tax relief to most taxpayers. Simultaneous enactment of spending programs left the government with record-breaking deficits.

Many economists have predicted that some increase in basic rates, perhaps only temporary, will come in the 1970s. In any case, the public demand for tax reform has not abated. Congress has been bombarded with reform proposals intended to increase revenues by closing more "loopholes" instead of raising tax rates, and to insure that all taxpayers carry their fair share of the burden. Reform legislation was foreseen, perhaps in installments throughout the 1970s. Yet simultaneously Congress has enacted new preferences, creating new tax leaks while plugging some old ones; opinions differ on what constitutes "reform."

The wise taxpayer, therefore, will keep a constant weather-watch on Congress. It is important to stay abreast of changes in tax laws and switches in IRS policy—and to shift the family's financial pattern, when possible, to cushion the impact of rising rates or take advantage of new tax breaks that will be coming.

Keep alert, because change is in the wind. Senator Wallace Bennett of Utah stressed that point in a 1972 speech to the American Bar Association. He said:

"On Capitol Hill we've succeeded in amending the old adage so that today nothing in this world is certain except death, taxes, and tax reform."

Is it ethical?

You should protect from the tax collector every cent you can, honestly and legally. You have no obligation to overpay the government. The taxpayer who exceeds requirements of the law hurts only himself.

On the other hand, the right to use the loopholes is not a license to cheat. The tax saving suggestions in this book are techniques of tax avoidance, not "tax evasion." Tax avoidance means making use of the preferences and advantages that the law provides. Tax evasion is stealing.

There is also the middle ground of legitimate difference of opinion. In a vast number of cases the taxpayer finds himself in a gray area: there is no clear answer whether certain income is taxable or tax-free, whether certain costs are deductible. Since the taxpayer has a positive right to pay no more than the law requires, he has equally the right to take a position on the disputed issue, assert his view, and use every weapon in the law, including resort to the courts, to minimize his tax liability.

Tax evasion is quite different. Willful, deliberate evasion of the tax law is a federal criminal offense. The tax law is perhaps more widely violated—and often in proportion to the misdeed the violations more lightly punished—than any other federal law. Tax evasion is theft, however, from those who pay their taxes honestly because it means that all tax rates are higher.

Occasionally someone is heard to boast of a feat of tax evasion: some income has been hidden successfully; a deduction has been inflated; an accounting of business costs has been doctored; or a vacation has been taken at the Treasury's expense. Even when big-scale cheaters are caught and punished, the penalties usually are comparatively light. They seldom involve prison terms, and the public is less outraged than it might be if, for instance, the same sum had been embezzled by a bank president or taken in armed robbery.

Sometimes tax evasion is condoned by those who engage in it on the ground that "the big boys get away with murder—I'm just saving a few dollars that I wouldn't owe anyway if the laws were enforced."

It is probably true that all Americans would pay taxes with better grace if more of the "big boys" were caught. But the honesty of taxpaying Americans still is a source of wonder in other countries. Some 97 percent of the $250 billion collected in all types of taxes is paid voluntarily or withheld at the source.

This remains true year after year, even though the nation's tax collector—the Internal Revenue Service—lacks either the funds or staff to police the taxpaying habits of most Americans. The IRS detects a relatively small percentage of the evasions with the help of experienced agents, informers and its technique of investigating, or "auditing," individual returns.

But Congress has shown willingness lately to tighten up some loose provisions of tax law which invite evasion. And more funds are being asked of Congress to build up the enforcement capability of the IRS.

A computer system now in nationwide operation catches obvious errors and pinpoints any returns that look odd. It helps IRS agents pick up about $3 billion a year in tax deficiencies through individual audits. It also is a deterrent to tax evasion because taxpayers know that employers, banks and corporations are sending in reports on wages, fees, interest and dividends paid. The time is nearing when all these can be matched up readily by computer with the income reported by taxpayers.

Consequently, there is increasing assurance that honesty is the best tax policy.

Tax avoidance is not cheating. Some taxpayers feel guilty about scraping up every possible penny of deductions. They feel it somehow unfair to take advantage of the tax breaks given them. They are wrong.

The fairness of the tax system as a whole can be questioned. As noted, the principle of the "progressive" or graduated income tax is defeated in part by tax preferences. Lacking opportunity to claim business deductions or use tax shelters, the low-income worker often pays a higher tax, in proportion to income, than the well-paid executive or upper-income professional. John L. Springer commented in his book, *Financial Self-Defense:*

"No one can deny that the tax system is unfair. But as President John F. Kennedy once said, life itself is unfair. And unless and until the law is changed, you are entitled to every legitimate way to minimize your tax load."

Though they were written in 1934, the words of the late distinguished Judge Learned Hand are often quoted by lawyers in this connection:

"Anyone may so arrange his affairs that his taxes should be as low as possible; he is not bound to choose that pattern which best pays the Treasury. Everyone does it, rich and poor alike, and all do right; for nobody owes any public duty to pay more than the law demands; taxes are enforced exactions and not voluntary contributions. To demand more in the name of morals is mere cant."

The taxpayer who ignores his opportunities for tax savings does himself, his family and his heirs a disfavor. His taxes are as high as Congress wants them to be. The exemptions, deductions and credits are part of the tax law. They were put into it by Congress deliberately, to serve some real or supposed public purpose. They remain in the law by the consent of Congress. They are accepted and honored by the IRS.

They are there to be used by you.

Where to find guidance

Many books and periodicals in the tax field carry a formal disclaimer advising readers that they do not purport to be rendering legal advice or accounting services or other professional assistance.

This book is no exception. For reasons of simplification it does not discuss legal complexities affecting only a few taxpayers. And for the sake of brevity it deliberately omits reference to many tax procedures plainly described in the Form 1040 booklet. Its readers, therefore, are advised to heed the "Declaration of Principles" jointly adopted by a committee of the American Bar Association and representatives of publishers. It says:

"This publication is designed to provide accurate and authoritative information in regard to the subject matter covered. It is sold with the understanding that the publisher is not engaged in rendering legal, accounting or other professional service.

"If legal advice or other expert assistance is required, the services of a competent professional person should be sought."

So the question arises: How do you choose the "competent professional person" who best suits your own needs, if your tax problems call for expert guidance?

No state licenses a profession called "tax professional" or anything resembling that. But there are two groups of licensed professionals whose training and qualifications have been rigidly supervised and whose conduct is subject to policing by their own professional organizations as well as by state licensing authorities.

The first is the attorney-at-law who specializes in the tax field. Four years of undergraduate training, three years of law school, some actual experience, and passing a state "bar exam" are among the usual requirements to practice.

However, not all attorneys have taken courses or had experience specifically in problems of the federal income tax. Your choice of an attorney to handle a tax matter probably should be limited to attorneys specializing in that field.

If you do not know a tax attorney who meets your need, the state bar association usually can help through its referral service. You will receive the names of three or more attorneys practicing in any specialty area. The final selection is up to you.

Most lawyers' fees range from $25 to $75 an hour for this kind of work. You should discuss the fee with the attorney before engaging him; he will appreciate settling the matter as much as you.

The other licensed professional who regularly deals with federal tax problems is the Certified Public Accountant, or C.P.A. He usually has had four to six years of college, plus one to five years of working experience under supervision of a C.P.A. before taking a formal examination which qualifies him to use the initials "C.P.A." after his name.

Almost all C.P.A.s have had training and experience in taxes, but in some cases a C.P.A. may feel it is desirable to work with an attorney. He will so advise his client.

The fees for a C.P.A. are similar to those of an attorney. If you do not know a C.P.A. you usually can find one through the state society of certified public accountants or by asking an attorney or banker for suggestions.

Some states permit persons who are not licensed as either C.P.A.s or attorneys to practice as "public accountants," "tax advisers," or "tax consultants." The lack of standing as a C.P.A. or attorney does not necessarily mean that such persons are not qualified; it simply means that their qualifications have not been certified by the agencies which prescribe and maintain professional standards in these fields.

Many unlicensed persons can meet your needs, usually at less cost. Members of a third group of licensed professionals, the "enrolled agents," share with lawyers and C.P.A.s the right to represent taxpayers at every stage of appeal. They are "enrolled" by IRS as qualified professionals after passing a difficult examination and meeting other strict requirements of the IRS.

Generally, in case of an audit the IRS will permit any individual who has signed a tax return as having assisted the taxpayer to meet with its agents to explain the items on the return.

Problems of estates and trusts should also be referred to an attor-

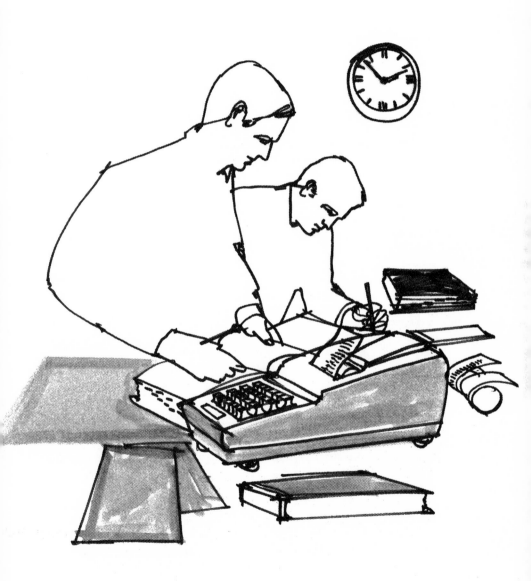

ney or a C.P.A., and matters involving a possible criminal prosecution by the government should be taken to an attorney.

A taxpayer should never sign a blank tax return at the request of a tax adviser. Any adviser who makes such a request becomes eligible for immediate dismissal.

Also, anyone who assisted in the preparation of your income tax return is required by law to sign it with you. If your adviser fails to do so, you should consider the omission a warning that something is amiss. *However, the responsibility for filing a true and accurate tax return remains always with the taxpayer, no matter who prepares his return.*

Some commercial tax preparing firms have been accused by the Federal Trade Commission of disclosing information from individuals' tax returns. In some cases, personal financial data have been sold for purposes of credit rating, mailing lists, or insurance sales.

The extent of such practices was uncertain, but in 1971 the FTC took legal action against two of the largest tax preparation companies and began cracking down or many smaller ones.

The IRS made an investigation of its own into operations of tax preparation firms, including "storefront" operators and "tax advisers" specializing in cheap and speedy returns. A number, it said, were taking as their fees a percentage of the money they saved their customers. In more than a few cases the "savings" were inflated by such tactics as reporting more dependent children than the taxpayer possessed. Quite often, when the taxpayer got a try-again letter from the IRS, the tax preparer had closed up shop and vanished.

Late in 1971 Congress made it a misdemeanor, punishable by up to $1,000 fine or one year in prison, for a preparer to disclose information given him for preparation of a return, or to use the information for any other purpose.

This did not solve the problem of ill-trained or unscrupulous sellers of tax preparation services. So IRS began a program which it hoped would make it unnecessary for most taxpayers to go to shoddy tax advisers.

IRS restored for 1972 the shortform tax return, Form 1040A, which had been dropped three years earlier. Johnnie M. Walters, who was then IRS Commissioner, said he hoped the seventeen-line form would prove so clear and simple that the great majority of taxpayers would never again pay others to make out their returns.

Walters personally rewrote much of the instruction booklet that went with Form 1040A. He took out legalisms and technical gobbledygook, even eliminating the word "spouse." He provided simple definitions of terms like "excess" and "adjusted gross income."

In the tax return season Walters drafted thousands of IRS staff people to work late hours and weekends in free tax-advisory services, sent mobile tax offices into crowded city neighborhoods and suburban shopping centers, and proclaimed the agency's willingness to do the computation job on returns of $20,000 or less. He also greatly expanded the free telephone tax information service available at all IRS offices.

The long record of attempts to clarify and simplify the income tax is strewn with failures, but Walters said he was convinced that at least "the average, knowledgeable American now can make out his own return unless he has some real complications."

"In those cases we don't object to help from competent tax preparers," Walters added. "They serve us well, as they do the taxpayers."

But the IRS itself is the biggest tax adviser and tax return preparer of all, and it does the job free. The aid-to-taxpayers program has been continued and expanded since Walters's departure from government.

... Tax policy is too important to be left solely to the experts. ... Taxation can and should be understood by the interested citizen.

Joseph A. Pechman, "Federal Tax Policy," The Brookings Institution, 1966.

CHAPTER 3

Some
ABCs of
Income
Tax

If the tax burden is to be shared equally, citizens must be taxed un-equally. This is the theory of the graduated, or progressive, income tax, as explained in the preceding chapter: everyone should be taxed accord-ing to his ability to pay. The higher a man's income, the greater his ability to pay taxes. Therefore he should contribute a higher proportion of his income to the support of the government.

The very poor pay no income tax at all. Those at the next higher eco-nomic level—persons having enough income to pay some tax but whose taxable income is less than $500 a year (or $1,000 for man and wife who choose to be taxed jointly)—pay a low tax rate, 14 percent of their taxa-ble income.

This is assumed to be as great a burden on a lower-income family as a 50 percent rate might be on a wealthy family.

The rate of tax goes up for each higher level, or "bracket," of income. A couple with $200,000 of taxable income could pay a maximum rate of 70 percent.

But that has a misleading sound. Actually, you do not pay a tax that is a flat percentage of your whole taxable income. You are taxed by your income bracket, with a higher rate levied on each bracket. (See Appendix III for Federal Income Tax Rate Schedules.)

This is how it works: John and Jane White, filing a joint income tax return, find they have a taxable income of $16,000. The tax rate in the $16,000 bracket is 28 percent. But the Whites do not pay 28 percent of $16,000, which would be $4,480. They pay much less, for the tax is built up in this way:

The first $1,000, taxed at 14 percent ....$	140
The second $1,000, at 15 percent	150
The third $1,000, at 16 percent	160
The next $1,000, at 17 percent	170
The next $4,000 at 19 percent	760
The next $4,000, at 22 percent	880
The next $4,000, at 25 percent	1,000
Total..	$3,260

The tax on $16,000 comes to $3,260, instead of $4,480. The highest rate which was applied was 25 percent, because the Whites did not quite get into the $16,000-and-up income bracket, which pays the 28 percent rate.

But if John White had earned one dollar more than $16,000—or $10 more, or $1,000 more—the additional income would have been taxed at 28 percent.

Assuming, for example, that the joint taxable income was $16,500, the Whites' tax would have been figured this way from the Tax Rate Schedule in their Form 1040 packet:

Tax on $16,000	$3,260
Plus 28 percent of $500 ...	140
Total tax ..	$3,400

Who files a return?

Some citizens need not file any federal income tax return. Their luck is not to be envied. They escape the annual ordeal, in general, only because their incomes are below the poverty line—that is, below the income level which the government in 1969 officially estimated to be necessary to maintain a decent standard of living.

Because of the Low Income Allowance provided by Congress in that year, several million Americans who used to fill out Form 1040 and mail it in no longer need do so.

The old rule said a tax return must be filed by every citizen or resident with a gross income of $600 or more, or, if age sixty-five or older, $1,200. For years 1972 and thereafter, Congress changed all that. The basic requirements went to $750 and $1,500; the poverty line had moved upward.

The table below provides all the present guidelines for filing. It has two columns of figures. The first column shows the gross income level at which various individuals were required to file income tax returns in 1974 and at which they would have to file in 1976 and thereafter. The second column shows the income level applying to 1975 only. In most cases the 1975 levels are higher, since they reflect the temporary tax relief provided by the Tax Reduction Act of 1975.

That same law also provided, for tax year 1975 only, a tax credit intended to offset the impact of Social Security taxes on lower-income workers with families. It is described later in this chapter. Returns for 1975 should be filed by persons entitled to this credit even if they had no tax to pay; it is the only way to claim the credit.

Who Files a Tax Return?

If you are a citizen or resident of the United States and had gross income of $750 or more in a year, you must file an income tax return unless you fall into one of the categories below. The following persons are *not* required to file a return:

Taxpayers who are	With incomes below these amounts	
	1974, 1976, and after	1975 only
Single	$2,050	$2,350
Single, 65 or over	2,800	3,100
Married, filing jointly	2,800	3,400
Married, filing jointly, one spouse 65 or over	3,550	4,150
Married, filing jointly, both 65 or over	4,300	4,900
Married, filing separate returns	750	750
Being claimed as dependent by another taxpayer	750	750
Surviving spouse	2,050	2,650

Note: Although not obligatory, it may be to your advantage to file a return if you have had tax withheld, or if you are entitled to the special 1975 credit for earned income, because the only way to claim your refund is by filing.

The basic requirement that a return be filed by everyone earning $750 or more applies to married persons who file separate returns and for married persons who live apart. It applies also to any married person whose wife or husband can be claimed as a dependent by some other taxpayer. This covers the increasingly common situation of a college student who is married but whose wife still receives most of her support from her parents.

Also still under the basic $750 rule are estates, which pay tax on their incomes as if they were people, and some small groups of taxpayers including aliens who are temporarily in this country but are not considered residents.

A self-employed taxpayer, a special case as already noted, must file a return if his net income from his business or profession amounts to as much as $400 for the year.

The rules apply to everyone, minor or adult, citizen or resident alien. A child who meets the gross income test must file a return. If he is not able to prepare his own, the parent or guardian does it for him.

However, any employe (such as a student with a summer job) whose earnings will not come up to the taxable level can now avoid tax-withholding. He merely certifies to his employer on Form W-4E that he expects to owe no tax for the year and owed none last year. Until 1970 the employer was obliged to withhold taxes just as if the youngsters were going to be paid the full-time rate the year around. The Treasury then kept the money the students did not owe—but needed for college costs—until refunds could be claimed the following year. Now such employes need no longer wait for months, or even file a tax return.

Gross income is the only test for filing. If it exceeds the stated limits, you must file a return even if your deductions and exemptions are high enough to relieve you of paying a tax.

You may also *want* to file, even if you are not required to. If you are entitled to a refund on taxes withheld from your paycheck, you will have to file Form 1040 or 1040A. It is, in effect, your refund claim.

Even if you are excused from filing under the foregoing general rules, you are required to file a return if you are in a special group, such as clergymen or U.S. citizens employed by international organizations. The latter two groups file if income is $400 or more.

Clergymen. Clergymen are accorded a special status. They may claim all the deductions available to professional persons; in addition, a congregation may designate part of a clergyman's salary as a parsonage allowance. This is excluded from the minister's taxable income. The amount may not exceed a fair rental value of the home, plus the costs of utilities. If the minister is purchasing the home, he may also claim the usual deductions for real estate taxes and mortgage interest.

A congregation can bestow another tax boon on a retiring minister by granting him a retirement bonus or retirement payments which are gratuitous—that is, not part of an enforceable contract or agreement nor of any established plan or practice of the church. If so given, the payment is wholly tax-free, provided the minister is not expected to perform any services for the congregation.

Foreign income. American citizens are taxed and required to file returns on income from foreign as well as domestic sources, with certain exceptions.

A U.S. citizen working outside continental United States may exclude earned income if he was actually in a foreign country for seventeen months out of an eighteen-month period. The limitation is figured on a daily basis; the 510 days, or seventeen months, need not be consecutive nor need they all be spent in any one country. IRS Form 2555, "Exemptions of Income Earned Abroad," may be used for computing the limitation.

Also, an American citizen who is a bona fide resident of a foreign country is entitled to exclude some earned income from foreign sources. The bona fide foreign residence must be for an uninterrupted period that includes one entire tax year, and the earned income must have resulted from services performed in that year.

The exclusion of foreign-earned income may not exceed $20,000 as a general rule. In the case of Americans who have been bona fide residents of foreign countries uninterruptedly for thirty-six months, the limitation is increased to $25,000. Taxpayers who have reason to believe that they may qualify for the exclusion should request a copy of IRS Publication 54, "Tax Guide for U.S. Citizens Abroad."

The exclusion does not cover any income paid by the U.S. government or any of its agencies.

Non-citizens. A person who is not a citizen but is a bona fide resident of this country is treated under the tax law almost exactly like an American citizen. The treatment of this "resident alien" differs mainly in these respects:

• He can claim a credit for taxes paid to a foreign country only if the country of which he is a citizen allows a similar credit to U.S. citizens.

• He is not entitled to exclude foreign-earned income.

• His tax rate may be doubled if his country is declared by the President to discriminate against American citizens.

"Residence" is strictly defined. Even the alien who has entered the country on terms which let him work but do not permit him to stay in this country is required to file a return and pay U.S. income taxes.

And a resident or nonresident alien who leaves the country, even for a brief time, may be required to get a federal income tax clearance from IRS, showing that he has paid his U.S. tax obligation. Many an alien traveler enroute from the United States to a week's holiday in Jamaica or Bermuda has been halted at the departure gate by officials demanding the "Certificate of Compliance," showing a clean tax record.

He can get one by taking to the nearest IRS office copies of his tax return and some proof of payment of prior years' taxes—such as W-2 Forms or canceled checks—together with a statement on his current year's income and taxes paid.

What income is taxed?

The income tax laws say that all income you receive is subject to tax and must be reported unless it is exempted specifically by law or regulations. Part of being a wise taxpayer is knowing what can be exempted, excluded, deducted, or otherwise relieved of tax.

Throughout this book, and throughout his experience as a taxpayer, the reader will find references to three concepts of income: gross income; adjusted gross income; and taxable income.

Gross income, speaking generally, may be considered as all the income you receive. When you subtract some "adjustments" and certain deductions which the law says do not count as income subject to tax, gross income becomes:

Adjusted gross income, which is the basic income figure used in computing your tax. The "AGI," as tax technicians call it, is the income figure from which a variety of exemptions and tax-saving deductions are subtracted, to arrive at:

Taxable income, which on your Form 1040 is the whittled-down total to which the tax rates are finally applied to determine how much tax you owe.

Some of the wealth that flows to you remains outside the definition of gross income. It is not reported on your tax return at all. Two basic kinds of income are so regarded. The first is called a "return of capital"; the other is "unrealized appreciation in the value of property you own."

A return of capital is not taxed because it is a return of your own money. For example:

The dividends you get each year on some life insurance policies are not taxable. You need not report them on your income tax return. Why? Because they are a partial return of your own money. You pay $200 in annual premiums on the insurance policy, and at the end of the year the insurance company notifies you that you are entitled to a $35 dividend. You may take it in cash, use it to reduce your next payment, or leave it on deposit with the insurance company to earn interest.

The $35 was not a payment to you but in effect a refund of part of the premium you paid. The company did not use all its policy-holders' money. Your policy actually cost you $165 instead of the $200 you sent to the company, so the company sends back the $35 overpayment.

You paid an income tax on that $35 when you earned it. Now that you have paid it out and it has been returned, it is not taxable again.

But if you decide to leave the $35 dividend on deposit with the insurance company and it earns interest, the interest is taxable. The insurance company will notify you (and the government!) of how much interest you have earned in the year. You must report the interest on your tax return.

Because of the "return of capital" principle, you need not report or pay tax on such receipts as accident insurance proceeds, dividends on life insurance policies, Social Security pensions and disability payments, unemployment benefits, or workmen's compensation.

The other kind of nontaxable income, "unrealized appreciation in the value of property you own," is important to the tax lawyers, but since you do not see it you need not worry about it now.

Let us assume you paid $2,000 for some stock and today's financial page tells you that it is worth $4,000. Do you have a $2,000 gain? Not yet. You have a $2,000 paper profit. There is no gain until you "realize" it by selling the shares. Then the gain is taxable.

The principle also applies to a work of art. Assume you paid $10,000 for it and a gallery wants to buy it from you for $25,000. Until you actually sell the painting you have made no profit on it. At the moment of sale your "unrealized appreciation" turns into a realized gain.

Still other kinds of income escape the income tax. Gifts and bequests are subject to different federal taxes if they are large enough, but not to the income tax. Servicemen's combat pay is excluded from tax liability also, and a Vietnam war provision extended this benefit even to those who performed war-supporting duties outside a designated combat zone, as in the case of U.S. operations in Cambodia.

Your gross income

Many taxpayers who overpay the Treasury do so because they take too literally the broad statement that gross income includes all income from whatever source.

Actually, as noted, many kinds of income are not included at all and other kinds are deducted from gross income before you get very far in computing your tax.

It is wise to find out which items are excluded because rather common kinds of income are involved: life insurance proceeds, gifts, some scholarships and fellowship grants, Social Security benefits, unemployment compensation and others.

On the other hand, some money you receive that you may not think of as "income" does go into gross income. This is in addition to such obvious items as wages, salaries, commissions, fees, rents, interest, partnership income, royalties and dividends. You must also include such payments as alimony and separate maintenance, annuities, pensions, income from trusts, most prizes and awards, and a good many more.

So the Form W-2 which you receive from your employer shows you the wage or salary that you were paid and the amounts that were withheld during the year, but it does not quite complete your job of reporting gross income.

In some cases, in fact, you must report income that never actually came into your hands. Most taxpayers who are not in business for themselves use what is called the cash method of keeping books and figuring their income tax (described in greater detail in our later chapter, "The Businessman and the Professional Man.") Income is reported in the year when received. It is mentioned here only because cash-basis taxpayers must report as income any money actually or "constructively" received during the tax year. This means that if income was available to you but you did not bother to pick it up by the last day of the year, it nevertheless was taxable in that year. Or, if money was paid to someone else for you, you "constructively" received it. This could happen, for instance, if your employer withheld part of your pay from you and gave that money instead to a creditor who had attached your salary. You never saw the money but you "constructively" received it and you are taxed on it.

Similarly, if money was paid to your real estate agent, or a stockbroker for your account, the payment is taxable to you in the year it was received by your agent or broker, even if you did not make use of the money or even know it was available to you.

If a dividend is paid by a corporation on December 31 and mailed to you on that day, you need not pay tax on it that year because it was not available to you. Since your Form W-2 from your employer does not include the money you earned between the year's last payday and December 31, that amount is not taxable. In both cases the amounts are taxable in the following year. But note: If your bank or savings and loan company credits your account with interest on December 31, you must report the interest in that year. The money was available to you, even though it may not have been entered on your savings passbook until the following year.

The tax law spells out a number of fringe benefits which you can receive tax-free from an employer. But some "fringes," some things of value other than cash, are taxable. If your employer gives you and your wife a trip to San Juan, Puerto Rico, as a prize in a sales contest, for example, the value of the vacation is taxable to you.

Nor can you escape tax by transferring earned income to some one else without first paying tax on it. This is called, curiously, the "fruit of the tree" principle. It grew out of a tax case in which a father tried to transfer some income to his son without first having paid tax on it. It seemed a good idea because the son was taxed at a much lower rate than the father. But the Supreme Court ruled that "the fruit of the tree cannot fall far from the tree on which it was grown." This was the Court's way of saying that once income has been earned you cannot avoid the tax on it by transferring it to another person. The individual who earns the income must pay the tax.

Adjustments

Not all items which must be reported in gross income are necessarily taxed. Some major ones, the "adjustments," can be deducted before the actual computation of tax ever begins.

These are most important tax savers, and they are among the benefits of the tax law most frequently slighted by taxpayers. Sometimes they are missed entirely. Other times, when not overlooked, they are entered at the wrong place in the tax return.

Four "adjustments to income" are listed specifically in the standard tax return, Form 1040. They are sick pay, employes' moving expenses, employes' business expenses, and payments made by self-employed taxpayers into their retirement plans.

The adjustments are simply deductions which are taken at this first step in the preparation of a return. They are called adjustments to avoid confusion, apparently, with the itemized deductions which come along later. Following are the groups of deductions—a more inclusive list than the four mentioned above—which are taken from gross income to arrive at adjusted gross income:

• Moving expenses of an employe and other expenses reimbursed by the employer; sick pay, if it is included in gross income; certain losses on sales or exchanges of property; 50 percent of the excess of net long-term capital gains over net short-term capital losses; and payments by self-employed persons to retirement plans.

• Ordinary and necessary expenses connected with carrying on a trade, business or profession.

• Ordinary and necessary expenses (and certain other deductions) in connection with property held to produce rent or royalty income; expenses of an outside salesman; travel, meals and lodging away from home, as well as local transportation expenses incurred by an employe.

These will be discussed in later chapters as they relate to tax-saving opportunities of executives, employes, professional and business men, and outside salesmen. However, the four most widely used deductions of this kind can be described here.

Sick pay exclusion. To qualify for the sick pay adjustment, an employe must have been absent from work because of sickness or injury and must have received either full or partial compensation under the employer's plan for continuation of wages.

If you were paid more than 75 percent of your regular pay, you must absorb the first thirty days of illness without any tax benefit. For the rest of your period of absence, you can deduct the sick pay you receive, up to a limit of $100 a week.

If you received 75 percent or less of your regular pay, the waiting period is only seven days before you can claim the exclusion. The deduction thereafter is the actual pay received, but not more than $75 a week. After thirty days you can deduct up to $100 a week.

If you were hospitalized for at least one day at any time during your treatment, you can begin deducting the sick pay from the first day of absence on, with no waiting period, provided you received 75 per cent or less of your regular pay.

Here's a handy way to tell how soon after the start of your absence the deduction can be claimed, under the sick pay exclusion rules:

If your employer paid you more than 75 percent of your regular pay, the waiting period before you can claim the exclusion is thirty days' wait in all cases. If you received 75 percent or less of your regular pay, there is no waiting period before you can claim the exclusion if you were hospitalized, but a seven-day waiting period if you were *not* hospitalized.

Here is an example of how sick pay is figured: Frank White broke his leg on April 1 and was off the job until May 4. His employer paid Frank's full $200 weekly salary throughout his absence. When making out his tax return, White had to absorb the first thirty days, up to May 1. He had four more days of absence, and could take the deduction for them. Because he normally worked a five-day week, his allowable exclusion came to $20 a day—one-fifth of the $100 weekly limit. For four days of absence he could deduct four times $20, or $80.

Moving expenses. This provision was liberalized greatly by the 1969 Tax Reform Act. The moving expense deduction now is an important tax break for employes, and has been broadened to cover self-employed men and women as well.

When an employe moves to another city because he is transferred by his employer—or goes on his own, to take a new job—he can deduct the actual, reasonable expenses of moving household goods and personal belongings, plus the cost of transportation, meals and lodging for the taxpayer and the members of his household enroute from the old home to the new one.

Other expenses only indirectly related to the move were made deductible in 1970 and thereafter. These include:

First, the costs of transportation, meals and lodging during house-hunting trips in the area of the new job site, not only for the taxpayer himself but for members of his family. This deduction is available only if the trip takes place *after* he has obtained the new job and if the principal purpose of the trip is the search for a new residence.

Second, food and temporary living costs at the new location for the taxpayer and his household while they are waiting to move into new quarters. Expenses for up to thirty days are deductible.

Third, qualified expenses of selling, buying or leasing a residence. The "qualified" expenses are the reasonable costs incurred by the taxpayer or spouse in the sale or exchange of a former residence, and the expenses incident to the buying of a new dwelling in the general location of the new job.

For these three kinds of indirect moving expense, the law limits the tax deduction to $2,500, of which not more than $1,000 may be attributed to the house-hunting trips and temporary living expenses.

If both a husband and wife begin work at new jobs in the same general location, the limit remains at $2,500 just as if there were only one new job. For married couples who file separate returns, the limit is $1,250 for each; the house-hunting trip and temporary living expenses are limited to $500 of the $1,250 for each.

The moving expense deduction covers the cost of rail, air, bus or other means of travel including your personal car. If you drive one car and ship another, the cost of shipping the automobile is deductible.

If you travel by automobile, you may deduct actual out-of-pocket expenses such as gasoline, oil and repairs (but not depreciation), or you may take a flat 7 cents a mile. In either case, the cost of bridge and turnpike tolls is an additional deduction.

There are three major restrictions on the moving-expense deduction:

First, the new principal place of employment must be at least fifty miles farther from the former residence than the old job location. If the taxpayer was not previously employed or self-employed, the distance is measured from the previous residence.

Second, the term "moving expenses" covers only the costs that are reasonable for that particular move. This means generally that the move must be made by the shortest and most direct route available by ordinary means, in the shortest period of time commonly required for the distance.

Third, the deduction is allowed only if you are employed on a full-time basis for at least thirty-nine weeks of the twelve-month period immediately following arrival in the general location of your new principal place of work. The thirty-nine weeks need not be with the same employer, nor with the employer for whom you made the move.

If you are self-employed, the time requirement is seventy-eight weeks in the twenty-four-month period following the arrival. The time limitation is waived in case of death or disability; or, in the case of an employe, a dismissal or other separation for reasons other than willful misconduct.

If your employer reimburses you for part or all of the moving expenses, the reimbursement must be reported as part of your gross income. If your moving expenses are greater than the reimbursement you may deduct the additional costs provided they are within the limits set by the law. If the reimbursement exceeds the amount fixed by the law, you may deduct the moving costs up to the limit permitted by the law, but is is questionable whether you can claim any deduction in excess of that limit.

As usual, special tax forms are involved. An employer who reimburses an employe for moving expenses must give the employe a filled-in Form

4782, "Employee Moving Expense Information," by Jan. 31 of the year following the move. He must also show any reimbursement for moving expenses on the employe's Form W-2. The employe who deducts an adjustment for moving expenses must attach either Form 3903, "Moving Expense Adjustment," or a statement of his moving costs.

The deductible expenses which are incident to the sale of the old residence are the real estate agent's commission, escrow fees and similar reasonable expenses necessary to bring about the sale or exchange.

The costs of fixing up the residence to promote the sale are not deductible, but they can be added to the cost basis of your old home, thus reducing any tax on your gain from the sale.

Costs that are incident to the purchase of a new dwelling include attorney's fees, title fees, appraisal fees and like expenses, including any "points" or loan-placement charges which are not equivalent to interest charges. Any "points" paid in obtaining a mortgage loan (in effect, extra interest charges) are deductible as interest.

Deductible expenses related to leases include the reasonable costs incurred in settling an unexpired lease on the former home, or the costs of acquiring a lease on the property which is to become the new home (but not of course, any rental payments or breakage deposits).

Employes' business expenses. Expenses incurred while traveling for your employer are deductible to the extent that your employer does not reimburse you. To the IRS, "travel" generally means being away from home at least overnight. You may deduct plane, bus, train and other fares as well as the cost of operating an automobile for business purposes. On overnight stays you may deduct the cost of meals and lodging.

Many other unreimbursed expenses of employes are deductible also, but most taxpayers cannot claim them as adjustments to gross income. Only the costs related to travel and transportation are entered at this place on the income tax return.

The other unreimbursed expenses incurred in behalf of an employer must be claimed as itemized deductions. They are not subtracted from gross income but from adjusted gross income.

The latter deductions may include business entertainment, postage, telephone and messenger costs, technical and professional publications, union dues, even the cost of maintaining an office-study in your home and part-time use of your personal car for business purposes.

Only those employes who qualify as "outside salesmen" may deduct all these business costs—and more—as adjustments to gross income. An "outside salesman" is the fair-haired child of the tax system; he gets so many special considerations that a chapter will be devoted to him. He is defined as an employe engaged in full-time solicitation of business for his employer away from the employer's place of business.

Retirement plans for self-employed. Self-employed persons can deduct 15 percent of earned income, up to $7,500 a year, for their contributions toward a retirement plan. The tax-free contribution is an important money-saver; in the 38 percent tax bracket the deduction for a contribution of $2,500 saves $950 in tax.

The actual cost to the taxpayer of the contribution therefore is only $1,550, but $2,500 is credited to his retirement fund. The interest it earns is tax-free every year until the money is withdrawn. Therefore the fund grows much faster than, say, a savings account.

The contribution of a business proprietor or employer for his self-employment retirement plan is deducted as an adjustment to gross income. A copy of Form 4848A must be attached to the income tax return to explain the deduction.

Watch your deductions

To attain even a modest level of tax planning, it is important to understand which deductions are taken from gross income in order to arrive at the adjusted gross income (AGI) and which ones are deducted from the AGI to find taxable income.

In general, the adjustments just discussed, which are used to arrive at adjusted gross income, are called the "business deductions." The others —such as your deductions for medical costs, taxes and interest paid, and charity—are the "itemized deductions."

It is highly important, of course, to classify your deductions correctly (again, the IRS will not do the job for you). Involved are tax savings to be secured by taking from gross income all the deductions that are possible at that point in your tax return, *before* arriving at the adjusted gross income.

One reason is that you may wish to claim the standard deduction. This is the automatic deduction of 15 percent, up to $2,000, which can be taken regardless of whether you have that much deductible expense.

(*Note:* The emergency Tax Reduction Act of 1975 increased the standard deduction to 16 percent for one year, with limits of $2,300 for individuals and $2,600 for those filing jointly. These temporary limits applied to 1975 tax returns only. An extension was possible, but the 1975 law specified one year only. Therefore our examples are based on the regular limit of 15 percent, up to $2,000.)

The standard deduction is taken from *adjusted gross income*. So if you can deduct some of your costs from *gross income* first, and then subtract the full standard deduction farther down, you will come out ahead.

For example, a married taxpayer has gross income from a salary of $25,000 in 1974. He could claim $500 in business travel costs but he has no other significant deductible outlays. He chooses to take the $2,000 standard deduction; it does not occur to him that the travel costs are deductible from gross income. This is the way his joint return looks:

```
Gross income ........................$ 25,000
Adjustments from gross income ........      0
                                       _____
Adjusted gross income ..............   25,000
    Personal exemptions .....$1,500
    Standard deduction ...... 2,000
        Total ........................  3,500
                                       _____
Taxable income.....................    21,500
Income tax .........................$   4,860
```

If, instead, he had subtracted his travel costs from gross income, this would have been the result:

```
Gross income ........................$ 25,000
Adjustment from gross income
    (the travel costs) ..................   500
                                       _____
Adjusted gross income ..............   24,500
    Personal exemptions .....$1,500
    Standard deduction ...... 2,000
        Total ........................  3,500
                                       _____
Taxable income ....................    21,000
Income tax .........................$   4,700
```

(A reminder: In these examples the regular standard deduction—15 percent, up to $2,000—is used instead of the temporary higher limits provided for 1975 returns only. See note, page 55.)

By using his adjustments from gross income, he saved $160. And note: The standard deduction has been made progressively more generous since 1970. Many more taxpayers now find it worth using; its usefulness is enhanced by taking as many deductions as possible from gross income, before applying the standard deduction.

There is a further reason to take deductions "at the top" (from gross income) whenever possible. When you itemize your deductions, the deduction for medical expenses covers only your costs that exceed 3 percent of your *adjusted* gross income. The smaller you can make your adjusted gross income (by deducting from gross income) the higher your medical deduction will be.

For example: Assume that you have an adjusted gross income of $15,000 and medical costs of $950. Three percent of your AGI is $450. Subtracting that from your $950 medical outlays, you have a $500 medical deduction.

Now suppose you had been able to take $600 in adjustments from your gross income, thereby reducing your adjusted gross income to $14,400. Three percent of that is $432. You can claim all medical expenses above that amount, or $518. Your medical deduction is $18 higher.

Two routes from AGI

After gross income has been pared down to AGI, the taxpayer must choose between two courses. He can itemize all of his deductible expenditures for the year, add them up, and subtract them from the AGI. Or, he can take off a flat percentage of his AGI, the standard deduction mentioned above, which is available to all taxpayers.

There is no "best" way. The goal is to arrive at the smallest possible taxable income. Whichever method does it is "the right way," for that means the lowest possible tax.

Calculating your return, you will also deduct the personal exemptions, but they offer little room for maneuver. You have one for yourself (for a couple, one each) and one for each dependent; you can add one for each spouse who is sixty-five or older, and one more for each who is blind.

The deductions can offer more difficulty. To find out whether it is worthwhile to itemize, you must go ahead and do it. Total up all your deductible outlays—for church and charities, mortgage interest, state and local taxes, doctor bills, casualty losses and a dozen other things—and match the dollar total against the standard deduction.

In ordinary years many families of moderate income find that itemizing does not pay. Millions of families simply do not have substantial costs of the deductible kind.

For these, the other route is made to order. The standard deduction permits you to claim a flat percentage of your adjusted gross income *whether or not you had any real deductible expenses.*

The new "standard"

The standard deduction is so much easier than itemizing that millions of taxpayers use it even when it is against their own interest. They simply do not bother to find out whether itemizing would save them money.

Some tax men have called the standard deduction "the give-up deduction."

For years the standard deduction stood unchanged at 10 percent of adjusted gross income, up to a maximum of $1,000 (or $500 for married persons filing separate returns).

Then came the major tax law changes of 1969 and 1971. When Congress finished, the standard deduction had become far more valuable to taxpayers. Over three years it was increased to 15 percent of adjusted gross income (AGI), up to a maximum of $2,000. A one-year increase in the limit was decreed by Congress for 1975 (see note on page 55), but the regular 15 percent limit, up to $2,000, is used in the following examples:

• If your AGI was $11,000, your automatic deduction would be $1,650 ($11,000 x .15), regardless of your actual deductible outlays.

• If your AGI was $18,000, you could claim the limit of $2,000, but no more.

• If your AGI was $13,000, and if you had itemized deductions that

How to Calculate Your Income Tax

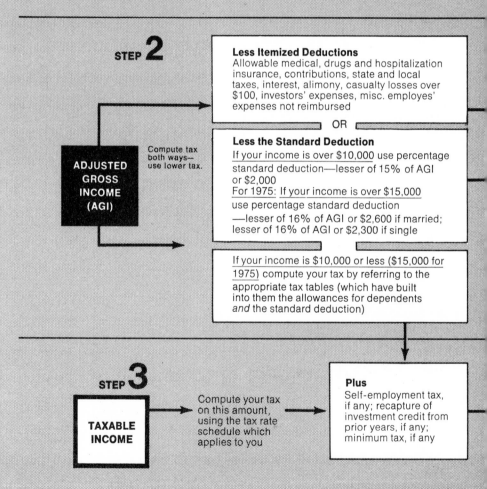

STEP 1

Gross Income From
Trade, business, farm, profession, rents or royalties and partnership income

Gross Income From
Salaries and wages plus any expense reimbursements not accounted for to your employer

Gross Income From
Annuities, pensions, interest, dividends (taxable portion over exclusion), alimony, tips, prizes, 50% of long-term capital gains over short-term capital losses, gains on the sale of other property, ordinary income from pseudo-corporations, income from estates and trusts and any other income

STEP 2

ADJUSTED GROSS INCOME (AGI)

Compute tax both ways—use lower tax.

Less Itemized Deductions
Allowable medical, drugs and hospitalization insurance, contributions, state and local taxes, interest, alimony, casualty losses over $100, investors' expenses, misc. employes' expenses not reimbursed

OR

Less the Standard Deduction
If your income is over $10,000 use percentage standard deduction—lesser of 15% of AGI or $2,000
For 1975: If your income is over $15,000 use percentage standard deduction—lesser of 16% of AGI or $2,600 if married; lesser of 16% of AGI or $2,300 if single

If your income is $10,000 or less ($15,000 for 1975) compute your tax by referring to the appropriate tax tables (which have built into them the allowances for dependents and the standard deduction)

STEP 3

TAXABLE INCOME

Compute your tax on this amount, using the tax rate schedule which applies to you

Plus
Self-employment tax, if any; recapture of investment credit from prior years, if any; minimum tax, if any

Less Business Deductions
Ordinary and necessary business expenses
related to the operation of your trade, business,
profession, farm; rents and royalties and certain
deductions you are required to pay for yourself
under the terms of your partnership agreement

Less Adjustments
Sick pay exclusion (employes only),
moving expense deduction,
self-employment retirement plan
payments, employes' travel, travel
and other expenses of a full-time
outside salesman to the extent they
exceed reimbursement (if any)

EQUALS →

ADJUSTED GROSS INCOME (AGI)

Less Exemptions
For taxpayer,
spouse and
dependents; plus
extra amounts
if over 65
and/or blind

EQUALS →

TAXABLE INCOME

Less
Retirement income credit;
Job development
investment credit;
Foreign tax credit;
Nonhighway gas tax credit;
Credit for your share of tax
on regulated investment
companies
For 1975:
Earned income credit

EQUALS →

YOUR TAX

Any balance due
after withholding tax,
estimated tax payments
and excess Social Security
tax must be paid with return.
Any excess will be refunded
or credited to next
year's estimated tax.

Chart by Martin L. Kamerow, CPA

added up to $1,990, you would be better off to itemize. The standard deduction ($13,000 x .15) would give you a deduction of $1,950. By adding up your interest payments, local taxes, medical bills, and other deductible expenses, your total itemized deductions would be $40 higher than that. By itemizing, you would save the tax on $40 of income.

But the outcome, in the last example, would have been different for 1975; it would have paid to take the standard deduction because Congress liberalized it for that year only. Taxpayers should be alert to changes in the tax law as well as to changes in their own financial status. It could be costly to go on taking the standard deduction from habit. It could also be costly to assume that you should itemize now simply because it was best for you a few years ago.

The standard deduction, or "percentage standard deduction" as it is officially called, is written into the permanent tax law as 15 percent, up to $2,000, with one exception: the maximum is half that much, or $1,000, for married persons filing separate returns.

However, the liberalized rules written by Congress for 1975 only, to combat a recession, not only raised the percentage to 16 percent but also provided different maximums for various classes of taxpayers. This table shows the normal standard deduction and the 1975 changes:

	1974, 1976, and after	1975 only
Single persons	$2,000	$2,300
Married persons filing jointly and surviving spouses	2,000	2,600
Married persons filing separately	1,000	1,300

Many persons who had graduated from the standard deduction to itemizing in the 1960s began shifting back in the 1970s. For them the easy way to take deductions had become the tax-saving way.

Moreover, the tax break given home buyers, because of deductions for property taxes and mortgage interest, is diminished. For many families it may have been wiped out entirely. It will, at least, take closer figuring to determine which way the tax advantage lies.

Itemizing and "alternating"

You may discover, when you work out a "dry run" tax return to determine whether itemizing is worthwhile, that either method brings the same result. Your itemized total may roughly match what the tax law gives you automatically in the standard deduction.

If that is a regular occurrence, consider itemizing every other year and bunching your deductible costs in those years. It is an almost sure way to save taxes in amounts of $100 to $200 or possibly more.

Let us consider the imaginary case of William Brown. He is married, files a joint return, and has about $13,500 adjusted gross income. His deductions usually total around $2,000; he normally takes the maximum standard deduction of $2,000 to save the bother of itemizing. (Note that this example uses the normal standard deduction instead of the liberalized level set for 1975 only; the "alternating" technique to be described here assumes that such fluctuations will seldom occur.)

If Brown has chosen to take the standard, he wastes his deductions when he incurs deductible expenses late in the year. He would be better off to delay those that can be deferred until next year, and in that year to itemize his deductions. So he arranges with the doctor and the dentist to delay payment of bills falling due late in the year. He defers having new dental work done until January. He delays payments to church and charities, telling the recipients that they will get his contributions just after New Year's. He defers buying a car to postpone paying the state sales tax, which must be paid in cash.

Now, having taken the flat $2,000 deduction in one year, he has a bundle of held-over deductions for the next year. These can be added to his usual total of deductible expenses for the second year; the itemized total substantially exceeds $2,000, so it will be to his advantage to itemize in the second year.

Now a pattern begins to emerge: Why not alternate year by year? In one year Brown can keep his deductible outlays as low as possible and take the standard deduction. Into the second year he can pack every possible deductible expenditure, and in that year itemize. Next year, back to the standard.

In the case of the imaginary but typical Mr. Brown, here is what happens: He finds he can postpone about $800 worth of deductions. He subtracts from his $13,500 AGI the flat $2,000 deduction as well as his two exemptions totaling $1,500 ($750 each for himself and his wife). That leaves a taxable income of $10,000. His tax comes to $1,820.

A year later Brown's income is the same; so is his tax rate. But this year he has paid the postponed bills, made the deferred purchases, and given the delayed contributions; these deductions total $800. In addition, he makes his usual $2,000 worth of annual deductible outlays. He also finds it possible to pay in advance some deductible costs for the following year, including the prepayment of part of his local real estate tax. His deductible outlays add up to $3,000.

So, on this second year's tax return, he itemizes. From his $13,500 AGI he subtracts his $1,500 worth of exemptions and his $3,000 worth of itemized deductions. The taxable income is $9,000. The tax is $1,600.

His tax is $220 less than if he had taken the standard deduction. Over the two years he has made his usual contributions to church and charity, paid the same interest charges and property taxes, and made the same medical outlays. But he has saved more than $100 a year; he has brought about a 6 percent reduction in his own income tax by alternating—simply by planning the timing of his deductible expenditures.

Up go the exemptions

For two decades Congress left the personal exemption at $600 for every taxpayer, his spouse, and each of his dependents. The idea of the exemption was that the government should not tax away any part of the basic amount needed to raise a child, care for an aged parent, or keep a disabled dependent. But the cost of raising a child rose 60 percent in those twenty years, and the $600 became something of a joke.

In 1969 Congress at last increased the personal exemptions. The two special exemptions also were raised; the taxpayer is granted an extra exemption if he is sixty-five or over, or if he is blind. These also can be claimed for his spouse.

Thus, a taxpayer who is over sixty-five and blind has three exemptions; if he files jointly with his wife, and she also is sixty-five, he can claim two more exemptions, or a total of five.

The increase was phased in by stages over three years. For 1972 and thereafter the exemption was fixed at $750. This increase of $150 per exemption obviously is a special boon to large families. For a couple with four children, the six exemptions totaling $4,500 mean that an additional $900 of income (which would have been taxed in 1969) has been removed from the tax collector's reach.

Retired persons also benefit substantially. A couple over sixty-five has four exemptions. In 1969, the exemptions shielded $2,400 of their income from tax. For 1972 and after, another $600 is exempted, for a total of $3,000.

(Note: In the emergency Tax Reduction Act of 1975, a temporary new $30 credit was allowed for 1975 for each taxpayer, spouse, and dependent, in addition to the personal exemption. Thus, for a family of four, $120 could be subtracted directly from the 1975 tax due.)

What is a dependent?

A dependent is a person who earned less than $750 and for whom you provided more than half the support in the tax year.

As always, there is an exception: The taxpayer can claim an exemption for his own child even if the earnings limit is exceeded, if the child is under nineteen years old or, regardless of age, is a student. In figuring whether he provides more than half the child's support, the taxpayer need not count any scholarships received by the child.

Other relatives may be claimed as dependents. The Treasury recognizes grandchildren, great-grandchildren, parents, grandparents, stepchildren, brothers, sisters, half-brothers and half-sisters, nephews, nieces, step-brothers, step-sisters and step-parents. Someone whose relationship is illegal under local law cannot be claimed; this might exclude a mistress. But all in-laws qualify.

The 1969 law gave a foster child the same exemption status as a natural child, if his principal place of abode for the entire year was the taxpayer's household. Thus the foster child can exceed the earnings limit and still be claimed as a dependent by a foster parent who provides more than half his support.

An exemption for your wife can be claimed even if you were married as late in the year as December 31. If her father had supported her during the rest of that year, he can claim her as a dependent—but not if you and she file a joint return.

If you were divorced in the year, you cannot claim an exemption for the divorced spouse. You can, however, file a joint return if the divorce has not become final at the end of the year.

Children of divorced parents. A problem frequently arises when divorced parents both claim a child as an exemption. The tax exemptions do not necessarily go to the parent who has custody of the children, though this is normally the case.

The other parent may get the exemption if he contributes at least $600 to the child's support and if a divorce decree or an agreement of separate maintenance gives him the exemption; or if he contributes $1,200 annually for support, regardless of the number of children. But in the latter case the parent having custody can retain the exemption if he shows that he provided most of the child's support.

Dependent parents. Many couples have one or more elderly parents in their households. The parent frequently has some income from Social Security, an annuity, securities or other sources. This may bring his gross income above the limit for a dependency exemption, or may represent more than half the cost of his support. In either case, the taxpayer cannot claim an exemption for the parent unless the financial situation itself is changed.

These are some ways in which a household's finances have been rearranged to make the exemption possible:

• If the parent's income is from securities, the parent may wish to solve the problem by simply making a gift to the taxpayer of some of the securities—enough of them to reduce his own income to the dependency level.

• Some income-earning securities may be shifted to tax-exempts. For example: Let us suppose that James Black provides most of his father's support, but Mr. Black, Sr. has $900 a year income from stock dividends. Even after he deducts the $100, which the tax law permits as a "dividend exclusion," he has $800 income—still too high for him to be claimed as an exemption. So Mr. Black, Sr. sells some of the stock and puts the proceeds into tax-exempt bonds. The interest income from the tax-exempts is not counted as part of gross income; the shift brings his gross income down so James can claim him as a dependent.

• John White's retired father has Social Security income of $1,250 a year. It costs $2,450 to support him. John provides the rest, but his $1,200 contribution is just short of half the cost of support. So John gives his father an additional $100 a year. He now provides more than half the support; Mr. White Sr., if he does not spend the extra money, can put $100 of his own Social Security income into a savings account. John now claims the exemption; his tax savings substantially exceed the extra $100 he has provided.

Note: The solutions will not work after the tax year ends. The income situation must be checked in the fall, when time remains to take action.

If children jointly contribute to supporting a parent but no one of them puts up more than half the cost, the exemption need not be wasted. Whenever two or more persons provide more than half the support of any dependent—and each puts up more than 10 percent—they can settle for themselves which one takes the exemption. The others sign a Multiple Support Declaration (Form 2120) saying they will not claim the exemption. The person taking the exemption files Form 2120 with his tax return. *When children are jointly supporting a parent, they can take turns year by year in claiming the exemption.*

Another plum: Low Income Allowance (LIA)

A tax break for lower income taxpayers was introduced by the 1969 tax law as a substitute for what used to be called the "minimum standard deduction." It is called the "low income allowance," and is claimed in addition to the personal exemptions.

The LIA in many cases can provide a substantially greater tax reduction than the device it replaced. Its express purpose, in combination with increased personal exemptions, is to lift the tax burden entirely from most families with incomes below the officially designated poverty line.

The allowance is normally a flat, across-the-board figure—$1,300 for 1972 and subsequent tax years, regardless of the amount of income or number of dependents.

(But note: The 1975 Tax Reduction Act increased the low income allowance for tax year 1975 to $1,900 for a joint return, $1,600 for a single return, and $950 for married persons filing separately. The tax withholding tables were reduced temporarily to reflect the change.)

The computation of the LIA need cause no trouble for taxpayers, because those with adjusted gross income of $15,000 or less can use the tax tables provided with Form 1040. Those who are benefited by the low income allowance will find it taken into account, along with their personal exemptions, in the tax computation.

This reflects a 1975 revision brought about by the Tax Reduction Act. Until that antirecession law was enacted, the use of the tax tables was limited to taxpayers whose adjusted gross income totaled $10,000 or less.

The optional tax tables are designed as a simplified method of computing the tax. The taxpayer using them need not worry about any temporary changes in the low income allowance or the standard deduction because the IRS revises the tables to take such changes into account.

For persons in the lower income brackets, the low income allowance shields more income from tax than the standard deduction. At higher income levels the standard deduction is the better choice.

Although one goal of the low income allowance was to relieve some seven million taxpayers of filing returns by erasing their tax liability, the 1975 tax changes—while giving further help to low-income families—could cause a greater number to file returns. That law included for the first time a variety of the long-debated "negative income tax." It was called the "earned income credit." Under this concept the tax mechanism is used to make direct cash payments to lower-income families. The special 1975 credit of 10 percent of earned income up to $400 was made payable in cash even if the taxpayer had no tax liability for the year. To get a refund it is necessary to file a return, even if the individual is not otherwise subject to the filing requirements.

Capital gains

As noted, the person who has accumulated property and capital gets preference in the tax laws over the one who is dependent entirely on his salary. The magic words are "capital gains." The special tax treatment accorded capital gains has opened the doors to wealth for many.

A capital gain is the profit made on the sale of a capital asset. Capital assets include stocks, bonds, your home and other real estate, your car, boat, jewelry and so on. They include practically anything of value except business property or inventory and some short-term government securities.

The tax law distinguishes two kinds of capital gain. One is "long-term"—the income realized from an asset owned longer than six months at the time of sale. It receives preferred tax treatment.

The "short-term" capital gain occurs when assets are owned six months or less at the time of sale. Short-term gains are denied comparable tax concessions. They are taxed as ordinary income.

The stock market boom in "growth stocks" and "glamor issues" in the 1960s was basically a quest for net long-term capital gains. Investors wanted stocks that would rise in price and could be sold at a profit.

The reason is clear. The tax rate applied to that kind of profit is never more than one-half the tax rate payable on wages, salaries and other ordinary income.

Until the 1969 Tax Reform Act, the tax on a long-term capital gain never exceeded 25 percent, regardless of the taxpayer's total income. For taxpayers in the highest rate brackets, this was *less* than half the rate on ordinary income.

Congress retained the ceiling at 25 percent for long-term capital gains up to $50,000 in a year (or $25,000 for married taxpayers filing separately) ; but on amounts above that, it raised the ceiling to 35 percent for 1972 and thereafter. These are still bargain tax rates.

For many investors, dividend earnings of stock therefore will continue to be of secondary interest. Dividend payments are treated like other ordinary income, to be taxed at the full rate (except for the first $100 worth of dividend income, which is exempt, or "excluded," from taxable income).

The investor who depends on his stock holdings to provide current income prefers big dividends; the investor who wants capital gains is happier to see the corporation reinvest its profits instead of paying them out as dividends to the stockholders. The corporation's growth makes his stock holdings rise in price, bringing the promise of larger capital gains.

And—perhaps the most desirable feature of all—the capital gain is not taxed until the investor sells the stock. If he holds it until he dies, his estate need pay no tax on the capital gain (though it may have to pay an estate tax). The taxation of capital gains at death is among the foremost goals of Congress members who favor broad tax reforms. Such a change could be enacted into law in the 1970s. Even so, capital gains will be sought by savings-wise taxpayers.

The average wage-earning householder, whose principal capital assets consist of his house, furniture and car, cannot do much to convert his assets into capital gains. His road to capital gains, therefore, is usually to purchase stock out of salary savings—and then hope the stock goes up, not down.

Even when it goes down, there is some compensation. The losses can be used to offset taxable earnings on other stock sales, and to offset a limited amount of ordinary income, as will be described shortly.

Gains, losses and carryovers. There is no such thing as a capital gains "rate" of tax. A long-term capital gain is taxed at half the taxpayer's ordinary rate, in effect, because only half the capital gain is taxed. It works this way:

If you held some stock for a year and sold it for $1,000 more than you paid for the shares, you would count only half of the $1,000 as income subject to tax. You would pocket the rest, tax-free.

In making out your Form 1040, you would report $500 as a net long-term capital gain. You would enter it on the special form, Schedule D, provided for reporting "Sales or Exchanges of Property."

The $500 is added to your ordinary income and is taxed at your regular bracket rate. But since you have reported only half of the actual gain, the effect is the same as paying half your ordinary tax on the full $1,000.

If you were in the 36 percent tax bracket, you would pay $360 on $1000 of ordinary income, but only $180 on the same amount of capital gain.

The purpose of the 25 percent ceiling on the capital gains tax was to insure that no taxpayer would have to pay more than a 25 percent effective rate on the full amount of his capital gains, however high his income.

The 25 percent ceiling is used, accordingly, only for taxpayers whose total taxable income is above the 50 percent rate bracket. This was not changed by the 1969 law, except for those taxpayers who have net long-term capital gains of more than $50,000.

Now the law sets the ceiling rate on long-term capital gains above $50,000 at one-half of the taxpayer's ordinary rate, whatever that might be. The tax could not be more than 35 percent because the highest ordinary rate bracket is 70 percent. So 35 percent has become the ceiling rate for big winnings in the stock market, real estate deals or other transactions producing capital gains.

In any year an active investor is likely to have some gains and some losses, especially if his investments are common stocks. The profit which is taxable at the favorable rate is the "net long-term capital gain."

What are net gains? To figure your net long-term capital gains, you start by separating all your year's sales of stock and other capital assets into two groups, short-term transactions (assets held less than six months) and long-term.

Find out how much you gained or lost on all your short-term transactions. Then do the same for all your long-term sales. Subtract one from the other, to see whether you had more gains than losses, or the reverse.

If this process shows you had an excess of short-term capital gains, the full amount goes into your return to be taxed as ordinary income, at full rates.

If the figures show you had an excess of *long-term* gain over short-term loss—a not uncommon investment situation—that margin is the net gain on which you will be taxed by the capital gains method.

For example: Suppose that your net losses on short-term transactions totaled $4,000 and that your net gains on long-term transactions total $6,500. You would have an excess of $2,500 net long-term gain. When you report this on Schedule D, you deduct 50 percent. In effect, you pocket $1,250 and you record the other $1,250 as your total net gain. If you are in the 50 percent tax bracket, you pay $625 tax on the gain—in effect, a 25 percent tax on your $2,500 net long-term gain.

If the taxpayer's total income is high enough, the top dollars would be taxed at an ordinary rate bracket higher than 50 percent. The effective tax on the capital gain therefore would be more than 25 percent—and the law says that should not happen on net capital gains up to $50,000.

So an "alternative tax" is provided. This has the effect desired by Congress of limiting the tax on each dollar of net long-term capital gain to 25 cents. The regular tax computation and the alternative method are shown in the box that follows.

If the "alternative tax" is lower than the tax computed in the regular manner, this is the figure that should be used and entered on the first page of Form 1040.

Computing the Capital Gains Tax

(For taxpayers with net long-term capital gains of $50,000 or less. Single taxpayer.)

A. *By the Regular Method*

Taxable income (excluding capital gains)	$70,000
Plus 50% of a net $10,000 long-term capital gain	5,000
Total taxable income	75,000
Amount of tax	$36,090

B. *By the Alternative Method*

Taxable income as computed by regular method	$75,000
Less 50% of a net $10,000 long-term capital gain	5,000
Total income subject to regular tax	70,000
Tax on $70,000	32,790
Add 25% of $10,000	2,500
Alternative Tax	35,290
Savings by use of alternative tax	$ 800

The steeper tax, 35 percent, which is now imposed on net long-term gains exceeding $50,000 complicates the figuring a bit. The same procedure is followed except that your "alternative tax" will be computed on Schedule D in this way:

First, find the regular tax on your ordinary income, without counting any net long-term capital gains; *plus*

$12,500, which is the 25 percent "ceiling" tax on the first $50,000 of net long-term capital gains; *then add*

35 per cent of the amount of net capital gain that exceeds $50,000.

Taxpayers with net long-term capital gains exceeding $50,000 will use the alternative method; at that income level it always works out to their advantage.

Deducting capital losses. If some investments turn out unhappily and you wind up with a net long-term capital loss when all your transactions are combined, the tax law provides a financial cushion. This is another area in which taxpayers must be watchful of changes made by the 1969 law. The cushion is not as ample as it used to be. Some of the net capital loss can be applied to offset up to $1,000 of ordinary income. But each $2 of net long-term capital loss will cancel out only $1 of ordinary income, up to the $1,000 limit; the other dollar is simply lost. Thus, $2,000 of losses are required to obtain this $1,000 maximum deduction.

However, if net capital losses still remain beyond the amount which can be applied two-for-one against ordinary income, the leftover loss can be carried forward to the following year. Then the process is repeated; the loss is applied first against capital gains, dollar-for-dollar, then against ordinary income, $2 for $1.

For example: William Thompson has a long-term capital loss of $3,500 and no other capital gain or loss. He uses $2,000 of the loss to offset $1,000 of his income from salary. He has $1,500 of loss remaining to carry over. The next year he again has no other capital gain or loss. He applies the $1,500 against his ordinary income; it offsets $750 of his income from salary.

The $2 for $1 provision was a change made by the 1969 tax law. Previously long-term capital losses could be deducted dollar-for-dollar from ordinary income, and this dollar-for-dollar offset is still in effect for *short-term* capital losses. Short-term losses are used to offset ordinary income before long-term losses are used.

For example: Henry Johnson has $2,000 of long-term capital losses and $500 of short-term losses. He uses the short-term losses first; dollar-for-dollar, they offset $500 of ordinary income. Then he uses $1,000 of his long-term loss; this offsets another $500 of ordinary income, or a total of $1,000. Johnson still has $1,000 of long-term loss remaining, which he can carry over to use the next year.

Two footnotes, also arising from 1969 tax law changes, are:

First, there is a break for taxpayers who receive *before 1975* long-term capital gains arising from sales of property made under binding contracts entered into on or before October 9, 1969. The 25 percent ceiling *continues* to apply to such gains over $50,000. This includes the proceeds of installment payments on sales made on or before that date. The new 35 per cent ceiling rate does not apply.

However, this "binding contract" rule does not apply to gains from the sale of timber or coal or royalties from iron ore taxed as capital gains.

Second, the step-up in ceiling rates on gains above $50,000 is not the only new curb on the profitability of large capital gains. Capital gains are among the "tax preferences" which are subject in some part to the new minimum tax, the "LTP," or "Limitation on Tax Preferences," to be discussed later.

Investment credit

The Job Development Investment Credit, usually called merely the investment credit, is designed primarily to encourage the purchase by industry of new equipment and machinery. But it is equally available to self-employed persons, small businesses, partnerships, and professional men and women. It is available for purchases of office machinery, tools, instruments and laboratory equipment as well as industrial equipment.

The legislation provides a 7 percent credit; that is, it permits the taxpayer to subtract 7 percent of the cost of the new equipment from the tax that otherwise would be due. The government, in effect, subsidizes the purchase with a 7 percent "discount."

The 7 percent credit was replaced by a 10 percent credit for the two years 1975 and 1976, under the Tax Reduction Act of 1975. The change was intended to provide stronger stimulation to capital investment. This section discusses briefly the regular 7 percent credit, then describes the two-year liberalization.

To obtain the full 7 percent investment credit you must buy equipment that has an estimated useful life of at least seven years. The credit is reduced by one-third if the life is less than seven years but at least five years, and drops another third if the life is less than five years but at least three. There's no credit if the useful life is less than three years.

To aid smaller businesses, the law permits use of the credit for purchases of used equipment, up to $50,000 a year.

A similar tax credit was adopted to encourage businesses to hire and train welfare recipients who are participating in the federal Work Incentive Program (WIN). The law provided a tax credit equal to 20 percent of the wages paid these employes in their first twelve months of employment, whether or not the twelve months are consecutive.

Under the Tax Reduction Act of 1975, the basic credit was increased from 7 percent to 10 percent of the cost of eligible equipment acquired after January 21, 1975, and placed in service before January 1, 1977. For property that was in process of manufacture or under construction on January 21, 1975, the higher credit applied only to the value added after that date.

The credit could be taken on used property costing up to $100,000 a year (instead of the permanent $50,000 limit) in each of the two calendar years 1975 and 1976.

Corporations that agreed to contribute 1 percent of the cost of acquired property to an approved employe stock-ownership plan could take an extra 1 percent credit, or 11 percent in all. This was designed to provide an extra infusion of capital for the corporation.

In cases where construction would take two years or more, "progress payments" made on the property or equipment became eligible for credit, provided that the new property had a useful life of seven years or more. Congress made this a permanent exception from the general rule that the credit could be taken only when the equipment or property is put in service. The change was designed to encourage major outlays.

Public utilities, formerly limited to a 4 percent credit in most cases, were made eligible for the 10 percent (or 11 percent) credit on property placed in service after January 21, 1975, and before January 1, 1977. The investment credit thus was employed to help ease the energy shortage.

The WIN credit was extended temporarily to employers hiring federal welfare recipients. This change was made effective for workers hired after March 29, 1975, and for service rendered before July 1, 1976.

Tax Reduction Act of 1975

This chapter has mentioned several of the tax relief provisions of the Tax Reduction Act of 1975. These were mainly temporary measures designed to combat the serious 1974-75 recession and applicable only to 1975 tax returns —although Congress, as always, reserved the right to change its mind and extend them for another year or longer.

The 1975 act provided small rebates of 1974 taxes; it also temporarily increased the standard deduction (note, page 55); provided a $30 credit against 1975 taxes for every taxpayer, spouse, and dependent (note, page 62); increased the low-income allowance (note, page 64); and liberalized the investment credit. Other provisions include:

Earned income credit. A special credit for 1975 only, intended to ease the burden of Social Security taxes, was provided for lower-income workers with dependent children. The law provided a credit amounting to 10 percent of earned income up to the first $4,000 of income earned, or a maximum of $400. Above that amount the credit was diminished by 10 cents for each added dollar of earned income; thus it was eliminated for those earning $8,000 or more.

The credit was declared to be "refundable"; that is, if any of the credit exceeded the 1975 tax due, a refund would be paid in cash. It thus became in effect a "negative income tax." Even if he had no tax withheld from wages and did not have to file a return, an eligible taxpayer would receive a cash credit by filing a return. "Earned income" includes wages, salaries, tips, and self-employment net earnings.

Payments to retirees. The Treasury made special one-time cash payments of $50 each to persons who in March, 1975, were entitled to regular Social Security or Railroad Retirement Act payments. The special payments were not to be considered income for tax purposes.

Rebates. The Tax Reduction Act gave each taxpayer a cash rebate on 1974 income taxes. It provided a $100 minimum or the amount of 1974 tax paid, whichever was lower; a 10 percent rebate of up to $200 for those with adjusted gross incomes up to $20,000; and a reduced rebate phased down to $100 for taxpayers with adjusted gross incomes of $30,000 or more. The rebates were not taxable as income.

*I think you will agree that the people
who complain about their income taxes
may be divided into two classes—
men, and women.*

Randolph W. Thrower, Commissioner,
Internal Revenue Service, June 25, 1970

CHAPTER 4

Don't Panic— It's Only Form 1040

Efforts to simplify the standard income tax return, Form 1040, have resulted in wider spaces to write in, annual changes in arrangement, a longer booklet of instructions, less technical language, and a simplified glossary of tax terms.

But Form 1040 still is formidable enough to dismay some quite experienced taxpayers and send them to commercial tax preparers—many of whom, IRS investigations show, have been incompetent and some downright dishonest, as noted earlier.

The government's answer is Short Form 1040A. It is a revival of the old punchcard Form 1040, abandoned in 1969, but it looks different and can be used by many more taxpayers. IRS has estimated that 33 million of the 77 million U.S. taxpayers can use the short form—mostly those whose income comes only from wages, salary or tips.

Short Form 1040A is half-page size, with questions on front and back. It can be used by any taxpayer, however high his income, who meets this test in the instruction booklet: "You may use Short Form 1040A if all your income . . . was from wages, salaries, tips, other employee compensation, dividends or interest, and you do not itemize your deductions."

Whether you use the regular Form 1040 or the Short Form 1040A, IRS will figure your tax for you free if your income is $20,000 or less. You must enter the figures on income, exemptions, withholding and so on, but you can leave blank the lines which call for the tax computation. The IRS will do the arithmetic, report to you the amount of your tax, and send a refund check if you are entitled to one—or a bill if your tax withholding did not match your tax liability for the year.

Note: You may gain a delay in paying your tax if IRS does the computation. You have thirty days to pay after IRS notifies you of the amount due.

The Short Form 1040A is not available for use to all small taxpayers. A taxpayer who itemizes his deductions, or who receives more than the prescribed amounts of dividend or interest income, or who receives any rental or other form of non-wage income, must use the regular Form 1040.

Check carefully before deciding to use the Short Form 1040A. Many who decide to use it to save themselves the annual tax headache will be cheating themselves. The shortcut can carry you right past the deductions you are entitled to take.

Two questions on each of the forms, 1040A and 1040, have nothing to do with your own income tax obligation. They were required by the 1971 Revenue Sharing Act, as part of the machinery for distributing federal tax funds to state and local governments. One question calls for a statement of your principal residency by state, county, locality or township; the other asks the number of persons who are listed as your exemptions but who file their own returns or did not live at your principal residence at the year-end.

Despite some genuine progress in clarifying the regular Form 1040, the complications of the tax law itself create many opportunities for error. One of the oldest and commonest taxpayer errors is still possible despite efforts to rearrange the form to eliminate it.

This is to report the total itemized deductions on the line which is provided for the "adjustments to gross income"—such as sick pay, moving expenses, employe business costs, and payments into self-employed retirement plans.

If you enter on that line, instead, the itemized deductions for taxes and interest paid, medical expenses and so on, your return will be rejected and sent back for correction. The itemized deductions should be listed on Schedule A and their total then entered in the "Tax Computation" section of Form 1040.

The other forms

The W-2 Form is as familiar to most taxpayers as Form 1040. Your employer prepares it and sends copies to you and to the government. It reports all the income he paid you, as well as all the income and Social

Security taxes he withheld from your pay. It provides the wage or salary figure which you enter as income on your Form 1040.

But it is not the only figure that must be entered. If you have income from other sources, all must be reported.

The W-2 Form serves another useful purpose. If you worked for two or more employers in the year, you may have paid more Social Security tax than you owed. You can get it back as a credit on your income tax return.

Add up the Social Security payments shown by all the employers. (They are under the heading "F.I.C.A. Employee Tax Withheld.") If the total exceeds the maximum prescribed under the Social Security law, you should report the excess payment. It goes into Form 1040 on the line labeled "Excess F.I.C.A. Tax Withheld." This will reduce your required tax payment or increase your refund.

Form W-4. For an increasing number of taxpayers the income tax normally withheld from their paychecks no longer comes close to matching the amount of tax they actually owe. That's because millions of families now have two breadwinners and two incomes, many have second income from rentals, investments, or side businesses, and growing numbers itemize their deductions.

The official withholding tables supplied to employers failed to deduct enough tax from millions of paychecks throughout 1971. The tables were steeply revised for 1972, and in that year millions of taxpayers had far too much withheld. The tax withholding continues to be excessive for many persons.

Form W-4 was devised to help taxpayers bring their withholding into rough balance with their real tax liability. It is filed with the employer, not with the IRS, and it can protect the wage and salary earner from serious cuts in take-home pay due to overwithholding, as well as from dismaying tax bills on April 15 caused by underwithholding.

Because the withholding maladjustments are most often a problem to families in which both wife and husband work, the use of the W-4 Form is described in the later chapter, "The Woman Who Works."

Form W-4P. You cannot escape tax withholding on your wages. But many taxpayers don't know that the law now also provides for withholding of the tax due on pension and annuity payments and some other non-wage payments.

Any person who receives a pension or annuity can ask the payer to withhold some portion for income tax. *The payer must comply,* whether it is an insurance firm or a corporate plan for employe retirement benefits.

The withholding request is made by filing Form W-4P with the payer. The request must be for at least $5 a month; but it may not be an amount that would cut any net annuity payment below $10.

Estimated tax declaration. The new withholding adjustment process can help you avoid an unpleasant surprise on April 15, but there's also a more familiar way to accomplish it. If it appears that your income and self-employment tax will exceed by $40 or more the tax to be withheld, you may be required to file declarations of estimated tax.

The declarations are made each quarter-year along with the quarterly installment of your estimated additional tax due. They are made on individual vouchers, one for each quarter, which come to you as part of Form 1040-ES. If you do not receive a set, obtain one from your local IRS District Director's office.

Filing voucher No. 1 is considered to be the filing of your tax declaration; it is due April 15, simultaneously with your annual income tax return. The second is due June 15, the third September 15, and the fourth on January 15. The rest of Form 1040-ES is a worksheet for your own records.

Making the quarterly payments is your responsibility. The IRS does not send a bill. But it can exact a 9 percent-a-year interest for underpayment of an installment of estimated tax or for failing to make a declaration.

You are subject to the penalty if the total of your estimated tax payments plus withholdings is less than 80 percent of your tax as shown on your final return.

You may escape the penalty if you can show that you have figured your estimated tax by using the current year's rates on your previous year's income less the exemptions you can claim for the current year. The penalty will be avoided, also, if your total tax paid in the current year equals or exceeds the total tax due for the preceding year.

It is not necessary to spread your estimated tax payment over four installments. If you wish, you may pay the estimated tax in full with your original declaration.

You can also amend your estimated tax if your income or exemptions change during the year. Just refigure the estimated tax and enter the new estimate on the voucher currently due; adjust your remaining payments to match the new total.

Remember that paying the estimated tax does not excuse you from making a tax return as usual on April 15.

Then you pay the difference, if any, between your final tax and the combined total of your withholdings plus your installment payments.

If you have overpaid, you can claim a refund or take a credit on your next year's declaration of estimated tax.

W-4E. To avoid withholding. Any employe who expects to have no income tax liability, such as a student doing summer work or a salesperson employed for the holiday shopping season, can avoid tax withholding by filing Form W-4E with his employer. It is a certification that he expects to owe no tax for the year and owed none in the past year. Withholding is eliminated; the employe need not wait until the year-end and file a tax return in order to get a refund of income taxes that he did not owe.

Filing your return

Your return is due April 15. It is on time if it bears a postmark of April 15 or earlier. If April 15 falls on a Saturday or Sunday the return is due on the following Monday.

The burden of proving that the filing was timely is on the taxpayer. To have proof, you can file by certified mail and get a receipt from the post office.

Many of the mistakes made on income tax returns are made by taxpayers who rush the job through at the last minute. Any tax professional will tell you that the taxpayer who gives early and careful consideration to his return is better off than one who prepares it in a last minute rush.

Extension of time. Since 1972 it has been easier to get an extension of time to file your return—but not a bit easier to delay the payment of your tax.

The IRS now gives automatic sixty-day extensions to taxpayers who file Form 4868, but there's a catch. Previously an extension of filing time also extended the time for paying the tax. Not so the automatic extension granted upon the filing of Form 4868. *The taxpayer must make a tentative estimate of his tax and send that payment along with his application for the extension.*

Further, any taxpayer who asks the IRS to compute his return for him is ineligible for the automatic extension.

Under the previous rules, a taxpayer who failed to meet the original due date for filing was subject only to an interest charge calculated at 9 percent a year. Under the automatic system, the 9 percent interest charge is made for any portion of tax unpaid on the due date, and an additional penalty is levied amounting to ½ of 1 percent a month on the late payment if it is 10 percent or more of the total tax shown on the Form 1040 when it is finally filed.

Form 4868 is titled "Application for Automatic Extension of Time to File U.S. Individual Income Tax Returns." Except in cases of undue hardship, the taxpayer cannot bypass the automatic extension and use the older, regular application first; it is Form 2688, and it also can obtain up to sixty days' extension for you if granted. But the taxpayer must use the automatic extension form first. Then, after the expiration of the sixty-day period it provides, he may request a further extension by using the regular form.

The automatic extension should be mailed not later than the due date for filing a return. It would be wise to send it by registered or certified mail. You should keep the U.S. Postal Service receipt to protect yourself against any late filing penalty if the application goes astray.

The District Director of Internal Revenue still has the option of deny-

What Forms Do I Use?

These are the schedules which should be attached to your Form 1040
to report various income items and claim deductions and tax credits

If you:	Use:
Are required to file an income tax return	Form 1040
Note—You can use the Short Form 1040A— and attach no other forms or schedules—if you do not itemize deductions or have sick pay, moving expenses, employe business expense or self-employed retirement plan adjustments. (You may have up to $200 of dividends and up to $200 of interest income and still use this form):	Short Form 1040A
Itemize deductions such as contributions, medical expenses, taxes, interest	Schedule A
Have dividends in excess of $100 or interest in excess of $100	Schedule B
Have income (or loss) from a business other than a farm	Schedule C
Have capital gains or losses	Schedule D
Have income from pensions, annuities, rents, royalties, partnerships, estates, trusts, small business corporations, other sources	Schedule E
Have farm income or loss	Schedule F

If you:	Use:
Claim income-averaging benefits	Schedule G
Claim a retirement income credit *(Schedule R is on the back of Schedule E.)*	Schedule R
Report net earnings from self-employment	Schedule SE
Claim the investment credit	Form 3468
Claim a foreign tax credit	Form 1116
Recompute a prior year investment credit	Form 4255
Claim sick pay	Form 2440
Claim moving expenses	Form 3903
Pay minimum tax	Form 4625
Have gains or losses from the sale of property other than capital assets	Form 4255
Request automatic extension of time for filing	Form 4868
Use the special ten-year averaging method for lump-sum pension or profit-sharing distributions	Form 4972
Correct a previously filed return	Form 1040X
Explain an underestimation of tax without penalty	Form 2210

ing your request for an extension; the IRS considers few things more important than the income tax. If he does deny it, he will notify you that your return must be filed on Form 1040 within ten days of the date of his notice.

Extensions will not be approved for taxpayers who were required to file estimated tax returns throughout the year but failed to do so; or who failed to pay the required installments on each due date; or who failed to file a timely return in each of the preceding three years.

In approving an extension, IRS sends back one copy of the application form. You should attach it to the tax return when you file.

A taxpayer who is out of the country on April 15 automatically gets a sixty-day extension for filing his return but not for payment of any tax he may owe. If abroad when the sixty days run out, he should apply for a further extension; this may be granted for up to six months if he remains abroad. When filing his return, he should note on it his absence from the country on the filing date, and should be ready to prove his absence by producing passport stamps or other travel records if asked.

"Borrowing" from the Treasury

It is possible to "borrow" from the government, if you are willing to pay 9 percent interest, by simply not paying your taxes on time. But the borrowing can be costly, for the IRS can also levy a penalty.

Because interest rates frequently have been higher than the Treasury's charge for late payment of taxes, some taxpayers used to file their returns on time but enclosed less than the full payment of tax. Thus, they avoided a late-filing penalty, and, in effect, went on using money that belonged to Uncle Sam.

Now there is a penalty of ½ of 1 percent a month, up to a maximum of 25 percent, for not paying tax when due. The penalty is imposed also for failure to pay a tax deficiency within ten days after the Treasury gives notice and demands payment.

The Treasury does not exact the penalty if the taxpayer shows there was reasonable cause for his delay, or if the taxpayer has obtained an extension of time for filing his return (unless the Treasury later finds that he misrepresented the reason for getting the extension).

Some corporations have used a similar device for low-cost borrowing, delaying payment to the Treasury of tax money withheld from employes' paychecks. There is also a flat 5 percent penalty for such late deposits— and the penalties, unlike interest, are not deductible.

By the same token, when you are entitled to a refund the government will either send you a Treasury check or credit the amount against your estimated tax for the following year. Usually it makes sense to take the check. Otherwise the Treasury is getting an interest-free loan of your money—which could be earning interest in your own savings account. However, if you make estimated tax payments, you might as well leave

it with Uncle Sam. Sometimes it takes sixty to ninety days to get a refund check, and you will have to make your first estimated tax payment
on April 15.

Splitting income

The more you can split up your income among family members, the
less income tax you pay. The basic idea is to divert part of your income
to someone else—perhaps a child or a parent who, because he has less income than you, is taxed at a lower rate.

The government sanctions this course by permitting husbands and
wives to file jointly. The wife may have little or no income, but the income earned by the husband is considered to have been earned by both.

So the total taxable income is split in half and the tax is figured on
two halves. For example, the tax in 1972 on a couple's $20,000 taxable
income, if they filed jointly, was $4,380. They were paying as if they
were two single persons, each with $10,000 income. The single individual
with $20,000 taxable income in that year, having no one to split with,
paid $5,230, or far more tax than the couple.

Clearly, husband and wife should file jointly, as a general rule. Just as
clearly, taxpayers should look about for ways to split the family income
further, if possible.

Creating a temporary trust is one way for a middle-income or high-income taxpayer to shift income from investments to someone who is in a
lower tax bracket, without giving up the investments permanently. The
beneficiary usually is a child or grandchild of the taxpayer.

Under one form of trust, for example, the law permits you to turn
over some income-producing property, such as securities or a house that
is rented, to a trust fund for at least ten years. The trustee who manages the fund will pay the income from the property to the child. The
taxpayer is not taxed on the income, and the property reverts to him at
the end of the trust.

The child pays income tax on the investment earnings at a lower tax
bracket, or pays no tax at all. The taxpayer still can claim a dependency
exemption for the child.

Here is an example of this method: John Wilson has two children,
Jack and Nancy. His taxable income is $40,000, of which $3,000 is interest from bonds. The tax is $12,140.

Wilson establishes a trust for each child to provide a college fund. He
puts half the bonds into Jack's trust, half into Nancy's. Now his taxable
income is $37,000 and his tax is $10,790.

He is saving $1,350 a year in taxes, $13,500 in ten years. Jack and
Nancy receive $1,500 a year each from their trusts. They will have to file
returns and pay some tax on this unearned income, under a tightening of
tax rules that took effect in 1972. But the tax is only a fraction of the
amount their father would have paid on the same income, because they

are in a much lower tax bracket. And after ten years and a day, Wilson regains possession of the bonds.

Trusts can do wonders in income splitting. They also can be tricky and hazardous. They will be discussed at greater length, along with other methods of giving-while-living, in our chapter, "Tax Planning for Family Security." The trust is available as a tax-saving tool only to the taxpayer who has assets—like stocks, bonds, or rental property—which earn income.

Professional guidance is advisable in setting up a trust. Start with your attorney; he can refer you to the proper specialist. It may be a lawyer, the trust officer of a bank, or a C.P.A. The decision will depend on your own circumstances and the special objectives you want the trust to attain for you.

Old Spanish custom. Joint filing began because some Western states retained a vestige of Spanish law, the community property system. Income and property were considered to be held in common: to belong equally to husband and wife.

A U.S. Supreme Court decision affirmed for these states the rule that, since a wife owns half her husband's earnings, she should pay tax on her half and he should pay tax on his. This gave residents of the community property states a thumping advantage in federal taxation over the rest of the country.

The states which had not passed such laws raised an outcry over the discrimination, so Congress eventually changed the income tax law to give married couples in *all* states the right to split their incomes.

Instead of each spouse actually reporting half the family income, the couple files a joint return, using the special rates for couples in the Tax Rate Schedules. The rates are computed as if the couples were splitting their income.

Once this was done, other groups of taxpayers complained. Why should married couples get a better tax break than widows and widowers who supported children? And why should they pay less than the unmarried persons who kept a household for aged parents?

Eventually the protesters won a partial victory. Congress created the "head of household" category, with tax rates cut to a level part way between single persons and married couples. Then, another amendment: a surviving spouse who supported one or more children was permitted to use the low split-income rates—those available to married couples—for two years after the death of the wife or husband.

Single persons were left in the cold, outside any tax rate shelter, until 1969. Then the Tax Reform Act eased that discrimination. The rates for heads of household were trimmed down, effective in 1971, to levels a good deal closer to the rates for married couples. Simultaneously rates for single taxpayers were moved closer to those for heads of households.

This bit of history explains the origin of the next topics, the tax status of couples, heads of households and single taxpayers, plus a few special considerations which still survive for taxpayers in the "community property" states.

It also provides a splendid example of how one tax preference breeds another—and how the effort to make the tax laws fair to everyone leads to ever more complicated tax laws.

Couples and singles: joint returns. Filing jointly is a "must" for most married couples. It is the first way to get the effect of splitting the family income to obtain a lower tax rate.

A couple can file jointly even if their wedding took place on New Year's eve and even if one of them had neither income nor deductions.

But divorced or legally separated couples cannot file jointly. So if a couple was married all year but divorced on December 31, each would have to file separately.

If the husband or wife dies during the year, the surviving spouse can file a joint return for that year. And for the two years thereafter, if he or she does not remarry and maintains a household that includes a child or stepchild, the taxpayer can get the cut-rate tax benefits of income splitting. This does not mean that the widow or widower can file a joint return for the two years; it means filing singly but using the same tax rates as are used by a couple filing jointly. The survivor cannot claim an exemption for the deceased spouse.

In the third year after the year of death, if still maintaining a household for self and child, the widow or widower files as a head of a household, and does so thereafter.

To file as a "surviving spouse" and use the tax rate for a married couple, you must have been entitled to file a joint return with your spouse in the year of death. Whether or not you actually filed a joint return is immaterial.

A couple may file a joint return if, even though not legally married, they are living together in a common law marriage which is recognized in the state in which it was initiated.

If married and living apart, but not divorced or legally separated, a man and wife can still file a joint return. An interlocutory (non-final) decree of divorce is not a legal separation for filing purposes.

If a husband or wife will be away from home or otherwise unavailable to sign the return, an authorization for the joint return should be obtained from the IRS, to be signed in advance by the spouse who will be away. But if the husband is on military service in a combat area, he need not sign; a simple declaration of the facts or statement of his whereabouts will suffice if attached to the return.

Separate returns. In a few cases, filing separately makes good sense for married couples. This can happen if a man and wife are in identical income brackets, each paying his own expenses and taking his own deductions. In such a case it is worthwhile to test separate returns. But, even then, joint filing is usually wiser. However, if a husband and wife file separate returns and one elects to itemize his deductions, the other spouse may not take the standard deduction or the low income allowance; nor may the latter spouse use the Tax Tables, in figuring the tax.

On the other hand, do not assume that filing jointly will save you money on your *state* income tax return just because it usually does on the federal return. In some cases—in the District of Columbia, for instance—it frequently pays for couples to file separately. It is beyond the scope of this book to analyze the varied and changing state laws; but couples will do well to compute their state income taxes individually as well as jointly to learn which way of filing holds a tax advantage.

Heads of households. For years a man or woman who qualified as "head of a household" has been entitled to about half the tax break granted to married couples; the tax rates have been about halfway between those of single taxpayers and married couples. As noted, the 1969 tax law reduced the rates for heads of households and single taxpayers, effective in 1971 and thereafter.

A person is the head of a household if he or she:

• Is unmarried. (An interlocutory divorce decree does not give you unmarried status for this purpose; only a final decree does.)

• Maintains a home for self and at least one child or grandchild, stepchild, adopted child or foster child; or for a parent or parents, or other relative or in-law who qualifies as the taxpayer's dependent. If the person for whom you provide the home dies, you may nevertheless claim head-of-household status for the year of his death. The parent or other dependent need not live in the taxpayer's home; he may, indeed, be in a rest home or home for the aged.

• Pays more than half the household expenses and, if the child or grandchild is married, furnishes more than half the support.

Single taxpayers. The orphan of the tax system, the single individual, has always paid a higher rate than others. Now, however, thanks to the Tax Reform Act of 1969, he pays rates not more than 20 percent above those of married couples in any bracket. The single person with just over $10,000 taxable income—who paid 32 percent in 1970—pays 27 percent. As income passes $20,000, the rate is 38 percent instead of 1970's 48 percent, for a tax saving of some $800.

For heads of households the rate readjustment brought similarly substantial savings. The household head with income just topping $10,000 pays 25 percent instead of 27 percent; if his or her income tops $20,000 the rate is now 35 percent, instead of 40 percent.

The reshuffle of rates brought one wholly unanticipated result. If both husband and wife work, a married couple now pays much more income tax than an unmarried man and woman. This encouragement for couples to live together without benefit of matrimony is discussed in the later chapter, "The Woman Who Works."

The "sin tax" was denounced in Congress but proved hard to correct.

Trusts, estates, and married couples filing separately. The rate relief for single persons was not granted to married persons filing separate returns. These rates continue unchanged at the same level as estates and trusts—except for those who happen to qualify for single-person rates under the following quirk in the 1969 Tax Reform Act.

Separated married persons. An important tax break for separated married couples results from the wording of the 1969 law. Congress meant to give tax help to wives abandoned by their husbands—and did so, by letting them pay single-person rates. But the wording applies equally to couples who have separated by mutual consent without divorce or legal separation. If either spouse maintains a principal abode for a child and meets other requirements, he or she (or both) may qualify.

The provision helps those who either cannot file a joint return because of a missing or unwilling spouse, or—in many cases—who prefer to file individually even though the separation was voluntarily and mutually arranged. The tax quirk is particularly helpful to those who can qualify, because married persons filing separately are in the most costly of all tax categories.

A husband and wife are both eligible for the single-person rates if each has one or more of their children. Husband and wife should each check to see whether they meet these four requirements:

First, he or she files a separate return.

Second, he or she maintains as a home a household which, for more than half the tax year, is the principal abode of a dependent—the dependent being a son or daughter or stepchild for whom the taxpayer is entitled to a dependency deduction.

Third, he or she provides more than half the cost of maintaining the household.

Fourth, the other spouse was not a member of that household during the entire taxable year.

An even better break comes to those who meet the foregoing requirements and also meet the test for head-of-household. If either husband or wife (or both) does, he or she or both can file as a head of household and pay rates lower than those for single persons. A spouse qualifies as head of household if he or she maintained the home as the principal place of abode of the child *for the whole year, not just the half-year mentioned above.*

Community property. The special rule for community property states —Arizona, California, Idaho, Louisiana, Nevada, New Mexico, Texas, and Washington—is that a wife may file a separate return showing half her husband's earnings as her own income, as well as half the income from their community property. (The property which either one owned before they were married remains his or her separate property, however, in all those states except Texas, Idaho and Louisiana.)

In filing separately, each claims half the deductions as well as half the income. If you live in one of these states you may or may not find an advantage in separate filing; figure your tax both ways.

The separate returns may show a lower tax if one of the couple has heavy medical expenses paid out of separate property funds.

Until the 1969 tax law changed the rules, couples in community property states might have found it cheaper to file separate returns if their net capital loss exceeded $1,000. Each spouse could have used up to $1,000 of loss to offset ordinary income. This advantage was knocked out by a new rule setting a $500 limit on the amount of capital loss which may be claimed by a married person filing a separate return.

Income-averaging

Some people's income fluctuates widely from year to year. This is often the case for lawyers, salesmen, self-employed businessmen, real estate agents, artists, doctors, actors, athletes and entertainers.

When a taxpayer has a very successful year financially, the graduated tax rates hit him harder. Taxes take a much bigger bite, proportionately, out of the higher income brackets.

Congress recognizes that it is not fair to give this taxpayer the regular tax treatment, just as if the high one-time earnings were his regular income. It devised "income-averaging" to cushion in part the tax blow. In 1969 it liberalized the income-averaging device: *Now, if your income is more than 20 percent greater this year than usual and if the excess above 20 percent is at least $3,000, check whether income-averaging will save you money.*

Take Joe Moore, for instance, the ballplayer mentioned in Chapter One. He has had a medium-to-good record for four years with a ball club. His income has averaged $14,000 a year. Then he has a hot season, gets a big raise, wins some cash awards and a piece of the pennant-winning team's bonus. For this year he has $44,000 taxable income.

Joe is supposed to pay $14,060 of it on his joint tax return. Joe is good at arithmetic, however, and he points out these facts: He has earned $100,000 in five years with the club, an average of $20,000 a year. The team's veteran shortstop, Pepper Peterson, who makes $20,000 a year as his regular pay, also has made $100,000 in the same five years.

But Pepper's total tax for the five years was well below Joe's. Joe's tax was pushed up by that big income bulge in the fifth year, which lifted him into a much higher tax bracket.

Joe's protests make the locker room ring, until the club lawyer tells him about income-averaging. The step-by-step method, and the results for Joe, are shown in the accompanying box.

Joe's tax turns out to be $11,549 instead of $14,060. He has saved $2,511.

Income-averaging can soften the tax impact for a person whose income

Income Averaging: How to Do It

This example assumes a $44,000 taxable income for a married taxpayer filing a joint return, with average taxable income of $14,000 a year in the preceding four years. The computation is done on Schedule G; to simplify, this example omits some references on Schedule G which concern few taxpayers.

a. Start with taxable income $44,000

b. Enter the income for each of the four previous years $7,000, $9,000, $13,000 and $27,000. You wish to find 120 percent of the average of those numbers; your Schedule G gives you a shortcut way of doing it: Add them up and take 30 percent of the total ($56,000 × .30 = $16,800). Enter the result on line 7 of Schedule G; this is the portion of income *not* subject to averaging 16,800

c. Find the income *subject to averaging* ($44,000 minus $16,800) 27,200

d. To the income not subject to averaging ($16,800) add one-fifth of the averageable income (20 percent of $27,200, or $5,440). The result, $22,240, goes on line 11 of Schedule G, and in most cases the same figure is repeated on line 13 22,240

e. Find the tax on that amount 5,097

f. Find the tax on the income not subject to averaging ($16,800) 3,484

g. Subtract the tax just above from the tax in step e ($5,097 minus $3,484); this goes on line 17 of Schedule G 1,613

h. Multiply the last figure by four (line 18 of Schedule G) 6,452

i. Add the last figure to the total from step e ($6,452 plus $5,097). The result is the tax after averaging 11,549
Without averaging, the tax would have been 14,060
The saving made through income-averaging was.. $2,511

jumps more than 20 percent above the average of the previous four years. What Joe did was to tax *all* the additional income above 120 percent of his four-year average at the same rate he would have used if it were only one-fifth as much.

Complicated? Yes, although simpler than the rules before the 1969 tax law. There are, moreover, special rules, limitations and exceptions, and some kinds of income are still excluded from income-averaging.

Thus, this may not be a job for the taxpayer who normally completes but one tax return a year, his own. He may need the help of a professional tax man.

But it takes no great skill to check whether income-averaging might save you money in a big-income year. Say that your income for the previous four years averaged $15,000. An income 20 percent higher would be $18,000. If your taxable income for the present tax year exceeds that amount by $3,000—that is, if the total taxable income is more than $21,000, then you are eligible for income-averaging. And it will be a tax saver.

This is a boon to the junior executive who gains a big promotion, an employe who receives a good bonus, a salesman who lands some hefty orders, a lawyer who wins a big case, a householder who wins a gasoline company's sweepstakes or the New York state lottery, a writer who finally hits the best seller list—or the self-employed professional or businessman who simply has a much better than average year.

At this point you can seek a tax adviser, or, if your income tax return is not a complicated one in other respects, you can obtain a copy of a special form, Schedule G, from the nearest IRS office and run through the computation, line by line.

Income-averaging may help for another two or three years after the first high-earnings year, if your high income continues.

Some types of income which formerly were barred from income-averaging, including capital gains, wagering gains, income from gifts and bequests, may now be included.

Young people just starting their earning careers cannot use income-averaging. It is available to those twenty-five or over who have not been full-time students during four of their taxable years starting after age twenty-one. A taxpayer under twenty-five may use it, however, if he furnished at least half of his own support in all four of the preceding years.

Some higher-income people who are eligible for income-averaging may find it gives them no advantage. That is because those who use it cannot take advantage of the new "earned income ceiling," or maximum tax on earned income. Congress has specified that earned income is not to be taxed at a rate higher than 50 percent. If your bracket is above that ceiling, it would be to your advantage to forego income-averaging and use the lower ceiling.

The liberalized income averaging helps the taxpayer who sells a house, a lot or other property. He formerly had to take his payment in install-ments to spread the capital gains tax impact over several years. Now he takes cash and usually still saves taxes; he "averages" his income bulge, as described in the later chapter, "The Home Owner and the Investor in Real Estate."

If you want to use the income-averaging device but do not have copies of your returns for the past four years, you can get copies by using IRS Form 4506, "Request for Copy of Tax Return," or you may write a let-ter to the District Director of Internal Revenue in the city where you filed the returns. For a charge of $1 a page, he will send copies of your returns for the missing years. Either way, you must personally sign the request for copies. However, a wise taxpayer will have kept copies of his tax returns on file.

*The first nine pages of the
Internal Revenue Code define income;
the remaining 1,100 pages spin the web
of exceptions and preferences.*

Senator Warren G. Magnuson, in the Senate,
May 12, 1966

CHAPTER 5

The
Itemized
Deductions

Tax men say millions of Americans have been losing money most of their taxpaying lives by assuming that their deductible outlays were not high enough to justify itemizing deductions. They have not bothered for years to find out by running down a checklist of their possible deductions. It may be time for you to do so.

Times change. Local property tax bills go up. New or higher state sales taxes are imposed. Cities levy new sales taxes of their own. Doctor bills have soared; dentist bills are not far behind.

All of these deductible costs have mounted steeply, as have many others: Interest rates in the 1970s climbed to historic highs; if you were typical, you used far more credit than ever before, and paid more interest for it. Your interest charge to finance a new car has risen—and it cost you more to repair an uninsured fender. These costs are legitimate deductions. If they were not worth itemizing a few years ago, they may be today.

Moreover, tax rules have changed. A lot of healthy taxpayers still do not realize they have an almost automatic medical deduction. Literally millions of them do not know that the medical deduction rules were changed a few years ago. Now, *everybody who pays for medical and hospitalization insurance can deduct outright half the cost of the premiums, up to $150.* The rest of the premium charge is also deductible, subject to the same limitation as other medical expenses, to be described later.

A trial run of itemization can be worthwhile. Through deductions, some of the family's worst financial burdens can be lightened.

Most homeowners, for example, bemoan their steep monthly interest payments throughout the year, but on April 15, when claiming tax deductions for mortgage interest, they can say: "Thank heaven for the mortgage."

The kids' tonsils, teeth, measles and broken arms are a family worry and a financial strain 364 days a year. On April 15, they are still a worry, but they turn into an overnight financial boon. If the doctors' and dentists' bills were high enough, some of the money comes back to you as a tax deduction.

Similarly, the ill wind that blew down your favorite flowering mimosa tree in December blows you some good in April: a tax deduction for a casualty loss.

The mortgage, the measles, the windstorm all help to illustrate why the personal deductions were put into the tax law.

Some deductions were designed to further social and economic ends that Congress considered desirable, such as homeownership and the support of churches and charities. Others were meant to cushion the family against crushing medical costs. The Appendix provides a list of deductions for all taxpayers.

One deduction eases the burden of local real estate taxes and state or city sales and income taxes. This helps the hard-pressed cities and states as well as the taxpayer; it makes it possible for local governments to levy heavier taxes than they could otherwise. Other deductions were designed to be a sort of insurance against fire, storm and natural disasters and against thefts and vandalism.

Owning vs. renting. The deduction for interest paid gives a lift to families in debt while also serving as a subsidy of homeownership. It benefits the home buyer by letting him deduct the heavy costs of a mortgage interest while buying a dwelling, a co-op apartment or a condominium.

The subsidy has grown as interest costs have risen. While it is harder now to buy a house, a bigger portion of the monthly mortgage payment is deductible from taxes.

Families who rent their homes pay the high interest rates indirectly. The landlord passes on to them his own interest payments and real estate taxes. But the renter, unlike the homeowner, has no way of getting part of his money back through tax deductions.

This preference of the tax law for homeowners over renters is not considered a fair arrangement. It was diminished to a substantial degree, in fact, by passage of the 1969 Tax Reform Act. But since it still exists, it behooves the family who rents to do some calculations.

Usually, it costs less per month to buy a house—once you have scraped up the down payment—than it does to rent the equivalent housing. You can, in addition, get back hundreds or thousands of dollars a year in tax deductions for mortgage interest and local property tax payments. When these are counted in, you might come out considerably ahead by buying a house instead of renting.

There are other reasons for buying. You will build an equity in real estate, which could be profitable. Real estate is usually an asset that gains in value. If you sell the house, your profit, if any, is taxed at the capital gains rate, far below the regular income tax rate.

The buy-or-rent question demonstrates how one of the biggest decisions confronting almost every family may be influenced by tax considerations.

Other considerations may of course be decisive: the size and ages of your family, the kind of work you do, whether you are a stay-at-home or a gad-about, whether you enjoy a householder's chores or detest them. You may decide it is worth the extra cost of renting to avoid mowing a lawn or shoveling snow. But you can hire a lot of boys with snow shovels and lawn mowers for what you might save in taxes if you owned.

Effect of the new "standard." In any case, do not fail to give careful consideration to the effect of the recent increase in the standard deduction. It could make itemizing a matter of less importance.

When Congress passed the 1969 tax changes it estimated that 11 million taxpayers who had been itemizing their deductions would stop doing so. It would pay them, the Treasury judged, to adopt instead the standard deduction as it moved up to 15 percent of gross income, to a maximum of $2,000.

The Treasury's guess was quite probably correct, although the rise in medical costs, state and local taxes and other cost-of-living elements indicated that part of the new tax break would have been eaten away by inflation before the higher standard deduction had taken full effect.

Nevertheless it may no longer be true—as it was for years—that the mortgage interest and property tax deductions alone make it worthwhile for almost all home buyers to itemize. So itemizers should make trial runs to find out whether they should switch to the standard deduction method.

"Average" deductions. The table following shows the average total of itemized deductions which have been claimed by taxpayers of various income levels. The figures do not represent deductions which IRS approves or allows, or which you can automatically claim. Taxpayers should not construe them as a measure of "what the traffic will bear." But the IRS computer might sound an alarm if deductions stray too far above these averages.

Average Deductions Claimed by Taxpayers
(Based on 1972 Returns)

Adjusted gross income	State and local taxes	Interest	Contributions	Medical expense
$9,000-$10,000	$810	$757	$304	$395
10,000- 15,000	1,030	931	344	333
15,000- 20,000	1,404	1,097	424	294
20,000- 25,000	1,778	1,208	544	291
25,000- 30,000	2,184	1,360	692	336
30,000- 50,000	2,983	1,686	1,031	393
50,000-100,000	5,145	2,855	2,092	462
100,000 up	14,499	8,372	13,444	673

Each taxpayer may claim *only the amounts actually spent* for interest, taxes, medical expenses, contributions and casualty losses. The Treasury may ask you to show proof of your deduction claims, whether or not they exceed these averages. Obviously, the higher the deductions shown on any tax return, the more likely is an audit. But if the amount you spent was greater than the average, you should certainly claim it.

The table, in fact, probably understates the average amounts now being claimed for each type of deduction. The figures are the latest breakdowns available from the Treasury, but do not reflect the latest increases in property taxes, interest rates or medical costs.

If, in December, it becomes clear that your total deductions will barely exceed the standard deduction, you may gain by deferring expenditures to the following year. Then you can add them to that year's outlays and take a larger deduction in the second year.

Just remember to keep receipts and canceled checks and make notations on your check stubs of deductible expenses. Also keep in mind that moving expenses for a new job, out-of-town travel costs, and sick pay are *not* itemized deductions. *They are adjustments to gross income and they can be deducted in addition to your itemized deductions.*

If you learn about a deduction you could have taken last year but did not, you have not lost the money. The IRS office will give you a special form, 1040-X, on which to make your claim. Taxpayers have up to three years to claim refunds for overpaid tax. Is it worth it for possibly only

$20 or $30? Many taxpayers find it the best return they will get on a postage stamp.

Deduction for taxes paid

The typical American family pays more for taxes, hidden or direct, than it pays for housing or for food. The personal deductions in the income tax law permit you to get a fraction of your tax outlay back, but you can also claim deductions for most of the state and local taxes you pay.

These are by far the most rapidly rising segment of your tax bill. Real estate and state sales and income tax collections are climbing at least twice as rapidly as federal taxes, and they will be doing so indefinitely. So if you have not added up your combined state, city and county tax bills for a few years, do so. The total may help you to decide whether to itemize your deductions.

Deductions may be taken for general sales taxes, gasoline and motor fuel taxes, income taxes, real property taxes and personal property taxes imposed by state and local governments, and for income and real property taxes levied by foreign governments.

Other state, local and foreign taxes are deductible *only* if they are paid as a cost of doing business or for the production of income. These include poll taxes, cigarette and tobacco taxes, alcoholic beverage taxes, driver's license fees, and state and local transfer taxes.

Real estate taxes are, of course, deductible. But generally you cannot deduct water and sewer assessments on your property because they are assumed to increase its value. If the assessment was for maintenance or repair, however, the amount may be deductible; your local tax collector can tell you.

If you sold real estate during the year, you can claim deductions for the portion of the year that you held the property; the buyer takes the deductions for the remaining days in the year.

State sales tax totals are computed by IRS, to a large extent. You may use the total taken directly from the Optional State Sales Tax Tables issued by the IRS district director in every state having a sales tax. These tables also appear in your Form 1040 booklet. They show typical outlays for taxpayers at each level of adjusted gross income, up to $20,000. If your sales tax deductions do not exceed these official estimates, your claim generally will be accepted without proof.

In using the state tables, start with your adjusted gross income to find the line which applies to you. But if you had some income which was not included in adjusted gross income, add that, too, before using the table to find your deduction.

For example, you may have income from Social Security or other tax-exempt pension income, or the interest earnings on tax-exempt municipal bonds, or dividend income (which is exempt from tax up to $100), or the

50 percent of any long-term capital gains which is excluded from income.

For example: The Grahams, a couple with two children, living in the District of Columbia, have adjusted gross income of $15,000. The table shows they can deduct $168 for the D.C. sales tax. But they remember they also have $700 of earnings in tax-exempt municipal bonds and $400 of nontaxable capital gain. Adding these to their adjusted gross income brings their total to $16,100. Again consulting the table, the Grahams find they are entitled to a $175 deduction, a gain of $7.

Those with incomes above $20,000 must also do some arithmetic. The sales tax table goes only as high as the $19,999 bracket. Persons with higher incomes should:

Start with the highest amount on the sales tax table for their family size;

Add 2 percent of that starting amount for every thousand dollars of income from $20,000 to $50,000;

Add 1 percent of the starting amount for every thousand dollars of income from $50,000 to $100,000.

For example: The Davises, a family of four in the District of Columbia, have income of $60,000. This is how Davis computes his sales tax deduction:

He starts with the amount shown on the D. C. table—$195. To arrive at the tax on the next $30,000 of his income, he adds 2 percent of $195, or $3.90, and multiplies by 30. The result is $117.

For the remaining $10,000 of his income, Davis adds 1 percent of $195, or $1.95, and multiplies that by 10. The result is $19.50.

He adds together the original $195, the $117 and the $19.50; his total deduction for D.C. sales tax is $331.50.

If you buy an automobile, you may add the sales tax on it to the deduction shown on the official table. The tax on the purchase of a new or used car is collected in many states by the state motor vehicle department at the time the new owner registers it.

Large purchases such as cars or boats are not taken into account in the Optional State Sales Tax Tables. In adding the tax to your deduction, you should make a notation of the special purchase in the section of your tax return for general sales tax. Several blank lines are provided on your return for such use. (In Vermont the sales tax paid on an automobile may not be added because it is not classed as a "general" sales tax.)

If for any other reason the official table falls short of your actual sales tax outlays, you should report the amount actually paid. Just be ready to substantiate your claim.

State gasoline taxes may be deducted in addition to the general sales tax. The IRS also provides in Form 1040 a state-by-state list of gasoline taxes, and a guideline table showing the deduction which can be taken for various totals of mileage driven during the year.

The table is computed for cars having six or eight cylinders, and averaging about fifteen miles to the gallon. If you drive a four-cylinder car, the gasoline deduction should be cut in half; but if you get less than fifteen miles to the gallon, you can increase the deduction. For example, if you drive 12,000 miles and pay a 7 cents state tax, the table shows you can deduct $63. But if your car gets only ten miles per gallon, your gasoline outlays are 50 percent higher, so your deduction is $95.

Transfer taxes imposed by states on the sale of real estate, stock or other securities may be claimed as an itemized deduction if paid in a transaction entered into for profit (as, an investor paying stock transfer taxes). However, if paid in connection with a trade or business, they are reported as business expenses, and are taken as an adjustment from gross income, not claimed as an itemized deduction.

Not deductible as itemized deductions are federal income taxes; estate and gift taxes; hunting and fishing licenses; water and sewer charges; auto inspection fees. If any of these are paid as business expenses, they are deductible as adjustments to gross income.

Some taxpayers wishing to bunch their deductions in a certain year have deliberately postponed payment of one installment of their real estate taxes from the previous year. The penalty for delaying a payment from September to January was insignificant compared to the tax saving.

Late payment of property taxes can hardly be recommended. But early payment is welcomed by the states. In the many states where the homeowner pays his half-year property tax installments in March and September, it is simple to pay in advance the March payment due in the following year. The prepayment permits you to crowd one and a half years' property tax payments into one year.

If your property tax is $600 a year, and if you are in the 36 percent tax bracket, the prepayment of one tax installment could save you $108.

You would have only half your usual property tax to pay in the following year; you could take the standard deduction, if it worked to your advantage.

Foreign taxes. Income taxes paid to foreign countries or U.S. possessions may be taken as an itemized deduction or claimed as a credit against the U.S. income tax, if the taxpayer itemizes. He cannot claim either the credit or a deduction unless he itemizes his deduction.

Note that if you received dividends on foreign investments, you are probably paying a withheld tax to the foreign country. You may deduct this tax in either of the ways mentioned.

Deductions for interest

For decades taxpayers complained that the "finance charges," "carrying charges," or "service charges" imposed by retail stores on their customers' credit accounts should be considered interest and should be deductible as interest.

The IRS finally agreed in 1972 that, in effect, such charges really *are* interest and are deductible. Previously IRS argued that the finance charge, which usually is 1.5 percent a month or 18 percent a year, could be deducted only if the taxpayer could prove that it was just interest—that it did not include a credit investigation fee or other non-interest cost. Few, if any, taxpayers could offer such proof. So IRS would permit a deduction of only 6 percent.

In effect, the deductibility of the charge depended on what the store called it. Now IRS says that the facts of the credit transaction govern the deduction, not the label applied to the charge.

The key ruling involved a retail store with a typical "revolving credit account" under which the finance charge is imposed only if the customer doesn't pay his full balance within thirty days after the billing. The charge is not a fixed fee but is based on the amount of the unpaid balance and is computed monthly. It is paid solely for the privilege of deferring payment. In short, it is interest.

The taxpayer may now deduct the full amount of the charge as interest. This applies also to the amounts levied on a customer's account by a bank under a credit card plan for a customer's failure to meet the payments, and to the finance charges on credit cards.

Though the ruling permits deduction of the full amount of a retail finance charge even when investigation and other costs are also covered, the IRS ruling makes a point of differentiating a service charge from interest.

It said: "A service charge is a fixed charge having no relationship to the amount borrowed or the time given to pay, whereas interest is based on the amount deferred and the time of deferral."

Interest on a mortgage, or on money borrowed from a bank, finance company or credit union is usually stated separately from any fixed charges involved in the transaction, so there is no difficulty in figuring the interest deduction.

The interest deduction can help a little in sending a child to college. Tuition contracts, under which banks or other lenders advance funds to pay for the costs of college or prep school tuition, fees, and board and room, are really installment purchases. The bank makes the required annual, semi-annual or quarterly payments to the college; the parent makes monthly payments to the bank. An interest charge is added to the amount of monthly payment; this is deductible on income tax returns. The interest charge usually is plainly stated; if not, the bank will give the information on request.

Mortgage interest

If you have a mortgage on your home or other property, you are entitled to deduct the interest paid. This is usually a home buyer's biggest deduction, and sometimes is sufficient in itself to justify itemizing—

although interest payments do decline as the mortgage matures. You must separate the interest expenses from the amounts you are paying on the principal and for taxes, insurance and so on. If necessary, get a statement of the interest total from the lending institution.

If you are charged a penalty for paying off your mortgage ahead of schedule, the penalty also is deductible as interest. This is true for automobile financing or any other loan.

In the late 1960s, an era of scarce mortgage credit and high interest, mortgage "points" became a sore issue to home buyers. *These mortgage interest "points" are now deductible.* Points, in real estate language, are deductions from the face value of a mortgage. Each point is a 1 percent deduction. You, as a home buyer who is getting a mortgage loan to pay for a house, will be paying interest on the full face amount of the mortgage, but you will not get that much money to put into your new house.

For example, if you are buying a house for $35,000 you might get a $25,000 mortgage at 8 percent interest, plus a lender's charge of five points. That means you will get 5 percent less than $25,000; the lender will keep $1,250 and give you $23,750. But you will repay him the full $25,000.

The IRS acknowledged in 1969 that the home buyer can deduct the "points" as interest if the points are really an extra charge for the mortgage loan, and not a fee for services rendered. The fact that the lending institution may call the points a "processing fee" or "service charge" is of no consequence if, in fact, you are paying them as an extra interest charge on your mortgage.

Whether you can claim all your deduction for points in the first year will depend on how you pay the points. There are two ways.

If the bank or savings and loan company simply gives you a check for your mortgage minus the points (in the example above, a check for $23,750), you have not actually paid the points. You have only undertaken to pay them as you pay off the mortgage. So each year during the life of the mortgage you will deduct from taxes as interest 5 percent of that year's payment on the principal of the mortgage.

But if possible, do it the other way. Pay the points out of your own savings account or other personal funds. The IRS has ruled that in such a case the entire amount can be deducted in the year paid. To the home buyer it is the same thing as adding that much to his down payment.

The importance of this choice is obvious. An extra deduction for interest would be a boon to almost any taxpayer who has just negotiated the buying and furnishing of a home.

Note: Points which are taken in place of specified service charges, such as appraisal fees, commissions, title reports or escrow fees, are neither interest nor part of the cost of the home. If they .are paid in connection with rental or business property, they are added to the cost of the property when you compute the depreciation.

You may also be able to build your interest deduction, in an install-ment purchase, by making a bargained adjustment of the price. For ex-ample, on a property sale the buyer in a high tax bracket may save money by agreeing to pay $80,000 at 8 percent instead of $85,000 at 7 percent.

Investment interest. For years an unlimited deduction for interest paid was a convenient tax shelter. Congress has now placed some limits on interest deduction, but the change affects only those taxpayers who make very large investments.

The limitation applies to interest costs which are incurred to make or carry investments. In the absence of such a limit, the interest deduction was a special boon to the real estate investor. He could borrow heavily on a mortgage to swing the purchase or construction of a building, then use his yearly interest payments as current deductions to shelter from tax the same amount of ordinary income, including his rental from the building.

This would help finance the investment. In many cases, in fact, the in-terest deduction plus deductions for rapid depreciation left him with money in his pocket while he was showing losses on his tax return.

Then, when the property was sold, the profit on the sale was taxed at the lower capital gains rate—a profitable arrangement, made somewhat less so by the 1969 tax changes.

The new law limited the deduction to 50 percent of the excess invest-ment interest. Excess investment interest is defined as the amount by which the interest payments on indebtedness incurred to purchase or carry investments exceeds $25,000, plus the taxpayer's net investment in-come, plus his net long term capital gains.

For example: Let us say that a taxpayer has $15,000 salary and $60,000 of net investment income. He pays $30,000 of investment inter-est. He can deduct the whole $30,000 because it is less than the total of $25,000 plus his $60,000 of net investment income.

Another example: A taxpayer has $40,000 salary and $20,000 of net in-vestment income. He pays $50,000 of investment interest. His interest deduction is $47,500. It was figured by adding $25,000 to his $20,000 net investment income; then adding half the $5,000 difference between that total ($45,000) and the $50,000 total of his investment interest.

Obviously, only a large investment generates an interest payment big enough to run into the limitation. At 7 percent interest, the taxpayer would have to borrow more than $350,000 to have a $25,000 interest out-lay.

However, the limitation could be quite costly to an investor with large investment deductions, large long-term capital gains, and no other net in-vestment income. Investment income includes the income from dividends, interest and rents.

The limitation on excess investment interest does not affect non-investment kinds of interest, such as interest on installment credit or home mortgages, or on money borrowed to purchase consumer goods. Excluded also is money borrowed in connection with a trade or business, including loans to build structures to be used in a trade or business. Nor does it apply to investment interest on property, if the debt on the property was incurred before December 17, 1969.

Prepayment of interest. The advantages of prepaying some deductible expenses in certain years have been stressed. In a year when tax rates are high, it is useful to crowd tax deductions into that year by paying taxes, interest, charitable contributions and medical bills ahead of time if possible. A word of caution is in order, however.

Until 1968, the Treasury permitted taxpayers to claim in one year a deduction for a prepayment of interest for as much as five years ahead. The rule then was changed.

Now a prepayment of interest for more than twelve months beyond the end of the tax year is not deductible in the year it is paid. The Treasury holds that prepayment for a longer period may "materially distort" the income of the taxpayer.

If you had paid in 1971 the interest due on a bank loan for 1971, 1972, 1973 and 1974, the Treasury would have denied a deduction for 1973 and 1974. You would have to deduct the appropriate portions of the payment in those years.

Presumably the Treasury would have permitted you to deduct the prepayment for 1972. But it is possible, if the amount is large in proportion to your taxable income, that even a twelve-month prepayment might be rejected as being a "material distortion of income."

Contributions

The government not only provides exemption from taxes for churches, schools and charities but also encourages private citizens to make gifts to them by treating such contributions as tax-deductible. The intent of this time-honored practice was to promote good works and thus presumably serve the national interest and help such institutions as hospitals, colleges and social service agencies perform a multitude of services which otherwise the government would have to provide.

However, the Tax Reform Act of 1969 altered some of the rules for charitable giving, and it seemed possible that further restraints on the charity deductions might result from the wave of tax reform sentiment in Congress in the early 1970s. Most of the 1969 changes resulted from widely held suspicions that some tax-deduction devices were being abused.

Most taxpayers need not worry about the changes because they do not affect the average donor. They do affect some forms of giving favored by upper-middle and higher-income taxpayers, such as contributions of appreciated stocks or property and "bargain sales" of appreciated stocks to charities at cost, or contribution of the rent-free use of property or the income from property. These devices have held substantial tax-saving benefits, and some still do, despite the sterner rules.

On the other hand, the limit on deductions for charitable giving has been boosted from 30 percent of adjusted gross income to 50 percent, generally. And the following deductible contributions remain unchanged in the law, if made to public charities without strings attached:

• Cash gifts

• Contributions of securities or real estate, but with some limitations on property which has appreciated in value

• Used clothing, appliances, furniture or other unappreciated property

• Expenses connected with fund-raising activities such as rummage sales, and theater parties

• Out-of-pocket costs incurred in performing services for charity

The last item highlights one of the discriminations of the tax laws. There is no deduction for the person who donates services instead of cash or property. The highly-paid performer-entertainer who entertains for charity gets no tax deduction; neither does the professional accountant who keeps a church's books nor the skilled editor who puts out a parish newspaper.

All that may be claimed by those engaged in charitable activities are deductions for actual out-of-pocket expenses, including transportation. If you use your own car, you may claim a flat 7 cents a mile; or, if you prefer, compute the actual costs of operating the car. (The 7-cents-a-mile allowance frequently does not cover the actual costs of using your own car.) If you are a designated delegate to the convention of a charitable organization, your travel expenses to the convention are deductible.

Long after kidney transplants had become quite common, IRS ruled that the donor of a kidney may deduct as medical expenses the surgical, hospital, laboratory and transportation costs involved, although the medical care is really that of the recipient of the kidney, not the donor's. IRS even agreed that a prospective donor whose offer was rejected could deduct the expenses involved. This seems also to apply to donations of other organs.

When blood is donated to the Red Cross, IRS says the donor cannot take a deduction for the value of the blood. But he can deduct his transportation and—presumably—other out-of-pocket costs.

Contributions in money or property are deductible if made to U.S. organizations operated solely for religious, charitable, scientific, literary or educational purposes or for the prevention of cruelty to children or animals; to veterans' organizations; to state, federal or local governmental units for public purposes; to qualified private organizations engaged in fostering or preserving natural beauty and to some nonprofit cemetery organizations.

Contributions to individuals are not deductible, with two exceptions.

Costs up to $50 a month are deductible for keeping a needy student in your home under a program sponsored by a charity. Also, outlays for movies, swimming, etc., for a "little brother" if the anti-delinquency group, Big Brothers of America, picks the boy.

It is an absolute "must" to keep a list of your larger cash contributions, together with canceled checks, receipts and acknowledgments. Most well-run churches provide a statement of your payments on your annual pledge; and the management of every fund-raising campaign, well aware that tax deductibility is one of their big talking points, is prepared to furnish proof of your donation.

Pledges and subscriptions do not count with the IRS. You must be prepared to show that the contribution actually was made. And if you buy tickets to charity bazaars, garden tours, dinners, or other fund-raising events, you can deduct only the portion of cost which exceeds the fair value of what you bought. If you paid $20 to see a benefit performance of a show that usually costs $10, you should claim a charitable contribution of $10, not $20, and keep your ticket stubs. Tickets to raffles are not deductible.

There is no deduction for contributions to social clubs or chambers of commerce. Memberships in tax-exempt museums, symphony societies or theatre groups, entitling the member to free or reduced admissions, are not deductible. However, the Treasury recognizes that frequently "sponsors," "sustaining members" and other persons pay dues much higher than the value of the benefits they receive. These members may deduct "that portion of the total payment that may be properly treated as a charitable contribution."

Gifts of used clothing, furniture, toys and other property to a church or charity are deductible, but not at a value anything like their original cost. The deduction is the "fair market value" at the time of the gift. The Treasury has argued that such value was what a *dealer* would pay for the same items. It lost that argument in a court case; the court held that the deductible value was what a willing retail buyer would pay.

If you are contributing used clothing or furniture, prepare a list for the charitable organization and keep a duplicate for yourself; if possible, have the organization's driver give you a receipt when he picks up the donation.

Small cash contributions, too numerous to record, are an almost weekly fact of life. Nowadays, some Internal Revenue district offices permit deductions up to $70, or as high as $94 in some areas, without substantiation. The IRS national office permits this forbearance without recognizing it as a national policy. And some courts have allowed larger deductions based only on the taxpayer's word.

But it is simpler and safer to have the records ready.

Giving appreciated property. Though Congress wrote into the 1969 tax law pages of new restrictions on deductions for charitable giving, it left one broad avenue of tax savings open to taxpayers at all income levels. This is the donation of property whose value now is greater than its cost when you bought it. Your tax deduction, therefore, could be greater than your payment for the property.

To qualify for this break the giver must give a capital asset—shares of stock, real estate, or other property which, if it had been sold instead of given to charity, would have produced a long-term capital gain. That means, in most cases, that it had been held six months or longer.

For example, James Jennings bought ten shares of stock for a total of $50 in 1954. The stock is now worth $450; Jennings donated the shares to his church. He claimed the full $450 as a tax deduction, avoiding tax on what would have been a $400 capital gain if he had sold the stock.

The advantage of this device over giving $450 cash, or even of selling the stock and giving the proceeds, is obvious. If a high-bracket taxpayer were to take the latter course, selling the stock and giving the proceeds, he would be taxed up to $140 on the sale and would have had $310 left for charity.

Any deductions for such "unrealized appreciation" in the value of a contribution must come within the old overall limitation on deductions for charitable giving—30 percent of adjusted gross income. Otherwise the limit, as raised by the 1969 law, is generally 50 percent. That was the only substantial liberalization in the rules for charitable giving. The new restrictions, as well as the tax breaks which remain available in spite of them, are discussed in the pages which follow.

The 1969 Tax Reform Act took a good deal of tax gimmickry out of giving. Several off-beat types of charitable deductions were either changed in ways that would divert more taxpayer dollars into the Treasury, or eliminated altogether.

Most of the changes affect tax maneuvers which few taxpayers would or should have attempted without professional advice in any case. They will be mentioned only briefly here.

• "Bargain Sales" to charity: It formerly was possible to avoid all taxable gain by selling property to a charity at cost; now some tax would be owed. Under the former rules, the giver could deduct the full market value as a charitable deduction, and pay no tax because he had no profit on the sale.

For example, John Block owned stock that he bought in 1964 for $14,000 but was now worth $20,000. He sold it to a charity for $14,000. He took a deduction for $6,000 charitable donation. That amount, of course, was what the charity gained when it resold the shares.

Under the new law, there is still a considerable tax advantage. The taxpayer is allowed a full deduction for the "bargain element"—in the case above, the $6,000 which actually went to the charity. But he no longer gets credit for the full cost, called "basis," or "cost basis," of the property. The law provides a formula under which only a portion of his cost is taken into consideration. Therefore, even though he might take no actual profit on the sale, he is considered to have made some gain—and it is taxable. The IRS will provide information on the computation method.

• Use of property: A giver who grants a charity the right to use his property cannot claim a charitable deduction for the rental value. A taxpayer who, for example, gives to a school the free use of a building having a $5,000 a year rental value cannot deduct the $5,000 as a charitable contribution.

• Appreciated property: The new law preserved the tax deduction for gifts to charity of appreciated property, if the property has been held six months or longer, but curtailed the tax breaks for donations of other property.

In general, there is no longer a tax advantage in contributing to charity any property which, if it were sold, would result in a short-term capital gain or ordinary income. That would include securities, real property or other capital assets held for less than six months. It also covers goods given from a businessman's inventory or produce donated by a farmer, as explained next.

• Gifts of merchandise: The new rule on appreciated property is broad enough to discourage merchants and businessmen from donating items from their shelves and inventories, and farmers from donating produce.

A retailer has a ready-made appreciation for every item in his stock —the difference between his cost price and his selling price. Until Congress acted in 1969 he could claim a deduction for the full selling price, however large his markup over the cost. Under the new law he could deduct only the cost.

The appreciation—the increase in value above the cost to the giver—is taxable in the case of any gifts made to a private non-operating foundation. It is taxable also in the case of such donated property as works of art or inventions created by the giver that would be taxed as ordinary income if the items were sold.

• "Unlimited contributions": A famous tax loophole which often figured in newspaper stories about millionaires who paid no tax at all was ordered phased out by degrees until completely eliminated in 1974. Formerly an unlimited charitable deduction was permitted if, in eight of the ten preceding years, the individual's charitable contributions, plus his taxes paid, amounted to at least 90 percent of his taxable income.

• Two-year trusts: Also eliminated was the "two-year charitable trust." Formerly an individual could put securities or other property into a trust, with the income to be paid to charity. Neither the charity nor the donor would pay tax on it. And the affluent taxpayer could avoid the normal limitation on overall charitable deductions. The two-year trust was ordered abolished.

• Private foundations: Contributions to private foundations are limited to 20 percent of the taxpayer's adjusted gross income, unless made to a private *operating* foundation. If made to a *nonoperating* foundation, they must be distributed to charity within two and a half months after the end of the fiscal year in which the contribution was made. An operating foundation is one which spends its income promptly for the charitable purposes for which the foundation was created; a nonoperating foundation is one which does not turn over its receipts to charity promptly enough to meet the IRS definition of an operating foundation.

Other special rules were applied to private foundations. Such foundations, a form of tax shelter favored by thousands of affluent executives, were severely restricted by the new law. An individual who has established one might be well advised to seek professional advice regarding its continued operation.

Political contributions. Taxpayers filing their returns for 1972 were permitted, for the first time, to take limited deductions or credits on contributions to political candidates, committees or national parties. The plan looks like a permanent fixture in tax law.

The limit for the deduction was set at $50, or $100 for couples filing joint returns. The limit for the credit was fixed at half the contribution made, up to a maximum of $25 of contributions for an individual or $50 for a couple. (In effect, that means ceilings of $12.50 and $25 on the credit.)

The question that immediately arises is: Which is more advantageous to the taxpayer, to take the itemized deduction or the tax credit?

First, if the taxpayer uses the standard deduction or low income allowance he cannot take a political deduction at all. But he can still take the credit if he wishes.

Second, if his taxable income is below $16,000, the credit is always the bigger tax saving. If his income is $44,000, the deduction is always better.

Third, the deduction is always your best bet if your taxable income is:

—$16,000 to $20,000 and your contribution exceeds $89.
—$20,000 to $24,000 and your contribution exceeds $78.
—$24,000 to $28,000 and your contribution exceeds $69.
—$28,000 to $32,000 and your contribution exceeds $64.
—$32,000 to $36,000 and your contribution exceeds $56.
—$36,000 to $40,000 and your contribution exceeds $52.

Fourth, at each of those taxable income levels the *credit* is more advantageous if your contribution is *less* than the amounts shown. If your contribution is the exact amount shown, the tax savings are equal for the credit and the deduction.

Raffle tickets purchased for political fund-raising do not qualify for credit or deduction; but deductions can be claimed for transportation costs or other out-of-pocket expenses of services performed for a candidate.

There is also a so-called check-off plan to encourage small contributions, though it got off to a controversial start. Taxpayers can designate $1 of their taxes ($2 if filing jointly) as a contribution to a general fund to be apportioned to the major parties for use in presidential election campaigns.

Congress seemed clearly to have intended that a box be provided on Forms 1040 and 1040A in which taxpayers could indicate whether they wished to make such a designation. But in introducing this device in 1972, the IRS required that taxpayers who wished to make the small contributions obtain and fill out a new Form 4875. The Democratic party leadership —which needed the money more than the Republicans in that particular year—fumed at this device, saying that the nuisance of getting the extra form undoubtedly discouraged many taxpayers from earmarking the dollar or two. A court action was filed, but by the time the Democrats could get into the courts the tax forms had been printed and mailed. In 1973, under congressional pressure, IRS did an about-face. Presumably the check-off will be a fixture on Form 1040 hereafter.

Public interest law firms. Contributions to public interest law firms— those which seek to promote social goals by legal action—are deductible if the firms meet the IRS guidelines for "charitable" organizations. The guidelines say that, to qualify, a group must be litigating something that could reasonably be considered "a broad public interest rather than private."

Many public interest law groups go to court to prevent alleged defilement of the environment; others, like some of the Ralph Nader groups, support consumer rights and consumer safety; some are even waging legal fights for more information from IRS about how tax decisions are made.

IRS indicates that it would not approve deductions for firms litigating matters in which the private stakes were large enough to justify private legal action. A firm could neither promote "a program of disruption of the judicial system," it said, nor accept "charitable donations" that were really fees from private interests.

Medical and dental expense deductions

If you go to a professional tax adviser to prepare your return, one of his first questions will be: "Did you or your wife have any major illness in the past year?"

This is because medical expense deductions can be among the most important tax savers available to ordinary taxpayers and, in the unlucky years when illness or accident pile up a tidal wave of doctors' bills, the deduction can be a financial lifesaver.

You can deduct those medical and dental expenses which exceed 3 percent of your adjusted gross income. Payments to chiropractors, osteopaths and Christian Science practitioners also are deductible within that limit.

Medicines and drugs are deductible to the extent that they exceed 1 percent of your adjusted gross income. Toothbrushes, toothpaste, feminine hygiene supplies, toiletries and deodorants do not count.

The Pill has been officially ruled deductible, even if used primarily from personal choice. The ruling seems to have been made simply because the Pill is purchasable only by prescription.

Everyone who pays for hospitalization or medical care insurance has a medical deduction. You can deduct half the premium cost, up to $150, regardless of how much your other medical expenses are—and even if you do not have any others at all. The portion of your premiums which you do not deduct under this special provision may be reported as part of your other medical expenses.

Some types of accident and health insurance are not deductible. These are policies which cover risks other than hospital bills, doctors' bills and other medical care. The Treasury does not recognize, for example, premiums paid on insurance against loss of income, loss of limbs or eyes, or indemnity for accidental death.

The optional monthly payments to cover doctor bills under Medicare are deductible, but not the portion of your regular Social Security tax payment which pays for hospital insurance. Premiums paid on policies issued by many companies to "supplement" Medicare are not deductible if they merely pay so many dollars a week while you are hospitalized. To be deductible, they must cover medical care expenses. The medical payments portion of your auto collision insurance premium is deductible.

Many outlays ordinarily nondeductible are deductible if a doctor prescribes or recommends them .It is advisable to get a doctor's statement when you claim such deductions as a bedroom air conditioner to relieve allergy; special chair, bed or mattress for an arthritic or cardiac patient; swimming pool or a bedroom or bathroom on ground floor level, central air conditioning, a garage nearer the house, or a home elevator when recommended for medical care. To the extent the addition or remodeling adds to the value of the dwelling, the cost is not deductible. An appraiser's valuation of the house before and after is your best evidence for a deduction. The appraisal fee is deductible.

A trip to a warmer or drier climate prescribed by a doctor to correct or relieve some specific ailment is deductible (but not the cost of lodging and meals while there). Reasonable expenses of a nurse to accompany a patient are deductible, if recommended by a doctor. A trip taken merely to improve general health or mental outlook is not deductible.

Transportation costs to a clinic, hospital or doctor's office are deductible; for use of your car the 7-cents-a-mile allowance may be claimed. Travel to a doctor in another city is recognized. So is the cost of a parent traveling with a sick child, and even a parent's trip to visit an ailing child if a doctor has recommended it for the child's therapy.

The expense of sending children to special schools for the handicapped —such as an institution where the deaf can learn speech or lip reading, or the blind can learn Braille—are deductible if the principal reason for the student's attending is to alleviate the handicap. Costs of a seeing-eye dog for the blind, or a "guardian dog" for the deaf, are deductible. So are outlays for special telephones for the deaf.

Your medical deductions are *not* limited to expenses for you, your wife and your dependents. You may also deduct your payments for anyone who could have been your dependent except that his own income exceeds the $750 dependency ceiling. For example, you may provide most of your father's support, but he has $800 of income from bonds. Though you could not claim an exemption for him as your dependent you can claim a deduction for any hospital, doctor, or other medical bills you pay for his care.

Sometimes the cost of room and board in a home for the aged is deductible as a medical expense. Courts have held that such costs "at an institution other than a hospital might constitute medical care." But this depends on the facts in the individual case: not on the kind of institution, but on "the condition of the person and the care he receives." A deduction was allowed recently for an elderly person who was unable to care for himself and was dependent on professional nursing at a home for the elderly. The deduction was refused in another case because no medical care was given.

Employes' business expenses

Millions of employes pay out-of-pocket expenses in connection with their jobs for which their employers do not reimburse them. Many are not aware that tax deductions are possible for some outlays they incur every day, week or month. The list is long and varied; it goes far beyond the categories of tools, uniforms and union dues normally mentioned in tax guides. (See "Employes' Business Deductions," in the Appendix.)

In many cases, these are exactly the same kinds of outlay which a businessman, self-employed person or professional man deducts as a cost of doing business.

The self-employed taxpayer, however, deducts these costs at the "top" of his Form 1040—as an adjustment to gross income. That is also where the outside salesman deducts the same kind of costs—and where the unreimbursed travel expenses of employes are reported.

The employe subtracts his unreimbursed business expenses among the "Miscellaneous Deductions" which he can itemize on Schedule A. They are subtracted from adjusted gross income, and the following list suggests the kind of deductions that are possible:

- Trade journals, technical studies and books needed in your field
- Dues and fees of professional organizations and unions
- Gifts and entertainment outlays for business purposes
- Supplies, tools, stationery provided by you
- Use of your personal car for business
- An office-at-home, when required for your work, or for a second income
- A portion of your home telephone expenses, if used for business—also telegraph, postage and messengers.

In this era of "moonlighting," when a high and rapidly rising percentage of workers have second incomes—part-time work for other employes, or small-scale businesses, or free-lance activity of many kinds—the office-at-home is becoming a familiar phenomenon. Such part-time activity, of course, helps to justify the office-at-home deduction.

It will not do, however, simply to declare that your den or playroom is an office. If the IRS ever investigates your tax return, the agent will want particularly to confer with you in that very room. He will expect it to have some of the attributes of an office and to look as if thoughtful work could be carried on there.

He may also want to see a letter from your employer indicating that you do take work home or do incur business expenses which are not reimbursed.

"Miscellaneous Deductions" include many other types of job-connected costs—employment agency fees, protective clothing, public stenographers, safe deposit rental, and the costs of tax guidance.

Casualty losses

A taxpayer's claim for casualty losses—the damage done by fire, storm, accidents or other destructive force (see Appendix for list) sets off an alarm buzzer at the IRS. If the loss involved is in any way substantial, an IRS agent may soon be inquiring into the claim.

Be prepared to prove any casualty loss you deduct. If possible, be ready with pictures taken before the damage was repaired.

"The camera can be a potent tax tool," according to one tax specialist. "Use up a roll of film in and around your own house every year or so," he advises. "Take pictures of your furniture, your piano, your study, your draperies, your workshop, your attic, garage and basement.

"Take pictures of your bookshelves and the books on them. If you collect rare coins, china, glass, stamps, paintings, photograph them.

"It's a good thing to have an inventory too, but pictures are quick, easy and indisputable.

"Then if you have a fire, or a bursting pipe that floods floors and ruins rugs, or a large-scale burglary while you are on vacation, you have evidence of what you owned and what condition it was in before the disaster."

Before-and-after pictures of your house and grounds, showing valued trees, shrubs and plantings, are the best evidence of any loss by hurricane, snowstorms, flooding rains, and falling trees. Losses from theft, embezzlement, vandalism, household accidents and automobile collisions also are deductible, to the extent not insured.

In each such case the deduction can be claimed only to the amount of loss which exceeds $100.

But any loss to business property, or to rental or income property, is deductible in full.

This raises an interesting point about your automobile. Suppose you use your car 75 percent for business and 25 percent for personal transportation. You suffer a $200 loss from vandalism or other casualty that is not covered by insurance. Your tax deduction for the casualty is not $100, as it would be if it were purely a nonbusiness loss. It is $150.

That's because the business loss is fully deductible; it comes to 75 percent of $200, or $150. The damage attributable to personal use, 25 percent of $200, is not deductible. It doesn't matter whether the car was in business or personal use when the damage occurred.

A related point: If your car is used for business and you claim a useful life of at least three years for it, you may be entitled to some investment credit. Check the rules relating to that credit.

If you use the automatic mileage allowance as a deduction for business use, you cannot take a separate deduction for depreciation on the car. But you could still take the investment credit if you qualify for it.

If you use your car for both family and business use, you can allocate the purchase cost and take the investment credit on the business portion. If the car is used 75 percent for business, and if the car cost $3,000, you would claim the 75 percent credit on three-fourths of the $3,000 outlay, or $2,250. That would save you $157.50 in tax.

Back to nonbusiness casualty losses: The $100 exclusion applies to each casualty, not to each piece of property damaged or destroyed. If a fire in the bedroom destroyed a bed worth $220, draperies worth $75, and did other damage totaling $180, the deductible loss would be the total of those items, $475, less the $100 reduction. You could claim $375 on your tax return.

The $100 limitation also means that if your camera worth $80 was stolen, you cannot claim any deduction at all. If your family car suffered $200 damage but insurance covered $100, you have no deduction because your actual loss just matched the $100 limitation.

If you are the victim of a theft or a robbery or an act of vandalism, report the loss to police at once. Otherwise the IRS may dispute your claim to a deduction. Without a police report on file, you may have trouble proving that you suffered a loss, or that your loss was actually a theft. And make sure that the loss you reported to police is the same as the loss you reported to IRS.

To claim a deduction for a loss by hurricane, fire, flood, storm or landslide, you must be able to show not only that you owned the property and that your loss was a direct result of the disaster. You must also have evidence showing:

• The kind of disaster and the time it occurred. Save the newspaper clippings; or get back copies of the issues describing the storm

• The cost valuation of the property, as shown by the sale contract or deed, along with canceled checks or receipts to show modernization or improvement costs

• The amount of depreciation you have allowed for your claim

• The extent of insurance, if any

• The value of the property before and after the damage.

The last item is a key one. In claiming deduction for trees or shrubs damaged or destroyed, for example, you must establish that there has been a decrease in the *total value* of the real estate.

This usually means obtaining an appraisal in writing from a qualified appraiser. Appraisers are easy to locate in any city; their fee usually is money well spent, in supporting your claim to a tax deduction. The fee is deductible.

Many taxpayers have little idea of the value of mature trees and ornamental shrubs which have been growing in their yards. One Washington, D.C., business writer lost three trees in a March fall of heavy wet snow. He did not know their value, but claimed $350 as a safely conservative estimate of his loss. Both the IRS and the District of Columbia tax collector challenged the claim. The writer belatedly called in an appraiser; to his surprise, and slight embarrassment, he found that he could and should have claimed a loss of $2,000 on the basis of the overall decrease in value of his residence. He filed an amended return.

Though your deductible loss on real property is the value before the casualty, less the value after the casualty, there is a catch. The claimed loss may not be greater than the cost, or "adjusted basis," of the property and must be reduced by any insurance recovered.

The term "adjusted basis" or "basis" usually means the cost of the property—whatever you paid for it. But if the property has been subject to depreciation or previous casualty losses, the cost must be reduced to reflect these changes. On the other hand, any outlays for capital improvements—say, the addition of a porch, or garage, or central air conditioning—should be *added*; the "adjustment" in this case is upward. The result of both the increases and decreases is the "adjusted basis" of the property. The term is also used for securities and other assets.

In computing the casualty deduction, the loss also is reduced by any recovery from insurance, as noted, and the $100 limitation still must come out of your claim.

For example: Your beach home was heavily damaged by a hurricane. It cost you $5,000 but was valued at $8,000. The value after the storm was $2,500. You collected $4,000 from the insurance. This is how you will compute your casualty loss:

Value of property before storm $8,000
Value after the damage 2,500

Decrease in fair market value 5,500
But loss is limited to your cost (basis), or .. 5,000
Less: insurance paid 4,000

Casualty loss 1,000
Less: $100 limitation 100

Deduction allowable .... $ 900

An inconsistency of tax law intrudes at this point. Since the Treasury insists that a casualty loss on real property is the loss in market value rather than the cost of repairs or replacements, one might assume that any loss in fair market value caused by natural disaster would qualify for the deduction.

But this is not so. The owner of a residence in the middle of a mudslide area tried to get a deduction though his own home was not damaged. Houses all around his were ruined and the prospect that a slide would destroy his home reduced its market value drastically. But a court said he could not claim a deduction unless there was actual physical damage to his own home.

There are special rules for computing casualty losses on business property and on property used partly for business and partly for personal purposes. They are explained in the IRS booklet called "Tax Information on Disasters, Casualty Losses, and Thefts." Ask your district director for a free copy of Publication 547. The "Tax Guide for Small Business" may also be helpful. Order it from the Government Printing Office, Washington, D.C. 20402.

Disaster areas. Tax help of an unusual kind—an off-season refund, in many cases—is provided for the victims of natural disasters. In states or regions proclaimed by the President to be "disaster areas," tax relief has been liberalized greatly.

Taxpayers whose property was damaged at any time during a year can claim the loss on last year's tax return, even if the return already has been filed.

Previously, if your property was hit by disaster before the filing date, normally April 15, you had a limited choice. You could wait to deduct the casualty loss on your next year's return, in the usual way. Or you could claim it on the prior year's return by filing an amended return if necessary, but only if the disaster occured before April 15.

In 1972 the deadly Hurricane Agnes struck the eastern U.S. seaboard in June, and drove home the message that more help was needed. Congress first made the retroactive help available on disasters up to mid-year; then it went the whole way with a law providing that those who suffer losses in declared disaster areas at *any time during the year* may file amended returns for the previous year.

They can, in effect, claim this year's losses against last year's income. Business and individuals who operate on fiscal years can get similar breaks. They could claim deductions for losses that occurred anytime in 1973, for example, by filing an amended return for a fiscal year that ended in 1973.

The IRS told flood and hurricane victims they could get faster refunds by marking "Disaster Area Loss" at the top of the refund claim. An amended return is filed on Form 1040X for an individual or Form 1120X by a corporation. Appraisals and photographs should be included to establish the amount of loss.

This is one possible situation: Your income tax last year was $7,500, of which you paid $6,000 by withholding. You would have to send another $1,500 with your return on April 15. But a flood struck your county on March 20 and the President proclaimed it a disaster area. Your house suffered $2,000 damage. You decide to claim the loss in the year already ended.

The result: You claim a $1,900 deduction ($2,000 less the $100 limitation). You no longer need to pay the $1,500 balance of your tax liability. Instead you get a cash refund of some of the tax already withheld.

If the flood struck in October—long after the tax year was closed, your return filed, and your $1,500 tax liability paid—you still could file an amended return. You would get your refund quickly—quickly enough, if the IRS machinery is working as planned, to help pay for repairing the house before the onset of winter.

Bad debts

These are not the same as thefts or embezzlements, and are not treated as casualty losses. However, this seems to be an appropriate place to consider them. They are deductible, but are not reported by the taxpayer among his itemized deductions.

A nonbusiness bad debt—a loan you made that became worthless—is treated like an investment that goes wrong. It is shown as a short-term capital loss, on the Schedule D sheet ("Sales or Exchange of Property") that comes with your Form 1040. Therefore, it is deductible whether or not you itemize deductions on your return.

A business bad debt—one arising in the course of your trade or business—goes into Schedule C, "Profit or Loss from Business or Profession." It is a deduction from your gross income.

To claim the bad debt deduction you must be able to prove that the debt was a valid one—not a gift, not a matter of "pay me when you can"—but a legally collectible debt. You must also show evidence that the debt became worthless in the year for which you make the claim—the debtor went bankrupt, for example, or disappeared.

Bad debts of relatives are eyed with suspicion by the Treasury. Loans to children or parents are usually regarded as gifts, as are loans to political parties or campaign committees.

However, if you guarantee a friend's note and are obliged to pay it because of his default, you can claim a deduction if you cannot collect from your friend.

Alimony

From the tax standpoint, alimony and separate maintenance payments amount to income splitting. The husband (or wife, if she pays the alimony) gets the tax deduction for the payments. The spouse who receives them is taxed on them.

This works out fairly well if the husband has the higher income, as is usually the case, because the deduction comes out of the high-bracket income and the payments are taxed at low-bracket rates.

To be deductible, the payments must be periodic and they must be mandatory under the divorce or legal separation decree, or under a written separation agreement or decree of support. Payments of other kinds made to her do not qualify.

For example: Suppose that Mr. Peterson borrowed $15,000 from his wife during their marriage. The divorce decree specifies that he repay the money in installments over fifteen years. He gets no deduction for the repayment.

As another example: Assume that Mr. Johnson agreed to pay $5,000 a year in alimony until Mrs. Johnson dies or remarries. He also agreed to make a final lump-sum payment of $15,000 if she remarries. The lump sum was not deductible. As it happened, Johnson made his final check out for $20,000, the annual payment plus the lump sum. He got no deduction for either. If he had made one check for $5,000 and another for $15,000, he could have deducted the $5,000 "periodic" payment.

Alimony payments must meet one of the several legal definitions of "periodic." One should be sure that his lawyer has the tax consequences in mind so that the payment plan adopted is one which makes the alimony payments periodic and therefore fully deductible. He has a number of choices, including:

• Installments of fixed amounts, such as $150 a month, over an indefinite period (until the spouse dies or remarries, for example)

• A fixed amount (such as $25,000) payable over a period of more than ten years, provided a deduction of more than 10 percent of the whole amount is not taken in any one year

• Payments of an indefinite amount (such as 15 percent of your annual income, whatever it may turn out to be) for a period of ten years or less

- Payments of a fixed amount for ten years or less, provided the payments end upon death or remarriage. Only the latter proviso makes alimony deductible. Otherwise a fixed amount payable in ten years or less does not qualify.

Unless a specified part of the payments is earmarked as child support, the entire payment is deductible as alimony. And the spouse would get the dependency exemptions for the children.

Alimony payments which are specifically designated for child support are not deductible by the husband, nor is the wife taxed on them. However, the husband can count these payments in determining who is entitled to take the dependency exemptions for the children.

Be particularly careful and conservative with claims for alimony deductions. Tax professionals say almost every taxpayer who has alimony deductions will be audited sooner or later, because IRS has found frequent rule violations in the past; it is a profitable area for audit. Many taxpayers have claimed alimony deductions which either did not qualify as periodic alimony payments or were amounts which were required to be paid as child support.

Child care deduction

If you must pay a maid, sitter, nursery school, or child care center to look after your child so that you can work, you may claim a deduction for child care. The deduction also may be claimed for the care of a husband or wife who is mentally or physically incapacitated.

Starting in 1972, very substantial increases in the child care deductions were authorized. The deductions can go as high as $400 a month. They are available to single taxpayers, widowers, divorced or legally separated persons, and couples in which both husband and wife work. But since the liberalizations were intended by Congress mainly to help working women with children, the deduction is discussed in our later chapter, "The Woman Who Works."

Education expenses

A deduction for educational expenses—including the cost of travel away from home primarily to obtain education—is allowed to persons who already are in a business or profession if the reason for the education is:

- To maintain or improve the skills required for the taxpayer's present job
- To meet the specific requirements of his employer
- To comply with the local law or regulations for keeping his present job, salary or professional status.

But, the expenses *cannot* be deducted if the education is primarily to qualify the taxpayer for a new job, or to set up a trade or business, or to further his general education.

If you are a teacher, you can deduct the costs of education designed to broaden your teaching skills and qualify you for promotion in your profession, even if this means qualifying you to teach courses you do not now teach, or to move from teaching into school administrative work.

For a teacher, the law permits a deduction for the summer courses which many school boards require be taken periodically to hold a teaching job.

Similarly, a doctor can take the courses that will qualify him for any specialty in the field of medicine. An engineer may take the courses needed to train him in such new fields as pollution abatement or rocket propulsion—or any of the long-established engineering fields, for that matter. A salesman may take courses to qualify him for an administrative job in his firm, and a production supervisor may take courses that would qualify him for his company's sales department.

How you report your deduction depends on your status as a taxpayer: If you are an employe, it goes as one of the "Miscellaneous Deductions," but the travel portions—including fares, meals and lodging—should be entered as adjustments to gross income. The travel is thus deductible even if you take the standard deduction instead of itemizing.

If you are self-employed, you should take the deduction on Schedule C ("Profit or Loss from Business or Profession").

The Treasury is a bit more lenient than formerly about travel deductions as an educational expense for teachers. It is still conservative, however. The trip must be shown to have a direct relation to the teacher's field of teaching. A music teacher might visit the great opera centers for study. An art teacher could justify visits to the galleries of Paris, Florence or Rome. A language teacher might deduct the cost of visiting countries for the improvement of linguistic skills. Like other unreimbursed travel costs connected with job or profession, these should be deducted as an adjustment to gross income.

It may be helpful, in substantiating a deduction for education expenses, to have a letter from your employer stating that advances in your field or speciality require further schooling in the new developments. There should *always* be a statement, in any case, attached to your return to explain the deduction and the connection of the education with your present job.

*Taxes should be proportioned
to what may be annually spared
by the individual.*

Thomas Jefferson, to James Madison, December, 1784

CHAPTER 6

The
Employe

Although employes on straight salary or wages have fewer tax-saving loopholes than some other taxpayers, a number of opportunities, already noted, are available to them. This chapter will discuss several more.

These include suggestions for splitting, investing and deferring income which usually are considered to be tax shelters of the wealthy. They also can be used, on a smaller scale, by taxpayers of modest income.

Employes' business expenses

As a general rule, an employe can deduct any expenses which are ordinary and necessary in performing his job. These may range from the cost of an engineer's slide rule to the depreciation on a writer's *Encyclopedia Britannica*. (See Appendix.)

An employe deducts *some* of his job expenses as adjustments to gross income, on page one of Form 1040. He takes the rest as "Miscellaneous Deductions," along with such assorted costs as alimony, child care and hurricane losses, on Schedule A, "Itemized Deductions."

A professional man, self-employed businessman, or independent contractor deducts *all* his business costs as adjustments to gross income, after listing and computing them on Schedule C, "Profit or Loss from Business or Profession."

For an employe, the only costs deductible from gross income are the "adjustments" described earlier. They include sick pay, moving expenses, all business expenses of an outside salesman, transportation costs other than commuting to and from work and travel expenses away from home. All these can be claimed even if you take the standard deduction instead of itemizing your other deductible expenses.

The business costs discussed in this chapter are all itemized deductions, so far as employes are concerned. If you claim them, you must not only be able to verify the outlays if challenged but also prove that they are necessary, normal and unreimbursed expenses of doing your job.

The fringes

Employes' fringe benefits are among the best of all tax savers. Because they are noncash, they are nontaxed as received.

If they are deferred-income pensions, annuities, profit-sharing and various other retirement plans whose benefits pay off in later life—the income is taxed, if at all, at the lower tax rates which you presumably will pay when your active earning years are over.

Unions have long recognized that hospitalization, medical and life insurance plans are often worth more to employes than cash pay increases because they are not taxed. They provide economic security which the prudent employe otherwise would buy for himself. Therefore, it is generally advisable for employes to accept the fringe benefits offered by many companies on a cost-sharing basis or, in many other cases, provided with no strings attached. The group plans provide economic security for the employe and family at lower rates than individual coverage. They also carry an invisible discount tag: the tax savings on that portion of your income.

Many employes have further fringe benefits more immediately available: use of the company infirmary, clinic, hospital and medical services, lower-priced meals in the company dining room or cafeteria, perhaps even use of the company swimming pool or tennis courts.

The corporate higher-ups, of course, may drive company cars, consult with customers at high-priced restaurants, golf courses and country clubs, entertain business contacts at night clubs, and attend sales conferences and conventions at plush resorts. "Expense account society," flourishing on tax-deductibility, keeps many high-priced restaurants in business. Although stringent limitations and accounting regulations are enforced by IRS, high living is very emphatically one of the "fringe benefits" of upper-level corporate employes.

For employes less lavishly favored, the list of desirable fringe benefits nevertheless is long and varied. In some union contracts the added fringe benefits each year exceed the cash wage increases. They amount to at least 20 percent, and perhaps more than 25 percent, of the average value of total compensation received by corporation employes.

Here are some of them:
Cafeteria; death benefits; bonuses and awards; discounts on goods purchased from employer; clinic and infirmary services; free parking; group life and disability insurance; holidays; medical and hospitalization insurance; outings and company picnics; paid vacations and sick leave; pensions; profit-sharing plans; stock bonuses and stock options; unemployment insurance; and workmen's compensation insurance.

Self-employed businessmen who incorporate their businesses may enjoy some of the same benefits as their workers—and that is one of the reasons why many do incorporate. The fringes are not limited to corporate employes.

A special pension break is provided for full-time employes of tax-exempt religious, charitable, or educational organizations—including, in some cases, teachers in public schools. Ask whether your employer qualifies under Section 501C3 of the Internal Revenue Code. If so, you can arrange with him for the purchase of a retirement annuity, with a contribution of up to 20 percent of the amount which is due you as compensation.

This can be done either by reducing your present salary or foregoing a future pay raise. The amount contributed escapes tax until you begin to receive payments from the annuity after you retire. Then the proceeds may be taxed to you—but at the much lower rate you will be paying then.

In case of retirement because of disability resulting from service in the Armed Forces, the U.S. Coast Guard and U.S. Public Health Service, the retirement pay is tax exempt. This also applies to disability retirement from a fire or police department.

Qualified plans. An employer naturally prefers a company retirement plan that gives him an immediate tax deduction for his contributions, while letting the employes defer any tax on the contributions until they actually start getting the retirement benefits.

Qualified pension and profit-sharing plans work that way. "Qualified" means approved in advance by the Treasury. The approval clearly establishes both the employer's eligibility to deduct his contributions as a business cost and the right of the employe to let the contributions accumulate untaxed until his retirement. Because the fund's earnings are tax-free from year to year, the fund grows much more rapidly than, for instance, a savings account.

The tax privileges would be permitted anyway, if the plan met official standards for financial soundness and the protection of employes' interests. But the tax deductions and exemptions might have to be proved to IRS after they were claimed. Getting the plan "qualified" provides such clearance in advance.

Pension. The pension reforms of 1974 limited the amount of pay that may be channeled into a pension fund to $25,000 or 25 percent of salary, whichever is less. The pension payments were limited to $75,000 a year, or 100 percent of the participant's average wage in his three best-paid consecutive years. But the dollar limits are revised each year to reflect changes in living costs.

The pensions are paid out according to a specified scale of benefits. The employer knows what his costs will be in any year, and the employe knows generally what livelihood he will receive in retirement—or what payment his beneficiaries will receive if he should die.

For employes whose firms lack pension plans, Congress authorized self-contributory plans, effective in 1975. Employes can contribute up to 15 percent of their income, tax free, into such "Individual Retirement Accounts," up to $1,500 a year.

Profit-sharing. This plan enables employes to share in the profits of the business, under a specific formula for apportioning the contributions among them. Up to 15 percent of an employe's salary may be so set aside and deducted from tax. If the employe participates in both a pension and a profit-sharing plan the limitation is 25 percent of salary, but not in excess of $25,000.

This plan is useful if the company's profits tend to fluctuate from year to year; the contributions can be omitted or reduced in low-profit years. Employes will have less certainty about how large their retirement income will be, but the plan is its own built-in incentive for hard work and profit-creating effort.

Stock bonus plan. This provides benefits similar to those of profit-sharing plans, except that the benefits may be distributed in the company's stock. The employer's contributions do not necessarily depend on his profits.

Restricted stock bonus. This is a popular plan in corporations wishing to give employes an incentive to remain with the firm. A high-level employe may accept a restricted stock bonus instead of a cash salary increase to avoid paying current tax at his ordinary income rate.

The employe's ownership of the stock may be "restricted" in various ways. He may be obliged to hold the shares until he retires, or sell them back to the company at a stated price if he leaves the firm. He is taxed each year on the dividends he receives from the stock, but pays no tax on the value of the stock itself until his retirement.

Some curbs were applied by the 1969 Tax Reform Act. The stock is taxed as ordinary income at the time it is issued to the executive (instead of when he retires) if the stock is either transferable—meaning that it can be sold by the executive before he retires—or is not subject to forfeit, meaning that he would keep his right to ownership of the stock even if he left the company. These provisions apply to stock issued to employes after June 30, 1969. The plan must be approached with caution; the restrictions are severe and the procedures are complicated.

Stock-option plans. These plans allow corporation employes—usually the key employes or executives—to acquire a certain number of shares of the corporation's stock at a specified price. If the stock rises in price, the executive gets a bargain; if it drops, he need not exercise his option to buy.

No tax is payable at the time the option is granted. If there is a gain, it may be taxed either at the time the option is exercised (that is, when the executive buys the stock) or when he sells the shares, depending on the terms of the option. The gain is taxed at the favorable capital gains rate.

Frequently stock-option plans have resulted in additional income for company executives amounting to several times their regular salaries and bonuses. But in recent years, because of periods of weak or erratic stock market trends, some options have dropped in value and many have not been exercised.

Annuity plans. These are pension plans under which the retirement benefits are provided through annuity or insurance contracts, without a trust managing the accumulation and investment of the contributions.

Bond-purchase plans. These are either pension or profit-sharing plans; they have in common the fact that only investment in U.S. Retirement Plan Bonds is permitted.

Your pension

Almost all large and progressive corporations and many smaller companies provide pension, profit-sharing or stock-option plans.

The advantage to an employe is that his equity or vested interest in the plan—his right to recover his own and his employer's contribution if he leaves before normal retirement age—increases each year. Yet he pays no tax until he retires or withdraws his equity in whole or in part.

In effect, it is a piece of income diverted into savings before it is taxed. And the interest on the savings is not taxed as it compounds.

A tax on at least part of the retirement income must be paid eventually, of course. But not until your retirement, when the pension checks begin to come (or when you withdraw your equity from the plan, if you leave the company).

But by the time retirement comes, your tax rate will be lower, you will have the benefit of the extra personal exemption for those sixty-five and over, and in some cases the retirement income credit. The tax bite will be smaller.

If you made no contributions into the pension, annuity, or profit-sharing plan, your payments from the fund normally will be taxable.

If you made contributions to the plan, your retirement payments will consist of two segments: A return of your own contributions, called your "net cost," *which is not taxed;* and the income on your investment in the program, *which is taxed.*

First you must add up the total contributions you paid, plus any contributions of your employer which you were required to count as income at the time. Subtract from that total any premiums refunded, or any rebates or dividends received before the starting date of the annuity. The result is your net cost.

Then, to determine how much of each pension payment you may exclude from tax, you must compute how much money the pension plan will pay you over your lifetime.

You know the amount of the pension you will receive each year, but do not know how long you will live. So the IRS provides an actuarial table which tells your life expectancy. Multiply the number of years of life expectancy by your annual pension income; that provides your expected lifetime return. Then divide your net cost (total contributions) by the expected lifetime return; that gives you the percentage of your pension income which is excluded from tax.

Next, multiply the amount of your yearly pension income by the percentage. That tells you the amount which is a return of your investment, and therefore is not taxed. Subtract that from your total pension payment for the year. What remains is taxed.

The Treasury supplies this example:

Your annuity (pension), in which you have made a total net investment of $9,000, will pay you $1,000 a year for life. You are a male, sixty-five years old; your life expectancy is fifteen years, according to the IRS actuarial table. You multiply the $1,000 annual pension payment by 15; your expected return is $15,000.

Divide your investment of $9,000 by your expected return of $15,000. The result is 60 percent. That's the percentage excluded from tax. On each year's tax return you will exclude $600 of your pension income (60 percent of $1,000), and will pay tax on the remaining $400 of income.

Of course, the computation is easier if your pension contract provides for payments to you for an exact number of years—say, ten years after your retirement. To figure your expected lifetime pension return, you would simply multiply the yearly payment by 10, then proceed as stated previously.

If your pension should be increased after you begin receiving it (some companies have made voluntary increases to help former employes cope with inflation), the amount excluded from tax does not change. In the foregoing example, you would continue to exclude $600 each year, while the taxable portion would rise.

If your annuity was completely paid for by your employer, and you did not report your employer's premium contributions as income when they were made, all the pension payments you receive are taxable. You had no investment in the plan.

The foregoing are typical annuity-type pension plans. If you buy an annuity for yourself, your cost (the untaxed part of the pension payments) is the amount of premiums you paid.

If your annuity was an outright gift to you, the cost (untaxed to you) was the cost paid by the giver.

Three-year rule. If the employer contributed part of the cost, and if the pension payments in the first three years of your retirement will cover your own entire contribution to the plan, a special rule applies.

The amounts you receive are not taxed until after your own investment has been recovered tax-free. Thereafter, all the pension payments are taxable as income.

Retired public school teachers, firemen, policemen and other former federal, state, county and municipal employes usually will recover their costs in the three-year period; then their pension costs must be reported as income.

Capital gains from pensions. When an employe takes his accumulated retirement fund as a lump-sum payment, instead of receiving it in monthly pension payments, part of it may be taxed at the low capital gains rate and the rest as ordinary income.

The pension reform law of 1974 specifies that all amounts accumulated in the fund before 1974 are treated as a capital gain and reported on Schedule D.

The part accumulated after 1973 is taxed as ordinary income; for this, Congress provided a special, elective, ten-year forward averaging rule to soften the tax impact of the one-year income bulge.

To qualify for this averaging the taxpayer must have participated in the qualified retirement plan for at least five years.

He must receive all that is due him under the plan (a lump-sum distribution of only part of the fund is considered ordinary income), and the distribution must all be made in a single tax year.

The recipient must either be more than fifty-nine and one-half years old or must have left the company because of retirement, death, disability, resignation, or discharge.

This allows an employe to take a lump-sum distribution after reaching fifty-nine and one-half years of age without ending his employment—something new in tax law. It helps key employes who retire but still want to work part-time for their employer. Formerly they had to become "contractor-consultants" to qualify for capital gains treatment of their lump-sum distributions.

But if a retiring worker takes annuity payments for a year or more, and then decides to take the rest in a lump sum, he cannot use the capital gains rate on part of the payout; his withdrawals were not all made in one year.

The rules cover members of any civil service retirement system that has a trust fund; the federal and many state and local systems are so qualified. A self-employed person also is covered if the distribution is made after age fifty-nine and one-half or after death or disability.

Computing the lump-sum tax. In computing the tax on the ordinary income portion of the lump-sum payout, a taxpayer can take advantage of not only the ten-year averaging rule but also a "minimum distribution allowance" of up to $10,000 to ease the tax load on those whose pension payouts are relatively modest.

The tax on the ordinary income portion of the payout is computed separately from the tax on all other income received in that year, and the rate for single taxpayers is used exclusively.

Form 4972 must be used to report the ordinary income portion; this should be attached to your Form 1040 when making a return. Form 1040 probably is being revised to provide a space for this item, but when this method was first introduced taxpayers were instructed to write the amount in the bottom margin of page 1 of Form 1040, identifying it as "Tax from Form 4972." The amount should be included in the total amount of tax entered on line 16 of Form 1040.

Minimum distribution allowance. The law excludes from tax 50 percent of the first $20,000 of a lump-sum payout, or $10,000; but this is reduced by 20 percent of the amount by which the payout exceeds $20,000.

Assume, for example, that a sixty-five-year-old taxpayer receives a distribution of $30,000. The excess over $20,000 is $10,000. Twenty percent of the excess is $2,000. The $10,000 allowance would be reduced by that much; the taxpayer could exclude only $8,000 from tax.

Or assume a much larger distribution, say $130,000. The excess over $20,000 would be $110,000. Twenty percent of that would be $22,000; this would wipe out the $10,000 minimum allowance entirely; the taxpayer would have to pay tax on the whole distribution.

Tax on ordinary income portion. After deducting his minimum allowance, the taxpayer divides by ten the entire payout which is subject to tax, including 100 percent of the capital gain portion. He computes a tax on this one-tenth, using the rate for single taxpayers; then he multiplies this tax by ten.

Finally, he multiplies that result by the percentage of his participation after 1973. For example, if he had participated in the pension plan for twenty years, and if five of the years were after 1973, he would multiply by 25 percent.

Here is an example, using $150,000 as the portion subject to ordinary income tax and 1978 as the year of the distribution:

Divide $150,000 by 10 .... $15,000

Compute tax at single rate on $15,000   3,520

Multiply that tax by 10   35,200

Multiply $35,200 by 25% (the percentage

of participation after 1973: 5 years

of post-1973 participation, divided by

20 years total participation .... $ 8,800

Tax on other income. To arrive at the rest of his tax, the taxpayer begins by computing the capital gain portion of the distribution. He multiplies the entire distribution by a fraction in which the numerator is the number of full pre-1974 years of participation and the denominator is the total years of participation. In the example above, the fraction would be 15/20, or 3/4; the capital gain portion would be $112,500.

This is added to the salary, investment, and other income; the deductions and exemptions are subtracted as usual (including the 50 percent of the capital gain portion not subject to tax); and the tax is computed in the usual way. The alternative capital gain method or regular income averaging can be used, whichever produces the least tax.

Your automobile

If your car is used to bring in income, it provides a deduction. Transportation costs are legitimate tax deductions when necessary to perform your job. These include local as well as away-from-home travel expenses, and they cover the business use of your family car as well as taxis, buses, and other public means of transportation.

What portion, if any, of your car expenses can be claimed as a business cost is your decision. One portion that does not apply is the cost of travel to work. Whether by auto or public conveyance or neighborhood car pool, that transportation is a personal expense.

But there are scores of deductible uses. You should arrive at an honest evaluation, make your claim, and prepare to defend it against an IRS agent who may have different ideas. Keep track of the trips or mileage when using your car to solicit business from customers, gain business information, collect bills, work on construction projects, interview applicants, visit patients, call on suppliers, use library or legal files, entertain customers, or inspect properties being sold, bought or remodeled.

You may divide your car costs between personal use and business use, probably on the basis of mileage. If you find that 40 percent of your mileage is business mileage, you may deduct 40 percent of your outlays for gasoline, oil, tires, lubrication, insurance, accessories, motor club membership, license plate fees, registration and driver's permit costs.

If you have two cars, you might decide, for example, that 75 percent of the costs of one of them is deductible. Then keep expense records separately for that car.

Depreciation on the cost of the automobile may be taken, as well as uninsured losses from theft or vandalism.

Repair charges are deductible. Make sure you keep not only the garage's bill which identifies the car, but also your canceled checks. Revenue agents take canceled checks at face value as proof of payment; the other records substantiate that the payment was for a deductible expense.

Parking charges, highway and bridge tolls incurred during business use may be deducted in full; regular wash and polish jobs are deductible on the percentage-of-use basis.

Instead of figuring the cost of business trips separately, an employe or self-employed person may choose to deduct 15 cents a mile for the first 15,000 miles of business usage and 10 cents a mile thereafter. Make records of each year's odometer readings, multiply the year's mileage by 0.15; then deduct the percentage allotted to business use. (This method may not be used by persons who operate fleets of cars or trucks, or those who rent out cars or use them as taxicabs.)

An important part of the auto deduction is a share of the depreciation. You can deduct each year a portion of the difference between the cost of the car and its probable trade-in value at the end of its usefulness to you. Then, if the car was used 40 percent for business purposes, claim 40 percent of the year's depreciation. If you use the 15-cent and 10-cent deduction you cannot claim depreciation. After a car is fully depreciated the flat mileage deduction is allowed, but at only 10 cents a mile.

Even if not used for business, cars provide these deductions:

Taxes. State and municipal property taxes on cars; license and registration fees in those states which base the fee on the value of the vehi-

cle; state or local sales taxes on the purchase of a new car, tires, batteries, accessories and replacement parts, where these taxes are part of a general sales tax.

Interest. The interest charges on your auto installment purchase; these almost always are set forth clearly in the sale contract.

Contributions. Seven cents a mile may be deducted as a charitable contribution for driving done in connection with church activities or philanthropic service.

Casualty loss. Damages suffered from fire, accident, storm or theft are deductible—after the first $100 of cost—if not compensated by insurance. They are not deductible if caused by the driver's willful act or gross negligence.

Medical deduction. The 7-cents-a-mile deduction also is permitted for trips to the doctor or clinic or other medical transportation costs. That covers only such operating outlays as gasoline, oil, tire wear and the like; it does not cover depreciation, insurance, registration and so on.

In fact, auto expense deductions sometimes are not altogether adequate. Commuting costs cannot be deducted, of course, and some allowable auto deductions fail to match the actual costs of many car owners. The 7-cents-a-mile deductions for medical and charitable use certainly fall into that category.

The 15-cent mileage allowance for business use is optional, and many taxpayers find it preferable to keep records of actual costs. For today's cars, just the costs of depreciation, license and insurance may exceed 15 cents a mile.

If you do use the mileage allowance, keep a record of the business use and remember that you can claim, in addition to the 15-cent mileage, the cost of parking, tips, bridge and turnpike tolls paid for business purposes.

Also, if you have a second job, you can deduct the cost of travel between your place of principal employment and your second job. This does not fall under the rule against commuting deductions.

And the tax code offers you one opportunity for savings. If your employer reimburses you on a mileage basis at a rate of up to 15 cents a mile, the arrangement is considered equivalent to an accounting of actual expenses to your employer. It need not be reported on your tax return.

If you now get less than 15 cents a mile, your employer can do you a favor by increasing the allowance. It is, in effect, a tax-free pay raise for you and a business deduction for your employer.

For years prior to 1974 the automobile expense allowance was only 12 cents a mile for the first 15,000 miles and 9 cents a mile for miles in excess of that. Recognizing the increase in fuel costs, IRS announced in late August of 1974 that it was retroactively increasing the allowance to the 15-cent and 10-cent per mile amounts for the entire year of 1974.

Effective for the year 1974 and thereafter, there is no longer a differential between an optional mileage allowance an employer can pay you and the amount you can claim under the optional method.

Again recognizing inflation, IRS increased the flat per diem rate for travel costs away from home up to $44 a day in the United States, effective January 1, 1974.

If your employer reimburses you for travel costs, you must make a detailed accounting to him to avoid reporting the expenses and reimbursements on your tax return.

You can skip all that bookkeeping if he gives you a flat travel rate allowance that does not exceed $44 a day.

Be sure to check the latest allowances on auto mileage and per diem travel reimbursements before filing your return. They are subject to change as gasoline and other travel costs rise. You may not notice newspaper items reporting such changes; they don't require Congressional action, merely a Treasury ruling.

Wherever the government's travel allowance for its own employes exceeds $44 a day, the Treasury ruled, private companies and their traveling employes can use the government's per diem figure.

When the higher alternative was authorized, the government allowance did not exceed $44 anywhere in the United States. But in a number of foreign areas the government allowance did exceed $44; and in these places travelers on private business also could benefit from the rates above $44.

Areas with rates over $44 included at that time:

Switzerland, Norway, Brussels, Belgium, Hong Kong, and Papua, New Guinea, $46; and Leningrad, $62.

Allowances ranging from $46 to $58 were posted for some Middle Eastern and African countries. Maximum rates ranging from $45 to $68 applied during the peak-tourism seasons in Antigua, Aruba, the Bahamas, Barbados, Cayman Islands, Grenada, Saint Lucia, and Saint Martin.

Gasoline tax credit. If you operate a motorboat, private plane for hire, power mower, or similar equipment, you can claim a 2-cents-a-gallon credit for every gallon of gasoline used. It is a partial refund of the federal gasoline tax. A 4-cent credit is given for gasoline used in non-highway farm equipment. A 6-cent credit is given for lubricating oil used for non-highway equipment. The credit is claimed on Form 4136, filed with your tax return.

The office-at-home

The taxpayer who has to do part of his work at home may be able to deduct part of his home costs, if he itemizes his deductions. The Treasury has strict rules on offices-at-home; it has insisted that taxpayers prove that regular work at home is a job *requirement.* Disagreeing, the tax court has upheld a deduction for a home-office that a salesman proved was "appropriate and helpful" in his job. But an appeals court ruled later that there must be a *business necessity* for the home-office, such as that the employer's office is unavailable or unusable for the purpose. This much is clear: the taxpayer must be able to show that the home-office is used regularly and unavoidably for his work.

An office-at-home may be a room added to your house or a room converted to business use. If you have an eight-room house and devote one room to the office-study, you could deduct one-eighth of the expense of your home. Or if the office takes up 200 square feet out of the 2,000 in your dwelling, you could deduct one-tenth.

If you should claim one-eighth, your deduction could include one-eighth of the depreciation on the dwelling, one-eighth of the light, gas and fuel, one-eighth of the upkeep expenses, and so on.

Personal or family expenses like a porch swing, landscaping, a power mower, a new kitchen range, of course, are not deductible. The painting of other rooms in the house could not be deducted, but the entire cost of painting the office-at-home itself—not just one-eighth of the outlay—would be deductible.

A telephone extension to the office-study would be deductible, at the full cost of that extra service. If business use represented half the total of your household telephone bills, that half would be deductible.

If the room is used only part-time as an office, that fact must show in your accounting. If it is used or usable part of the day for purposes other than business, the element of time must also go into the accounting. For instance, if the room is available for family use half the time, the deduction of one-eighth would be cut in half, and would become one-sixteenth.

Obviously, all your other necessary and unreimbursed outlays for business purposes also are deductible. Presumably your tools, typewriter, office machinery, files, reference material, technical journals and other items *required* for work at home would be kept in the office-at-home—but these would be deductible whether or not you had an office set aside for your work.

This is an illustration of how an office-at-home deduction might shape up for taxpayer Fred Graham, who converted the den in his eight-room house to office use:

Deductions for an Office-at-Home

Depreciation:		
Cost of home	$38,000	
Less cost of lot	6,000	
House less lot	32,000	
One-eighth business portion	4,000	
Useful life of house, estimated 20 years; annual depreciation		
($4,000 divided by 20)		$200
Household operation:		
Insurance	120	
Utilities, fuel	450	
Repairs to roof, gutters, front door	230	
Total	800	
Business portion, one-eighth		$100
Telephone Use:		
Year's bills	200	
Business use, one-half		$100
Improvements, office-at-home:		
New office-type lighting	100	
Bookcases	70	
Total		170
Total deduction for office-at-home		$570

For purposes of that example, it was assumed that Graham entered his deductions for real estate taxes and mortgage interest payments in the proper place on Schedule A ("Itemized Deductions").

If Graham were a professional or other self-employed person, or an outside salesman, he would take his office-at-home deduction "at the top"—it would be a deduction from gross income.

In such a case he should include one-eighth of his real estate taxes and interest as part of office-at-home expenses. By thus deducting them from gross income, he comes out with a smaller adjusted gross income—which would be helpful if he took the standard deduction or claimed a medical deduction.

A doctor or dentist whose principal place of business is the space set aside in his home obviously would have little difficulty substantiating his right to take an office-at-home deduction.

Others, however, must be prepared to prove their claim and back up their figures. A letter from the employer would be helpful. At the minimum, the employe must be ready to show all the necessary household records, receipts, canceled checks and other documents which substantiate his office-at-home outlays.

Even if you cannot justify an office-at-home deduction, you may be able to deduct part of your home telephone bill as an "ordinary and necessary" expense of your employment or business. Rules for this deduction are less rigorous than for the office-at-home. Entitled to use it, among others, are policemen, firemen, news reporters, repair crew supervisors and many others whose job requires them to be available for emergency service.

Home-office for your own benefit. If your office-at-home is not connected with your full-time job, but is set up to produce extra income for yourself, the rules are only slightly different. They are more liberal, in fact, and the tax saving could be large enough to be a factor in your decision whether to branch into part-time activity on your own.

Deductions would be available, for instance, to the newspaperman who regularly contributes articles to magazines, using his office-at-home for interviews and writing; a dentist employed in a clinic who sets up an office for part-time practice in his house; a lawyer who works for a utility corporation but has his own practice at home; a psychiatrist at a hospital who takes other patients in evenings and on weekends; or an employe of an electronics concern who runs a part-time neighborhood TV and stereo repair business.

Essentially the same rules would apply for allocating part of the household costs to the business use. However, the cost of lawn care, walks, fences and shrubbery might also be deductible.

A deduction for the costs of working at home to produce or collect your own business income would not be taken among the "Miscellaneous Deductions," but as a cost of producing your own business income. It would be computed on Schedule C ("Profit or Loss from Business or Profession") and subtracted there from gross business income.

Let us return to Fred Graham, our taxpayer who had a $570 deduction for an office-at-home. Let us change his status somewhat. He now has a small income-producing business going; his gross income is $16,000 a year, the income from his job combined with that from his own enterprise.

One question confronting him is whether to use the standard deduction or itemize his deductions. For our illustrative purposes we will use the normal standard deduction—15 percent of adjusted gross income, up to $2,000 —instead of the higher level permitted for 1975 only.

Because his expenses for an office-at-home are costs of producing income for himself, taxpayer Graham can deduct them from gross income to arrive at a smaller adjusted gross income. This is how he does it:

Graham's gross income $16,000
He starts with the office-at-home
   expenses previously listed, which come to $570
He adds one-eighth of the $1,200
   interest on his home mortgage, or 150
And one-eighth of his $480-a-year
   real estate tax bill, or 60
Plus his full business-connected
   transportation costs, which come to 120
For a total business expense of   900
Leaving an adjusted gross income of $15,100

At this point he must choose either to itemize his personal deductions or take the standard deduction. Let us itemize first, to see whether that provides any advantage.

A. *Itemizing the Deductions*

Adjusted gross income $15,100
Remainder of mortgage interest, not
   claimed as cost of office-at-home $1,050
Remainder of real estate tax, not
   claimed as cost of office-at-home   420
       Total itemized deductions ....$ 1,470
Taxable income (before claiming exemptions) $13,630

B. *The Standard Deduction*

Adjusted gross income $15,100
Less standard deduction 2,000
Taxable income (before claiming exemptions) $13,100

Graham's taxable income is $530 lower if he takes the standard deduction than if he itemizes deductions. (For purposes of simplification, these examples set aside the probability that Graham might have had other

itemized deductions such as medical costs and charitable contributions which would have altered the outcome.)

But note: If Graham had had the poor judgment to claim *all* his office-at-home and business-related deductions as itemized deductions, they would have added up to $2,370. When subtracted from $16,000 adjusted gross income (the same as his gross income, since he had taken no adjustments), he would have wound up with $13,630 of taxable income, before taking his personal exemptions.

The fact that he had failed first to deduct his income-producing costs from gross income would have made no difference to IRS; it would have accepted his return. But his taxable income would have been $530 higher.

The advantage of taking deductions "at the top"—from gross income whenever possible—is thus demonstrated. By doing it that way, you can still claim the standard deduction if it is to your advantage to do so.

Another advantage appears if there is serious illness in the family. Medical costs can be deducted only to the extent that they exceed 3 percent of adjusted gross income. Therefore it is advisable to make adjusted gross income as small as possible.

Retirement programs

Tax-sheltered, do-it-yourself retirement programs are available both to self-employed persons and to millions of employes who do free-lance work outside their regular jobs, and also—starting with the 1975 tax year—on a small scale to salaried workers whose employers do not offer pension plans.

The latter program was authorized by a 1974 amendment to the Keogh Act; it permits employes who have no private pension coverage to set up tax-free "Individual Retirement Accounts." They may contribute up to 15 percent of their pay, to a maximum of $1,500 a year, into Treasury-approved retirement plans and take tax deductions for the contributions.

The Keogh Act program remains primarily a retirement plan for doctors, lawyers, small businessmen and other self-employed persons who could not get the pension or profit-sharing plans usually available to employes of corporations. It is described in our chapter on "The Businessman and the Professional Man." But it is equally available to an employe who does some moonlighting as a side business of his own.

The taxpayer can earmark up to 15 percent of his income from such self-employment—within a maximum limit of $7,500 a year—as a contribution into a Treasury-approved master plan operated by a bank, mutual fund, insurance company, or professional association. A retirement fund can also be built by purchases of a special issue of U.S. Treasury bonds.

The deductions now are considerably higher than those under which the Keogh plan operated for years: 10 percent of net self-employment income, up to $2,500. Many professional men complained that those permitted contributions were too low and failed to provide adequate retirement programs. In the 1974 pension reform legislation, Congress responded by boosting the amount of deductible contributions permitted.

It also established a lower limit: a taxpayer can contribute up to $750 a year of his net self-employment income, tax deductible, regardless of the 15 percent ceiling.

The latter provision applied for 1974 and 1975 without question, but then the IRS ruled that the $750 limit conflicted with a general provision of the 1974 tax reform law which set a limit on annual retirement contributions of $25,000 or 25 percent of compensation, whichever is lower. Congressional tax technicians said the $750 was intended clearly to be an exception to the 25-percent limit, but the IRS held to its position. Beginning in 1976, it said, if you earned under $3,000, your minimum deduction of $750 would be reduced to 25 percent of your self-employment earnings.

There were indications that Congress might move to clarify the point before taxpayers began filing their tax returns for 1976; it would be wise to keep watch on this question.

Joining a self-employment plan is a simple matter. Your banker, broker, or accountant can tell you how. No matter what time of year you join, you can claim the full amount of your contribution—up to the 15 percent or $7,500 limit—as a tax deduction. The contribution is not taxed until it is paid back to you when you retire. Then, presumably, you will have a lower tax rate.

If a self-employed person has employes, he must usually include them in the retirement plan. If one of the employes is his wife, he can build up the deduction by including her contributions.

Other forms of individual savings must come out of what remains of your income after taxes, and the interest earnings are taxed as they are earned. The tax-sheltered plan builds the pension fund much more rapidly. For those with side businesses, it can provide an important supplement to a regular company pension.

Invested in a savings account at 5 percent annual interest, a Keogh plan investment would double every fourteen years. Its growth is fairly rapid because the interest earnings are not taxed. The growth might be still more rapid, however, if the contributions were put into various forms of approved mutual funds, insurance, or annuity plans.

*We have long had death and taxes
as the two standards of inevitability.
But there are those who believe that
death is the preferable of the two.
"At least," as one man said,
"there's one advantage about death;
it doesn't get worse every time
Congress meets."*

Erwin N. Griswold, Dean, Harvard Law School

CHAPTER 7

The Executive

The salaries of top policy-making executives range up to $450,000 or more in large corporations. Yet the salary is only part of an executive's compensation in most companies and not necessarily the most important part.

To attract and hold first-class executive talent, companies offer many nonsalary compensations, all with a single aim: to avoid or reduce the tax on the compensation, or defer it to later years when the employe's income is reduced and the tax bite accordingly smaller.

In some large corporations, the retirement income of a long-time top officer may actually match the after-tax income he was getting at the peak of his active working career. He may be benefiting from not one but several income-deferring schemes—pension, bonus, insurance, profit-sharing, stock purchase and possibly still other retirement plans.

Executives are covered by pension plans in probably nine out of ten corporations. Bonus plans exist in at least half. Most large companies also have stock-option plans for executives. Many have profit-sharing programs; some are tied in' with pension plans, others are separate. Health and hospitalization plans and other "fringes" abound.

Almost all companies pay moving expenses of key executives; some pay more than the actual cost, to compensate the executive for his inconvenience.

Many firms guarantee to buy the house of a company official, if he has trouble selling it when transferred. Some pay extra cost-of-living allowances in high-cost areas.

There are also a multitude of other privileges and side benefits that are actually remuneration; the executive enjoys comforts, luxuries and travel that he does not pay for.

The fringe benefits include company cars, country club and social club memberships, professional society memberships and expense accounts which, although explicitly restricted by law and subject to strict rules for proof of business purpose, provide a largely tax-free scale of living which few executives could or would sustain out of their taxable incomes.

Executive fringes

Comparisons of two styles of executive compensation reveal the very solid advantages of the nontaxable "fringes." Here are two hypothetical executives whose salary situations may be rare in real life but who will serve to illustrate the point:

J. P. Whitestone, fifty-three, earns $45,000 annually. It is his only compensation. Martin Bell, thirty-one, is paid $15,000 a year. At first glance, Whitestone seems to be three times better off than Bell, but a closer look indicates otherwise.

Assuming that each man has two exemptions, one for himself and one for his wife, and that each takes the standard deduction, $1,500 in 1971, here is their relative situation:

Whitestone	Bell
Salary $45,000	Salary $15,000
Income tax 13,172	Income Tax 2,297
After-tax income $31,828	After-tax income $12,703

Whitestone has seen 30 percent of his total salary go for income taxes. Bell lost 15.3 percent of his salary in taxes.

But that only starts to tell the real story. Martin Bell gets a number of completely tax-free benefits from his company. Here is the approximate annual value of each:

Full use of company car, per year $1,500
Interest-free mortgage loan from his employer 1,000
$50,000 paid life insurance policy 1,000
Free health insurance and annual medical examinations for self and wife 750
Total value $4,250

Now it becomes clear that Bell's true annual income, counting both after-tax dollars and untaxed benefits, has a value of nearly $17,000.

Whitestone, on the other hand, has to buy the same list of benefits—if he wants them—out of his after-tax income. Because of his higher tax bracket, it takes earnings of about $8,000 a year to buy the $4,250 worth of benefits which Bell gets from his company tax-free.

Moreover, Bell's company has a pension system and thrift plan under which the company matches the amounts that Bell sets aside each month in a fund to be paid out to him when he retires. Such tax as he eventually will pay on the retirement income will be at a lower rate; he has, in effect, postponed some income from the high-tax period of his life to the low-tax period. Whitestone, on the other hand, must set aside after-tax dollars to buy old age security.

What this will mean in dollars and cents cannot be estimated precisely in advance. But it is now clear that Bell's income is not really very far below Whitestone's.

That is why the fringes—insurance, health plans and expense account items (not taxed at all), or deferred income (taxed later in life), or stock plans (taxed as capital gains at bargain tax rates)—have become just as important as salary to executives.

Frequently, an executive can persuade his company to give him all or part of a planned pay raise, for instance, in the form of fringe benefits. Most companies are happy to oblige, because most fringes bless those who give as well as those who receive. They are not only tax-free to the employe but are deductible by the employer as a cost of doing business.

Life insurance

One of the most common tax-free fringes, and one of the most valuable, is group life insurance, deductible by the employer.

The amount of deductible coverage is now limited to $50,000. At one time some highly paid employes were insured for as much as $250,000 —a tax-free fringe worth as much as $7,000 a year in before-tax income.

Under a 1964 change in law, the employe now can receive up to $50,000 of group-term life insurance coverage tax-free; if more is provided, the employe must pay tax on the premium. But even this extra coverage is still a bargain.

This is why: The premium cost for tax purposes is set forth in an official table. The costs shown are one-third to one-half *less* in many cases than the employer has to pay for the coverage. And the employer's cost itself is well below the amount the employe would pay if he bought the policy himself.

For example: Wilbur Smith, forty-seven, an executive, has $100,000 of group-term life insurance under his company's plan. The first $50,000 coverage is tax-free to him. The cost of the other $50,000 coverage is taxable income; computed by the official table, the cost comes to $240 a year. He is in the 50 percent tax bracket; therefore his yearly tax on the amount is $120.

Actually his company paid $480 for the insurance, tax-deductible. In other words, Smith's cost is $120 for extra insurance coverage which cost his company $480 and would have cost him, buying it as an individual, a good deal more than that.

If the company drops the portion of an executive's insurance coverage which exceeds $50,000, the employe in effect takes a pay cut. For older executives, this may be quite a substantial setback.

For example: Lester Frye, fifty-seven, is in the 50 percent tax bracket. He received an extra $50,000 of insurance coverage which cost the company $1,162.50 a year. The cost to Frye was only $330 a year in taxes. The firm decided to drop the insurance and raise Frye's salary by the amount it had been paying for his extra coverage.

Frye was the loser. His additional income, after taxes, was only $581.25. For that amount he could get less than $25,000 of insurance coverage. To get $50,000 of coverage he would have had to pay more than $1,160 a year for the coverage that formerly cost him $330.

The law also permits an employer to provide tax-free life insurance coverage for an employe's wife and children, up to $2,000 each, in addition to the $50,000 of coverage which is tax-free to the employe himself.

Health insurance plans

A fringe benefit found useful by an increasing number of medium-sized corporations is an accident and health insurance plan. Many variations are possible under flexible Treasury rules, but the principle is the same.

The employer pays for insurance coverage for employes, their wives and children under individual or group insurance policies. The cost to the employer is deductible; the employes are not taxed on the premiums paid in their behalf.

An executive or owner-officer can be covered. If he is, the Treasury insists that the plan cover the employes as well. And it will not approve an insurance plan if the premium payments, when added to an employe's regular pay, exceed a reasonable compensation for his services.

A valuable variation is offered by some companies: They agree to pay, in addition, the uninsured medical costs of the employe and his family. These frequently amount to around $1,000 a year. The cost, again, is deductible by the employer as a business expense, and is tax-free to the employe.

This arrangement covers the costs which are excluded from most hospitalization and major medical policies, and costs which may be barred as tax deductions because they fall below the limit (3 percent of adjusted gross income) for medical expenses.

Cash from a corporation

It is sometimes feasible for an executive to borrow from his company. However, the IRS enforces strict rules to guard against the possibility that the "loan" may be, in effect, an untaxed dividend.

The executive must therefore make sure the loan is properly formalized, even if the corporation is a closely held one under his control. Interest must be paid, as in any legal loan. If IRS finds fault with the arrangement, the loan will be taxed as a dividend. The best way to stay trouble-free is obvious: pay the loan back.

Sometimes, if an officer-stockholder in a closely-held corporation has a large life insurance policy, he can obtain cash from the company by selling his insurance policy to it. The payment is not taxed if the sales price is equivalent to the value of the policy. If it is greater, the difference is taxable to the executive as ordinary income.

The transaction means that the company becomes the beneficiary of the insurance policy rather than the taxpayer's family. But in a small, closely-held company, it is assumed that the executive had arranged for his stock in the corporation to go to his family on death, so the family would move into control of the corporation. It then would get the benefits from the increase in the value of the corporation's assets: the proceeds of the insurance. If the corporation were liquidated at that time, the family would receive the money without tax.

The tax-exempt status of an insurance policy is not affected by the fact that the corporation is the beneficiary, even if the proceeds are greater than the price the company paid plus the subsequent premiums it paid to the insurance company. But obviously, such a plan would require the most careful consultation with a tax counselor.

Side businesses

A growing number of executives in high tax brackets have found it possible to establish side-business corporations which, in effect, serve the purpose of splitting income. They may also serve to absorb some deductible costs.

One investment specialist has established a "premium finance company." It provides financing for business insurance premiums. Another has set up a haberdashery shop. One executive who owns two horses operates his racing enterprises as two corporations.

The incorporated side-business company has an income that is taxable, but the owner sometimes can charge the operation of an automobile to the side business, and perhaps club dues and other business-generating expenses.

The tax structure favors small businesses; while not "progressive" in the same way that individual income taxes are, the corporation rate is much lower on small profits than on large-scale earnings.

Another expense-splitting possibility is to establish your wife in a business. Many a housewife has found a new career, and a tax break for the family, in a gift shop, book store, antique shop or some other business for which her experience and knowledge fit her.

One Washington, D.C., publicist set his wife up in a gift-importing and retailing business. Today, so successful has been the enterprise, hers is the family business, his the sideline.

Private foundations

Many wealthy executives and owner-officers of corporations have set up tax-exempt private foundations. Established presumably for charitable purposes, these have been used to cover numerous costs which otherwise might have been paid out of ordinary income.

Long under fire from Congress members, who complained that the foundations frequently were mere tax-dodging devices, more than 20,000 private foundations took a beating in the 1969 Tax Reform Act.

Their income from investments was taxed for the first time. Another tax was levied on "self-dealing" loans, payments or other transactions between foundations and their founders. The foundations' ownership and control of businesses were restricted. A penalty tax was decreed for foundations using any of their assets for investments that might jeopardize or bring into question their charitable purposes. Curbs were imposed on their lobbying activities, and many other restrictions were enacted.

Moreover, reform-minded Congressmen warned that they would seek further restraints if the 1969 changes did not cure past "abuses." The private foundation, in short, has become a dubious and precarious tax-saving device.

It could still be useful to an individual of substantial income and wealth who has already established a history of charitable giving, in providing maximum tax economy for a program designed to channel money and effort in a worthwhile direction.

The taxpayer who is thinking in such terms, however, must seek specialized tax counsel.

Stock options

Styles in executive compensation have changed as the rates and rules of income taxation changed. The practice of giving "deferred compensation" to help executives avoid current taxes became popular in the 1950s, when sky-high tax rates remained as a legacy of World War II. The topmost incomes were taxed up to 90 percent until the tax reduction act of 1964.

Even when the top rate was reduced to 70 percent by the 1964 tax law, companies felt they had to provide further "incentives" to key executives. One of these incentives, the "restricted stock option," became especially popular. A company could give its top officers and directors the right to buy the company's stock at cut rates immediately or at some later date. The price would stay low for these preferred buyers—as low as 85 percent of the market value of the stock at the time the option was granted—even if the market value had gone much higher by the time the executive chose to use his option.

When and if the executive sold the stock and pocketed the difference between the bargain price he paid and the market value at the time of his sale, his overall gain usually was not taxed at the high-bracket rate which he paid on his regular corporation salary.

That gain, as well as any additional profit made from a further rise in the value of the stock before he sold, was taxed at the capital gains rate. The maximum capital gains rate until 1970 was 25 percent; that maximum was increased somewhat by the 1969 tax law but still remains a tax bargain.

The restricted stock option—called "restricted" because of limitations specified on the sale or use of the stock—remained the vogue in corporate compensation until the mid-1960s. Then Congress eliminated the tax advantage in any purchase of stock at less than 100 percent of the market price.

Stock options continue to be a major form of executive compensation, but much of their attractiveness is gone. The stock market slump of 1967 and the even more painful collapse of 1969-1970 made many unused options worthless in their holders' hands and brought other techniques to the fore.

Deferring income

A multiplicity of plans—far too many to be described here—has been developed for the purpose of deferring part of an executive's income to later years. Increasingly, from the middle 1960s on, deferred-compensation plans have become the golden thread that binds executive talent to a company and the golden key to lifelong affluence for the executive.

"Deferred compensation" is not taxed until it is paid. It usually is not paid until retirement, when the executive's income has declined and his tax rates are lower.

Executive-rank employes usually have a wide choice of deferral methods. In many cases a deferred-pay agreement is made for an individual. Sometimes income can be deferred for as short a time as one year.

Some pension and profit-sharing plans are especially tailored to the circumstances of certain echelons of executives and key employes. Even though it is an IRS rule that tax-sheltered plans cannot discriminate in favor of employes who are also officers, supervisors, stockholders or in higher pay brackets, the IRS does not insist that *all* employes of a company be embraced in *every* pension or profit-sharing plan.

The IRS has accepted, for example, a company's profit-sharing plan that included forty salaried employes but excluded 110 others who would have been eligible except that they were paid by the hour. Those covered by the plan included four officers and eighteen supervisors, including a number who also were stockholders.

The Treasury held the plan to be nondiscriminatory. Apparently it did so on grounds that the pay of the salaried workers was substantially the same as those on an hourly scale; there was no discrimination, in other words, because of pay.

The executive can arrange—if he and the employer follow carefully some basic rules—to defer part of his pay for services to a future year, or spread it over a future span of years, instead of taking all the payment as the services are rendered. The payment to be deferred may be salary, commission, bonus or any combination of these. It may be paid in cash, stock or property.

The arrangements may contain some benefits for the employer. The contract can stipulate, for example, that the executive will forfeit the future payment if he leaves the company. This assures the firm of his continued service. The arrangement also retains cash for other company use; in effect, it is an interest-free loan to the firm.

The basic considerations are, first, that an agreement is made *before* the services are performed, and second, that the deferred portion is neither available to the employe nor controllable by him until he receives it.

The IRS looks with disfavor on plans which appear to challenge the "constructive receipt" rule. For a taxpayer who manages his affairs on a cash basis—as most executives do—IRS may take the position that income has been "constructively" received at the time that compensation is credited to his account, earmarked for him, or delivered into his control, even if no money changes hands.

In such a case, the tax benefit collapses. The future payment is declared by IRS to have been "constructively" received and the tax is currently due, though the money has not been paid.

So care is taken to avoid "constructive receipt." The Treasury says that the mere promise, or contract, of an employer to pay in the future for services is not a constructive receipt. There must be no note or other security, and the money may not be set aside in a trust fund. The company simply contracts to make payment at a later specified time.

Here are examples similar to some that have received the Treasury's approval:

• Wilfred Brown and the Ace Corporation make a five-year employment contract paying Brown $40,000 a year, plus a $10,000 annual bonus which is to be deferred. The bonus is set up in a bookkeeping reserve account. The money is not held in trust for Brown; Ace merely agrees to make annual payments, each amounting to 20 percent of the reserve, starting upon completion of Brown's five-year employment term.

• Joseph Green and the Ajax Corporation make a contract under which Green receives $35,000 a year for eight years, plus $15,000 a year of deferred compensation. The deferred portion is to be paid in annual installments of $15,000 starting after the eighth year, at which time Green will either retire or become a part-time consultant to Ajax.

There may also be a contract covering commissions or fees to be earned in the future, in which it is specified that only a certain amount will be paid in any one year, the rest to be paid in subsequent years under prearranged terms.

The only flaw in these plans, from the employer's standpoint, is that he cannot take a tax deduction for the deferred payments until the money actually is paid out. Then he gets the deduction and the employe pays the tax.

Still, the delay could very well have some advantages for the employer. As noted, he usually writes into the contract a provision that the payments will be forfeited under some conditions—such as if the employe quits, takes a job with a competitor when he retires, is discharged for cause, or engages in conduct detrimental to the company.

The device of granting bonuses has proliferated as a means of deferring income. The bonuses are paid in cash, but not at the time when they are awarded. They can be paid in such a form that they are essentially a claim on the corporation; the executive can leave them in the company's hands, in a fund, and take them later in life when it best suits his advantage.

For example: Able Corporation sets up a plan to distribute bonuses among certain top management employes in any year in which the company's pretax profits exceed $500,000. The bonuses are a share of the excess earnings, divided up according to salaries. But they are not paid currently. They are set up in separate accounts, to which a bonus is added in every year that profits exceed the specified level. The company also credits each account with any earnings received from investment of the funds. Annual payments begin when the employe reaches sixty-five or becomes disabled. Payments are made to the widow or other designated beneficiary if he dies.

Two 1970 Treasury rulings gave some additional leeway to the income-deferral plans that can be set up by employers for middle-income and higher-bracket employes. Here are two examples:

1. A company gives annual bonuses to employes chosen by a committee of the firm's board of directors. The committee has sole authority to defer all or part of the bonus until a date set by the committee. The only limit on its discretion is that no part of the bonus may be paid beyond ten years after the employe's normal retirement date.

2. Each employe aged forty or over whose salary is above a certain level can choose to defer 5 percent or 10 percent of his salary. The deferred amount is payable in installments for ten years after the executive ends his full-time employment.

There is no hard-and-fast rule on how far in advance an agreement must be reached before the income-deferment plan goes into operation. Apparently an executive could, in the middle of a year, ask his company to defer part of his income during the rest of that year until some future year. But in most cases, whether for individual or group plans, tax advisers say it is wise to make the agreement before the year begins.

Nevertheless, the 1969 tax law put a damper on many deferred-income, fringe, bonus and stock-option plans in two ways:

First, it made regular salaries, taxed at ordinary income rates, more attractive to highly paid persons. This was done by putting a ceiling on the tax rate on earned income (as distinguished from other income, such as capital gains and interest or dividend income).

Second, to insure that no wealthy person escaped tax altogether, it imposed a special tax—the "Limitation on Tax Preferences" or "LTP"—on some types of income which previously were sheltered from tax by various preferences. Some of the shelters used by corporations to protect the income of their executives were among those hit by LTP.

Other provisions of the 1969 law limited a variety of special tax preferences. The combined result of Congress' labors has upgraded the popularity of straight-salary compensation and downgraded the search for fringes and shelters.

Ceiling rate on earned income

Higher-paid executives, professional men, artists, writers, athletes, entertainers and self-employed persons in every field are the beneficiaries of the limitation on the taxation of earned income. The law decreed that the tax rate on earned income—compensation for personal services, such as wages, salaries and professional fees, as distinct from the income from property or invested capital—could not exceed 50 percent in 1972 and thereafter.

An old doctrine, that of tax preference for earned income, thus was revived, but hardly in a way to benefit an ordinary wage earner. It was a break for the affluent. For a high-salaried executive or a high-income professional the savings can be up to $200 for each $1,000 of earned income on all earned income above $52,000. The latter figure is the income level at which the 50 percent ceiling rate takes effect.

This ceiling shall apply, said Congress, no matter how much earned income a taxpayer receives and no matter how much other income he has. Any ordinary income which is not *earned income*—that is, income which comes from such sources as interest, dividends, or short-term capital gains—will continue to be taxed at the regular rates ranging up to 70 percent.

When a taxpayer has both earned income and income from capital, as in the case of an owner of a business, his earned income is reported as a reasonable allowance for the personal services he renders. The rules limit this allowance to a maximum of 30 percent of the net profits of the trade or business.

Earned income also includes any gains (other than capital gains) and any net earnings resulting from the disposition of property by the person whose personal efforts created the property. This would include, for example, an artist who sells a painting or a sculpture.

Most "deferred income" types of compensation were ruled excluded from the definition of earned income and therefore would be subject to the old rates. These apparently include any deferment arrangements made between an employer and employe, including even the usual benefit payments made from approved pension and profit-sharing plans. The rules still had not been clarified fully, however, when this book was written.

However, the law is clear that even if a company made a deferred-compensation contract with an employe before the rate ceiling took effect in 1971, the deferred payments would not get the benefit of the ceiling. So far as employes are concerned, deferred income does not qualify as "earned income"—it will be taxed at the regular rates ranging up to 70 percent.

Note that *only earned income* counts in qualifying for the ceiling rate. A taxpayer with $40,000 earned income and with $200,000 income from dividends, interest, rentals or capital gains would get no benefit. His earned income, by itself, is not sufficient to qualify under the ceiling.

The ceiling rate has diminished the need of highly paid executives to convert, defer, or shelter income for tax reasons. They may also be less eager to channel earned income into such investments as real estate, cattle, oil and minerals which provide immediate deductions to offset highly taxed income.

Some of the income shielded from tax by those devices is now subject to the special minimum tax on "tax preferences," to be described shortly. And for capital gains in excess of $50,000, the capital gains rate, previously only 25 percent at most, now stands at 35 percent for high-bracket taxpayers.

So the tax-saving margin between capital gains and earned income has been narrowed for higher-income taxpayers. There may be more emphasis among executives in future years on direct cash income and less emphasis on deferred income, capital gains and fringes.

The margin apparently remains wide enough, however, to continue to make it worthwhile for most affluent taxpayers to delay income or convert it into capital gains when possible.

The ceiling rate on earned income—sometimes called the "maxitax"— may also remove some of the incentive for high-income self-employed businessmen and professional men to adopt the corporate form of doing business for tax advantage. When the top-bracket rate on earned income for individuals and partners has moved down to 50 percent and the maximum corporation rate still stands at 48 percent, the margin is slim. But most self-employed businessmen and partnerships have other considerations in mind in making the decision to go corporate.

And for one very good reason capital gains will retain its allure and deferred income will keep its charm for the great majority of taxpayers. The reason is simply that few taxpayers ever make the exalted circle of top-bracket income earners. For them, the earned income ceiling is purely academic.

LTP—the minimum tax

While Congress was deliberating the "Limitation on Tax Preferences," a newspaper suggested that the initials stood for "Let's Tax Plutocrats." And, in fact, LTP was in large part a response by Congress to a public demand for reform of a tax structure under which many wealthy persons paid little or no tax. This pressure on Congress still prevails.

So Congress set out to make sure that practically everyone above the poverty line pays some tax. It did not go quite that far: The income from state and local bonds remains wholly exempt, for example. But a minimum tax of 10 percent was imposed on many of the other important shelters from taxation. The tax is imposed on this amount: all the income sheltered by the tax preferences which exceeds the actual tax otherwise due, plus a flat exemption of $30,000.

This is how the Limitation on Tax Preferences is figured: William Barton has tax preferences totaling $75,000. His regular tax is $35,000. That sum, plus the flat exemption of $30,000 adds up to $65,000. The total of his preferences exceeds that by $10,000. Therefore Barton pays the 10 percent minimum tax on $10,000 of preference income. He must add $1,000 to his regular tax.

If his regular tax had been larger, he might have escaped the LTP tax. For example, Joseph Morton also has $75,000 of tax preferences. He has a regular tax of $50,000. When he adds that to the flat $30,000 exemption, the total is $80,000. His tax preferences are $5,000 less than that figure, therefore the 10 percent LTP tax is not imposed.

Will the LTP serve to discourage the efforts of taxpayers to find tax-sheltered investments or convert their earnings into capital gains? Probably not in any substantial way. There are these reasons:

First, because many of the sheltering tax preferences remain untouched—$30,000 worth, plus an amount equal to your regular income tax for the year. Few middle-income taxpayers will ever feel the effect of LTP.

Second, because some tax-geared investments including tax exempt municipal bonds were not made subject to the LTP.

And third, because the LTP rate is low enough to leave the tax-saving investments still attractive, even though subject to the minimum tax. For example, if you make an investment in a housing project, you could deduct $5,000 a year for depreciation on a straight-line depreciation basis; but if you choose to take $10,000 on an accelerated basis, this choice saves you the ordinary tax on $5,000.

This $5,000 is added to your tax preferences and may be taxed at 10 percent, or $500. So you have paid $500 for the privilege of saving the much larger tax on $5,000 at your ordinary income tax rate.

Finally, a carry-over device softens the impact. If the taxpayer's regular tax plus the $30,000 exemption exceeds the total of preference items, he may "carry forward" the amount not used to offset tax preferences. This excess can be used as an offset to the LTP in any of the seven succeeding years.

The tax preferences

These are the tax preferences which were made subject to a minimum 10 percent tax on the amount that exceeds the regular tax plus $30,000:

1. *The "bargain" element in stock options.* Companies often give "restricted" or "qualified" stock options to their executives. These are options to buy company stock in the future at present-day prices if the executives remain in the firm's employ. The preference tax is imposed on the difference between the price paid when the executive buys the shares and the price he would have had to pay in the market at that time if he had not held an option.

2. *Reserves for bad debts.* Banks, savings and loan associations, and other financial institutions are permitted to make rapid build-ups of their reserves against possible future losses on loans. But if these reserves exceed the amount found to have been needed in past bad-debt experience, the amount of excess is subject to the preference tax.

3. *Excess percentage depletion.* When the owner of oil or mineral property has claimed his percentage depletion allowance over the years until the total deductions exceed the actual cost of acquiring and developing the property, the excess is subject to the minimum tax. "Intangible drilling costs" were not subjected to the tax; these are wages, machinery and tool rental, fuel and other expenses incidental to drilling a well which are deductible as current expenses. However, they are excluded from the computation of the actual property cost, thus increasing the margin of depletion allowance which is subject to the preference tax.

4. *The untaxed part of capital gains.* Only 50 percent of the taxpayer's net long-term gain is subject to tax. The 10 percent preference levy is imposed on the remaining 50 percent or untaxed half.

5. *Accelerated depreciation.* When "accelerated depreciation"—tax deductions for a rapid write-off of wear-and-tear and obsolescence—is claimed, the minimum tax is applied to the excess of the speeded-up deductions over the normal straight-line accounting method. This applies to real estate, personal property subject to a net lease, railroad cars and lo-

comotives, approved water pollution control facilities, and the rehabilitation of lower-income housing.

"Excess investment interest" formerly was a preference item; it has been dropped from the list of tax preferences, but may now be partially nondeductible.

Affluent investors often borrow large sums, put the money into investments which have good prospects but not much current income, and then use the interest payments on their borrowings as deductions to offset taxes on other income. When the investment—like an apartment house or office building—is sold, the gain in value is taxed at the preferred capital gains rate.

Now, if interest expense on the loan exceeds the current income of the investment, half of such excess investment interest over $25,000 may not be deducted. The effect is to subject the excess to half the taxpayer's regular rate; for individuals with large excess interest outlays this is a heavier tax than the 10 percent LTP levy.

There has been much agitation in Congress to increase the 10 percent LTP rate, and to extend the tax to some preferences not originally covered. Taxpayers who suspect they may be subject to LTP should keep abreast of tax law changes and take professional counsel.

Retirement plans

A big company may offer its key employes not one but several plans for retirement income. The following section describes the various pension and deferred-income plans in use in a single great U.S. corporation.

The company paid out bonuses totaling $75,000,000 in 1969. Officers and directors received bonus grants totaling $858,000 in cash and stock. Directors and officers also received options to buy company stock.

The bonuses in this case are paid in a form that really represents a claim against the corporation. If the employe wishes, the bonus grants may be set aside, earmarked for later payment, by a method explained in the company's annual statement: "Bonus grants in cash or in shares are settled either in full at the time of the grant or in not more than five annual installments, commencing at the time of the grant, except that settlement of grants may be deferred until the termination of employment, either in full or not more than ten annual installments, commencing at the termination of employment."

There is also a thrift plan for all employes, under which employes may make savings contributions ranging from 2 percent to 10 percent of their pay. The company makes contributions equal to 60 percent of the employe's contributions. This plan is available to directors and officers, and is used by most of them.

Still another program, a system of employe annuities, is available to all employes. One executive of this company, in 1969, received direct remuneration totaling $237,500. In addition, his bonus grants for that year totaled $120,000. He had exercised stock options having a purchase price of $242,200 and still held stock options, unexercised, with an aggregate market value of $309,000. He had aggregate contributions of nearly $100,000 in the thrift plan.

On retirement after thirty-five years this corporate officer would receive his pension annuity, a retirement income of $132,000, in addition to his bonus payments and the benefits of contributions to the company thrift plan.

His retirement income would easily match the after-tax take-home pay he received in his peak earning years.

Expense account deductions

Expense account living is less glamorous than before. In 1962, Congress enacted a much-publicized crackdown on widespread abuses of tax-deductible travel and entertainment expenses. But in terms of tax savings, it still offers great attractions. You need only abide by the rules.

To be deductible as business expenses, the costs of entertainment, amusement or recreation must not only be "ordinary and necessary" expenses of doing business, but must also conform to either of two standards.

They must be (1) "directly related to . . . the active conduct of the taxpayer's trade or business"; or (2) if directly preceding or following a business discussion, they must be "associated with the active conduct of the taxpayer's trade or business."

Within those boundaries, almost anything in the ordinary categories of entertainment is acceptable, including nightclubs, theaters, cocktail lounges, clubs and assorted other fun spots.

It is harder to meet the first test—"directly related" to business—than the second, "associated with" the conduct of business. Usually, it is wise for the taxpayer to try to identify his outlays as being "associated with"; if he can do so, virtually all his entertaining expenses for business purposes will qualify for deductions, despite the fairly tough rules laid down for substantiation and documentation.

The taxpayer must be mindful to plan his business entertainment sensibly and to retain the receipts, vouchers and notes which he made at the time or shortly thereafter. These must pinpoint the business nature of the meeting, the time, the place, and the name and business connection of the person entertained.

It is basic that you have a "substantial" and "bona fide" business discussion with the customer, prospect or client, directly preceding or following the entertainment. It is not necessary to have made an actual deal; it is simply necessary that there be reasonable expectation of future income or other benefit from the conversation. This applies whether you are hoping to form a new business connection, or whether you merely expect to foster the continuation of a present business relationship.

The expression "directly preceding or following" is interpreted as being a bit more liberal than it sounds. The IRS has indicated the discussion may take place on the same day, or even on the morning after the entertainment, if the business guest or guests have come from out of town.

This interpretation makes a nightclub, however noisy, an acceptable place for a "business interview." You need not have discussed business at all during the entertainment.

It would be more difficult to prove the conversation was "directly related" to a business purpose; the IRS in such a case requires that the business discussion occur *during the period of entertainment*. The Treasury holds that race tracks, nightclubs and cocktail parties are unlikely places for serious business discussions. The taxpayer will be wise to claim his deduction under the "associated" rule.

You may also claim a deduction for entertaining the wife of a customer, along with the customer himself, in many common situations. And your *own wife, too,* if she joins the group for the entertainment. It is much harder to prove to IRS that a wife should be deductible on a business trip. Her travel costs are not deductible unless it is shown that she provided substantial services directly and primarily related to her husband's busines. The fact that she entertained his business guests or clients does not usually suffice.

"Directly related." This is what must be proved to back up a deduction for entertainment outlays that are "directly related":

First, that you had more than a general expectation of earning income or some definite business benefit at some indefinite future time; also that you engaged in a meeting, discussion, or other business transaction during the period of entertainment; and finally, that the principal purpose of the combined business and entertainment was to transact business. It cannot have been merely incidental to the entertainment purpose.

If the expenditure does qualify as "directly related," then any money spent on a person or persons who are "closely connected" to those engaged in the business transaction may be deducted also under the other test; they are "associated with" a business purpose.

A wife (or husband) is specifically mentioned by IRS as a "closely connected" person. Her expenses can be deducted by the taxpayer. There is no further indication as to what the expression covers. It may mean friends or children, employes, lawyers, or professional advisers, even if the latter are not actively taking part in the business discussion.

"Quiet meals." The "quiet business lunch" or other "quiet meal," as it is designated in IRS regulations, is exempt from the stern rules governing expense accounts. That means that almost all business lunches, dinners, breakfasts, cocktail hour meetings and coffee breaks at hotels and

restaurants are deductible. The deductibility stands up even if the only aim is to maintain or cultivate general goodwill with business associates, customers, clients or prospective business contacts. There need be no actual discussion of business at all.

Two standards must be met, however, to nail down the deductions.

First, the guest must have a business relationship with you which provides the reason for entertaining him for business, rather than social, reasons. Examples would be: a salesman buying lunch for a prospective customer; an insurance agent buying lunch for a client; a manufacturer entertaining the owner or a dealer or distributor of his products; a reporter taking a news source to lunch; or a public relations man taking a reporter to lunch.

Second, the meal or drinks must have been taken in a restaurant, lounge, club, or similar place where there were no distractions or noise such as an orchestra or floor show. This makes most hotels and restaurants eligible, but rules out nightclubs, race tracks, large social gatherings and cocktail parties.

One kind of "quiet lunch" is definitely rejected by the Treasury: the "reciprocal" arrangement among two or more business associates who take turns picking up the tab for lunch so that they enjoy deductible lunches every day.

Entertaining at home for business associates is a deductible expense, but is subject to the IRS rules for dining-out. The Treasury does make one important concession. The cost of "quiet business meals" served to clients, customers or business contacts at home is deductible. You must be prepared to show that the motive in entertaining them was a business, rather than a social motive, and you must keep a record of the costs, names of guests, and business affiliations. You need not discuss business. But if personal friends are present, the deduction may be endangered.

Business gifts. The deduction for business gifts generally is limited to $25 for each recipient in a year. The allowance covers business gifts made to customers, business associates, employes, and others who provide services or are prospective sources of income.

You are not prevented from making gifts much larger than that, but the income tax deduction may be no more than $25 for each person to whom you made business gifts in a year. The limit is based on what the gift cost you, not its worth to the recipient.

Gifts to employes may be deducted up to $100, if the gift is in recognition of length of service or other presentation of the nature of a recognition or award and is clearly distinguished as such.

Use of car. If you use your car for business, you can deduct depreciation. Either of two methods may be used, the straight-line or the declining-balance. The straight-line method gives an equal amount of depreciation each year. If your income is high in the first year of the car's life, you may want a larger deduction that year. If so, elect the declining-balance method. Here are examples:

• Straight-line method: You buy a car for business use costing $3,500. You estimate its useful life as four years. Its salvage value, $300, is less than ten percent of the cost and can be ignored. You will divide the cost of the car by four and take a deduction of $875 in each of the four years.

• Declining-balance method, 200 percent rate: This method may be used only on a new car with a useful life of three years or more. Figure it as follows: Find the rate you would use under the straight-line method; in this case it would be 25 percent. Double that rate, which gives you 50 percent. Apply the 50 percent to the new car cost; your first-year deduction is $1,750. In the second year, deduct 50 percent of the remaining $1,750 cost basis; the deduction is $875. And so on: The third year deduction will be $438, and the fourth year $219.

If you can get by on $44 a day while traveling on business, you can save yourself a lot of record-keeping. The employer can give an executive or salesman an expense allowance not exceeding that amount daily. The employer must maintain satisfactory audit control; if so, the IRS will consider that the amounts are automatically accounted for to the employer. A fixed mileage allowance of not more than 15 cents a mile also will be permitted on the same terms.

Clubs and "facilities." Dues paid to country clubs, golf clubs, athletic clubs, hunting or fishing clubs and social clubs are deductible if two tests are met. First, the taxpayer must have used the club primarily for the furtherance of his business, meaning more than 50 percent of the time.

Second, even if the club is used more than 50 percent for business purposes, only that portion of the club dues which is "directly related" to the active conduct of business is deductible. In other words, to deduct the costs of entertaining a business guest at a club—even a social club —requires that serious business matters were under discussion and the meeting was not merely to promote goodwill.

However, taking a business associate or customer into the club's restaurant or dining room qualifies as a "quiet meal" and there is no requirement that business be discussed at the luncheon.

The 50 percent rule applies not only to club expenses, but to "recreational facilities" or "entertainment facilities." These might include automobiles, if more than 50 percent of the mileage for the year is ordinary and necessary business travel; airplanes, if 50 percent of hours flown is for business purposes; and a long list of other facilities— yachts, hunting lodges, summer homes, tennis courts, swimming pools, bowling alleys, and fishing camps—if more than 50 percent of the number of calendar days the facility is used during the year is for business use.

The "directly related" rule also applies to the use of recreational facilities and it complicates the claiming of a deduction. Even though the taxpayer shows that the primary use of the facility—more than 50 percent—is for business purposes, the rules usually bar him from claiming as much as 50 percent of the expenses as a deduction.

A business man might use his yacht 70 percent for business purposes during a year, including "goodwill" entertainment which is a business use. But he can deduct only the portion of his expenditures which is "directly related to the active conduct of his trade or business."

That narrows the deduction possibilities, because goodwill entertainment is not considered to be directly related, under the rules. And the IRS regulations presume that directly related entertainment cannot take place on a yacht or any other place where there are distractions. Yachts, therefore, are in the same category as nightclubs, race tracks or cocktail parties.

So it becomes difficult to deduct the operating cost of the yacht—or tennis court or swimming pool—because depreciation and maintenance costs including repairs and insurance can be taken only if the "directly related" test is met as well as the 50 percent test.

However, the actual costs of goodwill entertainment are deductible if the entertainment follows or precedes a business discussion, even if the entertainment takes place on a yacht or in a hunting lodge, resort cottage or other recreational facility.

The goodwill entertainment costs include the fuel of the yacht, the drinks and refreshments, fishing bait and other out-of-pocket expenses.

Business, vacation, travel. It is perfectly possible and legal to combine a vacation with business travel. These are the rules to follow to claim the maximum business expense deductions:

• If the trip is within the United States, the entire transportation cost of the combined business-pleasure trip (including meals while actually traveling) is deductible if the trip was taken primarily for business reasons.

• If the trip is outside the United States and lasts for a week or less, or if the entire trip is longer than a week but your personal activities take up less than one-fourth of the whole trip, you can deduct your entire transportation costs. Again, this assumes the trip was primarily for business.

• However, if the trip is outside the United States and lasted for more than a week, and if 25 percent or more of the total trip time was for personal activities, the deduction for travel costs is limited to the percentage of the time spent on business.

However, the Treasury has fairly liberal rules in this connection. Most business travelers might still get a deduction for full fare instead of only part-fare. There are two conditions under which a business traveler

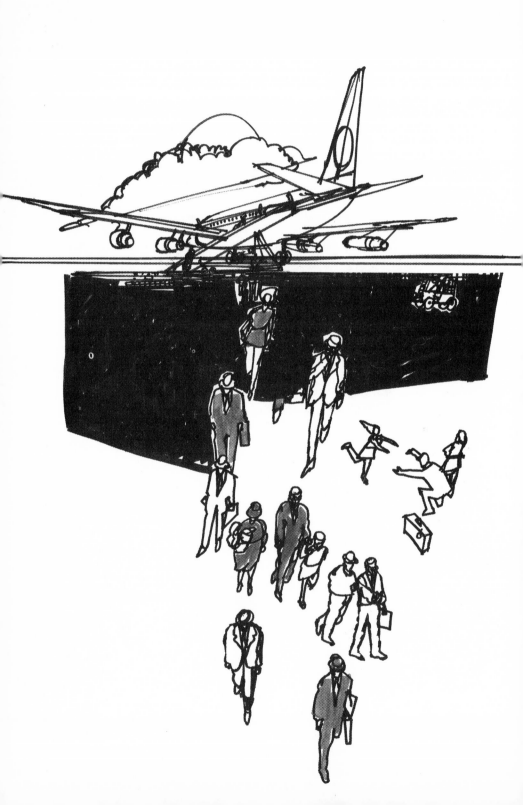

could deduct his entire transportation expense even if the trip outside the United States lasted more than a week and 25 percent or more was for personal reasons. They are:

First, the traveler did not have substantial control over arranging his business trip; or second, that getting the chance for a vacation was not a major consideration in the decision to make the trip.

The Treasury automatically assumes you lacked control over the business trip if your employer reimbursed you for your expenses on the business portion of the trip.

But, there is a limit to this liberality: It does not apply to employes who own more than 10 percent of the stock of the corporation employing them, or who are related to the employer, or who are "managing executives" of the employing firm. A "managing executive" in this case is one who has enough authority to decide whether he needs to make a business trip, without getting it approved by anyone else in the organization.

But if this executive can prove that he did not have substantial control, or that a vacation was not a major consideration, he, too, may deduct his entire round-trip transportation costs, even if gone for more than a week and even if 25 percent or more of the time was spent vacationing.

If your travel is primarily for pleasure, you may not deduct the trip expenses. But if you make side trips for business purposes, those costs are deductible. For example, a New York taxpayer spends his vacation in Maine, but travels to New Hampshire for three days to call on business customers. The expenses from New York to Maine and return are not deductible, but the costs of the trip to New Hampshire are.

Records and proof. Travel and entertainment costs are among the deductions most frequently challenged in IRS audits. Records must be complete and readily available.

The Treasury requires that the taxpayer keep some kind of account book, diary, date book or other record of expense which will be available for inspection in case of an IRS examination.

This would be the source for information about weekly, monthly or other expense account statements required by an employer or client. For self-employed persons, it is the basic document which a revenue agent will wish to see in any examination of business deduction claims.

A page-a-day desk diary can be made to serve as an account book. The hour and place can be entered when the appointment is made. On return from the luncheon, the entries of cost, business purpose and other required data can be entered. Stubs from restaurant checks or other receipts may be slipped into the pages or filed elsewhere.

The information should be entered daily, or at least on each day that expenses were incurred. If it is obvious you have been catching up on entries only once a week or so, the Treasury may reject your records as providing an untrustworthy record of expenses.

Keep the substantiating evidence of your outlays. The proof should include every paid bill or receipt from a hotel or motel while traveling on business. Receipts will be required for every separate expense account item of $25 or more, except for transportation if the railroad, bus line or other transportation company does not generally provide receipts. Plane fares of $25 or more require receipts.

As in every other situation in which proof of an expenditure is required, the IRS will not accept a check made out to a payee as sole proof on an expense deduction. An itemized or receipted bill is required as well as the canceled check to show the actual items or services purchased by the payment.

The Treasury provides examples of acceptable ways to keep records of business entertainment outlays.

Here are two of them: For entertainment expenses, an architect has submitted plans to an investment trust for an apartment building. He invites four trustees of the fund to lunch to discuss and promote his plans. This might be the record in his account book:

> 12-17-73: Lunch and tip—$17.00; Cafe Plaza, New York, N.Y.; with Jones, Brown, Green and Smith, trustees of Modern Real Estate Investment Trust, concerning architectural plans for Clarement Village Apts.

He need not obtain a receipt from the Cafe Plaza since the amount of the expense is less than $25.

For entertainment following business discussion, the promoter of Y Corporation holds a business discussion with officers of the Acme Corporation. Then the promoter takes the Acme group to drinks and dinner. This might be his record:

> 12-27-73: Taxi and tip ($2.25); drinks at bar & tip ($14.50); dinner ($24) and tip ($4) at Flair Club, Washington, D. C.; entertainment of President Black, Vice President Chum, and Treasurer Drew of the Acme Corp., following business meeting with them at my office all afternoon concerning proposed distributorship arrangement between Y and Acme Corporation.

He need not obtain a receipt for either the dinner bill or the bar bill, since both are less than $25. (Tips can be excluded from the calculation.)

Most taxpayers *do* save money by keeping *good* records, even if many think that they gain by relying on estimates and memory.

The old "Cohan rule" proved costly to a lot of taxpayers. It resulted from a celebrated tax case won by the late entertainer, George M. Cohan. The Supreme Court said the IRS was bound to allow "fair and reasonable deductions for travel, entertainment and promotional expenses for a taxpayer who was reasonably able to prove that he had incurred such expenses, but who was unable to substantiate the amount of the deduction to which he was entitled because he had neither records nor receipts."

Later Congress hardened the law, spelling out the requirements for records and proof and overruling the Cohan rule. One C.P.A. recalls that some of his firm's clients relied on the Cohan rule, against the firm's advice, until the law was changed. Then the C.P.A. firm refused to prepare those clients' tax returns unless they kept adequate records. When they did, *most* were surprised to find they had been cheating themselves.

*Even though we have striven to make
the instructions simple, we have missed
the boat. For instance, we shouldn't use
the word spouse. We don't think it's
fair to the American taxpayer to think
we are talking about a water fountain.
Between this and Women's Lib,
we have a difficult problem because
we can't say husband, or he, all the
time. We have to say husband-wife
or he-she or something like that.*

IRS Commissioner Johnnie M. Walters,
interview with the Associated Press,
March 25, 1972.

CHAPTER 8

The Woman Who Works

More and more women work. At least one-third of them are wives and mothers who want to build up the family income. Equally compelling, in many cases, is the reason that they simply don't want to waste the abilities that God and college gave them.

But sometimes the psychological rewards are greater than the monetary gain. It sounds good for a family to earn two incomes, but often the result is only an income-and-a-fraction.

Taxes and hidden costs frequently consume much of the working wife's pay. Many a woman's job has cost the family as much as it brought in and sometimes more.

The problem was mentioned briefly in earlier pages of this book, with a tax chart showing how the federal income and Social Security taxes alone can eat up a third to a half, or even more, of a working wife's income.

When married women go to work they become the country's most heavily taxed wage earners, because the first dollar they earn is taxed at their husband's highest rate bracket. Their rates go up from there. There's no help from the standard deduction; the law gives only one of these to a couple, unless the couple is living together without matrimony.

Tax law changes of recent years have eased somewhat the problems of single women and working mothers, although some new and almost absurdly discriminatory results have come along as byproducts of the reforms.

The high tax rate which formerly discriminated seriously against unmarried women—and single men—is now no more than 20 percent higher than the married couple's rate. Even more favorable tax rates are now available to the many who become heads of households because of divorce, desertion, death, a mutually agreed parting of spouses, or the necessity of supporting an aged or invalid parent.

And a substantial increase in the child care deduction now eases the burden of millions of women who, in order to work, have to pay steadily rising costs for this service. Such costs often amount to 20 or 30 percent of a woman's income.

Now, such outlays may be deducted, up to a maximum of $400 a month. The rules should be studied carefully; they can provide an important tax break for working wives and single women—or men—but there are several new catches in the law that bear watching.

These and other tax developments will be discussed shortly. Right now, this warning should be heeded by women who see a job as more than a cure for boredom and an escape from dishwashing and vacuuming: If the pay is an important consideration, check carefully in advance into the tax consequences.

In the first place, the pay will usually be lower than a man would get —about 35 percent lower for a woman college graduate than for a man of equivalent education, the Census Bureau says. The job entails extra costs, too—transportation, clothes, dry cleaning—and the family has to start paying for laundry, sewing, and other chores that the wife used to perform.

One householder with $20,000-a-year taxable income found that his wife's $4,000-a-year job was no bargain. It necessitated a thrice-weekly maid for laundry and housecleaning at $1,600 a year, plus her $100 bus fare. The wife's bus fare added about $165; her lunches and incidentals came to $400; her bills for shoes, clothing, dry cleaning, hair dresser and cosmetics went up $400 a year. The kids bought their lunches instead of coming home for them.

The family budget went up about $2,900 a year. The biggest blow came at income tax time. The federal income tax was $1,280 higher because of the added income, and the state income tax rose proportionately. The "second income" wound up as a loss of about $200.

The magazine *Money* in October, 1972, explored the case of a wife with $177 weekly pay before deductions, whose salary came to $9,200 a year. Her husband earned $14,400. Taxes and special costs cut her take-home pay to about $70 a week, or $3,640 a year.

The tax collector dealt another blow in the spring. The tax withholding was calculated separately—as it always is—on the husband's salary and on the wife's. But the tax was payable on their joint income, $23,600. They owed another $818 on April 15.

Only $2,860 remained of the wife's $9,200 "second income," or $55 a week.

Social Security is a growing problem; it is the fastest rising federal tax, and a wife who works long enough to earn the maximum Social Security benefits gets a retirement pension as big as her husband's. But she'd get half that much, as a dependent spouse, if she never worked at all.

Still, what does a wife do when the bills are piling up each month, the kids are big enough to take care of themselves, and boredom is driving her up the wall? She rustles up a job, of course.

But she might do well to adjust her sights in job hunting. She might consider taking a job in the community library or recreation center or in the paid secretaryship at the church, or becoming the news and ad assistant in the neighborhood newspaper. The sense of service and fulfillment can perhaps be just as great. The costs of clothes, eating out, bus fare and beauty shop will be lower, the hours can be shorter.

The pay will be lower, too, but so will the tax rate. She just might come out ahead.

The Sin Tax

One tax irritant that resulted from Congress' effort to reduce the single taxpayer's rate is a definite bias against working married couples. As revised, the tax law favors working couples who live together without marrying.

The ink was hardly dry on the 1971 tax reform law when a young Virginia housewife, Kathryn B. McGrath, wrote a letter to the chairman of the House Ways and Means Committee, Representative Wilbur D. Mills of Arkansas. Mrs. McGrath said she and her husband John would be paying at least $1,000 more to the IRS than if they were single taxpayers.

"The United States Congress," she scolded, "has provided us, and all other married taxpayers where both husband and wife work, with a strong economic incentive to obtain a divorce and thereafter to live more prosperously 'in sin.' "

Mrs. McGrath cited as an example a husband and wife with $14,000 income each, a total of $28,000. Under a joint return, the 1971 tax due was $7,100. If they had been living together but using the single taxpayer's rate, they would have paid $3,210 each or a total of $6,420. The combined tax of the unwed couple thus was $680 less than the married couple's tax. Wrote Mrs. McGrath:

"I can see no rational basis for this discrimination against working wives, and I believe that this new tax rate table may well be susceptible to attack in the courts on constitutional grounds."

The Ways and Means Committee conceded that the bias existed at most income levels. But it was not frightened badly enough by Mrs. McGrath—or by many hundreds of column-inches of newspaper criticism —to recommend any immediate amendment to the House. Some members predicted, however, that a revision of this so-called "sin tax" might be incorporated in the next tax reform bill, whenever it might come.

Unless that happened, the tax-writing committee admitted, the built-in discrimination would be worse for 1972 and thereafter. In that year the standard deduction rose to 15 percent, up to a maximum of $2,000.

Two single persons living together therefore could each claim a standard deduction of up to $2,000, or a total of $4,000. A husband and wife with exactly the same combined income could claim only one standard deduction, or $2,000.

Thus the standard deduction alone would give an unmarried pair up to $2,000 less taxable income than a married couple.

The Senate-House Joint Committee on Internal Revenue Taxation did issue an explanatory "Blue Paper" on the tax schedule. It said the new tax rate for singles was enacted in response to the complaints from single persons that the rate structure favored couples. The change was justified, it said, "on the grounds that although a married couple has greater expenses than a single person and hence should pay less tax, the couple's living expenses are likely to be less than those of *two* single persons, and therefore the couple's tax should be higher than that of two single persons."

The joint committee apparently preferred not to think about the possibility of an unmarried couple living together and sharing expenses without benefit of matrimony.

For two unmarried persons with incomes of $20,000 each, the tax cost of getting married would be around $2,000 a year. If one of the two was a "head of household" with two children, the financial setback of marriage would be even more dramatic, for the tax rate of an unmarried head of household is lower than the single taxpayer's rate.

Two Tax Traps

Married couples must watch out for two further tax traps when both husband and wife work. These, too, illustrate how an attempt by Congress to patch up one tax inequity can create a new inequity.

One is the possibility of "underwithholding." When both man and wife work, the employer may not withhold enough income tax from the weekly or monthly paychecks. Then the couple winds up the year with a large and unexpected tax payment due. More about this tax trap shortly.

Overwithholding. The other hazard, *over*withholding, was created when Congress tried to remedy the underwithholding problem. It wrote new tax withholding tables for employers to use in 1972 and thereafter.

In literally millions of cases, particularly those of taxpayers with relatively high incomes and itemized deductions, the amounts being withheld from workers' paychecks suddenly jumped to levels far above the amount of tax due. The effect in early 1972 was much like that of a sudden tax increase. Consumer buying power was reduced as paychecks became smaller; an incipient business recovery was temporarily slowed.

Since then the Treasury—fearful of this deflationary effect but also fearful that its refunds totaling billions of dollars in the spring would cause a spurt of inflation when taxpayers claimed them—has pushed a continuing publicity campaign encouraging taxpayers to get their withholding adjusted to realistic levels.

Most of the taxpayers who were worst hurt—meaning, in most cases, those with the highest incomes and highest itemized deductions—took the Treasury's advice and arranged with employers to scale down their withholding to the approximate level of tax actually due.

But millions either failed to get the message or preferred not to heed it. It finally dawned on the Treasury that many taxpayers were treating overwithholding as a kind of forced saving. Apparently they liked the idea of having the government hold their money until they claimed a refund on their next April 15 tax return.

From a purely economic viewpoint, it makes little sense to use the Treasury as a Christmas Savings Club. The government is happy, of course, to keep a taxpayer's money for months. But if the taxpayer has learned that he can get along with less take-home pay, he would do better to put the extra money to work earning interest in a savings account than to let the Treasury use it as an interest-free loan.

Underwithholding. Taxpayers who have once been clouted by the effects of the reverse problem, *under*withholding, usually need no urging to adjust their withholding rate. The penalty for failing to do so is a serious financial setback when tax-filing time comes.

This problem is caused mainly by the low-income allowance. The LIA is available to married couples who file jointly. Each couple can claim only one allowance on Form 1040, but in the readymade withholding tables used by their employers the allowance is given to each and every worker. The husband's employer gives him the benefit of one allowance, the wife's employer gives her another full allowance.

The pay withholding of both man and wife is scaled down accordingly. The IRS feels it would be impossible for employers to adjust the withholding accurately by keeping tabs currently on which employes had wives or husbands working.

"The result is that if both husband and wife work, not enough tax is withheld," said an IRS warning notice.

"At the end of the year the couple may face a large tax bill to make up the difference between the withholding and the actual tax."

A stream of warnings, advice and instructions on how to adjust withholding came from IRS in 1971 and 1972. Finally a Form W-4 was evolved which, IRS hoped, would help all taxpayers figure out how much should be withheld from their paychecks. The W-4 is to be filed with the employer, not with IRS.

The Form W-4 was intended primarily to cope with what had become the major problem, overwithholding. But it was designed also to correct underwithholding.

It is titled "Employee's Withholding Allowance Certificate." Once you have filled it out, it remains in effect until you change it. It provides for the use of a certain number of "withholding allowances" which, in effect, are like so many personal exemptions.

By using a worksheet that is part of the W-4 form, taxpayers can correct the distorting effect of the low-income allowance on the withholding of families in which both husband and wife work. This eliminates some underwithholding. The form also permits employes to take enough "withholding allowances" to offset the itemized deductions they will claim; this helps to correct overwithholding.

Employes whose companies fail to distribute the W-4 forms should ask for them or, if necessary, obtain them from local IRS offices.

Child care

If a bigger burden than the income tax drags down the working mother, it is probably the high cost and acute shortage of good day care facilities.

Women's rights organizations for years have done battle in the lobbies of Congress for larger child care deductions and greater federal support for the establishment of day care and nursery school facilities. They scored gains on both counts beginning with the 1972 tax year.

The full amount of expenses now may be deducted up to a limit of $400 a month, or $4,800 a year, for the care of a child or other qualified dependent in your home, if the outlays are made to enable a taxpayer to work. The old deduction was $600 a year for one dependent, $900 for two or more.

For services outside the home—such as a day care center, private school or nursing home—the maximum deduction is $200 a month for one dependent, $300 a month for two, or $400 a month for three or more.

One basic rule applies to both types of care, and it is unchanged from former years: To be deductible, the expenses must be incurred to permit the taxpayer to be "gainfully employed"; this term is defined by the IRS as meaning (1) employed by another for pay, (2) actively looking for such employment, or (3) employed in your own business.

Virtually all other pre-1972 provisions were liberalized, so working parents should read the new rules carefully. There are other important concessions, and a major restriction. In tax years through calendar year 1975 this deduction could be claimed in full only if the taxpayer's adjusted gross income—or the combined adjusted gross income, for couples—was $18,000 or less. (For later years this limit was liberalized greatly, as will be described a few paragraphs below.)

For every dollar of adjusted gross income above the $18,000 level, Congress decreed, the amount of deduction must be reduced by 50 cents. At $27,600 of income the deduction thus vanishes entirely. The $18,000 limitation, moreover, was applied over the year on the basis of $1,500 a month, so the taxpayer earning more than $2,300 in any month could not claim any deduction for that particular month. The following schedule shows the maximum deduction that could be claimed at various levels of monthly income:

Monthly Adjusted Gross Income	Limit of Maximum Deduction
$1,500 or less	$400
1,700	300
1,900	200
2,100	100
2,300 and over	None

These are among the major liberalizing provisions:

• The age limit for a dependent child has been raised from thirteen to fifteen; that is, the deduction can now be claimed for children fourteen and under. The eligibility rules were not changed for dependents who are physically or mentally incapable of caring for themselves.

• Expenses for care of a disabled husband or wife can be deducted, but the deduction must be reduced by the amount of any disability payments received.

• The full amount paid to a maid or housekeeper may be deducted, as long as part of her time is spent caring for a qualified dependent. It is no longer necessary to separate housekeeping time from child-care time, even when the housekeeping is not directly related to the care. Previously, only the costs attributable to dependent care were deductible.

• All single persons and married couples are eligible for the deduction, provided the other tests are met. Formerly bachelors were ineligible; a man could claim the deduction only if he was widowed, divorced or legally separated from his wife, or if his wife was incapacitated or in an institution for at least ninety consecutive days.

Effective for tax years begining after March 29, 1975—but not for calendar year 1975—Congress boosted the $18,000 limit to $35,000 of adjusted gross income, thus making the deduction available to more affluent families.

The restrictions. The child care deduction is allowed only to taxpayers who itemize their deductions, not to those claiming the standard deduction. To be eligible to claim he or she is maintaining a household that includes one or more of the qualifying dependents, the taxpayer (or couple) must furnish over half the cost of the household.

These other restrictions were written into the new rules:

• Married couples can claim the deduction only if they file a joint return for the year.

• If a person is married during any portion of the year, the deduction will be allowed for employment-related expenses during that married period *in which both spouses were employed on a full-time basis or one spouse was disabled.*

• A "full-time basis" has been interpreted to mean that both spouses must be employed at least 75 percent of a normal work week, or thirty hours, unless one spouse is incapable of self-care.

(However, a married person living apart from husband or wife and filing a separate return may claim the deduction if, for more than half the tax year, he or she maintained a home for a qualified dependent.)

• In the case of a physically or mentally incapable dependent, a taxpayer may qualify for the deduction even if the dependent has over $750 income and thus would not qualify as a dependent for tax exemption purposes. But in such a circumstance, the deduction must be reduced by the amount of any income or disability payments in excess of $750.

• Although the deductible outlays for maid, babysitter, or caretaker may cover services not related to child care, the deduction cannot cover amounts paid to an individual who is employed predominantly, for example, as a gardener, bartender, or chauffeur.

• In permitting use of the deduction for expenses incurred outside the taxpayer's household for one or more dependents fourteen years old or younger, no deduction can be claimed for any portion of the cost of normal schooling.

• Nor can any child care deduction be claimed if the payment is made to someone related to the taxpayer. The babysitter, in other words, may not be an older child, a grandparent or an aunt.

Finally: The deductions are allowable only to the extent that the taxpayer can prove he has actually paid the expenses. It will be necessary to keep good records, not only to prove that the money was paid but to show that the child care was necessary for the mother to be gainfully employed.

Women's groups

In liberalizing the child care deduction, Congress responded to strong pressure from many organizations, including women's liberation and women's rights groups. These are still dissatisfied; some have demanded that the child care costs of a working mother be treated as business expenses, like a lawyer's library or an electrician's tools.

Congress has not been visibly impressed with that particular argument, but the door is not closed to further liberalizations. Some sentiment has been voiced, for example, for relaxing the rule that married couples cannot deduct the expenses unless both spouses are gainfully employed on a full-time basis. Women's groups contended that this unfairly penalized the part-time working wife.

Further steps were being considered, also, to improve the number and quality of child care facilities. Congress made a start in the 1971 legislation by providing a tax incentive for companies to install day care centers for working mothers.

The company is permitted to write off the cost of the facilities in depreciation over sixty months, regardless of the actual useful life of the day care center. A similar incentive, permitting the firm to recover rapidly the cost of the facilities, is provided for a company's outlays for on-the-job training centers for adults.

The child care facilities must be specially designed for the personal care, protection and supervision of children. A general-purpose room—such as a room used as an employe recreation center at night, or part of a room screened off for daytime child care use—would not qualify for the rapid depreciation benefit.

Contributions made to women's liberation groups, and the out-of-pocket costs of services performed for them apparently are deductible; at least one such group has been declared by IRS to be a tax-exempt charitable and educational organization.

The particular women's group approved was not named in the official announcement, and the IRS said other women's rights groups should not consider themselves automatically entitled to the same exemption. Each group must apply for it individually.

But the IRS ruling described the organization it had approved and thereby gave some guidelines for others. The approved group promotes equal employment rights for women, investigates cases of apparent discrimination, offers counseling to women and companies on equal treatment, and holds seminars to educate women "with regard to their socioeconomic image in society." It gets most of its support from public contributions and, IRS added, does not engage in economic boycotts, reprisals, or picketing.

Another difference between death and taxes is that death is frequently painless.

Anonymous

CHAPTER 9

The
Outside
Salesman

Short of paying no tax at all, the employe who is an "outside salesman" lives in the best of all possible worlds from an income tax standpoint. His is a distinct classification that he shares with no other taxpayer.

In an earlier discussion of the structure of a tax return we reviewed the advantages of taking as many deductions as possible "at the top," subtracting them from gross income. Everyone starts with gross income, the total of receipts from all sources. Those who can subtract substantial "adjustments" from gross income, instead of taking their deductions further down from "adjusted gross income," generally come out ahead.

One reason for the advantage is that you still can claim the standard deduction, no matter how much you have already subtracted as "adjustments" from gross income. The outside salesman, unlike other employes, can deduct *all* his business expenses from *gross income.* (See Appendix, Deductions for the Outside Salesman.)

If you meet the rather rigid definition of an outside salesman, you make out your return in the same way as one who runs his own business and deducts his expenses, except that he must use Schedule C. You need simply attach a statement of business expenses or, if you wish, fill out

Form 2106, which you can obtain from the IRS office nearest to you.

Most employes have a very limited opportunity to make business expense deductions from gross income; they can claim only local transportation expenses connected with their work, plus travel and living expenses away from home overnight on business.

Who qualifies?

Who is an outside salesman? For federal income tax purposes, he is an employe who does his selling away from his employer's place of business. His principal activity must be the outside solicitation of business on a full-time basis. You can not be an outside salesman if you work primarily at your employer's office or business place.

Incidental duties performed at your employer's place of business, like writing up reports and orders and making telephone calls, do not disqualify you, so long as your primary duty is outside selling. But you do not meet the definition if you are required to do some inside selling for regular periods.

If the salesman's principal duties include service and delivery as well as sales, he does not meet the definition. A driver-salesman with a milk or bread route does not qualify. Neither does an insurance agent who serves a fixed territory as a debit manager. The Internal Revenue Service is prickly about seeing that every taxpayer who claims "outside salesman" status actually meets the requirements.

This is understandable, for, in effect, the law gives the outside salesman a double identity. He is treated as a self-employed person who can deduct all his business-related expenses from gross income. At the same time, he enjoys the status of an employe, which permits him to shape his income as favorably as possible to divert some earnings to tax-exempt or capital gains status.

The sales representative who does not quite qualify as an outside salesman because he does some inside selling should consider the question: Would he be better off, for tax reasons, to seek a change in assignment to outside selling only—even if that involves some loss of commissions?

Salesman's fringe benefits

Since he is still an employe on a payroll and not an independent contractor, the outside salesman may seek employe-type fringe benefits of the kind that are fully deductible by the employer and tax-exempt to the employe.

A company-paid accident and health plan is a "best buy" from a tax standpoint. Even if he agrees to take an equivalent deduction in his salary or commissions, the outside seller comes out ahead. He is swapping fully taxable income for nontaxable income.

The employer generally will not object. He can deduct the full costs as

a business expense, without taking into account the limitation on medical deductions which applies to employes when they pay their own medical bills.

The outside salesman also may seek a "sick pay," or wage continuation plan. It guarantees that his income will continue if he misses substantial time at work because of illness or injury, and it provides a tax deduction to help out with the incidental costs of serious illness.

The benefits of life insurance plans and Treasury-approved retirement programs are likely to be of interest to the outside salesman, as to other employes. These, too, may provide a worthwhile trade-off, even if commission or salary are reduced.

Another possible substitute for cash would be payment of dues and memberships in clubs, chambers of commerce, trade associations and civic groups which obviously enhance the prospects of sales return. There is probably more justification for the employer to provide this pay-substitute to an outside salesman than to any other group of employes. The personal benefits to the salesman, and often to his family, are obvious.

Timing of income

The outside salesman is in a better position to control the timing of his income for tax advantage than almost any other taxpayer. Much of his income is paid in commission checks. Within reason he can govern the timing of their arrival.

And he could take advantage of his special payroll status to set up—by agreement with his employer—a schedule for deferring the receipt of some income.

This deferment might be arranged, as described in the examples in the chapter, "The Executive," on particularly large commissions which otherwise would put the salesman in a significantly higher tax bracket.

The rules previously described should be carefully observed. If the company's lawyer is not thoroughly familiar with the tax rules on such plans, a tax specialist might be consulted. One cardinal rule: the agreement should be settled and formalized before the full commissions are due for payment.

The newly simplified system of income-averaging may provide another device for avoiding the big tax bite that comes with a sudden bulge in income resulting from a big sale. That device probably is better for the once-in-a-lifetime kind of windfall, however, than for the year-to-year fluctuations that many salesmen experience.

Other techniques may serve better to smooth out the peaks and valleys of commission income. The outside salesman is in good position to vary his tax tactics. For one thing, he can keep a close check on his commissions in the closing months of each year so that he can either defer or accelerate receipt of some commissions.

The "alternating" device, described in our chapter on "Some ABCs of Income Tax," is made to order for the outside salesman. He can control better than most employes the total amount of gross income he will receive in a given year. He also has some control over his deductions from gross income. The alternating year device, or some variations of it, could be adapted to avoid high-bracket tax years.

Record-keeping

The Treasury exacts a price for the preferred status it gives to the outside salesman. It demands precise record-keeping on all expenses and complete substantiation of deductions which he claims.

Particularly severe are the standards for reporting travel, entertainment and business-gift expenses. Approximations, which might be acceptable for other types of expenses, are seldom allowed.

The record-keeping must be performed at the time the expenses are incurred and must not only indicate the amount (verified through receipts, bills and canceled checks) but also report all the facts substantiating the business nature of the outlays.

The rules recited earlier, applying to executives' expense account requirements, apply to the outside salesman, who is expected to be even more meticulous.

He grumbles. He has to write and send reports to his home office every night when he is traveling. He is tired. He does not have time to do all this bookkeeping for the IRS.

But it pays off at income tax filing time.

Beyond some point, which our budget plans already reach, everything that the Government gives out with one hand it must take back with the other, in higher taxes or more inflation or both.

President Richard M. Nixon,
Economic Report to Congress, January 31, 1973.

CHAPTER 10

The
Investor
in
Securities

The tax results are an important factor in any investment decision. *But they are not the most important factor.* The aim is not less tax but more after-tax income.

Many an investor has postponed taking a substantial capital gain because he could foresee that his tax would be lower next year, and the gain would be taxed at a lower rate. But when next year came, the market had slumped and he had no gain to be taxed.

So this warning should precede any discussion of securities investment and taxes: Never let the tax considerations alone dissuade you from a sensible market move.

As noted, there are two significant benefits from investment in common stocks and securities. One is that dividends paid on most profitable issues are partly tax-exempt. The first $100 in dividends received annually is excluded from tax. On the joint return of a husband and wife, if each owns stock which produced $100 or more in annual dividends, the couple can exclude $200 in dividends from income.

The other and usually more important benefit is that profit gained from the sale of securities is taxed under the favorable capital gains formula. The computation is done on Schedule D ("Gains and Losses from Sales or Exchanges of Property"), which is filed along with Form 1040 to report investment transactions in stock or other property.

Capital gains and losses

Several pages of our early chapter on "Some ABCs of Income Tax" were devoted to the tax advantages of taking income in the form of capital gains. The paragraphs following will summarize the general rules on capital gains and losses, as a quick refresher preceding a longer look at the tax considerations of securities investment.

• The tax law recognizes two kinds of sales of securities and other assets—short-term and long-term.

• A short-term sale is one made within six months after the securities are purchased. If a profit results, this "short-term gain" is fully taxable as ordinary income. That means the gain is lumped together with wages and other income from ordinary sources, and it is taxed at the taxpayer's full regular rate.

• A long-term capital gain is the profit made on the sale of assets (stock, bonds, real estate or other property) which have been held *longer than six months*. It gets much more favorable tax treatment; namely:

• If the taxpayer's long-term capital gains exceed his short-term losses, half of this excess—the "net long-term capital gain"—is not taxed at all. The other half is taxed at his regular rate.

• But the overall tax may not exceed 25 percent *unless the net long-term capital gain exceeds $50,000 in the tax year*. The top tax on gains in excess of $50,000 is 35 percent, which is half the highest rate of ordinary tax that anybody pays.

Because of this preferred treatment given capital gains, it is usually sensible to hold profit-making securities longer than six months before selling them.

But there are many reasons why one might depart from that principle. Foremost is the fact that it may be wiser to cash in on the investment when a profit is within grasp than to risk losing the profit by hanging on for a tax saving.

An investor's decisions are conditioned, too, by the aims of his investing. The prudent taxpayer whose investments are designed to conserve money or build an estate for wife and children would cash in promptly, instead of holding on, if there were any substantial risk of loss.

An aggressive risk-taking investor might sell and take his profit, regardless of whether there was any substantial risk of later price decline. He wants to stay liquid, keep his money working. Says a veteran investor of the latter breed:

"If you sock away all your money in tax shelters it is safe and it is low-taxed. But it is not available for use in making more money."

Frequently it is wise to take a loss on a weak stock—instead of hanging on in hope that an upturn will bring a capital gain—and use the loss to offset some of your capital gains, if any, or some of your ordinary income. In that way, your tax savings will help cushion your market loss.

Some guidelines. Your attitude toward investment may be influenced by your tax bracket. The higher your tax rate, the more attractive speculative investments can be. There's just as much risk but, if you lose, your loss is smaller because the IRS would have taken a bigger percentage of it anyway.

The lower your income bracket, the less you should speculate. More of the money you risk is your own.

Stocks which pay little or no dividends, such as "growth stocks," cost their holders less in taxes every year than stocks paying fat dividends. If dividends are paid in stock, they cost you less in taxes than cash dividends.

If you plan to use your investments to finance something specific, like your children's education or a son's start in business, it might be wise to give the securities to the children now. The taxes on the interest or dividends earned—or on the capital gain if the securities are sold—will be paid at the children's much lower tax rate. For this purpose, many taxpayers set up custodial accounts with a broker.

Tax loss time. When the leaves fall each year, it's tax-loss season. You should consider then—well in advance of New Year's Eve, when the books will close on your tax year—whether to sell some losing issues and use the loss to reduce the tax on your capital gains or other income.

Here are some questions and answers on specific situations; each answer assumes that all other conditions are equal—that a tax saving is the only consideration involved:

Q. I expect my total income to be substantially higher next year, but I have some stocks that are losers. Should they be sold now?

A. Hang on to them until next year, then sell. The capital losses will be worth more then because your income tax rate will be higher.

Q. I expect my total income to be lower next year.

A. Sell your losing securities now, while the capital loss is worth more to you.

Q. I have some stocks whose value has climbed, some which have gone down; I haven't made any sales yet, but I can see my tax bill is going to be high.

A. Sell some of your recently-purchased losers. You can use short-term loss to offset up to $1,000 worth of your ordinary income.

Q. I don't have any potential short-term losses that I can take, but some of my older holdings have weakened; they would give me long-term losses if sold.

A. You can sell and take the capital loss. But $2,000 of net long-term loss will offset only $1,000 of ordinary income, and the $1,000 is all that can be thus offset in any one year.

Q. I have a heavy net loss. I can use $2,000 of it to offset $1,000 of my salary income, but what about the rest of the loss?

A. Sorry, no additional loss deductions this year. But you can carry over this excess of loss—in effect, set up a "loss bank"—and use it in future years to offset capital gains plus $1,000 of ordinary income in each year until it is used up.

Q. I have only a long-term gain.

A. Don't make a move. No reason to sell unless you think your gain may diminish or disappear.

Q. I have sold my house for a profit and don't plan to reinvest the money in another house. Can I use losses on stocks to offset some of the profit?

A. Yes. Losses on investments can be used to offset any capital gains, not just profits on securities investment. They also can be used to offset ordinary income, but only 50 cents on the dollar can be used against ordinary income, up to $1,000 a year.

Q. I have taken some long-term losses this year.

A. That means you have a ready-made offset for your profits if you decide to sell some recently acquired securities and take the short-term gains.

Many of the larger securities firms publish detailed guideline booklets to advise investors on market moves in the tax-loss season. Or a telephone call to your broker usually will produce guidance for specific problems.

Establishing a loss. "Establishing a tax loss" merely means selling a stock whose value has declined below the level at which you bought it.

Frequently an investor wants to establish a loss to cut his tax bill, but does not want to give up his investment in a certain company or industry. There are ways for him to keep his "position" in the market.

One method is to sell the stock, wait thirty-one days, and then buy it back. The law requires that more than thirty days must elapse between the sale and repurchase, in order to establish the loss.

The same time period must be allowed even if a different kind of security is purchased from the one sold, provided the purchased security is exchangeable for the one disposed of, like a convertible bond or convertible preferred stock of the same company.

If a stock is bought back or replaced with an exchangeable security in less than thirty-one days, the IRS considers that no sale was made at all. The taxpayer loses the tax benefit of his loss. The sale is called a "wash sale," not acceptable as a bona fide disposal of the stock for tax-loss purposes. (It is also a "wash sale" if a relative buys your stock to hold for you during the waiting period.)

Take the case of an investor who owns 100 shares of stock in which he has a loss and who sees a chance that the stock might rise in price shortly. He does not want to let go of the stock for thirty days before buying it back. So he can buy instead an additional 100 shares of the same stock, hold it thirty-one days, and then sell the first 100 shares. He must tell his broker to specify on the sales order that the sale is made against the first 100 shares.

IRS does not recognize losses on stock sales if equivalent securities of the same company are bought within thirty days *before or after* the date of sale. So if the investor decides to buy 100 shares as a replacement, he must buy them before the end of November. Otherwise the loss sale cannot take place before the end of the tax year.

Unfortunately, this method requires money to buy the additional stock. And if the stock goes down instead of up, the investor loses twice as much.

An alternative technique is to buy stocks in the same industry group to hold during the waiting period. An investor in Armco Steel, for example, might sell Armco and buy Bethlehem Steel. If economic developments cause steel stocks to rise as a group, the investor is protected. Most brokers can provide lists of such "stock switches."

If you have more losses than gains, you may wish to sell some appreciated stocks to acquire tax-free gains. When offset by your losses on securities, these gains may be taken tax-free. The waiting period, incidentally, does not apply to establishing gains. If a stock is sold at a profit, shares in the same corporation may be purchased immediately, but the repurchase must be made from someone other than the person who bought your original shares.

There are other methods of establishing losses and maintaining positions in stocks, but most of them tend to be more complicated and more liable to question from the IRS.

Some financial experts contend that tax selling is overdone. What frequently happens, they argue, is that investors sell to establish losses, fail to repurchase the stock, and lose out on subsequent price rises.

Perhaps so. But obviously millions of investors, seeing the prospect of making Uncle Sam share in their losses, as well as in their profits, are going to go on making tax-loss sales.

For the foregoing reasons and several others, it is a good idea to keep a record of exactly which shares were bought on what dates. The dates on the stock certificates are not necessarily accurate, and the exact date can be important.

For example: Suppose you bought 200 shares of Ace Corporation eight months ago at 20, and another 200 shares four months ago at 10. You now sell 200 shares at 16. Depending on which shares you sold, your tax could be greatly different. If you sold the longer-held shares, you would get a long-term capital gain on the disposal and a lower profit on which the gain would be figured. If you sold the shares you bought only four months ago, you have a bigger profit, taxable at the full ordinary rate.

If you hold your stock certificates yourself, record the date and the price when you receive them. Then, when you sell some of the stocks, give your broker the certificates which actually represent the shares you sell. Ask your broker to identify them by the date of purchase and the cost in his own records.

If a security becomes worthless, the loss is treated as a capital loss as of the final day of the tax year in which the stock became worthless—the year, for example, in which the company that issued it went out of business. The loss may only be deducted for that year, but claims for refunds or credit as a result of deducting the loss may be filed within three years of the due date of the return for that year.

"Against the box." As the year-end approaches, you may find you have securities with considerable price gains, but you may not wish to sell them immediately for tax reasons. However, you run the risk of a drop in price by holding them. There is a way to sell them at a profit but delay the tax until the following year.

In such a case you can "sell short against the box." In the usual short sale, the seller sells a stock he does not own; he borrows the required shares. Under certain circumstances, the investor can borrow them from his broker. Later he buys shares to replace those he had borrowed.

In "shorting against the box," the seller need not actually buy the shares to replace the borrowed ones. He repays the shares by going to his own safe deposit box, taking out shares that he already owned and delivering them. The tax is thus deferred to the following tax year.

Using the deductions

The law provides many deductions for investors; some are easily overlooked. For instance:

Commissions paid to brokers are part of your investment cost; they can help cut your tax bill. Visits to consult your broker provide a deduction for taxi or other transportation costs, unless you are merely visiting to watch the board.

If you took your broker, tax lawyer, or C.P.A. to a business lunch, the costs are deductible; also, your fees to your attorney or tax adviser, and the costs of postage and telephone calls involved in investing.

The interest charge on margin accounts—purchases made on credit—is a deductible cost, as are any state transfer taxes and the cost of a safe deposit box if you keep securities in it or use it for any other investment purpose.

Even the cost of newspapers, magazines, or other periodicals or books bought for information on investments is deductible, as well as tax publications.

Charitable deductions. Making charitable donations of securities which have appreciated in value can help you make larger gifts to churches or philanthropies, at less tax cost to you.

Stock or other securities which you have held for more than six months and which have risen in value can be given to church or charity. You can deduct the present higher market value as a charitable contribution; the appreciation in value is taxed neither to you nor to the church.

If the stock has declined in value, sell it and give the cash to the church instead. You will be able to deduct the capital loss and the charitable deduction as well.

Creating a charitable remainder trust is a way of giving the stock away, yet letting you enjoy the income from it during your lifetime. It is particularly useful if you hold some stock which has greatly increased in value—so much as to make its sale a painful tax problem.

Instead, you can set up the charitable remainder trust, under which the stock will go to a charity upon your death, or upon the deaths of you and your wife, if you so wish. Your tax deduction is based on the present value of the securities, yet you and your wife can take the income from the holdings until you both die. The trustee, in the meantime, can reshape your portfolio of securities by disposing of some or all of your holdings without incurring capital gains tax along the way.

More of the tax-saving possibilities of charitable deductions are described in the booklet, "Give Till It Helps," published for investors by the brokerage house of Merrill Lynch, Pierce, Fenner and Smith.

Don't forget that there is a relatively new tax-saving tool for the investor who scores a big capital gain. If the gain exceeds $50,000, he may be able to lower his tax substantially by income averaging. This could save him from the 35 percent top tax on capital gains. The 1969 tax changes made capital gains eligible for income averaging; they had been barred before.

Investment clubs

There are investment clubs everywhere. They may be as insignificant as four or five housewives joining together to buy and sell stocks with a total investment of $300 or as sophisticated as forty or fifty senior business executives, each investing thousands.

Whatever the size or success of the group, an investment club is taxed exactly like a partnership. The tax regulations that apply to it are the same as apply to partnerships generally.

The clubs may or may not have written agreements or by-laws. Some operate with a committee to gather information on investments; others are advised by investment specialists, and most require a vote of members before a purchase, sale, or exchange. They may invest in real estate as well as securities.

As a partnership, the club pays no tax, but it must file an information return on Form 1065. That shows each partner's share of the club's income, credits and deductions. Each partner must report them on his own tax return as if he had realized the gains or incurred the losses personally.

If the club makes such outlays as payment of investment counselors, or purchase of investors' publications, the costs are not deductible by club members as business expenses; they are itemized deductions, to be listed on Form 1040 as "Miscellaneous Deductions." If the investor does not itemize, he cannot deduct the expense.

Some variations

Following are a number of other tax considerations for investors to bear in mind:

Stock dividends. Dividends are not always paid in cash. A company may distribute additional dividends in the noncash form of shares of stock. This dividend is not taxable ordinarily, except in such cases as when a stockholder has the choice of taking the dividend in cash.

There is also no tax on stock received after a stock split.

When the stockholder sells such stock, the proceeds are treated as in any other stock sale. To find your cost basis per share, on which you will figure your capital gain or loss when you sell, you add the number of new shares to the number of shares originally held, and divide the total number into the original cost.

This area was complicated by the 1969 Tax Reform Act. Stock distri-

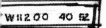

butions now are taxed under certain circumstances, such as when all shareholders do not gain equally in the distribution, or when some common shareholders get preferred stock and others get common stock.

Get tax advice before assuming your stock dividend is tax-free.

Capital gain dividends. Portions of the dividends from mutual funds and other regulated investment companies may be designated as "capital gain dividends," or "capital gain distributions."

These can be reported by the investor as long-term capital gains, regardless of how long the mutual fund stock has been held.

Tax-exempt stocks. A number of corporations, mostly utilities, issue stocks whose dividends are termed tax-exempt. Usually only a portion of the dividend is tax-exempt. When such amounts are received they reduce the cost basis of your stock by a like amount. A taxpayer who owns such stock will be advised annually as to what portion is nontaxable.

Bonds

A bond is merely a certificate that says the holder has made a loan to the company which issued it. The investor who buys stock owns a part of the company; the investor who buys a bond is simply a lender to the company.

The stockholder shares in the success or failure of the firm; if the company makes profits he will get dividends, and the price of his stock is likely to rise. The bondholder gets the same interest return on his investment no matter how successful the company is, but the price of the bond may rise, within limits.

The bondholder runs less risk of losing his money. He also has fewer opportunities for major tax savings, but some do exist.

If you buy a corporate bond on the open market at a price lower than the amount you will receive when the corporation pays off the loan—that is, redeems the bond—you report your profit when the company redeems the bond as a capital gain. The interest paid on the bond is taxable as ordinary income, like any other interest. For example, if you buy Ajax Corporation bonds for $9,000 in the open market, and hold them for any period longer than six months, you will receive $10,000 when Ajax redeems them—a long-term capital gain of $1,000.

Under the capital gains tax rules, half the gain is excluded from taxes; you will pay tax on only $500, at your regular tax rate (plus the ordinary tax on the interest yield).

The same treatment would apply if you sold the bonds on the open market before maturity, assuming that you held them six months or longer. Bonds fluctuate in price, as stocks do, but in a narrower range.

Assume that a major corporation issues a bond when interest rates are high; it has to offer 9 percent interest in order to attract buyers. If interest rates generally should start downward during the life of the bond, would-be buyers would bid up the price of the bond because of the high interest return.

The $10,000 bond might conceivably rise in price until it cost $11,000. The guaranteed interest rate would be paid only on the $10,000 face value of the bond. But it still would return the same earnings, even to the investor who paid the higher market price.

The excess of what you pay for a bond over what the issuing corporation must pay on maturity is called the bond premium. Tax law permits you to amortize the premium yearly over the remaining life of the bond. That is, you can deduct in installments the extra cost of the bond premium. For example: You pay $11,000 for a $10,000 bond maturing in five years. You can deduct $200 each year, for the five remaining years until the bond is redeemed by its issuer.

While the interest on the bond is taxable in full, the amortizable premium is claimed as a "Miscellaneous Deduction" on your income tax return.

So in periods of shifting interest rates, taxpayers can find opportunities for substantial savings through bond investments.

For example, Joseph Winters, a lawyer in the 50 percent tax bracket, paid $8,000 for a $10,000 bond which has risen in market value to $11,000. He sells the bond for $11,000 and immediately repurchases it (or a similar bond) at that price—$11,000.

He has made a $3,000 gain, the difference between the $8,000 purchase price and the $11,000 selling price. Since it is a long-term capital gain, Winters pays tax on only half that amount, or $1,500. And since he is in the 50 percent tax bracket, he pays a tax of $750.

The sale has permitted Winters to pay a $750 tax on a $3,000 gain. He paid a 25 percent effective rate, instead of his ordinary 50 percent tax.

In repurchasing the bond, Winters had to pay a $1,000 premium. This he can deduct at the rate of $200 a year for the five remaining years to maturity. At his tax rate this saves him $100 a year, or a total of $500.

Other bonds. There are many kinds of bonds, but for tax purposes most corporation bonds have the same features. Some bonds are called debentures. These are backed only by the faith and credit of the issuing corporation. Convertible bonds or "convertibles" carry the privilege of exchanging the bond into a stated number of shares of the corporation's common stock. Mortgage bonds are secured by a mortgage on property, such as land or a company building or factory. Because of the security, mortage bonds are considered higher-grade investments.

Among the safest bonds of all, though not the best-paying investments, are securities of the U.S. government. Marketable U.S. securities may be sold in the same way that stock shares are sold.

The nonmarketable U.S. bonds—Series E and Series H U.S. Savings Bonds—have the advantage of complete absence of risk, even if the bond certificates are lost, burned, destroyed or stolen. But they carry relatively low interest rates.

The investor in U.S. Series E bonds pays an initial price of 75 percent of the amount the bond will be worth upon maturity. He can choose either of two methods to report his annual interest earnings—yearly, as the interest accumulates, or in a single amount, reported as a total sum when the bond is redeemed.

Your choice is determined by your own circumstances. If you plan to cash the bond at a time when your income should be higher, you will be better off to report the interest annually as it accumulates. Your tax rates will then be lower than when the bond is redeemed.

On the other hand, if you plan to redeem your E bonds on reaching retirement, or at some other time when your income will be lower, it probably would be wiser to report your total interest at the time of redemption.

You may similarly defer reporting until maturity the income from another bond—for example, Series H—into which you may convert your E bonds. This means that even after your E bonds mature you need not report your accumulated interest as taxable if you convert the proceeds into an H bond. The entire reporting will be postponed until the H bond matures.

However, if any cash interest payment is received at the time of the conversion, the amount must be reported then.

Tax-exempt bonds. In 1973, the cost of living rose to a level about 8 percent above that of 1972. You would have had to earn 8 percent on a savings investment that year just to stay even with inflation.

If you did find an 8 percent investment, you had only the illusion of staying even. Each $1,000 of saving earned $80 for you, but you still had to pay tax on the $80. Thus, if you were in the 32 percent tax bracket, you lost about another $25 to the tax collector.

You had to be earning more than 11½ percent on your savings to keep as much purchasing power as you had when you started.

If your top tax bracket was 50 percent, you had even less chance of finding a return that would keep you abreast of inflation.

Though the rate of inflation may decline gradually, it is likely to stay high enough to erode savings and incomes seriously for years to come. During those years the quest for long-term security will be a constant struggle against rising prices and taxes.

In what we have known as normal times, securities paying 10 or 12 percent interest or higher—enough to offset a steep inflation—are rarely to be found by an investor of moderate means.

But a taxpayer whose taxable income is above $20,000, putting him in the tax brackets of 30 percent and higher, may find that the bonds of states, cities, counties, or other public authorities—the so-called municipals—may provide at least a part of the answer.

At first glimpse this seems improbable. The tax-exempt municipal bonds carry interest yields well below those of good corporation bonds. But their charm is in their tax-exempt status. Their interest earnings are free of taxes.

They are an ironclad shelter against taxation. Consequently, the higher the tax rate you pay, the greater your benefit from securities that are exempt from taxes.

In some recent tight-money periods, municipals have paid up to 7 percent, while corporate bonds yielded 9 to 10 percent.

A taxpayer in the 30 percent tax bracket—including federal, state and local taxes—would find that a 7 percent municipal was roughly equal to a 10 percent corporate issue in its net value to him. The tax saving makes the difference.

In the 40 percent tax bracket—meaning a taxable income somewhere above $30,000—an untaxed 7 percent municipal would match the after-tax yield of a corporate issue paying 11.67 percent.

Taxpayers in the 50 percent bracket would have to find a 14 percent investment for a comparable return; those in the 70 percent bracket would have to look for something paying 20 percent taxable interest.

The following table shows for taxpayers in various brackets, including federal, state and local income taxes, how much interest a taxable security must pay to match the lower but tax-free income of state and municipal tax-exempt securities:

Tax bracket (Percent)	5% tax-free rate equals: (Percent)	6% tax-free rate equals: (Percent)	7% tax-free rate equals: (Percent)
20	6.25	7.50	8.75
30	7.14	8.57	10.00
40	8.33	10.00	11.67
50	10.00	12.00	14.00
60	12.50	15.00	17.50
70	16.67	20.00	23.34

Not many taxpayers in the 20 percent bracket may have large sums of money available for investment in tax-exempts, but the bonds are still available in units of $1,000 despite a recent tendency to make $5,000 the minimum for new issues.

Bear in mind that if you buy a tax-exempt bond at a discount—that is, at less than face value—only the interest is tax-free; the profit you make when cashing the bond at face value is taxed as a capital gain. Also, the interest paid on money borrowed to purchase or carry tax-free securities is not deductible.

It should be remembered, moreover, that not all tax-exempts are top-grade investments. Consult your broker or banker before buying.

On the other hand, tax-exempt bonds escaped Congress' assault on tax shelters in 1969. The Tax Reform Act may even have made the municipals relatively more attractive than before. They are among the few tax shelters which were not penalized under "LTP"—the minimum tax levied under the "Limitation on Tax Preferences."

Some investment houses have contended, in fact, that the reform law moved tax-exempts to the fore as an investment vehicle. Some advised clients to use tax-exempts in many cases where trusts formerly had been used. These included supporting elderly parents, providing for a child's education, or paying alimony.

One firm of certified public accountants, endorsing this view, noted that the use of tax-exempt income to support a parent, for example, would avoid the legal costs of a trust, continue to maintain the parent as a dependent (providing a tax exemption to the taxpayer) and retain in the taxpayer's hands (instead of being sealed off in a trust) the control of his own income-producing assets.

Anti-pollution bonds. There's a way to invest in tax-exempt bonds and fight pollution simultaneously. More and more cities and towns are issuing anti-pollution bonds. The money raised by the bond issues is used to buy pollution-control equipment that is leased to the corporations which have caused the pollution.

This has become a major method of financing the enormous cost of cleaning up the environment. The bonds are exactly the same as the "industrial development bonds" which thousands of localities issued in the 1960s to build plants for private companies—until Congress stopped them cold. The bonds were so popular that the Treasury asked Congress to halt the drain on tax revenues.

So Congress ruled that it was illegal for cities to sell bonds to build factories for private industry. But it left a loophole. Communities can sell as many such bonds as they like if they use the proceeds to build sludge handlers, dust baghouses, desulphurization towers and similar pollution-abatement facilities.

The volume of such issues has mushroomed since 1969. Some predict it will taper off as the deadlines for pollution cleanup are reached. Others expect that urban and industrial growth and stricter controls will keep this form of financing expanding indefinitely.

Other tax-sheltered securities

There are other kinds of investments which produce tax-free or tax-sheltered income. Here are some of them:

Tax-free notes. These are like municipal bonds except that the tax-free notes pay off the face amount in less than one year. They are favored by affluent investors who use them as a way to keep their money earning a tax-free return between major investments.

Municipal bond funds. These are similar to mutual funds except that the pool of securities is made up of many different municipal bonds, instead of many different stocks. So the income yield is exempt from federal taxes.

Deep-discount bonds. These are bonds which sell for much less than face value because they were issued when interest rates were low. Deep-discount bonds have this tax advantage: When they mature and pay off at the face value (which usually is $1,000), the profit is taxed as a capital gain, not ordinary income.

Flower bonds. These are U. S. government bonds which can be bought at a discount. But the Treasury will accept them in payment of federal estate taxes at full face value. They are frequently bought by persons stricken with incurable disease: hence the name, flower bonds, suggesting a funeral. They are also called death bonds.

Self-employed retirement programs. These are described in other chapters. Self-employed persons can get current tax deductions up to 15 percent of income, to a maximum of $7,500, for contributions made into a Treasury-approved retirement program. Note that persons who have businesses of their own, outside their regular salaried jobs, also can set up such programs. They can make tax-sheltered contributions each year of up to 15 percent of their self-employment income.

Tax-sheltered investment plans. You can buy an interest in a limited partnership which invests in such businesses as real estate and cattle feeding. Depreciation write-offs in early years usually lead to tax savings. An investor should consult with his tax adviser first, even if he has the substantial amount of funds needed to join.

Mutual fund rule

The problem of determining the gains or losses of taxpayers who own shares in open-end mutual funds has been simplified by the IRS.

Investors who buy shares at different times and prices usually leave them in custody of a bank or agent. When an investor decides to sell some, he may have difficulty later in identifying exactly which of his various blocks of shares were sold. The IRS has required that he either identify them or assume that the shares he bought first were those sold first.

That assumption may work to the taxpayer's disadvantage, since the shares held longest may have had the greatest increase in value—and therefore, when sold, result in the highest tax.

The new regulation provides a method by which a taxpayer can determine his average outlay for the shares he owns. If he elects this method, he can use the average cost in determining his gain or loss. When he chooses to average in any year, however, he cannot change his method in some later year.

IRS—Den of Inequities.

Bumper sticker, Washington, D.C., 1972

CHAPTER 11

The Home Owner and the Investor in Real Estate

Real estate provides not only a shield against inflation but also one of the best shelters against high taxes. The 1969 Tax Reform Act curtailed this shelter somewhat, but without seriously lessening its usefulness.

In more recent years tax reformers' eyes have turned again to the real and supposed abuses of the tax concessions in real estate. Wary taxpayers will keep watch on the progress in Congress of legislation which could abolish or curtail some of the tax-saving devices described in this chapter.

One of the important sheltering devices is depreciation. Tax laws permit the owner of rental dwellings, apartments, office buildings, and other real estate to deduct from their income amounts that represent depreciation of the property—the money value lost through the wearing-out and obsolescence of the property.

Depreciation rarely reflects the actual decline in the market value. But it provides a deduction which, in effect, cuts down your cost of buying the property. Frequently, the market value of the property does not decline at all. It may even increase. In some real estate ventures, the depreciation charged off is equal to or greater than the amount of the rental income from the property. The result: no tax to pay on that income. On paper, the property may even seem to be losing money, because the depreciation is entered on the tax return just as if it were a cash outlay. The owner adds this theoretical loss of value to such cash outlays as fuel, repairs and mortgage interest; if the total is greater than his income from rentals, he uses this apparent loss on the rental operation to offset his income from other sources, and thus to reduce his income tax.

He wins in two ways: He pockets an untaxed cash gain on his real estate venture, and he cuts the tax on his other income.

Depreciation is a key to tax savings. It is often a boon to the real estate buyer and sometimes a burden to the seller. It has tax usefulness, and sometimes tax headaches, for anyone who builds or buys a house for rental, a factory or an apartment house, and for any professional who buys instruments, any businessman who buys a typewriter, any retailer who buys a showcase, any writer who buys an encyclopedia. All those things depreciate.

Depreciation deserves a chapter by itself. The present chapter will touch on depreciation in only enough detail to provide a background for discussing tax aspects of home ownership, rentals, and real estate investment.

The following chapter will describe the several methods of depreciation, tell how to compute them, and provide some suggestions for using depreciation as an avenue to tax savings.

The real estate investor usually uses a form of "accelerated depreciation," or "rapid write-off," to help cover the initial costs of the purchase or construction of a new building.

This means that instead of subtracting an equal amount of the building's value each year through the estimated useful life of the structure— the usual "straight-line" method of depreciation—the owner can deduct greater amounts in early years and correspondingly smaller amounts in later years.

The rate of write-off permitted by law varies according to the type of structure. The government encourages the building of new rental housing, for example, by letting the owner of an apartment building deduct twice as much in the first year as he would under the straight-line method. In each year thereafter the deduction would be smaller; in the last year, if the same owner still held the building, the depreciation deduction would be only half as much as under the straight-line method.

That is called the "200 percent declining balance" method of depreciating. For other types of building a "150 percent declining balance" is allowed; the owner can deduct one and a half times as much in the first year as he could under the straight-line method. There is also a 125 percent declining balance method, and a variation called the sum-of-the-years digits method. All are explained in the following chapter.

If the investor has built the structure mainly with borrowed money, avoiding a large cash payment, the 200 percent depreciation method usually permits him to recover his cash investment within a few years. Some projects, in fact, have earned a 20 percent return on the cash outlay in their early years. The big mortgage is no problem. It helps; the mortgage interest also is deductible.

Use of the 200 percent depreciation for commercial, industrial and other nonresidential construction was barred by the 1969 Tax Reform Act.

New property of those types was permitted a depreciation write-off starting at 150 percent of the straight-line rate—in other words, half again as much as normal at the start.

On used housing with a remaining useful life of twenty years or more the law has authorized a 125 percent write-off. The normal straight-line depreciation must be used for other used property.

When rapid write-offs are used in the early years of depreciation, there is always an equivalent cut in the amount of depreciation deducted annually in the later years of the building's life. Usually, however, the original builder has sold the structure before the depreciation write-offs dwindle away. The new owner starts depreciating over again.

With the 200 percent method, the builder can usually expect to recover through tax write-offs roughly two-thirds of the building's cost in the first half of its estimated useful life.

By the end of the structure's useful life, the builder would be claiming only half as much depreciation as normal. The government in theory has simply postponed its taking of some tax revenue. Yet this is a real subsidy to the builder; even if he retains ownership until the end of the depreciation schedule, he has had the use of tax money that belonged to the government; it was in effect an interest-free loan.

Congress has favored the "accelerated depreciation" device because the various higher-than-normal rates provide an incentive for home building and for job-creating investment in new commercial and industrial projects.

Selling your house

You probably bought your house for a home, but the purchase nevertheless was a real estate investment of some importance. As both a dwelling and an investment, the property is accorded some special tax concessions when the time comes to sell or to rent it.

If you sell at a profit after owning the residence for at least six months, the profit is taxed at the capital gains rate. Let us take, as an example, a homeowner in the 25 percent tax bracket who makes a profit of $10,000 on the sale of his house. Half the gain is free of tax; only the other $5,000 is taxed at the taxpayer's regular rate. The capital gains tax means that he pays only $1,250 in tax on the $10,000 gain. In effect, he pays a 12½ percent rate instead of the 25 percent rate he would pay on ordinary income.

Once you reach sixty-five, the federal income tax law gives you a rare opportunity: It permits you to exclude from gross income any gain attributable to the first $20,000 of the price you receive on the sale of the residence. Details of this provision will be found in the chapter, "The Retired Taxpayer."

The capital gains treatment is available on any other real property you buy and sell, such as a resort cottage or a "second home" at the beach or in the mountains. It also is available for any real estate you may purchase for investment.

If you take a loss on selling your home, you owe no tax, but your loss is not deductible. In the more pleasant circumstances of profit, you can defer the tax by investing the proceeds from the sale of your home in the purchase of another residence within a fixed time limit. The limit, established permanently by the 1975 Tax Reduction Act, is eighteen months before or after the sale of your home, if you are buying a new or used dwelling. If the new residence is being constructed, the time period is extended to two years, provided the construction begins within eighteen months from the time of the sale of your former home. If the new home costs as much as, or more than, the price you get for the old one, you pay no tax at this time, even though you may have made a handsome profit on your old house. The eighteen-month and two-year limits apply on dwellings sold after December 31, 1974; they replaced former limits of twelve months and eighteen months respectively.

The homeowner is taxed on his sales profit only to the extent that the price he received exceeds the cost of the new house. In figuring the price received, he is entitled to deduct his costs of fixing-up for the sale, as well as the real estate agent's commission and other selling costs.

The fix-up jobs must be done within ninety days before the sale and paid for within thirty days after.

The price thus reduced is called the "adjusted sales price."

If the homeowner pays as much for his new dwelling as he receives for the old one, he has no tax to pay at that time.

The tax is simply postponed until some future day when he sells a residence without replacing it. If that never happens, he never pays a tax.

For example: Will Jones sells for $32,000 a residence that cost him $22,000. His broker's fees and other selling costs were $1,800, so his net profit was $8,200.

Jones pays $39,000 for a new house, thus avoids paying any tax on his profit. It is deferred until he sells the second home—and then, perhaps, again and again.

Any gain not taxed in the year you sell the residence is subtracted (for tax purposes) from the cost of the new residence; the "adjusted cost basis" is reduced by that much.

The Housing Tax Credit of 1975

One of the short-time benefits of the 1975 Tax Reduction Act was a tax credit of 5 percent, up to $2,000, on the purchase of a new home. The credit helped builders dispose of many newly constructed but unsold dwellings in the mid-1970s recession, but it was available only briefly. These were the rules:

- The dwelling could be a condominium, a cooperative unit, or a mobile home, but it had to be a new principal residence of the taxpayer.
- Construction must have begun before March 26, 1975, but the dwelling had to be new—that is, never lived in before.
- A binding contract for the purchase had to be entered into before January 1, 1976 (except in the case of a dwelling constructed by the taxpayer himself).
- The residence had to be acquired and occupied after March 12, 1975, and before January 1, 1977.
- The tax credit was reduced to $1,000 in the case of a married taxpayer filing a separate return; it could not be larger for any taxpayer than the purchaser's tax liability for the year.

If the taxpayer occupied the property before January 1, 1976, he could take the credit on his 1975 tax return; if he entered a binding contract in the specified portion of 1975 but did not occupy the residence until 1976, the tax credit would apply to his 1976 tax liability.

The IRS specified that the credit must be claimed on a new Form 5405, to be attached to the income tax return on which the credit was taken. Except in the case of self-construction, taxpayers were required also to attach a certification by the seller that the price was the lowest at which the residence was offered for sale after February 28, 1975.

A taxpayer who built the dwelling himself and started it before March 13, 1975, could claim the credit only on the portion of the cost that represented the construction done after March 12, 1975, and before January 1, 1977. Thus, if a taxpayer had put $10,000 of cost into the structure before March 13, 1975, and finished it at a total cost of $40,000, he could claim the credit on 5 percent of the difference, $30,000. His credit would be $1,500.

In Will Jones' case, his net gain of $8,200 is subtracted from the $39,000 cost of the new house; when and if he sells it, he will have to compute its cost basis as $30,800 instead of $39,000.

If Jones should die before paying the postponed tax, the tax is waived. His children or other heirs would take the house at its market value as of the time of his death. They could sell at that price without incurring any tax liability.

The tax deferment is possible only on the sale of the home-owner's *principal residence*. It could therefore be a boat instead of a house, or a condominium or cooperative apartment, or a mobile home.

But it could *not* be a summer cottage, beach house, or other structure which was not the principal dwelling.

What if your new house costs less than the old one? You will have a taxable gain on the sale—the amount by which the selling price exceeds the cost of the replacement house. First, find your gain on your old house:

Selling price	$34,000
Less real estate agent's commission	2,200
Net sales price	31,800
Cost of old house	28,100
Gain	$ 3,700

That is what you would be taxed on if you were not replacing the house. Now figure your taxable gain this way:

Sales price of old house		$34,000
Real estate agent's commission	2,200	
Fixing-up cost:		
painting and new gutters	1,700	
Total selling costs		3,900
Adjusted sales price		30,100
Cost of new home		28,000
Gain taxable in year of sale		2,100
Nontaxable gain (the portion of gain on which tax is deferred, $3,700 less $2,100)		$ 1,600

Note that in figuring your overall gain ($3,700) on the sale of your old house, the selling price is reduced by the selling expenses ($2,200). The costs of fixing the house up to make it more saleable ($1,700) are not subtracted from the selling price.

But in figuring the part of the $3,700 gain on which tax is deferred, the selling price of the old house ($34,000) is reduced by both the real estate commission ($2,200) and the fixing-up cost ($1,700), or a total of $3,900 in selling costs. That leaves a reduced selling price of $30,100 and a taxable gain of only $2,100.

To sum up: If you replace your old house with another one, you can deduct the costs of making the old one saleable. If you don't replace, you can't deduct such costs.

These examples are simplified. Frequently the homeowner's original cost of a house is increased by capital improvements, such as a porch, a bathroom or central air conditioning. In such cases the cost figure used in the above example would have been increased, and the total gain on the sale would have been smaller.

Similarly, the price paid for the new dwelling is increased by the amount of any capital improvements made by the new buyer, plus any purchasing expenses (such as lawyer's fees) incurred in buying the new house. If such outlays totaling, say, $2,000, had been incurred in the preceding example, the cost of the new home would have been $30,000 ($28,000 plus $2,000) and the gain subject to tax would have been reduced to $100.

Installment sale. If you do not reinvest in a new home, but sell your old residence on an installment contract, you may pay your tax over a period of years as the payments come in. Each payment is in part a "return of capital" (not taxed) and in part profit (taxable).

The great tax advantage of an installment sale is that the tax payments are spread over the same period of years as that during which installment payments are received. The taxpayer thus avoids a steep rise of income in any one year which boosts him into a costly tax bracket.

To qualify the contract as an installment sale, the down payment plus other payments made in the year of sale must not equal more than 30 percent of the sales price, and the payments must be extended over at least two years. This is how to figure the tax:

You sell your residence for $40,000. The buyer agrees to pay $10,000 down, followed by $5,000 in each of the next six years. Your cost for the house was $28,000; your gain is $12,000.

Divide the $12,000 gain by the $40,000 selling price to find your percentage gain; it is 30 percent.

Therefore 30 percent of each payment you receive is gain. In the first year you receive $10,000. Thirty percent of that, or $3,000, is taxable at the capital gains rate.

In each year thereafter you receive $5,000. Thirty percent of that is $1,500; you will pay tax on the $1,500 each year for six years as a capital gain.

The installment method of taking a gain and paying tax on it is a lifesaver, especially when a substantial sum of money is involved.

But don't decide on this method until you have checked its tax results against an important new alternative, a description of which follows.

A new tax saver. The 1969 Tax Reform Act provided a device which may prove to be even more helpful than installment reporting for paying the tax on sizable capital gains. Congress made capital gains one of various types of income now eligible for income averaging.

If you make a profit on the sale of a house—or business property, or any other capital asset—you may be able to reduce your tax by reporting the entire gain in one year, then averaging the gain with your income of the four preceding years under the income-averaging rules.

This method requires that the full tax payment be made in one year. But the tax may be substantially smaller, in total, than if you spread it in installments over the years following the sale. And you will have the cash in hand to pay it with.

The choice depends wholly on the circumstances in each case—especially on whether your income was relatively low in the four years preceding the sale. If it was, the bulge in your income will be taxed at a relatively lower rate under the income-averaging formula.

Income-averaging is not always possible, of course; the buyer may be unable to pay cash. But if the opportunity presents itself, make sure your tax adviser computes the results in both ways before making up your mind.

It is wise to do that, in fact, before the negotiations get to the final stage; it could improve your bargaining position. It is even possible that you could trim your price a bit to get payment in cash and still come out ahead financially.

The liberalization of income-averaging may prove to be one of the major tax breaks provided by the 1969 legislation, though it went almost unnoticed in news accounts of that new law.

Enacted in December, 1969, this provision took effect almost immediately in 1970. For one watchful taxpayer it provided a windfall. He had been offered $775,000 for a piece of industrial property. He had contemplated spreading the payments over eight annual installments to diminish the tax impact.

He closed the deal in 1970, but on a different basis. He settled for cash, used income-averaging to minimize the boost in his 1970 income, and saved $80,000 in capital gains tax.

Exchange of property

If you plan to sell one piece of property and invest the proceeds in another, consider instead the possible tax advantage of an exchange. You can trade property without recognition of any gain or loss on the transaction.

The property you receive in the deal assumes the cost basis of the property you traded for it; you calculate the original cost less the depreciation you have taken plus the improvements you have made in the years you held the property. That becomes the adjusted cost basis you will use on the new property; it is called a "substituted basis." If you pay cash in addition, you add the amount to this cost basis.

A trade is usually more advantageous if your property is now worth more than its original cost, or basis. The exchange gives you an equivalent value, but you escape the immediate tax you would incur on the appreciation of value if you sold the old property to buy the new one.

If your property is worth less than its cost, you might be wiser to sell it outright and take the benefit of any deductible loss on your tax return,

Renting real estate

If for any reason you decide to rent a dwelling, the tax considerations will change markedly. The rental of your own house can provide a glimpse of the possibilities for profit and for tax savings in the rental of residential or commercial property as a business or an income-producing sideline. One welcome discovery is that the deduction of depreciation and expenses can sometimes work out so favorably that, though you put money in the bank every month from the rent you collect, your tax return can show a loss on the rentals. The business of being a landlord can be a headache, but it also can provide tax-free income.

This is largely because of the liberal treatment provided for depreciation on rental or business property—the annual deductions taken each year on the theory that the house is wearing out and will become completely without value in a certain number of years.

In theory, a property owner could save up these amounts and, over the years, build up a fund for the purchase of a new structure when the old one actually wore out or collapsed. In real life, however, the depreciation rate usually exceeds the actual wear and tear, and may even exceed the profit from rental. If so, you will be pocketing money while showing a loss on your income tax return.

For example, Jane Morrison rents her $30,000 home for $300 a month. Mrs. Morrison's outlays for taxes, interest and operating costs are $250 a month. Her profit averages $50 a month, or $600 for the year. But her depreciation is $750 for the year, so her income tax return shows a loss of $150.

A taxpayer is not allowed any deduction for the depreciation of his home if he just lives in it. The deduction is permitted only for property used in business or held for the production of income.

As soon as an owner rents his house, or moves out and makes a genuine effort to rent it, he can start claiming depreciation. The property does not actually have to be income-producing to qualify for the deduction, if it is being "held for the production of income."

When the owner rents only part of his house—for a store, an apartment, business office or other use—a deduction for depreciation is allowed on the rented portion. (If one floor of a three-story house was converted into a rental apartment, for example, the owner might take a tax deduction of one-third of the depreciation.) If he uses part of his residence for his own business purposes, a depreciation deduction is allowed on the portion used for business.

If you convert your dwelling to rental property, you must determine a "depreciation basis." It is substantially the same idea as the cost basis which you must determine when you sell a home or any other property. In this case it is reduced by the value of the lot.

The depreciation basis is the amount you paid for the house, plus the costs of any permanent improvements you made in the structure, as well as fees, commissions or other costs incurred in the purchase of the house. You arrive at the depreciation basis by adding all those items together and subtracting the value of the lot.

If the resulting figure is higher than the fair market value of the house when you convert it for rental, you must use the market value as your basis for depreciation. This might be the case, for instance, if your house stood in a deteriorating neighborhood, or if you had installed extensive improvements involving costs which could not be recovered from the new owner. Normally, however, a new porch, an added bathroom, the finishing of a basement, erection of a fence, or other improvements add to the "depreciation basis" of the property.

In a situation where the fair market value has *increased* since your purchase of the property, you are limited to using your *actual cost*, which is the maximum amount which may ever be used as your basis for depreciation.

Each year's repairs and maintenance on rental property are deductible as current expenses. Also deductible are property taxes, mortgage interest, costs of advertising a vacancy, utilities, insurance and other normal expenses of operating and renting a property.

If only part of the house is rented, you deduct only half of the depreciation, taxes and other expenses as a cost of your rental operation. The other half of the mortgage interest and taxes can be taken as a personal deduction, in your listing of itemized deductions.

The same general principles that apply to the renting of a family residence apply to other rental investments, whatever the scale of the operation. The tax treatment of depreciation in larger real estate operations will be discussed further in the following chapter.

The condominium. A phenomenon of modern real estate investment— whether in city, suburbs or resort areas—is the condominium. Condominiums are bought in many cases neither as residences nor second homes but mainly as investments.

The tax benefits of resort condominiums have been widely advertised, and for that reason this brief discussion of condominiums will touch mainly on those built at beach or mountain resorts. The tax benefits have been curtailed sharply by the Treasury, as noted in the following section, but in most cases the prospects for both profit and enjoyment remain good.

A management company sells you a villa, cottage, apartment, or even a hotel room at a vacation area and rents it out during the period when you are not using it. You share the rental profit.

You can specify the period of the year when you and your family wish to use the condominium. You escape the regular charges on your vacation; you pay a comparatively small service fee to the management firm.

Prices range from quite modest figures up to $60,000 and above. One desert resort offers "super-suites" at $275,000 each.

Quite apart from their allure as investment properties or second homes in resort areas, condominium apartments have gained high popularity as fulltime residences for city dwellers and suburbanites. Tax deductions are a major reason why—along with the obvious inducements of management services, upkeep and repairs.

Condominiums provide the same deductions for mortgage interest and real estate taxes as separate houses. These bring the annual housing costs of the owner down to about the level of a comparable rental apartment—well below that level, for higher-income taxpayers—and the owner gains a steadily rising ownership equity in a highly salable asset.

Let us compare the net after-tax costs of buying a $50,000 condominium ($10,000 down payment and $40,000 mortgage for twenty-five years at 8 percent interest) with an apartment renting for $350 a month.

The first-year cash outlay before taxes for the condominium is $5,305. It breaks down as follows:

Mortgage payments	$3,705	(of which $3,280 is interest)
Condominum costs	600	
Real estate taxes	1,000	
Total	$5,305	

That is larger than the yearly total of $4,200 cash outlays for the $350-a-month rental apartment. But the condominium gives back part of the annual cash outlays in tax deductions.

It works this way: The $1,000 of local real estate tax is deductible; for a taxpayer in the 50 percent bracket, that's a tax saving of $500. Mortgage interest payments totaling $3,280 in the first year are also tax deductible, for a tax saving of $1,640.

The high-bracket taxpayer thus recovers in tax savings about two-fifths of his total cash housing outlay for the first year of condominium ownership. A taxpayer in the 30 percent tax bracket would recover about one-fourth. The tax saving diminishes a bit each year, of course, as the owner pays off more principal and less interest.

But at the end of five years the condominium owner in the 40 percent tax bracket will have paid $20,381 for housing (including the 6 percent annual interest earnings he might have received on $10,000 if he hadn't made the down payment). That is $619 less than the apartment tenant paid in rentals. Meantime the condominium owner has added $3,090 to his $10,000 equity in his dwelling. A taxpayer in lower brackets does less well; a taxpayer in higher brackets does much better.

Here are comparative tables covering the first five years of condominium ownership (and including in the condominium costs the after-tax income on the $10,000 down payment computed at 6 percent a year, compounded annually):

	Apartment	Condominium			
		Condominium: Net cost after taxes			
Year	Annual rental	Tax bracket 30%	40%	50%	Annual gain in equity
1	$ 4,200	$ 4,470	$ 3,992	$ 3,514	$ 524
2	4,200	4,508	4,032	3,554	567
3	4,200	4,550	4,073	3,596	614
4	4,200	4,595	4,118	3,642	665
5	4,200	4,640	4,166	3,692	720
		Condominium: Cumulative cost after taxes			
Year	Cumulative rental	Tax bracket 30%	40%	50%	Cumulative gain in equity
1	$ 4,200	$ 4,470	$ 3,992	$ 3,514	$ 524
2	8,400	8,978	8,024	7,068	1,091
3	12,600	13,528	12,097	10,664	1,705
4	16,800	18,123	16,215	14,306	2,370
5	21,000	22,763	20,381	17,998	3,090

The taxpayer in the 30 percent bracket has paid $1,763 more for his five years of condominium housing than he would have paid in apartment rentals ($22,763 as against $21,000). But he has built up a $3,090 equity in the property, plus the appreciation in value.

Part-time rentals of "second homes." The government has closed the door quite firmly on a tax-saving device that gained some popularity in the 1960s among middle- and upper-income folk. They bought resort property, used it for their own vacations, and rented it to others for the rest of the season or year.

Quite frequently the cottage-owner enjoyed a double benefit—first, the rental income and, second, an operating "loss" to be claimed as a tax deduction against his ordinary income. The tax saving, in turn, helped him make his payments on the cottage purchase.

Beach and ski resort developers advertised such second homes as "tax havens." Their salesmen were glad to explain how the beach cottage, ski lodge, resort condominium or fishing cabin could become a shelter from the income tax as well as from the sun, wind, and rain.

The pitch was simple: Uncle Sam would help you buy a piece of resort real estate. The Treasury's subsidy was in the form of a cut in your income taxes.

This was the technique: You used your cottage for your own family vacation one month in the summer, for example, and rented it the other two months. You took a tax deduction for two-thirds of your expenses— your mortgage interest, taxes, utilities, maintenance, and depreciation. These costs—in most or many cases—added up to more than your income from rentals largely because of the depreciation deduction. You showed a "loss" on your rental operation, even though you actually pocketed some cash income. And on your tax return you claimed the loss as a deduction against your regular income.

Some courts denied the tax deduction in cases where buyers of vacation homes were held to be investing primarily "not for profit." The practice became widespread nevertheless.

In mid-1972 the IRS issued final tax regulations on this haven. The announcement caused some dismay not only among those planning the double-purpose shelters but among many persons who already owned them and were enjoying the tax benefits. The regulation was made effective as of Jan. 1, 1970. It thus applied to tax returns already filed for 1970 and 1971; it also covered properties bought before 1970.

The crackdown affects those whose investment is considered to be primarily nonbusiness in nature; whose ownership of a beach cottage, for example, is held to be mainly for personal enjoyment and not for business profit.

The new rule cuts two ways. It states first, that the expenses of the investor in this situation will be counted only up to the amount of rental income received. The "loss" deduction no longer can be applied to salary or other income.

Second, the owner is required to allocate all of his mortgage interest and property taxes on the cottage to the rental venture—even though they would be deductible whether or not he rented the property.

Here are before-and-after examples of what the change in regulations means to the owners of resort property who are part-time renters:

Before:

The owner used his cottage one month, rents it for two. He charges $1,000 a month; his rental income therefore is $2,000 a year.

His expenses were $3,900, of which he charged off two-thirds against the rental income. The breakdown looked like this:

	Total	Charged to rentals	Charged to personal use
Interest	$1,200	$ 800	$ 400
Taxes	600	400	200
Maintenance	600	400	200
Utilities	300	200	100
Depreciation	1,200	800	400
Totals	$3,900	$2,600	$1,300

Though he only took in $2,000 in rent payments, the owner charged $2,600 of his total costs to the rental operation. On Schedule E of his income tax return he reported a deductible $600 loss for the year. Actually, he would have paid all the taxes and interest anyway, whether or not he rented the property. And since the depreciation was not an out-of-pocket expense, only $600 of the outlays could be attributed directly to the rental—the maintenance costs ($400) and the utilities ($200).

So he received $1,400 more in cash than he paid out (the $2,000 rental income less the utilities and maintenance) on the rental operation, while taking a tax deduction for a $600 loss. If he was in the 50 percent tax bracket, the loss saved him $300 in tax.

And he still could deduct the $400 in interest and $200 in taxes that he allocated to his personal use of the cottage.

After:

The owner must apply *all* his mortgage interest, $1,200, and *all* his real estate taxes, $600, to the rental venture, even though he could deduct them whether he rented the cottage or not.

And since his expenses can be counted only up to the amount of the rental income he receives, he finds himself with this result: His mortgage interest and taxes total $1,800; his rental income was $2,000; he can deduct only $200 of the other expenses. He is considered to be breaking even on the rental operation.

The silver lining: The tightening-up, says the IRS, does not hurt the taxpayer who buys a beach cottage, ski lodge or condominium almost entirely as an investment. If he does not use the property for himself or his family, or if his use of it is incidental to the rental business, the old rules will continue to apply. But if he is using the tax laws to help himself acquire a second home, the Treasury says it means to see that the same laws apply to him as would apply to his first home.

How can you show that your vacation-property venture was launched for profit, not for personal use and enjoyment? The IRS has announced these general rules: If you can show a profit in two out of five years, your investment will be considered a business investment. The old rules will apply; but then, if you are showing a profit, you are not deducting any losses against your ordinary income anyway.

Since the owner of a new enterprise has no five-year record to show, he is given five years in which to show two profitable years. If he cannot make it, he must forfeit retroactively any special tax benefits he has gained. Or he can try to persuade the IRS that he really made a good-faith effort to turn a profit and had reason to believe he could do so.

One more interesting angle has been raised by tax analysts. Some have pointed out that if you eliminated the mortgage interest from the costs of your rental operation, you could use more of the other deductible expenses to cut your tax bill. You could eliminate mortgage interest by not mortgaging the cottage in order to buy it.

You might finance the purchase of the cottage by putting another mortgage on your principal residence, or by borrowing on insurance, or by getting a personal loan from a wealthy relative.

You could still deduct the interest, it was argued. But this interest cost would not be generated by the beach cottage, and you therefore would not have to use it to reduce your deductible business expenses on the rental venture.

But the IRS quickly discovered this new loophole. Now it says that if a resort cottage purchase is financed by *any* borrowing—such as a personal loan or an insurance loan—it will treat the interest on that loan exactly as if it were mortgage interest on the cottage itself. The interest would have to be charged against the rental income of the cottage.

Selling a rental property

If a rental property is held for more than six months and then sold, the profit on the sale is a capital gain, taxed at the preferred rate. If the property is held for less than six months, the gain is taxable at the ordinary income rate, at least twice as high. Obviously, it is wise to keep property long enough to qualify for the tax savings.

When sold, the cost basis of property is determined by totaling the purchase price and permanent improvements, then subtracting the depreciation taken on the building.

The proceeds from the sale are the selling price less your costs of making the sale, including commissions, advertising, and fixing-up expenses, if any. The difference is your gain; it is a capital gain and it is taxed generally at the low capital gains rate.

However, there is one situation in which part of it may be taxed at your ordinary income tax rate. This will happen if, by using one of the rapid depreciation methods described in the next chapter, you have taken larger depreciation deductions than you would have obtained under the straight-line method.

The IRS has a procedure called "recapture" by which it recovers some or all of the tax you avoided by taking the rapid write-off. A description of the "recapture" procedure is given in the next chapter.

If you hold the property long enough—200 months, or sixteen years and eight months—the recapture process is eliminated; the entire profit on the sale is treated as a capital gain. This applies only to residential buildings, however; for other types of property the "recapture" of any excess depreciation is the invariable rule.

The "recapture" device might seem to erase any advantage for the taxpayer using the rapid depreciation rate; if you used straight-line depreciation all along you would never face the recapture problem.

But that is not true. By taking a fast early write-off you gained the current cash benefits of a tax postponement; you had the use of the Treasury's money at no interest cost, at the time when you needed it to help finance the building project. And, presumably, when you sold the property you paid the "recaptured" tax in dollars that were worth less, because of inflation, than the tax dollars you had saved in the earlier years.

If the sale of a piece of rental property results in a loss, it is deductible. The loss on any investment property is a tax deduction, although the law provides no such benefit for a loss on your residence.

The sale of depreciable business property is a special type of transaction which, if losses exceed gains, can be treated as an ordinary loss against other income. This can be most helpful in offsetting some of the effects of your actual loss and can result in a substantial tax savings.

If net gains from such transactions exceed net losses, they are treated as long-term capital gains and losses, except, of course, whatever already had been written off as depreciation in earlier tax years.

There are other methods of deferring the tax in cases where you do not qualify for installment treatment. These are complex, seldom-used rules on which you should receive advice from your professional adviser.

Pooling investments

The most profitable real estate ventures frequently require investments much larger than most individuals can swing.

So investors combine their funds with those of like-minded investors. The simplest way is to form a partnership in which each partner contributes his capital and perhaps his efforts and experience. Each takes a share of the earnings in proportion to his contribution, and each pays taxes on the income as an individual taxpayer.

Other arrangements permit larger numbers of investors to participate in bigger-scale enterprises. A brief description of these, and the tax arrangements peculiar to each, follows:

The syndicate. A syndicate or "limited partnership," is basically a partnership of a large number of investors. Normally the syndicate limits itself to single properties, such as an apartment building, a shopping center or a resort structure.

Each participant in a syndicate owns a fraction of the total invested. He is a "limited partner." That means that if he has bought a 5 percent share in the syndicate, he is liable for 5 percent of the syndicate's debts.

The syndicate frequently obtains a high rate of return. It thus became an exceedingly popular investment device during the 1950s. State laws vary widely on the liability rules, scope of investment permitted, and exact legal status.

One rule prevails, however: The syndicate or limited partnership is not, itself, subject to tax; the profit or loss is reported and taxed on the individual returns of the partners.

One possible tax problem, however, is the possibility that the IRS may decide the "partnership" is really an association that should be taxed as a corporation. Or the partnership may have losses which exceed the amount that the partners are allowed to claim on their individual tax returns.

Special care is required in this type of organization, because if the return of any one of the partners is examined by the IRS and any deficiencies are found, or any changes are required in connection with the partnership interest, *it is mandatory that the examining agent examine the returns of all the other partners.*

The audits of the other partners will not be limited to examination of the partnership matters alone but will extend to all the areas generally covered in an audit.

For this reason, if not simply because of the general complexity of this area of taxation, the best available professional tax advice should be sought before entering into a limited partnership.

The real estate corporation. Like the syndicate, the real estate corporation is engaged in buying, selling and owning real estate, and possibly in the building of investment structures.

The basic advantage of a corporation over a syndicate is that the risk in the investment is smaller. The shareholder is not responsible for any of the debts of the corporation.

But the return on the investment is likely to be smaller, also, because the income from the corporation's business is subject to double taxation. The profits of the corporation are taxed at the regular corporation rate before any dividends are paid out to the shareholders; when the dividends are received by the stockholders, they must pay tax on them as ordinary income.

The taxes cut down profits, obviously. But here again, the liberal deductions for depreciation, taxes, interest and operating expenses may offset the tax bite to a considerable extent.

Real Estate Investment Trust (REIT). The Real Estate Investment Trust is almost a counterpart of the corporation, except that, as its name implies, it is managed by a board of trustees. The investors are called the beneficiaries.

The great advantage of the REIT is a tax advantage. The income of the trust is taxed only once, instead of twice as in the case of a corporation.

The REIT owes its vast popularity to tax law amendments which took effect in 1961. The aim of Congress was to give small investors in real estate the same advantages as were gained by investors who purchased shares in mutual funds.

In a REIT, the small investor puts his money into a pool, reduces his risk because the trust can diversify its investments and becomes a participant in deals too big for small investors or partnerships to undertake alone.

Tax is paid only on the income distributed to the investor-beneficiaries. This gives a REIT essentially the same tax advantage as a small syndicate, plus the advantage that it can spread its investments.

To qualify for the tax advantages, Congress set up many requirements. A REIT must have at least 100 investor-beneficiaries; more than half of the trust cannot be owned by fewer than six persons. The REIT must pay out at least 90 percent of its net income to the investor-beneficiaries each year. At least three-fourths of the income must be from real estate investments. Also, the REIT cannot manage directly any property it owns.

Although specifically written to provide advantages for small investors, the act of Congress establishing REITs provided a great attraction also for higher-income taxpayers. The depreciation allowance, as in most real estate matters, is of key importance.

This is how a group of investors might make money without paying taxes in a REIT:

The REIT buys an office structure for $2,000,000, of which $1,800,000 is for the building and $200,000 for the land. The payment is $800,000 in cash, with a mortgage of $1,200,000 covering the rest of the cost at a 6 percent interest charge.

Annual payments on the mortgage are $90,000 in principal and interest. The income from office rentals in the building is $200,000 a year. Real estate taxes, operating expenses, insurance and management costs average $38,000 a year.

A profit-and-loss statement for income tax purposes would read as follows:

Rental income	$200,000
Expenses:	
Mortgage interest	72,000

Depreciation (5 percent a year)   90,000
Operating expenses   38,000

Total expenses $200,000
Net profit or loss ....   None

Thus, the office building shows no profit and pays no taxes. But here is how the statement of "cash flow"—the actual income and outgo of the property—reads to the investor-beneficiaries.

Rental income $200,000
Cash expenses
 Mortgage (interest & principal)   90,000
 Operating expenses   38,000

Total expenses   128,000
Balance for distribution to beneficiaries .... $ 72,000

So, the building which shows no profit at all for tax purposes gives its investor-beneficiaries a 9 percent return on the $800,000 they put in.

There are good REITs and bad ones. The tax advantages are obvious, but some promoters rush in so recklessly to take advantage of them that they misjudge their market or build the wrong kind of structure for a given location. Many REITs suffered losses and defaulted on loans in the recession and interest-rate squeeze of 1974-75.

Depreciation. The tax-free deduction of a specified amount of "depreciation" each year permits the builder, in theory, to accumulate the money which eventually will replace the worn-out building, as already noted.

Actually, of course, the owner seldom keeps the building to the wearing-out stage. He sells it; the new owner starts a new and presumably shorter period of depreciation.

The IRS estimates the useful life of an apartment building to be forty years and an office building, forty-five years. This is how depreciation works:

You buy an apartment structure for $1,500,000. The land is worth $300,000 and the building, $1,200,000. Since land does not depreciate, depreciation is taken only on the $1,200,000 represented by the building itself. It has a remaining useful life of twenty-five years. If you use the simple, straight-line method of depreciation, you would write off 4 percent a year, or $48,000 in each of the remaining twenty-five years.

If, in the meantime, the building earned a return of $100,000 each year, you would be offsetting almost half that amount with the depreciation allowance: you would pay tax on only $52,000 a year, despite a $100,000 return.

Investment interest. The real estate investor who makes a small down payment and assumes a big mortgage gets current tax deductions for his payments of interest on the mortgage. The deductions, which formerly could be claimed for the full amount of interest paid in any year, were limited by an act of Congress that took effect in 1972. The interest deduction continues nevertheless to be an inducement to real estate investment. Together with the depreciation deduction, it helps to offset ordinary income that would be taxable at the taxpayer's full rate. It contributes to producing income even while the tax returns suggest losses.

The new limit on interest deductions was described in our chapter, "The Itemized Deductions." It cuts the deduction for "excess investment interest" in half. Only a 50 percent deduction can be claimed on the "excess investment interest," which is defined as the amount by which investment interest payments exceed the sum of three items—$25,000, the taxpayer's net investment interest, and his long-term capital gains, if any.

Since it would take a borrowing of more than $300,000 at 8 percent to produce a $25,000 interest cost, the limitation will not be a deterrent to most investors.

Investment in land

Will Rogers advised people to invest in land "because they ain't making any more of that stuff."

Rogers never knew how good his advice really was. One reason for buying land is the capital gains rate; you get a favorable tax rate on your land's *appreciation*. Unlike buildings, land has no *depreciation*. Because it never wears out, land differs from buildings in tax treatment.

When land is "improved" by the addition of a building, or grading, or paving, the tax deduction for depreciation can be taken only on the improvement, not the raw land.

Otherwise the tax treatment of an investment in land which is rented out on an unimproved basis, for example, as a trailer camp site or a parking lot, is much the same as if you had rented a building. The income is declared, and the expenses including mortgage interest, taxes and maintenance are deductible.

But you do have a choice. As long as the land is simply held in unimproved and unproductive condition, you may either deduct your taxes, mortgage interest and other expenses each year (providing you with a deductible loss), or you may "capitalize" them. That means the outlays may be added to the cost of the land on your books. This would reduce your bookkeeping profit, and your tax, when you sell the tract.

If you can reduce your current tax costs by taking the loss as an annual deduction, that might be the best choice.

Once the property has begun to produce income, it is no longer possible to capitalize the expenses; they are used to offset the rental income.

If you subdivide the land holding and sell the lots, you ordinarily will qualify for capital gains treatment—unless and until you sell enough lots to be considered a land dealer. At that point you may be taxed at the ordinary income rate.

To maintain your right to capital gains treatment you must have held the property for at least five years and made no "substantial improvement" on the land. Moreover, you must not have been holding any other property for sale to customers as an ordinary trade or business.

Any improvement in the property which increases the value by more than 10 percent is considered by the Treasury to be a substantial improvement, unless you can persuade the IRS agent otherwise. Building your own residence on one of the lots is not viewed as a substantial improvement, however.

If you have held property ten years or longer, you can make considerably more extensive improvements without being considered a land dealer. You can, for instance, install water and sewer facilities, hard-surfaced roads, drainage and gutters. But building a commercial structure would be adding a "substantial improvement."

By meeting these conditions you can avoid being taxed at the ordinary rate on your sale of lots so long as you sell five or fewer lots in any year. If you sell a sixth lot in the same year as the other five, or sell any number of lots beyond five, you are taxed at the ordinary income rate on 5 percent of the combined sales price of *all* the lots sold, and at the capital gains rate on the rest of the total sales price.

Oil and mining

High-income taxpayers—usually those in the 50 percent bracket or higher—frequently are attracted to oil-well and mining investments. The reason is the tax write-off of current expenditures and the much-publicized depletion allowance.

The depletion allowance was a sacred-cow tax shelter for years until the 1969 and 1975 tax acts chipped away much of the shelter.

The theory of depletion is that the developer of an oil or mineral property has created a valuable asset. Therefore, he is allowed to recover each year, free of tax, a portion of the value which is being depleted by taking out the oil, metals or minerals.

In this way depletion is similar to depreciation: In theory, the money can be accumulated to replace the oil well, mine or other property when its value is exhausted.

There are two kinds of depletion: cost depletion and percentage depletion. You can change from one to another in any year.

Cost depletion. Divide your cost by the number of barrels of oil (or other units) to be produced and sold in the year. For example: You paid $20,000 for a share in an oil well. The geologist estimates the well's total output will be 200,000 barrels. Divide your cost by that number of barrels. Your depletion deduction is 10 cents a barrel. So if you take out 40,000 barrels in the first year, you multiply 40,000 by 10 cents; your deduction is $4,000.

Percentage depletion. This has been the quicker, cheaper, and more popular method. Its use by the oil and gas industry was curtailed drastically by the 1975 Tax Reduction Act, however.

Under this method you simply apply the percentage depletion rate allowed by law to your gross income from the property. For oil and gas the rate was 22 percent. If you received $2,000 from the production of a well, you multiplied that by 22 percent to find your depletion deduction—$440.

Much criticized as a tax loophole, the depletion allowance was hit heavily by Congress. It was eliminated entirely for large oil companies. Some small, independent firms may still claim the deduction, but the rate was ordered to be phased down to 15 percent by 1984 on a smaller volume of oil.

The allowance for many other minerals, metals, and ores was not changed. Congress left it at 15 percent for copper, silver, gold, and iron ore, and at 22 percent for asbestos, bauxite, mica, chromite, and the ores of lead, cobalt, nickel, mercury, tin, platinum, and zinc. However, there has been serious talk in Congress of curtailing the allowance on all minerals; it could happen in some future tax reform wave.

One tax boon to the oil industry—the second biggest after depletion allowances—was not disturbed by the Tax Reform Act. This is the right to deduct "intangible drilling costs." In an oil-drilling enterprise the operator may choose to take current tax deductions for many of the drilling expenses, instead of following the usual course of adding them to the capital investment and taking depreciation on them year by year. This creates immediate, sizable tax deductions for such outlays as labor, supplies, hauling fuel, materials, rental of equipment and hiring of seismological teams.

There are limitations on the deduction of intangible expenses, but not severe enough to detract from the lure of oil investment for high-bracket taxpayers. This deduction, like percentage depletion, has long been a target of tax reformers.

Royalties. Land having oil or mineral deposits can be leased to oil or mining operators for the payment of royalties. The royalty usually is based on the amount of oil or minerals produced. Royalties are taxed at full ordinary income rates, but the tax may be reduced by depletion allowances.

The owner of timber lands may claim depletion on the cost of the timber (but not on the cost of the land), taking the deductions as the timber is cut.

Both coal and timber royalties usually are taxed as ordinary income, but there are conditions under which the royalties can be taxed at the lower capital gains rate.

This could be the case if the holder of the lease owned the coal for more than six months before it was mined, and took the gain on the difference between the royalty payments he received and the cost of the coal that was sold. In this case, however, he could not claim percentage depletion, only cost depletion.

When there is an income tax, the just man will pay more and the unjust less on the same amount of income.

Plato, circa 400 B.C.

CHAPTER 12

The
Art
of
Depreciation

A deduction for depreciation is a return to the taxpayer on his investment in business property or income-producing property over the period of its useful life.

The property can be buildings (but not including the land), machinery, vehicles, office furniture and equipment of a relatively permanent nature; farm buildings and equipment and some draft, breeding or dairy animals; and even such intangible property as contracts, franchises and patent rights when their useful lives are definitely limited.

Depreciation should be taken on business assets even when they are not in use. This would apply, for instance, to a plant shut down for lack of sales or a rental dwelling lacking a tenant.

But a vacant house or other building awaiting resale is not depreciable because it is neither "used in the trade or business" nor "held for the production of income." A merchant's stock in trade provides no depreciation allowance; losses are shown in his inventory.

By taking the depreciation deduction, the property owner indicates that part of the receipts from his business is a return of his invested capital, instead of taxable income. A return of capital is never taxed.

As noted earlier, the deduction theoretically permits the owner to accumulate the money needed to replace the house or factory or tool or machine when its usefulness is ended.

If the useful life is a year or less, as in the case of many tools or reference books, the full cost is simply deducted as part of the operating expense for the year.

When the useful life is longer, the government considers that each yearly depreciation deduction taken is an amount subtracted from the original investment value of the property. The worth of the asset has been depreciated by that much; the owner already has recovered that much of his investment.

So when the property is finally sold, the gain that is taxed is the difference between the sales price and the depreciated cost. This is a larger amount than the difference between the sales price and the original cost; the profit is greater and the tax is higher accordingly.

The Supreme Court has described the deduction in these terms:

"The theory underlying this allowance for depreciation is that by using up the plant, a gradual sale is made of it. The depreciation charged is the measure of the cost of the part which has been sold. When the plant is disposed of after years of use, the thing then sold is not the whole thing originally used."

For example: A summer cottage cost $15,000 ten years ago (not counting the cost of the land). Its estimated useful life is 30 years; the owner takes $500 each year as a depreciation deduction. After five years he sells the cottage for $18,000. His profit is not $3,000, the difference between what he paid and what he received. It is $5,500—the difference between $12,500 ($15,000 less $2,500 depreciation) and $18,000.

The seller owes more tax, therefore. But the tax is paid at the low capital gains rate. And the deductions taken have reduced his regular, full-rate income tax over a period of five years.

How to "depreciate"

A taxpayer may use any of the methods of computing depreciation described here, so long as it is the method consistently used by him for any similar items he is depreciating.

He need not use the same method for all his assets, and he need not use a method in one year simply because he used it for similar property in an earlier year.

But once he has chosen a method for a particular asset he cannot change without getting permission from the IRS. There are exceptions. You can shift from the 200 percent or 150 percent declining balance methods to the straight-line method in any year. Just attach a statement to your tax return reporting the change.

If an asset is expected to have any salvage value—either by cash sale or trade-in allowance—when its useful life to the taxpayer ends, the total amount of the depreciation deductions must be reduced by such salvage value.

A piece of property cannot be depreciated below a reasonable salvage value by any of the depreciation methods. Since salvage value is an estimated resale or second-hand value, its amount will depend on how long the owner keeps the property in use. If his policy is to use an asset until its useful life is exhausted, the salvage value might be no more than junk value. If he disposes of assets while they are still in good condition, salvage value could be a substantial percentage of the original cost.

You may *ignore the salvage value* in four kinds of situations:

First, if you estimate that you will exhaust the useful life of the asset;

Second, if you elect to use the Treasury's depreciation "guidelines" to be described later in.this chapter;

Third, if you use a declining balance method of depreciation;

Fourth, if the property is *personal property*—that is, not real property or stock in trade—which has a useful life of at least three years and an estimated salvage value that is less than 10 percent of the cost of the property. If the salvage value is more than 10 percent, only the amount above 10 percent is counted. For example, if the estimated salvage value on such an item is actually 15 percent, you would count it as 5 per cent —the excess over 10 percent.

Following are the most-used methods of depreciation:

Straight-line method. You deduct the same amount each year over the useful life of the item. If a compressor cost you $1,000 and will last ten years—and will have no salvage value—you can deduct one-tenth of the cost each year, or $100 annually.

If the compressor will have a $200 salvage value at the end of the ten-year useful life, the $200 is subtracted from the cost. You then have a "depreciation basis" of $800. Each annual deduction is one-tenth of $800, or $80 a year. The depreciation rate is 10 percent.

200 percent declining balance method. This method, as well as the sum-of-the-years-digits method which will be described next, can be used on any new property with a useful life of at least three years. It is calculated without subtracting the salvage value at the start. You do not *finish* the depreciation any faster by this method than by the straight-line method. But the first-year depreciation is twice as great; from then on the deductions taper off, each year's depreciation being smaller than the last.

Take the same $1,000 compressor, with a ten-year life. Take twice the straight-line rate, or 20 percent, and apply it to the $1,000 for the first-year depreciation. The deduction is $200. In the second year, after subtracting the $200 from the original cost, you have an $800 depreciation basis. Take 20 percent of that; the second-year depreciation is $160.

Then: third year, 20 percent of $640, or $128; fourth year, 20 percent of $512, or $102.

And so on. You could change to the straight-line method at any time, deducting what remains in equal amounts. When the depreciation gets down to a "reasonable" salvage value it must stop.

Although limited to property with a useful life of at least three years, the declining-balance method works better for assets having a relatively short useful life than for longer-lived assets. It can produce a recovery of about two-thirds of the cost in the first half of the estimated useful life.

If used on a building having a fifty-year useful life, for example, the first year write-off would be only 4 percent (twice the straight-line rate); the allowance would not result in recovery of most of the investment in the early years.

150 percent declining balance method. This works like the 200 percent depreciation, but less rapidly; it starts with 150 percent instead of 200 percent, again without subtracting salvage value at the start.

This is the fastest depreciation now permitted on new, non-residential property. On a $100,000 office building with a forty-year life expectancy, the starting straight-line deduction would be 2½ percent. The 150 percent method would start at a rate 1½ times that, or 3¾ percent.

125 percent declining balance method. This method, with a first-year depreciation 1¼ times the straight-line depreciation, is the fastest method now permitted on used housing.

Sum-of-the-years-digits method. This method with the baffling name also provides a fast write-off at the start and slower depreciation later on. Using the $1,000 compressor as an example, the method is as follows: Since the machine has a ten-year life, add up the years' digits—1 plus 2 plus 3 plus 4 and so on up to 10. The total is 55. In the first year, 10/55 of the $1,000 would be claimed; in the second year 9/55; the third year, 8/55, and so on, down to the salvage value.

Here's how it would work on an asset with shorter useful life, a light pickup truck bought for business use. It cost $4,000 and will have $400 salvage value at the end of a three-year useful life.

The total of the years-digits is 6 (adding 1 plus 2 plus 3) and the depreciable cost is $3,600 (subtracting $400 from $4,000). The depreciation deduction for the three years will be:

First year	($3,600 × 3/6)	$1,800
Second year	($3,600 × 2/6)	1,200
Third year	($3,600 × 1/6)	600
	Total	$3,600

For easier computations of the years-digits when the asset has a long useful life, use a shortcut method: Square the useful life, add the useful life to the result, and divide by two. The sum of the years-digits for an office building with a useful life of forty years thus would work out to 820, as follows:

$$40 \times 40 = 1{,}600$$
$$1{,}600 \text{ plus } 40 = 1{,}640$$
$$1{,}640 \text{ divided by } 2 = 820$$

Then the annual deductions are computed as in the preceding example.

Depreciation of real property

Congress has pulled the brakes on accelerated depreciation of both new and used real estate. The 1969 Tax Reform Act specified that the 200 percent declining balance and the sum-of-the-years-digits methods could be used only for new residential rental property.

Nonhousing property—commercial, industrial, religious, business and other—is limited to methods no faster than the 150 percent declining balance, and this only if the structure is new.

All *used* real property *except used housing* must be depreciated by the straight-line technique. Used housing may be depreciated by methods no faster than the 125 percent declining balance method, and this may be applied only if the used dwelling or apartment structure has a useful life of twenty years or more.

To encourage the rehabilitation of slum or deteriorated buildings for low cost rental housing, a special five-year depreciation write-off is permitted. The straight-line method must be used; no salvage allowance is required. The outlays must exceed $3,000 in any two consecutive tax years but may not exceed $15,000 per dwelling unit in the building.

Write-Off Percentages for Real Property

Here are the most rapid depreciation methods now permitted:

New residential rental property	Can use 200 percent declining-balance and sum-of-years-digits methods
Other new property	150 percent declining-balance method
Used rental housing, if useful life at least twenty years	125 percent declining-balance method
Other used property	Straight-line method
Rehabilitation for low-income rental housing	Straight-line, with five-year useful life

The table herewith summarizes the real estate depreciation rules, and this example illustrates some of the principles:

William White buys a house for $27,000, as an investment. He plans to rent it. It is almost new, with an estimated life of forty years. But, having been lived in, it must be depreciated under the 125 percent formula.

White can charge only $20,000 off in depreciation. The other $7,000 is the cost of the land, which does not depreciate.

If White were using the straight-line method, he would deduct $500 a year throughout the life of the house. Under the 125 percent accelerated depreciation, he can take off 25 percent more in the first year, or $625. The second year's depreciation would be $605.47. It would become progressively lower in subsequent years. In the last twenty years, the depreciation deductions would be smaller than under the straight-line method.

The same principles apply to the write-off rules for other real estate, whatever the scale of the investment.

A $200,000 apartment structure with a forty-year useful life would be depreciable at 2½ percent a year, or $5,000 in annual write-off, if the straight-line method were used. The building would be depreciated $5,000 in the first year.

Under the 200 percent declining balance method, still permitted for rental residential property, the building could be depreciated $10,000 in the first year.

An office building of the same size and cost, also with a forty-year life expectancy, could not be depreciated more than $7,500 at the outset because the fastest allowed depreciation method for nonresidential property is the 150 percent declining balance technique.

The furniture, equipment, air-conditioning and machinery in a building are depreciable, too. Their useful lives are shorter, so the owner finds himself dealing with a whole range of depreciations.

The Treasury helps by providing special depreciation guidelines covering many classes of property. IRS offices can provide you with a booklet of the estimated life of many items used in many businesses and industries. A section of this chapter is devoted to the guidelines.

Since the present rules on depreciation of real property were part of the Tax Reform Act of 1969, they do not apply to property acquired before July 25, 1969. New property constructed before that date was eligible for the 200 per cent declining balance method and the sum-of-the-years-digits method.

If used rental housing was acquired before July 25, 1969, the 150 percent declining balance may be used; for used rental residential property purchased after July 24, 1969, the 125 percent declining balance is the most rapid depreciation method permitted.

Used residential rental property with *less* than a twenty-year useful life must be depreciated under the straight-line method unless the IRS Commissioner permits otherwise.

To qualify as residential real property, at least 80 percent of the income from the building must be rental income from dwelling units, other than motel, hotel or other transient-type units. Thus, an apartment building with ground-floor stores could be classed as residential if less than 20 percent of the total rental income came from the stores. But an all-apartment structure would not qualify if some of the apartments were rented on a transient basis and these provided 20 percent or more of the gross rental income.

As was noted in the preceding chapter, the taxpayer who converts his dwelling into rental use must determine a "depreciation basis"—in effect, the cost basis on which the depreciation is figured. It differs from the cost basis which must be determined when you sell a residence or other real estate in an important respect: The land does not depreciate, so the value of the lot must be subtracted from the price you paid.

You may add to your purchase price the costs of any permanent improvements and the fees and commissions paid in purchasing the property. But if your total cost and the improvements add up to an amount greater than the fair market value at the time the property is converted to rental use, the market value must be used as the depreciation basis.

The "recapture" problem

Many an unwary seller of income property has fallen into the "recapture" trap—the device by which the IRS in some circumstances may tax part of the profit at the seller's full ordinary income rate instead of treating it all as a capital gain.

Taxpayers who own rental property and have used one of the accelerated depreciation methods may run into the recapture problem if they sell the property at any time before the useful life has expired. The owner will have taken more total deductions than would have been permitted under the straight-line depreciation method.

The excess represents income on which he would have been taxed at his full ordinary rate if it had not been shielded as a deduction. So the IRS "recaptures" this avoided tax when the property is sold. That amount of the gain is denied the capital gains treatment; the ordinary rate must be paid.

A reminder: The recapture problem washes out if you hold a residential rental property long enough. After 200 months, which is sixteen years and eight months, the recapture procedure is eliminated and the full profit on the sale is taxed as a capital gain. This is not true of non-residential properties; for commercial, industrial or other structures the recapture rules are enforced indefinitely.

In some cases the owner who would incur a large depreciation recapture if he sold his property might find it advisable to borrow money on the property instead, or to refinance a present mortgage with a larger mortgage.

In this way, money could be realized on the property with no tax liability at all. The taxpayer would continue to take rentals from the property, would still take depreciation deductions on it, and would deduct the interest paid on the loan.

He could thus hold on to the property until the recapture liability has been lessened or disappears, so that the profit from his later sale—when the mortgage falls due, for example—would be largely or entirely a capital gain.

Recapture has sometimes dealt a particularly hard blow to the owners of poorly planned projects which failed to attract and hold tenants. Such a scenario might go like this:

The project was built mainly with borrowed money; the owner was relying heavily on his tax deductions for interest and depreciation to swing the deal. When rental incomes failed to meet expectations after a few years, he could not meet the mortgage payments. His depreciation deductions got smaller each year; he faced the prospect of losing the building by foreclosure. But he could not simply give up and walk away from the failure, because the IRS considers a foreclosure a sale, and it would insist on recapture of the excess depreciation taken. The owner finally is forced to "sell" the building for the amount of its mortgage balance. He gets nothing from the sale; nevertheless he has to pay the tax on the recaptured depreciation at his ordinary income rate.

Recapture can be avoided by adopting the straight-line depreciation method, assuming that a realistic "useful life" is used. But there are many situations in which accelerated depreciation is both safe and desirable.

For example, ailing persons and older taxpayers sometimes elect an accelerated write-off on property which will be part of their estate. If they die, the fact that they have taken excess depreciation is wiped out; the inheritor of the property need never undergo a "recapture."

Also, a high-income person may buy a house with the intention of moving into it in later years. A sixty-year-old executive, for instance, might buy a place in Florida and rent it to tenants continuously for five years, with the idea of moving into it when he retires. He faces no problem of depreciation recapture.

Even under the straight-line method, your deductions for depreciation bite into your profit when the time comes to sell income-producing property.

Suppose you bought a house for $50,000 to provide yourself with some rental income. Of the total price, $10,000 was for the land, which is not depreciable; the house itself cost you $40,000. You have a twenty-five-year mortgage.

The house has a presumed useful life of thirty-five years. (A twenty or twenty-five year useful life would probably have been questioned by the IRS; after all, the mortgage company gave a twenty-five-year mortgage, and it surely expected there would be some residual value in the house if the company had to foreclose at any time in the life of the mortgage.)

On the straight-line basis, you deduct 1/35th of the cost of the structure each year. Your depreciation deduction is $1,142.85 a year.

After ten years you decide to sell the property. By that time you have deducted a total of $11,428.50 for depreciation. You have in effect been paid back that much of the cost, and in computing your tax you subtract that much from your original cost. That gives you a remaining cost basis, or "depreciation basis," of $38,571.50. (Note that the lot provides no depreciation deduction, but its value *is* included in computing your basis for sale.)

You sell your house for $75,000. This at first glance looks like a profit of $25,000, since you had paid $50,000 for it. But it looks otherwise to the IRS. Your gain for tax purposes is $36,428.50. It consists of the selling price ($75,000) less your original cost ($50,000) plus the depreciation already taken ($11,428.50).

The profit is thus increased; so is the tax you must pay on the deal.

You come out ahead, nevertheless. The depreciation deductions had sheltered from tax $11,428.50 of your income that would have been taxed at your full ordinary rate. But when added to your profit on the sale, that $11,428.50 becomes part of your capital gain; you pay only half as much tax on it.

This is how it works:

If you have been in the 50 percent income tax rate bracket during your ownership of the house, your annual depreciation deductions saved you 50 percent of $11,428.50, or $5,714.25, in federal income tax alone (not counting the similar deductions on your state income tax).

Now that you are selling the house, you lose part of the saving. The $11,428.50 is subtracted from your cost, as if it were a part-payment on the sale of the house taken in advance. It becomes part of your capital gain, and only half of a capital gain is taxed at your regular rate. Half of it is $5,714.25; the tax on that much at your regular rate is $2,857.25.

So here it is in capsule: During your ten-year ownership of your rental dwelling you saved $5,714.25 in federal tax by your depreciation deductions. When you sold it, Uncle Sam took only $2,857.25 back in capital gains tax. Your net saving is $2,857.25.

If you had taken accelerated depreciation on the property, there would have been a recapture; you would have saved more in taxes during your ownership, but lost a great deal more of it when you sold, because of recapture.

How would a taxpayer with smaller taxable income fare in the sale of a depreciated property? This way: If the owner described above had been in the 30 percent tax bracket, he would have saved $3,428.55 in taxes during his ten years of depreciation deductions. The depreciation total would have been the same, $11,428.50, by the time he sold the building. Under the capital gains treatment, the tax would have been levied on only half that amount ($5,714.25); the tax on that at the 30 percent rate would be $1,714.28.

This is only half of his tax savings from depreciation during his ten years of ownership. And the $1,714.28 which Uncle Sam did collect in tax was money which had been, in effect, a ten-year interest-free loan from the government.

The Treasury's guidelines

The Treasury has provided a set of general depreciation guidelines that save taxpayers time and trouble and sometimes money.

They were designed to help taxpayers avoid the painful detail work of trying to estimate accurately the useful lives of all the items of machinery, office machines, and other equipment in a factory, or the various items of furniture, heating and cooling equipment, carpeting and other items that go into an office building or apartment structure.

The guidelines were intended to provide a reasonable overall result by grouping seventy-five types of items into broad industry classes. These replace old, arbitrary rules which specified the useful lives of hundreds of different items for every industry.

The guidelines provide several advantages. There are fewer categories to deal with. The useful lives are 30 to 40 percent shorter than in the old rules, on the average. Therefore they provide greater annual depreciation deductions.

The guidelines provide for a built-in salvage value; it is therefore not necessary, when using them, to limit the depreciation by subtracting from the cost an estimated resale, trade-in, or junk value.

Taxpayers are not required to use the Treasury guidelines. You can compute depreciation on a shorter useful life than the guidelines provide if you are prepared to show that you do replace the items as frequently as you claim. But the guidelines simplify the depreciation problem because they save arguments with revenue agents. They are accepted without question by the IRS.

The Treasury's booklet of depreciation guidelines includes some single-industry guidelines which cover all the equipment used in an industry. There are also guidelines for assets which are in general use by all industries; here are a few of them:

Office machines, fixtures, equipment	10 years
Transportation equipment:	
Automobiles	3 years
Light trucks	4 years
Heavy trucks	6 years

Land improvements (sewers, walks, paved surfaces, etc.)	20 years
Buildings:	
Apartments	40 years
Dwellings	45 years
Factories	45 years
Office buildings	45 years
Stores	50 years
Theatres	40 years

In some cases the guidelines for an industry cover all the equipment used in that industry. For example:

Services (includes accountants, beauty shops, doctors, dentists, lawyers, engineers, hotel, laundry, photo studios, and so on)	10 years
Wholesale and retail trade	10 years
Recreation and amusement (billiards and bowling establishments, etc.)	10 years
Agriculture:	
Machinery and equipment	10 years
Cattle, breeding or dairy	7 years
Horses, breeding or work	10 years
Hogs, breeding	3 years
Construction contracting:	
General	5 years
Marine	12 years

The foregoing examples are merely illustrative. The booklet presents much greater detail. And since the guidelines are used mostly by business organizations whose depreciable assets fall into two or more of the four broad groups listed by the Treasury, the instructions for using guidelines are considerably more complicated than might be supposed from this brief description.

This should be remembered also: The estimated useful life of any depreciable property is based on the useful life it will have in *your* hands. A printing press in the shop of a small job printer who uses it every day will have a shorter useful life than the same press would have in a large factory where it is used once or twice a week. Similarly, the owner of a business car who puts 60,000 or 70,000 miles on it each year should claim a shorter estimated useful life than the car owner who travels only 15,000 miles a year.

Two depreciation bonuses

There are two important depreciation bonuses in the tax law. The first is an additional first-year depreciation allowance. The second is a liberalized depreciation for equipment or instruments used in a business or profession; this is the "asset depreciation range," or ADR.

A taxpayer in a trade or business may deduct an *extra* 20 percent of the cost of many items in the year he buys the item.

This extra first-year depreciation is available on tangible personal property, a term which covers machinery, equipment, vehicles, refrigerators, and other items which are not *real* property. The bonus is in addition to the regular depreciation allowance.

The property must have a useful life of at least six years, and the total amount eligible for this bonus depreciation cannot exceed $10,000 (or $20,000 for a couple filing a joint return) in any one year. The maximum deduction therefore is $2,000 (or $4,000).

For example: You buy $2,000 worth of gas ranges for an apartment building. They should last ten years. You start by subtracting the extra 20 percent first-year depreciation, or $400, from the full $2,000. That reduces the depreciation basis to $1,600. Then apply any method of depreciation you choose.

Another example: John Martin, operator of a cleaning and dyeing shop, buys equipment costing $15,000. He is married, so the amount is within the limits of eligibility for the bonus depreciation. The equipment has a useful life of ten years and a salvage value of $1,200.

Martin figures his depreciation allowance, using the straight-line method, as follows:

Bonus first-year depreciation:	
20 percent of $15,000	$3,000
Regular first-year depreciation:	
10 percent of $12,000 ($15,000	
minus $3,000; salvage is ignored	
because it is less than 10 percent	
of cost)	1,200
Total first-year depreciation	$4,200
Depreciation in later years:	$1,200 per year

A second depreciation bonus, the "asset depreciation range," or ADR, has provided still another way to speed up the early years' depreciation of business assets.

ADR is optional. A taxpayer can elect to depreciate business equipment, machinery and furnishings within a range that is up to 20 percent shorter than the useful lives of such equipment listed in the Treasury's depreciation guidelines. Or he can *lengthen* the depreciation period up to 20 percent, and take smaller yearly deductions, if that suits his situation better.

You make the election every year on Form 4832. Your election is binding within a given year, but you do not have to make the election next year just because you made it this year.

If the guideline life for an asset is ten years—as it is for office furniture, fixtures, machines and equipment—you may reduce its useful life to eight years (by subtracting 20 percent of ten years, or two years), or you may increase its life to twelve years by adding 20 percent.

The ADR has been a particular target of tax reform advocates in Congress since its birth. The Nixon administration introduced it by executive order in 1971, and Congress subsequently enacted it into law by close votes late that year, after eliminating some features. But ADR has been under criticism ever since as an unfair tax boon to business and a generator of inflation.

Despite the "boon to big business" label applied to the liberalized depreciation rules by some critics, the changes can be a great tax help to very small firms and self-employed individual businessmen and professional men.

Here is a sample: Suppose you are a small businessman. You discover, in the fall, that you are having an unusually good year. You face a big tax bill unless you can find some unusual savings. One solution is to seize the opportunity to modernize quickly and start using the new equipment by December 31.

If you buy $10,000 worth of new office or shop equipment, you can get:

- A 7 percent investment credit, worth $700 of cost.
- A 20 percent "additional first-year depreciation," worth $2,000.
- A regular depreciation deduction of up to $1,000.

You have escaped or postponed the tax on $3,700 of income. Though the optional $2,000 first-year depreciation means that your deductions in later years must be smaller, you have received in effect an interest-free loan from the government. And if you use the ADR system of figuring regular depreciation deductions, you can write off the new equipment in eight years. Even if you don't start using the new equipment until the last day of December, you can take a half year's depreciation on the year's tax return.

One of the major characteristics of our tax system, and one in which we can take a great deal of pride, is that it operates primarily through individual self-assessment. The integrity of such a system depends upon the continued willingness of the people honestly and accurately to discharge this annual price of citizenship. To the extent that some people are dishonest or careless in their dealings with the government, the majority is forced to carry a heavier tax burden.

President John F. Kennedy, to Congress,
April 20, 1961

CHAPTER 13

The Businessman and the Professional Man

There are headaches as well as rewards in being self-employed. If the rewards are success and profits, one of the headaches is income tax.

From the tax collector's standpoint, there is not much difference between the corner druggist and the famous surgeon; the auto dealer and the lawyer; the dentist and the dry cleaner; the self-employed salesman and the owner of a potato chip factory or bottling plant. Their tax problems and solutions are startlingly similar. This chapter will examine first the problems that are common to all, whatever the particular activity. Then it will identify the special advantages and problems of the professional, whether he practices as an individual or has incorporated; and of the small businessman, whether he operates as a partner, corporate owner, or self-employed sole proprietor.

Launching a business

Just having money, ability and ambition is not enough to start a business. Planning is essential.

Before you begin, review the requirements that you may have to meet. Most states demand that contractors, electricians, plumbers and many others be licensed before they set up shop. Frequently bonds must be purchased from insurance companies. Zoning laws may require an occupancy permit, even if your business is in your own home. Furthermore, the federal government is not the only government that is interested in levying taxes on you. This book cannot explore the problems of collecting and forwarding state and local sales taxes, paying a business privilege tax, a real estate tax, personal property tax, a business franchise license, or any of the many state and local levies on employers. Decisions made on the basis of federal tax law could be the wrong ones in the light of your particular state and local laws. Obviously, these should be considered carefully before you invest your time, money, and reputation in launching a business.

Who is self-employed?

If you are a doctor, lawyer, dentist, engineer, architect, economic consultant, writer, artisan, certified public accountant or other professional, you have no trouble deciding whether you are self-employed. But in some careers, the answer is less simple.

Sometimes taxpayers who think they are self-employed are not. What if you work in Baltimore as a sales representative of a New York clothing manufacturer and you incur travel, entertainment and promotion expenses for which you are not reimbursed? You are an employe if you are working under the "direction and control" of the New York company. It does not matter that you do not work at its place of business and only visit there now and then. Your wages are subject to income tax withholding and Social Security deductions, and you do not qualify for the sometimes valuable federal tax advantages which self-employed persons claim.

If instead of representing just one company, the clothes salesman also represented other manufacturers, and if none of the manufacturers could tell him where, when or how to sell, he probably would be self-employed.

It is possible, however, to be the employe of more than one company at a time and still not qualify as a self-employed taxpayer. If you are in doubt, ask IRS. Better to know now than to find out the hard way later.

Deductions

Once you are actually "in business," you may deduct the ordinary and necessary expenses directly connected with the business even before you have received any income. For instance, if you established your business in November but did not receive payment until January for the jobs performed, you may deduct the expenses in one year—even with no income received in that year—and report the income in the next year's return. This is also true for a salesman who sells for several months but does not receive his first commission check until the following year. In situations like these, it is wise to attach a note to your tax return, explaining the circumstances and stating that the expenditures will produce future income.

The expense of training or qualifying for a new business or profession is not deductible. For the law student, school costs and bar examination expenses are generally personal costs. They are not deductible because the student is not yet engaged in his profession.

Similarly, money spent investigating a possible business enterprise is not deductible. It is not an "ordinary and necessary" business expense because you are not yet engaged in business. Nor can you treat the cost as a loss on a transaction entered into for profit, because there is no transaction until you acquire the business.

Do not forget that you are considered a completely new enterprise, so you may need a new identity as a taxpayer. As an individual taxpayer, your Social Security account number was your "taxpayer identifying number," used on all tax returns. But if you are engaged in a trade or business, an "employer identification number" is generally required. Apply on Form SS-4, which may be obtained from your local IRS District Director's office.

Unhappily, some of the decisions you might prefer to postpone until you know the ropes must be made first. The choices, known as "elections" in tax law, will often bind the self-employed taxpayer throughout his professional or business career.

In your first year of business, an accounting method, a plan for taking depreciation and a tax year must all be selected.

Sometimes some changes can be made by the taxpayer himself but, for other changes permission from the IRS is needed.

Records and accounts

Accounting is the language of business. Every business and professional man should maintain a complete set of books. This need not be as formidable as it sounds.

Most businessmen seek professional guidance in preparing income tax returns; it is sensible to select a Certified Public Accountant or other qualified accountant before starting a business, and consult with him on the methods of maintaining records.

Usually, he can show you a simple set of books for item-by-item entries, called journals, to record your daily transactions. He can use the journals at the year's end, along with bank statements, canceled checks and other data, for a full and accurate accounting of the year's business.

This, in itself, is a basic tax-saving technique. It also provides the information you need to measure the success of your enterprise, to determine your financial standing and to back your application for outside financing, if necessary. It serves to establish the value of your business if you decide to sell it and serves as the basis for planning to arrive at the lowest legal income tax.

But you have not solved all your tax problems merely by getting a professional to prepare your tax returns. You must understand enough about your own tax goals, possibilities and problems so that you can ask your adviser the right questions and understand his answers.

Here are a few time-tested rules for staying out of trouble with the tax collector. Each steers you away from a pitfall into which many a taxpayer has fallen.

• Keep copies of your income tax returns forever. They should never be destroyed; they can be of invaluable help.

• Keep your records updated on a daily basis. These are your tax proofs of business transactions. To let them get behind is to invite extra work and confusion; many a taxpayer has simply foregone a deduction or a credit rather than invest the time, effort or expense involved in substantiating it.

• Open a separate bank account for your business. If you have more than one business, open a separate bank account for each. Be certain your business records reflect clearly any non-income deposits that go into this business account, such as bank loans or your own contributions to the business.

• Make every payment by check, if possible. Make a note on the check, and on the check stub, of the invoice number, order number or other identification of the outlay. (This is vital for tax purposes; it also can help if disputes arise over the payment of bills.) Consider buying a "one-write" check system. The check has spot carbon on the back; when you make out the check you create its stub and the journal entry at the same time. If you write more than thirty checks a month the cost is minor by comparison with the effort saved and accuracy gained.

• Do not use the business checking account as a personal checking account. Even though a sole proprietor is taxed on the net profit of his business, not on how much he withdraws from it, the accounts should be kept separate. It is better to withdraw one check a week from the business account, for your personal funds. This should be deposited to your personal checking account, to be used for your personal and household expenses.

• When you buy furniture, fixtures, autos or other depreciable assets used in business, maintain the bills separately in your record of business assets, and keep each bill at least three years *after you dispose of that asset.*

• Classify your outlays in your records in appropriate descriptive categories such as rent, purchases of merchandise for resale, repairs and supplies.

• Keep canceled checks and bank statements, paid bills, cash register tapes or daily reports, monthly statements and other records. They are the supporting material that will substantiate the accuracy of your books and tax returns. Store them in a clean, dry, clearly marked place; keep them *at least* three years from the time you file the tax return which they support.

Accounting method

One of your first decisions is to choose an accounting method. Once selected, you must remain with it unless IRS grants permission to change.

The IRS is not particular *which* method you use, provided certain basic conditions are met. It will accept any method which clearly reflects your income through consistent use of the accepted accounting principles that are in accord with the usage and conditions of your trade or business.

But taxpayers are expected to follow certain guidelines, including these:

• If you are in the business of producing goods or if you purchase merchandise for resale, you must make an inventory (an itemized listing of your stock in trade) showing the value of your goods or merchandise remaining at the end of the tax year. You may not deduct the cost of inventory items remaining in your inventory at the end of the tax year.

• Your outlays must be classified in two categories. They are either "ordinary and necessary expenses" of doing business, or they are "capital expenditures," such as outlays for machinery, furniture or equipment. The term "ordinary" means an expense that is a common and accepted practice in your field of business; "necessary" means appropriate and helpful in developing and maintaining your business.

• Any outlays made to restore your property or prolong the useful life of a building, machine or other depreciable assets are capital expenditures. They must be added to the cost basis of the property and depreciated over the years, rather than deducted as an expense when the outlay is made.

Usually the business or professional man will choose between two basic accounting methods: cash or accrual.

Cash method. The full name is "cash receipts and disbursement method." It is available to any businessman who does not have to keep inventories.

Income is reported when it is received, and expenses are reported when paid. (Under the accrual method, income is reported when your bills go out to customers, not when you receive payment; and your expenses are reported when you get a bill from a creditor or supplier, not when you actually pay.)

The cash method is popular because it gives greater flexibility in delaying or advancing the time for reporting income and outgo. It helps, in other words, in shifting income and expenses so as to give you the smallest net tax impact.

The cash basis is easier for most businessmen because you are not obliged to calculate your accounts payable and receivable at year's end.

If you are in a professional practice, like law or medicine, you will tend to have accumulations of receivables, but only small amounts of payables at any one time. Under the cash system you are not paying tax on income you have not received.

Most professional people and most service businesses like repair shops, plumbers and electrical contractors find it better to use the cash method. But use of the cash method does not excuse you from reporting income when it is "constructively" received.

A "constructive receipt" occurs when a sum is credited to your account or set aside for you, even though you do not actually have it in your possession. If it is subject to your control and you may draw upon it at any time, you have received the income, unless there are some substantial limitations or restrictions on the time or manner of payment. For example, if you were an entertainer and a night club paid $2,000 to your booking agent on December 31 for your appearances to be made the following January, you are required to report the income in the year ended December 31, even though you may not have known the money had been received in your behalf.

Usually expenses must be deducted in the year in which they are paid. But capital expenditures and some other costs attributable to more than one year are treated differently.

If you pay interest in advance for three years, for instance, or pay rent in advance for more than one year, you do not deduct the outlay in the year when you make the payment; you must deduct in each year only the portion of the payment that was due in that year.

Some court decisions have excepted fire and other business insurance policies, which sometimes are written for three-year periods. A number of taxpayers who use the cash method and have consistently charged as an expense the entire three-year premium in one year have been successful, but most courts have required that the expense of the premium be prorated over the life of the policy.

Accrual method. If inventories are necessary to reflect your income accurately, as in a store or lumber yard, you must use the accrual method of accounting to determine your purchases and sales. You may also use this method to determine expenses like taxes, rent or repairs.

The IRS requires that a physical inventory be taken, with each item tabulated, at the beginning of your tax year. No approximations are accepted. The books also must show the cost of all merchandise purchases in the course of the year. The entries provide a basis for fixing the exact cost of all goods sold.

Under the accrual method, all income items are included in gross income for tax purposes when earned, even if the payment is received in another tax year. You are required to include income in a particular year if that was when all the events fixing your right to the income occurred and if the amount could be determined with reasonable accuracy.

For example: You own an appliance store. You sold a refrigerator to Mrs. Durham on December 2, with the understanding that she would pay for it out of her husband's Christmas bonus. She did not pay until January 4 of the next year. You must include that account receivable as part of your sales for the preceding year, because the income was earned in that year.

It works the same for expenses. They are deducted when incurred, whether or not you make payment in the same tax year. All events fixing your liability must have occurred, and you must be able to ascertain the cost with reasonable accuracy. For example: You place an advertisement for your appliance store in the *Morning Times* for the week before Christmas. The *Times* does not send you the bill until January 3. You pay the bill on January 10. But you can deduct the cost for the year in which the ad was placed because there was a fixed and determined liability as of the date the ad appeared. This would be true even if the paper normally gave you terms permitting the payment of bills by the tenth of the following month.

It is essential for the accrual-basis taxpayer to make his tally of accounts due and bills payable as of the last day of the tax year. If he waits, the task of trying to reconstruct this information sixty or ninety days later, when the tax return deadline date may be hanging over his head, can be formidable.

If you operate more than one business, you can use a different accounting method for each. A merchant who runs a clothing store and a dry cleaning business could use the cash basis for the cleaning shop because no inventories are involved, even though he would have to use the accrual method for the store. Each must be a separate and distinct business, however, with its own set of books.

Other methods. You might be advised that in your particular business the "installment method" of reporting income would be useful. It has advantages for businesses whose customers pay on time-payment plans.

Under this method, you report income only as the cash is collected. The amount of each payment reported as "income" is a percentage of each installment payment. The percentage is the same as your margin of anticipated gross profit on the total selling price.

For example: You sell a home humidifier for $100. It cost you $70. Your prospective gross profit is 30 percent of the selling price. Therefore, you report as gross income 30 percent of each installment collected on that sale.

The tax advantages are twofold. The method helps to stabilize gross income from year to year, leveling out the humps and valleys of the accrual method; it therefore saves you the high-bracket tax payment that hits your peaks of income. And since the tax is not due until the cash is received, the means of paying is at hand when the tax falls due.

Combinations of the foregoing methods are permitted if the combination—known as a "hybrid method"—clearly reflects income and is used consistently without variation from year to year.

There are other ground rules. A businessman using the accrual method for figuring his gross profit may use the cash method in computing all other items of income and expense.

Also, even if you use the accrual basis for your business, you may use the cash method for reporting other income such as salaries, rents, and interest, and for claiming personal deductions like contributions, interest on your home mortgage and your personal real estate taxes.

With both cash and accrual methods, however, you are required to segregate your personal expense items. They may not be deducted on the business tax return. For instance, a clothier must record any personal items taken from store inventory, and he may not include their costs among his expense deductions.

Similarly, a doctor may not deduct that portion of his automobile expenses which represents personal use or traveling to and from his office. He can, of course, deduct the portion used in making house calls, hospital visits or trips to the clinic or laboratory.

Fiscal or calendar?

Another early decision is the choice of an accounting period: Should you choose the calendar year basis, from January 1 to December 31 each year, or a fiscal year?

A fiscal year is an accounting period of twelve months that ends on the last day of a month other than December. A fiscal year might run, for instance, from March 1 to February 28.

Selection of the most advantageous fiscal period will help you maintain a relatively stable net profit period from one year to the next. This can be important because of the proportionately larger amount of tax required when the income level rises.

The nature of the business will play a part in determining the period. If you are in a seasonal business it might be unwise to pick an accounting year that brings most of your receipts into your bank account in one tax year and most of the expenses which produced that income in another tax year.

For example, in operating a ski lodge, many expenses are incurred before December 31 each year. But receipts will come largely between January 1 and the end of March. Similarly, in a gift shop, the bills for incoming holiday merchandise will pile up in October, November and December, but your customers may not pay their Christmas shopping accounts until January or February. In both cases it might be wise to choose a fiscal year ending March 31.

Since the accounting year you use for an unincorporated business must be the same for all your other income and deduction items, you must change the period for your individual income tax return to correspond to your business accounting period. The change requires a prior written request to IRS to secure approval.

"Fiscal" savings

While most sole proprietorships and partnerships are taxed by calendar years, a new corporation can elect a fiscal year ending on the last day of any month. The first fiscal year of the infant corporation can be only a few months long, and taking advantage of such circumstances can produce tax savings.

This is how it works:

Rogers and Able were operating a small wholesale house as a partnership. Most of the sales and profits came late in the year because their lines included much Christmas merchandise.

After consultation with professional advisers, Rogers and Able decided to incorporate as of July 1. Because the partnership usually was active only in the latter half of the year, Rogers and Able had only a small amount of tax to pay on the partnership earnings of the first six months.

They decided to close the fiscal year of the new firm on January 31, giving the new corporation a first fiscal "year" that was only seven months long. Rogers and Able drew only nominal salaries from their new corporation in those months. But on closing their books in January they decided to award themselves substantial bonuses. The bonuses were almost equal to the full amount of profits earned by the corporation in the seven months.

The bonuses were deductible by the corporation as costs of doing business, so the corporation had little profit left, and little or no tax to pay in its first fiscal year. Rogers and Able had income tax to pay on the bonuses, but the tax was not due until after the following December 31, almost a year later, because, as individuals, they could still pay taxes on a calendar year basis.

Thus they spread over two years income they had earned in thirteen months and virtually eliminated their tax for the year of incorporation. If they continue to use the bonus plan in future years, their tax liability would always come almost a year after they collect their money.

Deferring income

Arrangements for deferring income are simpler for professional and self-employed persons than for employes or executives. A well-paid actor, writer or independent businessman has no need to persuade an employer to withhold some reimbursement for payment in a future year. He can negotiate the timing of income along with the price of his services.

An architect, for example, takes on a $200,000 job with a development corporation to design a luxury resort community. He arranges to take the money payment at $40,000 a year for five years. The Tax Rate Schedule for married taxpayers shows why he does it that way:

Assuming he accepted payment in a lump sum and had no other income that year, the tax on $200,000 would be $92,060, even after his taking advantage of the 50 percent maximum rate on earned income. But the tax on $40,000 a year for five years adds up to $60,700. He would save $31,360 by deferring much of the income. (This example is grossly oversimplified for purposes of illustration. There would be deductible expenses in executing the job, so the architect would not pay tax on the full $200,000.)

Shifting income. The self-employed taxpayer has a better opportunity than the salaried man or wage earner to shift income and expenditures for tax advantage.

For some hints on how to shift income and expenditures, consider the following instructions written by a Norfolk, Virginia, pediatrician to his secretary at the end of November, 1969. Here is an example of a self-employed man planning ahead, in time to beat the year-end deadline for his tax year. The memo by Dr. Forrest P. White was published in the magazine, *Medical Economics*:

Dear Debbie:

The tax reform bill should lower my income tax rate next year and, with the surtax also slated to be phased out, it's to my advantage to pay as many tax-deductible expenses as possible before Dec. 31. I also want to defer receiving income where possible until after Jan. 1. So please take the following steps at once:

Check the inventory of all the office supplies, stationery, stamps, and everything else in your domain, and have Vonnie do the same for her medical supplies. Without absolutely glutting all the storage space, order and pay for supplies for several months ahead.

Send routine bills to patients; to do otherwise would, I believe, be poor business practice. However, defer billing of Blue Shield and other third parties until January.

Since things always get a bit confused in the office during the Christmas holidays, be prepared to implement the following after Dec. 25 and before Dec. 31 without further reminders from me:

Pay the January rent, the January fee for the answering service, and any other charges we pay at a flat monthly rate.

Don't wait for January bills. Take out all invoices from our drug supply firm, stationer, office supply companies, and the like. Total each one and write checks for my signature.

Remind me to give you copies of all charges to gasoline credit cards, and pay them.

Make out salary checks for the period ending Jan. 2.

Write checks for my personal account for my first quarter of 1970 payments on my church and United Fund pledges.

Call our family dentist and Traylor Optical. My son is due for dental work and for new glasses during his holiday from school. Have them send us the bills, and pay them.

Pay the January bill at the nursing home for Aunt Hattie.

Remind me to bring in the final quarter bills for my real estate taxes and for my personal bank loan. They should arrive at my home just after Christmas.

Send all the above checks out before Dec. 31.

Continue to record all checks received through Dec. 31.

Forms of business and their tax aspects

Being self-employed does not necessarily mean being a lone operator. The man who is his own boss can employ dozens or hundreds of others.

Nor is the professional practice of a doctor, lawyer or other professional man necessarily a solo performance. Lawyers more often than not work in "firms" of partners. Doctors increasingly are joining other doctors in professional corporations, with tax savings as a principal incentive for doubling-up.

Many choices are open to the business or professional man setting up his own office. The same choices are open to other self-employed persons, even including writers, artists, artisans and entertainers. Each form of business has its pros and cons; this list of the major forms of business organization indicates briefly the basic tax characteristics of each:

• Sole proprietorship. This is the classic form for a small, independent business. Profits are taxed only once, when the owner files his return. The opportunities for tax-saving retirement, "fringe" and deferred-income plans are limited.

• Partnership. Whether there are two partners or fifty, the partnership keeps the virtue of simplicity. Each partner is taxed as an individual on his share of the income; double taxation is avoided. However, tax benefits for pension and fringe benefits are few.

• Corporation. The corporation form has many business advantages, including limited risk to its stockholding owners, ease of raising capital by stock sales, permanence and centralized management. But its income may be taxed doubly. The corporation pays a tax on its profits, then the stockholders pay income tax when they receive the remaining profits if they are paid out as dividends. But the owner-officers can participate like employes in qualified pension, profit-sharing, and deferred-income plans with liberal tax treatment.

• Subchapter S corporation. (Also called tax option corporation, pseudo-corporation, small business corporation or "electing small business corporation.") This is corporate in form and provides many of the benefits of a corporation, but the shareholders avoid double taxation by being taxed as if they were partners.

• A partnership or proprietorship which elects to be taxed as a corporation. This form is seldom used. One attraction is that corporation tax rates are lower than the individual rates paid by high-bracket tax-payers. But most businessmen feel that if they are to be taxed as a corporation they might as well get other corporation benefits such as limited liability for debts, pension rights and fringes.

The sole owner

The simplest form of doing business, the sole proprietorship, is also the most hazardous. If the business fails, the personal belongings of the owner are subject to attachment by business creditors. The sole owner, therefore, is gambling all he owns that he will succeed and will not incur debts to jeopardize his present assets or future earnings. But neither tax problems nor legal expenses are encountered in setting up a sole proprietorship, and all profits belong to the owner. They are reported on his individual Form 1040.

If he incurs an operating loss, he may claim a deduction. "Salary" payments or other funds he withdraws from the business are not considered business deductions; they are not to be included in other expenses or salaries paid.

Like any other business, the sole owner whose operating loss exceeds income can carry the loss back to the third preceding year, apply it as a deduction, and claim a refund for that year. If there is loss remaining, it can be carried to the second and then the first preceding year. If some balance of loss still remains, it can then be "carried forward" to the next five years as an operating loss deduction. The tax benefits of such a loss can be substantial. If the loss is large, the taxpayer can claim as much as all the income taxes he has paid in the three preceding years. Computing carry-backs and carry-forwards, however, is a complicated matter; it should generally be done in consultation with a professional tax adviser.

To protect businesses from possible insolvency, IRS has provided a special procedure whereby the taxpayer can expect that the refund for operating losses will be paid within ninety days after his application.

The partnership

A partnership does not pay taxes. It files a return on Form 1065, advising the Treasury of each partner's share in the profits, losses, deductions and gains of the joint enterprise.

Each partner pays his tax accordingly on his personal income tax return. The same rules, in general, apply to various business devices which are partnerships but go by other names, such as syndicates, joint ventures, pools, even investment clubs.

The partnership agreement of co-owners in a trade, business or profession may be oral, written, or merely implied by the action or conduct of the members. There is no need to file a "certificate of partnership" in most states.

For tax purposes, profits and losses are divided in accordance with the

agreement of the partners. Profits need not be divided equally, and losses need not be divided in the same ratio as profits, although they will be so divided unless the partners agree to the contrary.

Any "salary," "interest on capital account," or other payment to a partner for his services is really part of the method of dividing the partnership's profits or losses.

Despite this looseness of structure, it is usually desirable to have a partnership agreement in writing prepared with legal advice, because partnerships have their troubles, too. Sometimes these grow out of the death or withdrawal of a partner; sometimes out of the fact that the partnership is a high-risk way of doing business, since the partners are jointly and individually responsible for the debts of the firm.

Partnership problems can arise when one partner wants to drive a Cadillac and the other a Volkswagen. Some partners are willing to travel economy class on business, others insist on first class. Problems between partners can be avoided by a written agreement providing that each partner pays his own automobile, travel, entertainment, promotion and other expenses. Each partner then can deduct his own expenses in arriving at his gross income for tax purposes, and can still take the standard deduction if this is an advantage.

The necessity of raising funds to acquire a deceased partner's interest is a problem for which some partnerships prepare in advance.

Sometimes partnerships buy life insurance payable to the surviving partner or partners to provide funds to purchase the interest of a deceased partner from his estate. Or, the proceeds of the policy may be paid directly to the estate. In either case, the costs of the premiums are not deductible by the partnership and the proceeds of the insurance are not taxable to the deceased partner's heirs.

Partners in a profession or business may be able to take the capital gains tax treatment on the money they receive from a newcomer buying into the partnership.

This is a recent development. Formerly IRS held that when a law firm, a doctor, or other professional took in a new partner, the incoming partner was buying a share in future earnings of the partnership. His payment to the original partner or partners was taxable as ordinary income.

In a more recent decision, IRS has accepted the view that the sum received by the seller may be considered a payment for good will. Payment for good will is a capital gain, taxed at half the ordinary rate.

However, IRS warned that such cases will be carefully scrutinized to make sure that good will, in fact, exists. The guidelines on what standards it may use to appraise "good will" are not yet clear. So before taking this course, talk to your tax adviser.

An investment club is also a partnership and should apply for a taxpayer identification number like any other. The number should be supplied to the club's stockbroker or securities dealer so that dividends or interest earned by the club are duly reported to IRS.

There can be trouble when a club buys stock in the name of an individual member if the broker reports the dividends or interest to IRS under that member's number instead of the number of the partnership. The broker may report the whole club income going to that member's number. The member will report only his share of the gains, and because of the discrepancy the computer will throw out his card for examination.

The Keogh plan

We have spoken of the limited opportunity that exists for a self-employed person to set aside tax-sheltered income for his own retirement. There is one important program, usually called the "Keogh Act plan," or "Keogh plan."

Until the Self-Employed Individuals Retirement Act was enacted in 1962, the federal government gave tax help in retirement planning only to those who worked on someone's payroll.

The Keogh plan, named after its author, Representative Eugene J. Keogh of New York, permits a self-employed person to shield from current taxes as much as 15 percent of his earned net income, up to a maximum of $7,500 a year, if the money is put away in a retirement fund approved by the Treasury.

The money thus set aside earns income, and this income also is tax-free while it is building up. Tax must be paid eventually. But the tax payment does not begin until the taxpayer retires and begins drawing his benefits. For most, these are the low-taxed years. Tax-rate brackets are usually lower, additional exemptions are available to those over sixty-five, the retirement income credit comes into play, and other preferences take effect.

Obviously, much of the money thus tucked away will never be taxed. On that which is taxed, the rates usually will be lower. And in the meantime, the plan represents a sizable discount in your cost of investing in a retirement plan.

For example: You are in the 42 percent tax bracket. You invest the maximum amount in a Keogh plan, $7,500 a year. Your deduction cuts your tax bill by $3,150 a year. Your actual investment in old-age security therefore is $4,350, but your retirement fund is built up by $7,500. The earnings on that fund are tax-free until you withdraw the money in your retirement.

For several years after Representative Keogh's bill became law, comparatively few of the self-employed took advantage of it. The amount which could be set aside untaxed was too small to interest many affluent professional men, and the red tape was plentiful.

Fewer than 10,000 new Keogh plans a year were started up to 1967. In that year, and again in 1969, the rules were liberalized. In the latter year more than 132,000 plans were started. And further liberalization has been enacted. The tax-deductible contribution is now 15 percent, instead of 10 percent, and the maximum in a year is $7,500, instead of $2,500. With each liberalization the number of persons voluntarily setting up their own retirement plans has risen sharply.

The Keogh plan is much more attractive now to accountants, architects, authors, artists, composers, consultants, dentists, engineers, lawyers, ministers, pharmacists, physicians, plumbers, restaurateurs, veterinarians and many others.

The Keogh rules. A sole proprietor or a partner who owns more than 10 percent of his business, known as an "owner-employe," is eligible to make contributions in his own behalf and to take tax deductions for them up to $7,500.

The law permits him to set up a qualified retirement program patterned after the pension, profit-sharing or other type of employe benefit plans usually reserved for corporate employes. The owner must include in the plan all regular employes with three or more years of service, without discrimination in contributions or benefits.

The contribution may be paid into a trust account or custodial account set up in the saver's own name with a bank or stockbroker, or invested in a special type of U.S. securities called "retirement bonds." Or, the funds may be used to buy an annuity contract from a life insurance company.

If employes are covered, the money set aside for them is theirs with no strings attached. If they quit, die, or become disabled, the money goes to them or their heirs; it does not revert to the owner.

Employes may make contributions of their own to the fund, when the plan permits, but they may not take tax deductions for their own contributions. If this arrangement is available to his workers, the owner may make extra contributions for himself, within certain limits. However much he sets aside for his retirement in a year, his tax deduction cannot exceed $7,500. The added contributions make his retirement fund grow faster, while its earnings accumulate tax-free.

The IRS gives advance approval to proposed plans. Owner-employes are not obliged to submit them in advance, but they usually do.

Individuals who are not "owner-employes" or partners and who have no employes to worry about, may also get advance approvals. But these persons may find it easier to join an approved "master plan" that has already been established by a bank, insurance company, trust company, mutual fund or professional firm. You can then choose a master plan tailored to your investment preferences. Under some insurance company master plans, disability or life insurance coverage at group rates may be added, but this is not always available to the employer himself.

There are also approved "prototype" plans worked out by a sponsor organization, such as a professional or trade association. The organization does not take custody of the funds or administer the plan; it merely offers a standardized plan for adoption by any individual who wishes to use it.

Advance approval of a prototype group plan by IRS does not necessarily mean that IRS will approve the personal plan of the individual who enters into such an arrangement. So it is usually recommended that self-employed persons seek IRS approval in any case.

Some Keogh problems. The master and prototype plans have caused a boom in Keogh retirement programs. But there are shortcomings.

The biggest complaint of professional men is that the limit on their contributions is too low. Many established physicians, for example, have incomes substantially exceeding $25,000 a year. In many cases, they want to invest a greater proportion of their net income than 15 percent, or at least a greater total amount than the $7,500 which is the maximum deductible.

The requirement of contributions for employes may also cause difficulties. The cost of their coverage may offset the owner's tax savings. On the other hand, a retirement program has some rewards in employe good will and loyalty, and may be appreciated by employes as much as a pay increase.

Finally, the Keogh plan lacks many elements of the complete retirement benefit packages available to owners and officers in the qualified plans of corporations.

If a businessman is in a position to do so, there are generally tax advantages in incorporating his business and installing the usual pension or profit-sharing plans.

Since enactment of state laws permitting the incorporation of a professional practice in most states, doctors and other professional men may also find it advantageous to incorporate. The self-employed business and professional man who is interested can obtain from his professional tax adviser a judgment on the desirability of incorporating.

However, the liberalization of the Keogh rules which Congress enacted in 1974 could have important effect in delaying the rush of professional men to incorporate their practices for tax reasons.

A minimum tax-deductible contribution of $750 a year, authorized by Congress for any person having that much self-employment income or more, regardless of the 15 percent limit, was in force for 1974 and 1975. The IRS ruled it out for 1976 and after on a legal snag (see page 139), but new legislation was being studied to extend it indefinitely.

The corporation

Ironically, one reason the boss may decide to incorporate is to become an employe—for tax purposes.

Like any other worker on his corporate payroll, he can get tax-sheltered pension, profit-sharing and bonus plans to pile up deferred income along with life insurance, hospitalization, health and accident insurance, lump-sum death benefits and various other valuable fringes whose cost the corporation can deduct.

There are dozens of other reasons, some having nothing to do with taxes. For example, once the corporation is formed and the capital stock is paid for, the stockholders no longer have a personal responsibility for debts of the corporation. And the death of even a major stockholder does not end the corporation; unlike a partnership or sole proprietorship, it lives on.

The great drawback, as mentioned, is that its earnings are twice taxed, once as profits of the corporation and again as dividends paid to stockholders.

This tends to be of less importance to small and growing businesses than to big ones. The salaries taken by the corporate officers, replacing the partnership shares they formerly drew, are deductible as business costs from the corporation's earnings.

Salary payments and the reinvestment of earnings in any typical growing concern could well reduce earnings to the point where the corporation would pay only the 22 percent "normal" corporate rate. The normal rate is paid on earnings up to $25,000; a 26 percent "surtax" is added for all profits above that amount, for a total rate of 48 percent.

(The Tax Reduction Act of 1975 made a temporary revision. For 1975 only, the first $25,000 was made taxable at 20 percent, the next $25,000 at 22 percent, and the rest at 48 percent.)

Unlike partners, who are taxed on their firm's full profit even if some is reinvested in the firm, the owners of a corporation can draw salaries while leaving plowed-back profits in the firm.

Usually, the process of incorporation lets the owner-stockholders split income with the company. They are taxed only on what they actually draw in salaries; this means not only less taxable income but a lower tax bracket rate. Meanwhile, the profit left in the corporation is taxed at the comparatively low "normal" rate.

The IRS levies a stiff penalty tax on a corporation's undistributed profits if the total grows too large. However, the 1975 Tax Reduction Act provided that accumulations up to $150,000 are permissible without penalty, instead of the former $100,000 limit on undistributed profits. This is a permanent change.

But there is considerable flexibility, especially if the firm is a service industry such as an advertising agency, public relations firm, fashion designers, business consultants, or employment agency. The company can keep its undistributed earnings down by delaying the mailing of bills to clients at the year-end, letting its accounts receivable pile up. It can pay bills ahead of due dates. It can pay Christmas bonuses to deserving members of the firm.

It can also provide "key man insurance" for the firm's top officers. This not only would help the firm maintain itself if a key man should die; it also helps to reduce the cash surplus. Many other devices are available.

The premiums on "key man insurance" are paid by the company out of its after-tax earnings; there is no tax deduction. But the value of the policy remains among the company's assets in reserve, while the premium costs help keep the firm's undistributed earnings below the penalty level.

As mentioned earlier, borrowing from a corporation by an officer-stockholder will be watched most closely by IRS. The loan must be a bona fide business transaction; otherwise IRS may decide it is actually a dividend.

An extraordinarily high salary is also a red flag to the IRS. Unjustifiably high payment to a stockholder-executive will cost the company its deduction for the amount that IRS considers to be in excess of a "reasonable" salary.

The corporation should be ready to show that the salary level was fixed well in advance, was not dependent on high profits, is consistent with the value of the services rendered, and is not out of line with the salaries of other executives with comparable duties in similar companies.

If the corporation fails to make such a showing satisfactorily, the salary may be ruled to be a dividend to the officer-shareholder. It will be taxed twice, once as a corporation earning, again as income to the officer-stockholder. But there is a way to avoid that outcome.

The board of directors can adopt a resolution—before setting up the salary schedules—whose wording has been approved by IRS. It says:

"Salary payments made to an officer of the corporation that shall be disallowed in whole or in part as a deductible expense for federal income tax purposes, shall be reimbursed by such officer to the corporation for the full amount of the disallowance. It shall be the duty of the board of directors to enforce payment of each such amount disallowed."

The corporation thus promises to correct any potential infraction of IRS rules on executive salaries before the infraction is even committed.

If you decide to incorporate, discuss with your tax adviser the possible advantages of investing only a minimum of permanent, paid-in capital and lending the corporation any added amounts needed to carry on the business.

The advantages are twofold: the corporation can then deduct interest payments it makes to you for the use of your money; when the corporation starts paying you back, the payments would not be taxable to you because they are the return of a loan.

This requires the preparation of a formal long-term note. And to insure that the IRS does not consider the repayments taxable to you, the amount lent to the company should be carefully matched to the normal business needs of such a corporation. This will require the counsel of a competent tax adviser.

Another good idea, if you are starting your own business or incorporating a going business: discuss with your adviser the advantages of conforming to Section 1244 of the Internal Revenue Code. By meeting some minimum requirements and inserting a few words in your corporate papers, you can establish that if you sell the corporate shares at a profit, you will be taxed at the preferred capital gains rate as on any other stock sale. But if you take a loss on all or part of the stock, a sizable part of the loss may be deducted as ordinary loss against other income.

The important fringes. Finally, the most important single advantage in incorporating a profitable business or profession is the opportunity to install profit-sharing or pension plans, open to the officers and stockholders who are company employes.

To this may be added numerous fringes: life insurance, group hospitalization, health and accident coverage, sick pay plans, death benefits and others described in some detail earlier.

Recent studies indicate that a business or professional man with about $75,000 income can save between $6,000 and $7,000 in taxes in his first year of incorporation by his untaxed contributions toward retirement. This does not include the tax-free accumulation of earnings in the pension trust.

But note: The question whether to incorporate is more than a matter of taxation. No one should ever incorporate a business or dissolve a corporation without careful consultation with a business lawyer. Almost always, there are considerations fully as important as, or more important than, the apparent tax advantages.

Subchapter S corporations

More than 200,000 companies now are organized in the hybrid form called Subchapter S corporations (after the section of the Internal Revenue Code which authorizes them).

The law allows small corporations to elect not to pay the regular corporation income tax, but to be taxed in the partnership pattern. Income of the corporation is treated as if it were the income of the stockholders.

The variety of names given the hybrid Subchapter S form may be confusing. But all of them—pseudo-corporation, tax-option corporation, small business corporation, even "electing small business corporation"—describe the same form of business.

The rapid increase in the number of Subchapter S corporations was slowed by the 1969 Tax Reform Act. One big attraction of Subchapter S was diminished—the opportunity to set up qualified pension and profit-sharing plans as liberal and diverse as those open to stockholders employed by large corporations.

Effective in 1971, the law restricted the deductible contributions made to such retirement plans for "shareholder-employes"—officers or employes owning more than 5 percent of the stock—to the Keogh plan limits, which were then 10 percent of the employe's earned income or $2,500, whichever was less. This discouraged adoption of the Subchapter S corporate form, but only temporarily.

The pension reforms made in 1974 increased the contributions to the new Keogh levels—15 percent of compensation up to $7,500. It appears that a number of firms, including some that had switched to corporate status, are finding the present Keogh limits adequate and are now electing to take the partnership tax pattern with its exemption from the corporate income tax.

Corporations may elect the pseudo-corporation form if they have ten or fewer shareholders (a couple is counted as one stockholder if they own any shares jointly) and meet various other conditions.

There are some deviations from the partnership pattern. For instance, stockholders who are employes of the corporation are still paid a taxable salary as they would be if they were working for any other corporation.

The protections normally afforded stockholders of ordinary corporations, such as protection against liability for debts of the company and the build-up of some surplus in the corporation treasury, exist also for the shareholders of the Subchapter S firm.

Only for tax purposes is the pseudo-corporation a partnership. The stockholders not only get the full income of the firm as if they were receiving partnership shares but also share any losses.

One favored tax-avoidance device of pseudo-corporation stockholders is to make gifts of the stock to their children. Since the children rarely have other income, their share of the profits is taxed at low rates or goes untaxed entirely. The parents can still claim the dependency exemptions for supporting the children because the children do not live on their pseudo-corporation income.

In one instance, three partners looked into the possibility of forming a pseudo-corporation. Their adviser found that there were seven children in the three families. He recommended a Subchapter S corporation. By giving some of the stock to each of the children, the income of roughly $200,000 was split ten ways. Thirteen personal exemptions were possible, including the wives of the owners. Salaries were drawn up by the three officers; the remaining profits were reported on ten separate tax returns. The brothers saved about $17,000 in tax in the first year; the average, over-all tax paid was about 29 percent.

The law bars a "shareholder-employe" from avoiding the new limit on retirement-plan deductions by giving or selling enough stock to children or other family members so that he personally holds less than 5 percent. For retirement plan purposes, his children's stock is considered to be owned by him.

Any contributions made for a shareholder-employe by the company which exceeds the new limits must be reported as gross income by the stockholder. When he retires and starts receiving retirement benefits, he will not be taxed again on that amount.

If he quits the company before he gets back the amount which he thus reported as income, he can claim a tax deduction for this amount in the year he leaves the company.

Several tax-avoidance practices made possible by Subchapter S came under attack during the consideration by Congress of the 1969 law. But the only major change made was to apply the Keogh limits on deductible contributions to the pseudo-corporations' retirement plans, as described above.

However, the Treasury is likely to keep on trying. In view of this uncertainty and the curbs already imposed on the pseudo-corporation form, it is most important for a proprietor or partnership to seek specialized advice before joining the parade into Subchapter S.

Selling a business

Getting good tax advice before selling all or part of a business is almost essential. It is possible for a businessman to wind up with no cash from the sale of his enterprise after paying his taxes. And there is no way to go back and do it over.

Two areas of concern are important in arranging the sale.

First, remember that when you sell an unincorporated business you are actually selling the separate component parts. Each may have a different tax treatment.

Gain on the sale of your inventory and accounts receivable is treated as ordinary income. The sale of good will, furniture, fixtures and equipment, or the rights to your lease on the business property may be treated as a capital gain, with greater tax advantage to you.

With judicious negotiation of the sale contract it is possible to shift some items that might otherwise be regarded as ordinary income into the capital gain treatment. This may complicate the bargaining, since what is to your advantage may be a disadvantage to the buyer.

Sometimes, however, your interests will coincide. The sale of your lease, for instance, can be teated as a capital asset by you, but can be depreciated by the buyer over the remaining life of the lease.

The second consideration is *when* your tax will be paid. Most businesses are sold on terms calling for payment over a period of years. Unless you take steps to qualify for an installment or deferred-payment method, you may be paying tax on a profit you will not collect for years to come.

The answer provided by the tax law is the installment procedure: If you collect 30 percent or less of the selling price in the year of the sale, you may spread the tax over the entire period in which you will be receiving the installments.

The DISC. A tax break for big or small companies that sell overseas is the relatively recent device, the Domestic International Sales Corporation, or DISC. A DISC makes no products; it is simply a selling arm for exports of its parent corporation.

An indefinite postponement of U.S. taxes is allowed on 50 percent of a DISC's income, if 95 percent of its receipts and assets are related to exports. The law provides that DISCs may use their tax-deferred profits to make "producer's loans" to their parent companies.

The DISC device was designed to boost exports and encourage U.S. companies to produce export goods at home instead of setting up subsidiaries overseas. This country's trading partners in Europe and elsewhere have attacked it as an export subsidy which violates international agreements. The DISC benefits were terminated in 1975 for oil, coal, timber, uranium, and other products for which depletion allowances are permitted. There was considerable debate about whether the DISC plan should be repealed entirely.

Controls

Anti-inflation controls caused some bending of the tax rules in 1971-72. Since such controls could be a fact of national life at least intermittently for years to come, businessmen should remain watchful.

For example: A presidential order ruled that any person or business who knowingly paid wages, prices, salaries or rents in excess of the Economic Stabilization Act ceilings might be subject to a criminal penalty of up to $5,000 for each violation.

The Treasury made such violations doubly costly. It said the IRS would disallow any such excess payments as deductions for business or trade expenses. And the disallowed amounts could not be included in computing the cost of goods sold, or of inventory.

Further, under the controls program, the government limited the payment of dividends by corporations. Accordingly, the IRS ruled that a company would not be subject to the penalty tax for unreasonably accumulating surpluses if it failed to pay dividends in excess of those allowed under the anti-inflation controls.

But the immunity was lost, said IRS, when controls were lifted.

. . . Unincorporated businesses which may desire maximum retirement plan benefits should give serious consideration to whether incorporation provides the best alternative, particularly from the overall *financial and tax viewpoint.*

"If incorporation is not feasible or desirable, self-employed retirement plans might be preferable to no retirement plan at all."

Stuart R. Josephs, C.P.A., "Tax Planning Techniques for Individuals," American Institute of Certified Public Accountants, 1971

CHAPTER 14

The
Professional
Corporation

For professional men the biggest tax news in years is the opportunity to incorporate. After decades of resistance in the Treasury, the courts, state legislatures, Congress, and some professional organizations, the legal way was opened by the IRS in 1969 for professionals to conduct their practices in corporate form.

Doctors took the lead in changing their status. They have been "going corporate" by the tens of thousands.

The tax advantages they gain are available also to other professionals, although other groups have been slower to take advantage of them—dentists, lawyers, architects, certified public accountants, engineers, veterinarians, and many others.

The chief attraction for well-to-do physicians is the ability to invest substantial portions of their incomes in tax-sheltered retirement plans, as noted earlier. When a doctor incorporates his practice he becomes an employe of his own company, entitled to all the tax advantages which key employes of corporations can obtain through pension and profit-sharing plans.

Since 1962 professional men have been eligible for retirement benefits under the Keogh plan. These were so limited at first that few professionals bothered to take advantage of them. A 1964 liberalization permitted the self-employed professional to take a tax deduction for amounts he contributed to an approved retirement program up to 10 percent of his income, but not more than $2,500.

That was 100 percent better than the original maximum, but it came nowhere near matching what any non-professional small businessman could gain by incorporating his business. Many feel that even the latest upward revision of Keogh, to 15 percent and $7,500, is insufficient.

As corporations, professionals can claim tax deductions for contributions to profit-sharing plans up to 15 percent of their income; or they can deduct contributions to pension plans with no specified income limit. They also can take advantage of some or all of an attractive array of tax-sheltered insurance and medical protection plans and other fringe benefits.

This is the reasoning behind these tax rules: As the employer, the incorporated professional deducts as a business cost the amount he contributes into a pension or profit-sharing plan for an "employe"—himself—who is not taxed on that money until the funds are actually paid to him.

This usually means upon his retirement or in the case of disability. At such time his income probably will be substantially less, so the payout of this investment will be taxed at lower rates.

In the meantime the funds set aside are earning interest and other income which accumulates tax-free. Best of all, some of the benefits which are finally paid to the retired professional from the pension or profit-sharing fund may be taken in a form that is taxed as a capital gain, subject to rates much lower than the ordinary income rate. (See the section on pensions in the chapter, "The Employe.")

A taxpayer who is considering setting up a self-employed retirement (Keogh) plan will usually be advised by his lawyer or certified public accountant to study carefully the possible financial advantages that he may gain by incorporation.

A number of persuasive arguments favor incorporation, and the self-imposed barriers which formerly deterred some professional groups from endorsing incorporation, in the form of codes of professional ethics, are being rather rapidly dismantled.

The Internal Revenue Service fought the trend toward the professional corporation for years despite repeated defeats in the courts; it finally gave up in 1969, announcing that it would treat a professional person or organization as a corporation if the change was made in compliance with state professional association laws.

All fifty states have adopted enabling laws since 1960 permitting professionals to practice in corporate form, and Congress has bestowed the same privilege on the District of Columbia.

Professionals who convert their individual practices or partnerships into corporations of this special form are required in some states to use special designations.

For example, if Drs. Ready and Willing, who have been partners in a practice, decided to incorporate, they would not necessarily become Ready and Willing, Inc. In Maryland they would be Ready and Willing, P.A.; the letters stand for Professional Association. In Ohio they would be Ready and Willing, L.P.A., (for Limited Professional Association). In Virginia and many other states, they could be Inc. or Ltd., like commercial enterprises.

A more important distinction is made by most of the states. Their laws undertake to maintain continuity with the principal that a professional must always remain personally responsible for his own acts.

So the laws almost always provide that a professional who errs in his professional task is still personally liable to his patient or client. He can be sued for damages, regardless of the fact that he was performing the services as an employe of the corporation. If he were an employe of a business firm or a government agency, only the company or agency might be sued; in the case of the professional corporation, both the corporation and the erring professional could be sued.

This has an advantage over the partnership form of practice for the other doctors or lawyers who are associated with the erring practitioner. Only the corporation itself and the doctor who is actually involved in the professional error can become financially responsible. Under the much more common partnership form of practice, all partners are equally responsible for the professional errors of one partner.

In its August 8, 1969, announcement acknowledging that it would recognize the corporate tax status of professional corporations, the IRS specified that the professional corporations could elect, if they preferred, to be taxed only at the shareholder level—in other words, not as corporations but as if the shareholders were partners. This is the tax pattern for the Subchapter S corporations described in the preceding chapter. Such a corporation does not pay the regular corporate tax; its income is treated as if it were the income of the shareholders.

That arrangement has a major drawback. The incorporated professionals would forego the larger tax benefits available under corporate pension plans. The Keogh-style limitations would apply.

Acting like a corporation

The Treasury has given warning: A professional service corporation must not only be organized as a corporation but *operated* as a corporation. The organizers must hold themselves out to their clients, patients, and the public at large as a corporation.

They are subject to the same searching tax examination that might be applied to any business enterprise. The Treasury plainly means to make sure that "incorporation" means what it says.

A Washington, D.C., certified public accountant who has helped to set up more than forty professional incorporations says: "When a professional partnership consults us about incorporating we always warn them: 'If you are going to be a professional corporation, make up your minds that you are no longer Dr. X, Dr. Y, and Dr. Z. You cannot go into this on the basis of merely sharing facilities and dividing the money as you did in your partnership days.' "

The incorporating professionals must hold regular stockholders' meetings if required to do so by state law. They must comply with all the formalities specified by law for the creation and preservation of a corporate charter.

If more than one professional man is involved, the patients or clients should be given legal notice that the corporation has the right to assign any of its qualified and licensed professionals to serve its patients or clients; some lawyers and certified public accountants insist that newly incorporated clients post a notice to that effect.

The idea here is to avoid violation of the personal holding company rules. The personal holding company was a flourishing tax-avoidance gimmick of the 1930s. Movie stars and athletes "incorporated their talents" by setting up corporations whose stockholders were themselves and their agents or lawyers. The corporations made the contracts, collected the earnings, paid the actors a salary, and held the rest for investment. Other wealthy persons of the period were incorporating their yachts and racing stables.

At the insistence of President Franklin D. Roosevelt, Congress slammed the door on the major abuse—the locking of untaxed income into the corporation for money-making investment instead of distributing it to the actor or the entertainer whose talent had earned it. To force the corporations to distribute the income to the stockholders, a steep penalty levy was imposed on the companies' undistributed funds— 70 percent of such income, plus the regular corporate taxes.

That has taken the fun and profit out of "incorporated talent." The tax remains; it helped to cause state legislatures and professional organizations to move slowly in endorsing the professional corporations, and it still serves as a go-slow signal for those tempted to abuse the new taxsaver. This problem need only concern the sole practitioner who has incorporated and who leaves earnings in his professional corporation after paying salaries, bonus, pension, profits, and other outlays. A corporation formed by two or more professionals is not vulnerable under the personal holding company rules.

There seems to be no doubt that the professional corporation is now solidly established. At least a dozen different federal courts have rejected the arguments of the IRS in opposition to the new-style corporation; some courts called the IRS opposition "discriminatory" and "patently arbitrary."

But Congress still could trim back some of the benefits, if the lawmakers decide incorporation loads the tax dice too lopsidedly in favor of professional men.

That almost happened while the 1969 Tax Reform Act was being drafted. A newspaper story quoted an unnamed California heart specialist who termed incorporation "the hottest thing to happen to us doctors since penicillin."

Then the story showed, in a step-by-step computation, how one wealthy physician with $176,700 annual income could—as an employe of his own corporation—put away $23,950 a year in a tax-sheltered investment plan. As an independent practitioner, he could have invested only the maximum permitted by the Keogh plan, then $2,500.

The difference in the payout, when the doctor retired at sixty-five, was eye-opening. The doctor could have expected a retirement income of $10,400 a year under the Keogh plan. As a corporate retiree, he would get over $99,000 a year!

There was nothing wrong with the arithmetic, but the story had some flaws. First, not one in a hundred doctors made that much money, or could afford to put so much into a retirement plan; and second, anyone who had that much money probably could have found other ways to invest it that were equally or more lucrative.

Nonetheless, the Senate Finance Committee was jarred into an overnight decision; it voted to impose on the professional corporations the Keogh Act limit on deductibility of contributions, then $2,500. There was consternation and a storm of lobbying activity by the professional groups. They prevailed; the amendment was killed.

But the episode was a lesson to professional organizations: what the law giveth, Congress can take away. And Congress still is watchful; if there is widespread abuse of the corporate form, sooner or later some of the benefits surely will be curtailed.

What savings are really possible?

The foregoing illustration, as noted, is less than realistic. What, then, are the real possibilities?

With careful planning, a professional man may establish a retirement program to which his own corporation can contribute as much as one-quarter or one-half of his salary. The income is not taxed to him at the time; it can be set aside for investment, to earn more money tax-free.

There is more: The professional can serve as the trustee of these funds. He can use the set-aside money for almost any type of investment he chooses; there are few restrictions. Yet in case of disaster or disability, the funds can readily become available to him or, in event of his death, to his family.

As the law now stands, if funds are built up in a pension or profit-sharing plan for the benefit of a corporate employe—meaning the incorporated doctor, lawyer or other professional—and if these funds are subsequently paid to a wife, child, or other named beneficiary when the employe dies, the money is not subject to the estate tax.

The exclusion of such pension and profit-sharing fund accumulations from the gross estate, for inheritance tax purposes, is in itself a substantial benefit to the professional who has accumulated considerable wealth. However, this provision has long been under attack in Congress. Some changes may be made; if so, they probably will affect all corporate employes, not just the employes of professional corporations.

Dr. Robert Robertson has a taxable income of $52,000. As a married taxpayer filing a joint return, he pays a federal income tax of $18,060.

Dr. Robertson incorporated. He decided to put $12,000 each year into a retirement plan. That reduced his taxable income to $40,000 and cut his federal income tax to $12,140.

By putting away $12,000 in trust for his own future use, he saved $5,920 in federal income tax while reducing his actual, spendable take-home pay by only $6,080. The simultaneous reduction in his state income tax may have added as much as another $1,000 or $1,200 to his take-home pay, depending on the state of residence.

Now, it can be assumed that a man with $52,000 in taxable income is investing some of that money anyway. Does he do better by incorporating and investing through his own deferred compensation plan?

In all probability, yes. Because he pays no tax on the money that goes into a deferred compensation plan, he can afford to invest almost twice as much. And his investment will earn more, because the income that a pension trust earns each year is not taxed; it all stays in the trust and grows.

How to incorporate

The professional who is thinking of incorporating should consult a tax attorney experienced in forming and serving professional corporations as well as an equally qualified certified public accountant. Since some important benefits of incorporation involve insurance, it is frequently desirable also to obtain the advice of a qualified insurance adviser.

The attorney will explain that the first step is to apply for a corporate charter. This is done by filing with the appropriate state authority the Articles of Incorporation, properly prepared. That document gives the corporation its right to exist, to do business, to issue stock, and to carry on other corporate activities.

The Articles for a professional corporation are likely to differ from those of other corporations in two ways. They will require that the stockholders be licensed professionals, and will provide that shares of the corporation's stock can be transferred only to other licensed professionals.

Another required document—which may be equally important, if more than one professional is involved in the formation and ownership of the corporation—is called a Stockholder's Agreement. This is similar to the partnership agreement mentioned in the preceding chapter. It spells out the rights, duties, and privileges of each stockholder, and it provides for the disposition of stock, payment of wages, and other arrangements to be carried out if a stockholder dies or becomes disabled.

Once the corporation has been formed, the attorney will help prepare the by-laws. These govern the procedures to be followed in the day-to-day practice of the profession. Also usually to be prepared with the attorney's assistance are the following:

• The initial minutes of the corporation, an official record of the proceedings.

• A contract of sale, covering the transfer to the corporation of the assets of the sole proprietor or the partnership which preceded the new entity.

• Ratification of the sale of assets, through the corporate minutes.

• An employment agreement by which the corporation hires its key professionals.

• A notice to suppliers, the landlord, professional associates, and others, notifying them that all future professional affairs will be conducted in corporate form.

• The full and formal notice mentioned previously—that, if more than one professional is associated in the office, the corporation retains the right to designate which one of them serves any client or patient. The reason for this last step—protection from possible penalty tax as a personal holding company—suggests another precaution which should be taken by any sole practitioner who incorporates: He should take care to plan his corporate activity so that on the last day of his fiscal year substantially all profits have been paid out—as salary, bonus, or contributions to the employe benefit plan—so that only a small amount is left in the corporate treasury. Then, if the penalty tax were to be imposed on undistributed earnings, the blow would fall lightly.

With the help of an attorney and a certified public accountant experienced in retirement planning, a "deferred compensation plan" should be chosen. The available plans are the profit-sharing and ordinary pension systems, both described in the chapter, "The Employe," and the money-purchase plan. A money-purchase pension plan is one in which a certain percentage of current income is set aside annually for a future retirement benefit whose amount has not been predetermined.

The advantages of each plan—or of a combination of them—can be judged only after careful evaluation of the earnings, age, and prospective future earnings of each of the professional men who are incorporating. The evaluation must also take into account the number of nurses, clerks, technicians, receptionists, and other employes who will be needed, the potential employe turnover, the employes' wages, and the employes' wages in relation to the salary of the owning professional person. The latter must also make a judgment on how much income he will have left over, after meeting his living expenses, for contributions toward his own retirement income.

When the most desirable plan has been chosen, approval should be sought from the IRS. Having the plan "qualified" helps avoid possible future questions over tax deductions.

Obviously, no single retirement package can be best for all doctors or all lawyers or all architects. Every corporate plan and matching retirement program must be tailored to the needs of the individual or group of individuals joining in the corporation.

Any nurse, technician or other employe of the corporation who works twenty hours or more a week and more than five months a year is considered a full-time employe and must be included in the pension program on a non-discriminatory basis. The pension costs for these lower-income employes usually are relatively small.

However, the expenses of incorporating and qualifying a retirement plan are substantial. They are likely to be in the neighborhood of $2,000 or $2,500. In many areas the fee to the attorney or C.P.A. is usually not paid in full until the IRS has qualified the plan, but this practice may vary.

Should you defer income?

Of the various other advantages of incorporating, the first may be a so-called "permanent deferral" of income taxes, a one-time tax gain which some tax attorneys recommend and some do not.

The professional who incorporates his practice usually assigns his accounts receivable to the corporation, so that the payments collected immediately after the incorporation will go into the corporation. The new corporation thus will have income almost from the day it is born.

Now, assume that a Dr. Smith has formed his own corporation around midyear, by which time he has earned enough money to see him through the rest of the year. He takes no pay from the corporation during the rest of that calendar year. And since he pays taxes on the calendar year basis, his income is much smaller than usual—and so is his income tax.

His new corporation need not operate on a calendar year basis, however. If it were incorporated on September 1, for example, it could end its fiscal year on the last day of any month up to and including the following August. Its first fiscal year need not even be twelve months long. So let us assume that Dr. Smith's new professional corporation ends its fiscal year on January 31, five months after it was incorporated.

Now Dr. Smith is in the same advantageous position as Rogers and Able, the wholesalers who incorporated their small business in our preceding chapter. If he did not draw any salary out of the corporation until January—just before the end of the corporation's fiscal year—there is no tax due on that salary until a year later.

Assume that Dr. Smith is married, filing a joint return. Assume he normally had $64,000 in taxable income each year and paid a tax of $24,060 on that amount. In the year he incorporated he drew no pay after the September 1 incorporation date.

If his patients paid about the same amount month in and month out, his tax on the $42,000 he earned in the first eight months of that year would be $13,100, or $10,960 less than his tax would have been without incorporating and postponing the income.

There would be a proportionate gain on his state income tax. And the advantage can be retained indefinitely, as long as he similarly defers some taxable income from one year into the next.

As noted, some tax attorneys recommend against this "income deferral" device; others take only limited advantage of it. They find no provision in the Tax Code or regulations forbidding it; they simply feel that its widespread use might invite a crackdown. They suspect IRS might seek to classify the income which is left in the corporation (but perhaps available to the doctor if he chooses to take it) as income that is "constructively received." (See the section on "Deferring Income" in the chapter, "The Executive.") If IRS made such an interpretation stand up, the newly incorporated professional might find himself with tax problems that outweighed his one-time gain in deferring the income.

Advantages if you incorporate

There are cons as well as pros to the question whether a professional should incorporate. The cons will be discussed shortly; meantime, here is a summary check list of some of the quite persuasive pros. Some were mentioned earlier in this chapter, some not; all are in addition to the basic benefits attainable through tax-sheltered pension or profit-sharing plans.

Estate tax-free. As the law now reads, the value of the professional's share in his corporation's qualified pension or profit-sharing trust, when payable as a death benefit to a named beneficiary, is not included in the professional's gross estate; it is not subject to the estate tax.

Sick pay exclusion. Like other employes, the professional can deduct as a sick pay exclusion up to $100 a week received as salary from his corporation during a period of illness, after the initial thirty-day period. The rules for sick pay are discussed in the chapter, "Some ABCs of Income Tax."

$5,000 death benefit. At the professional's death, a death benefit payment of up to $5,000 may be excluded from taxable income by the widow, child or other beneficiary, and the corporation may take a deduction for the amount of the benefit. This type of benefit, when provided under a contract with the corporation that makes it payable solely by

reason of the death of the employed professional, may be treated for tax purposes as if it were part of the employe's investment in his pension.

Medical payment plan. The corporation may adopt a Medical Expense Reimbursement plan, providing a substantial reduction for the professional in his cost of routine medical care. The plan gives the corporation a tax deduction for the medical, dental, and hospitalization insurance bill for the professional and his family, without regard to the regular 3 percent limitation on itemized medical deductions. This fringe was discussed in the section, "Health insurance plans" in the chapter, "The Executive." Since many professionals are in relatively high income brackets, the 3 percent limitation ordinarily bars them from claiming medical expenses (except for half the first $300 of hospitalization insurance) among their itemized deductions. The medical expense plan must be carefully prepared and drawn, and must provide some benefits to some other employe or employes.

Dividend exclusion. The corporation may exclude from its income, for corporate income tax purposes, 85 percent of the income it receives from investments in other domestic corporations. This is a privilege of corporations generally.

Voluntary contributions to pension plans. The professional may voluntarily contribute up to 10 percent of his after-tax earnings as additional payments into the corporation's pension trust in addition to the regular contributions made by the corporation. The earnings of these contributions in the pension trust are not taxed.

Limited liability. Already mentioned as a non-tax benefit is the limitation on legal liability of the incorporated professional. The professional practicing in corporate form is protected personally from financial responsibility in a lawsuit resulting from an error made by an associate in the corporation.

Fiscal year. Because the tax year of the professional man and the fiscal year of his corporation may differ, he may be able to defer taxes on some income and some tax liability from the year in which he incorporates, as described in the preceding section.

Continuity of corporate life. By forming a corporation the professional can perpetuate his practice beyond his own lifetime. This is possible through a stockholders' agreement, in the case of a corporation with two or more professionals, or through the hiring of other professionals if the deceased professional was a sole practitioner.

$50,000 group life insurance. The sole proprietor or partner, not being an employe, cannot take advantage of the group life insurance coverage that is available to most employes. The incorporated professional can do so; the cost of up to $50,000 of group term life insurance coverage is deductible by his corporation; the corporation's outlay in his behalf is not taxable income to him.

Insuring with before-tax dollars. The corporation's pension or profit-sharing trust may, with careful planning, be able to purchase life insurance protection on the life of the incorporated professional. The professional thus may be relieved of the cost of life insurance he is paying for out of his after-tax income. The corporation could deduct the cost; and for a professional in the 50 percent tax bracket this could mean saving half the cost of some or all of his life insurance protection. This is personal insurance protection, apart from the group coverage mentioned above.

Accumulation of retained earnings. When the corporation is formed by two or more professionals, the earnings of the corporation above the amounts paid out in salary and fringe benefits may be retained by the corporation. There they will be taxed at the normal corporate rate of 22 percent—which is usually much lower than the individual income tax rate paid by the professionals. Up to $150,000 of earnings may be accumulated on this basis if there are two or more professionals. This can be most useful, for instance, to doctors who must buy and replace expensive equipment.

Obviously, the tax consequence is only one of a number of considerations in the decision whether or not to incorporate.

Many doctors in recent years have found group practice appealing for other reasons. Business matters can be arranged more efficiently and economically, better equipment can be acquired, holidays and vacations can be arranged without inconveniencing patients.

The arguments against

The drawbacks to incorporation seem to have had more deterrent effect on lawyers, accountants, engineers, and other professionals than on doctors.

Lawyers have seemed reluctant to abandon the ancient partnership tradition of their craft. The partnership idea seems to help the image of dignity, respectability, and stability. And lawyers may be more cautious about the possible legal or legislative traps that may still lie ahead for the new-style corporations.

Also, some professional organizations have given their members less encouragement than did the American Medical Association. The AMA Newsletter said in 1969: "A major plus is that corporate practice offers physicians a greater potential economic benefit than any other single element in the financial environment." In New York and elsewhere the state medical societies were the front-line fighters in the struggle to get legislatures to pass enabling laws.

But many doctors and other professionals find incorporation distasteful despite tax-sheltered pensions, profit-sharing, and fringes. These are among the objections named by some:

  • Patients or clients may object to being served by a corporation. Incorporated physicians scoff at the idea; patients usually don't know or care, they say.

• The new corporations will have to pay the taxes and fees imposed under state income, corporation, and franchise tax laws.

• The initial cost in legal and other fees is substantial, and after incorporating there probably would be higher overhead costs of bookkeeping and accounting.

• The professional must sacrifice some take-home pay if he is going to take full advantage of the tax shelter by diverting a substantial slice of his income into the corporation's pension or profit-sharing trusts. A doctor with a growing family, a big mortgage and children to send to college, and with heavy insurance or investment commitments made before he incorporated, may find it hard to meet the new pension plan payment schedule. A doctor with a going investment program might have to curtail that program, without absolute assurance that the long-run financial outcome would be better.

• The historic hostility of IRS to professional corporations suggests that the revenue agents will be giving more constant and intensive scrutiny to professional corporations than to individual practitioners—and that the Treasury will be supporting proposals to amend the tax laws to make incorporation less profitable.

• There would be difficulties in breaking up a corporation of two or more professionals who decided to split up and go their separate ways. The co-owners would have difficulties in disposing of the funds accumulated in the pension trust, and there might be a tax liability for the individuals ending their corporate employment. The funds which accumulated tax-free in the corporate pension trust would become taxable when paid out to the individual practitioners.

• If a professional returns to individual private practice upon the liquidation of the corporation, it is possible that IRS might contend he received some "good will" value from his corporate connection—and that this good will has a monetary value that is taxable as income. The chance that such a tax actually will be levied seems remote, but at least the possibility of litigation exists.

• Wage-price control brought an unforeseen problem to those in the allied medical professions. The salary ceilings made it difficult for an incorporated physician to increase the salary paid him by his corporation, no matter how rapidly his practice was growing. Yet if he failed to increase his own pay, the earnings piled up in the corporation. Such accumulations could make the corporation subject to the steep penalty rates of the personal holding company tax. The doctor faced a dilemma: If his corporation obeyed the salary guidelines, its taxes soared; if it did not, the doctor was in violation of the wage-price rules.

It is obvious that problems and pitfalls remain. But the professional corporation is here to stay, and by now a good number of tax attorneys and certified public accountants have had ample experience in helping professional men set up the new kind of shop. Most of the headaches, apparently, can be avoided by the professional who spends the time, money and effort needed to obtain full information and qualified guidance.

To tax and to please,
no more than to love and be wise,
is not given to men.

Edmund Burke, British statesman, 1729-97

CHAPTER 15

The
Farmer

The farmer gets some tax advantages not granted to salaried or hourly-paid employes, or even to other self-employed persons. The unique tax benefits were meant for dirt farmers, to simplify their bookkeeping. But they are equally available to high-bracket taxpayers whose chief aim, frequently, is to cultivate losses.

Many a "hobby farmer" or "gentleman farmer" may relish the joys of rural life, but may also wish to cut his tax costs while doing so.

An individual with high income—say, a corporation executive, self-employed businessman, well-to-do doctor or lawyer—may buy a farm with the expectation of rebuilding, re-equipping and restocking a rundown property. He buys machinery for cultivating the soil and livestock for breeding. Under the liberal tax rules for farmers, he can deduct many of the heavy outlays from current taxes in full, instead of simply taking depreciation on such investments like other taxpayers. Thus, he shows losses that reduce the tax on his income from business or profession.

When the farm has been rebuilt into a healthy operation, he can sell at a substantial profit, which is taxed at the favorable rate provided for a capital gain.

Even if no such ambitious program of restoration is undertaken, a farm is generally a good investment. Prices of farmland have been increasing at the rate of 6 to 7 percent a year for more than a decade; and they are likely to continue rising at an even faster rate.

There is thus an opportunity to hedge against inflation and, when the time comes to dispose of an appreciated property, to benefit from the capital gains tax treatment.

Ordinarily the farm owner's outlays on buildings, fixtures, trucks and machinery must be capitalized—that is, treated as an investment on which depreciation is claimed over the span of years which represents the useful life of the property. But the farmer is permitted to take current deduction for such items as soil and water conservation outlays, feeds, supplies, land-clearing, fertilizer and lime. The Appendix contains a list of deductible farm costs.

It is wise not to clear more land at one time than is needed. There is a limit on the land-clearing outlay which may be deducted as current expenses in any one year. The farmer can choose the deduction, rather than taking depreciation, by attaching a statement to his return describing the land-clearing costs and showing his "taxable income derived from farming."

The ceiling on the deduction is 25 percent of the taxable income derived from farming, up to $5,000. The 25 percent ceiling increases in dollar amount, of course, as your income from farming goes up from year to year. By waiting until farm earnings are higher, you can deduct larger outlays for clearing, up to the $5,000 flat limitation. It is not necessary to adhere to this method year after year. You can capitalize the costs in any year when you do not need the deduction to offset income.

In the development stage, or "preproduction" period, while the farm is being built up, the farmer has some other helpful choices. Many ordinary and necessary expenses, including certain taxes, irrigation water, orchard-keeping costs, interest, spraying, cultivation and repairs, may be either capitalized or "expensed." To "expense" an outlay is to claim it as a deduction for the year in which it occurs.

When the farm reaches its productive stage this option is lost; these expenses cannot be capitalized but must be claimed as deductions.

"Expensing" obviously would suit a short-time "hobby farmer," who could use the deductions to offset heavily taxed income from other sources. But if you are in the business in earnest, and are not just sheltering outside income, you might want to take the slower write-off through depreciation. Otherwise you could waste your deductions by using them when you have no income, or not enough to be offset.

Soil and water conservation costs are deductible up to 25 percent of gross income from farming; there is no $5,000 ceiling or other arbitrary limit. This includes earth moving, ditches, grading, dams, channels, contour terracing, ponds, dikes, levees and windbreaks.

Cattle can be an important tax shelter because they are treated as capital assets; the profit on their sale is taxed as a capital gain if they have been held at least twelve months. Investing in a dairy herd has become a rather popular tax shelter; usually a hired manager takes care of the cattle and handles the sale.

Investors may also use horses, oxen or mules for shelters, because the rule applies to any animals raised for breeding, draft or dairy purposes. In each case the profit from the sale qualifies as a capital gain. But if tax considerations seem to be the sole motive, IRS may challenge this tax treatment after at least twelve months.

The IRS also frowns on farming ventures which show losses year after year. It may crack down on such operations as "hobby farming." The law requires that there must be a bona fide intent to make a profit, and IRS insists there be "reasonable expectation" of a profit. But it recognizes that many new businesses take some years to graduate from red ink into black.

Breeding and dairy animals

A farmer's income from the sale of breeding, draft or dairy animals qualifies for the lower-taxed capital gains treatment. In effect, the taxpayer need report no taxable farm income from the sale of such animals until the price he receives for them *is more than twice the costs incurred in raising them.*

For example, one farmer put $100 into raising a breeding cow which he later sold for $200. He shows the income on his tax return as a long-term capital gain. But he pays no tax on his profit because the $200 sales price is treated as a long-term capital gain; only half the cash he received, or $100, is recognized as taxable income. And this $100 is offset by the $100 deduction he claimed for the expenses of raising the breeding cow. He has collected $100 tax free.

If the sales price were less than $200, the farmer would have a tax loss. If, for instance, he sold the cow for $120 and qualified for capital gain treatment, he would report only half that amount, $60. He thus has made a sale in which he gained no taxable income. He shows a "farm loss" of $100 because that is the money that he put into raising the animal. He has a capital gain of $60. Combined, these two items result in a $40 loss.

If the taxpayer has other income, his "farm loss" may be used to reduce his taxes on the other income. To oversimplify, if the farmer in the foregoing example had a nonfarm salary of $100, the $100 of "farm loss" on the cow could be deducted from his salary. It would reduce his income to zero. In other words, instead of having a taxable income of $220—made up of $120 from selling the cow and $100 of salary—his taxable income would be only $60, the one-half of the capital gain which he is required to report.

The 1969 crackdown

For many years the liberal tax treatment of farm losses raised questions of tax equity. One was the charge that the system brought unfair competition to those farmers whose farming income was their primary source of livelihood.

Underlying this charge were the abuses of the special farm rules, usually by those who had "tax losses" which were not genuine economic losses as well as sizable nonfarm income against which to offset those losses.

The farm-tax benefits are considerably smaller for those with only farm investment to live on. So the high-bracket, nonfarm taxpayers with sideline farm investments enjoy a competitive advantage.

They quite conceivably may bid up the price of farmland. They compete in the market place with those who must have profits to survive as farm operators, yet they may be happier if they lose money than if they make it. They would be content to take a lower price for their crops than the neighbors who farm for a living. The Treasury (like some Congressmen) was irritated by the growing number of investment advisers who advertised their willingness to arrange farm tax-loss plans.

In 1969, Congress undertook to discourage "tax farming" by setting new boundaries on farming losses. But, not wishing to penalize legitimate farmers in the process, it did not crack down very hard.

The tightening of tax rules for farmers in 1969 resulted partly from the Treasury's complaints about "the liberal deviations from good accounting practices" that were permitted for farm operations.

The Treasury told Congress that the tax rules for farming not only

support money-losing operations, which were more than covered by tax savings, "but also fail to tax even profitable farms."

The Treasury supplied an example of exactly how it is done. It can still be done, even after the reform law, though the new capital gains rate and other revisions would make the tax profits somewhat smaller.

This is a simplified version of the Treasury's example:

A farm operator who was in the 70 percent tax bracket incurred expenses of $200,000 in raising a breeding herd. For this he claimed current deductions from his overall income from all sources. This resulted in a $140,000 saving on his total tax bill (70 percent of $200,000).

He sold the herd for $220,000. On his income tax return this was all profit; he had claimed his $200,000 in costs as current deductions, so the entire proceeds of the sale was treated as a capital gain. The tax came to 25 percent of the gain, or $55,000.

The farmer thus paid less tax on his profit from sale of the herd than he had saved in tax by deducting his expenses in raising the herd. His tax was $55,000, his deduction was $140,000, his "tax profit" thus was $85,000. On top of this he pocketed his actual $20,000 profit on the herd (the $220,000 sales price less his $200,000 in actual costs). His combined sales profit and tax savings were $105,000.

The Treasury's report added: "In the typical situation, the taxpayer will then begin the entire cycle again by starting a new breeding herd which is later sold at capital gains rates."

It said that similar advantages are available to developers of such ventures as citrus groves, fruit orchards and vineyards.

Though the 1969 Tax Reform Act did not interfere, generally speak-

ing, with the deduction of farm losses, it provided a way for the Treasury to "recapture" lost revenue when a farmer ultimately sells his assets and reports his capital gains. These are among the major farm provisions of the 1969 law:

• *The EDA.* The total amount of farm losses can continue to be deducted, but taxpayers who have an adjusted gross income of more than $50,000 from nonfarm sources must comply with a special limitation. They are required to keep a record of farm losses which exceed $25,000 each year.

The excess loss goes into this EDA or "Excess Deductions Account." Then, if the farmer sells any farm property which would normally give him a capital gain, like a breeding bull or orchard, the profit on that sale is taxed as ordinary income up to the amount which is in the EDA.

The EDA account goes on from one year to the next. If the owner reports a net farming profit in any year, the EDA is reduced by that much. The EDA account is reduced, also, to the extent that the balance in the account in any year is used to offset that year's gains on the sale of breeding livestock or other farm property.

This, for example, is how the account would be kept by Will Morgan, an executive with an $80,000 salary from his advertising agency. He owns a cattle farm, which shows this record for 1970 and subsequent years through 1975.

EDA
account
balance

1970

The farm's ordinary deductions are $45,000 greater than its ordinary income; the net loss of $45,000 exceeds the $25,000 limit by $20,000. This goes into the EDA.....$20,000

1971

The farm earns $3,000 of ordinary income. It is subtracted from the EDA account, leaving a balance of 17,000

1972

The farm earns $1,500 of ordinary income. Also, Morgan sells breeding livestock which he has held more than two years. His profit of $12,000 normally would be a capital gain but there is more than that in his EDA account. So it is taxed as ordinary income; the EDA balance is reduced by the $12,000 plus the $1,500 ordinary farm income, or $13,500. The balance 3,500

1973

The ordinary farm loss is $7,000.
This does not affect the EDA because it is
less than $25,000. The EDA balance
remains at   3,500

1974

The farm's ordinary income matches
expenses. Morgan sells a breeding mare,
making what normally would be a capital
gain of $2,200. But because the EDA balance
is larger, it must be reported as ordinary
income. The EDA is reduced by the $2,200,
leaving a balance of $1,300

1975

The farm shows ordinary income of $1,300.
That coincides with the EDA balance.
Morgan's next breeding livestock profit can
be a capital gain because the EDA shows....   0

Individuals with nonfarm income less than $50,000 or with farm losses smaller than $25,000 are not affected. These figures drop to $25,000 and $12,500 respectively for a married individual if his spouse also has non-farm adjusted gross income and they file separate returns.

For corporations operating on a cash basis and for trusts, the conversion of capital gains into ordinary income applies for every dollar by which the ordinary farm deductions exceed ordinary farm income. For a "pseudo-corporation" or "Subchapter S" corporation the rules for individuals apply with some exceptions.

• *Holding period for livestock.* Formerly the law allowed a gain on the sale of livestock held for breeding, draft or dairy purposes to be treated as a capital gain if the animal had been held by the taxpayer for one year or longer.

The Treasury thought this period was not enough to decide whether the taxpayer was holding the animal for breeding or simply for sale in the ordinary course of business. Congress changed the provision so that horses and cattle must be held at least two years to qualify for capital gains treatment. Other livestock remains subject to the one-year holding period.

• *Hobby losses.* To discourage "hobby farms" and other businesses which were operated mainly to produce losses that could be deducted from other income, the law formerly set a $50,000-a-year limit on the amount of losses from an individual's business which he could use to offset his other income. The limitation, however, was effective only if the farming losses exceeded $50,000 a year for five consecutive years.

The 1969 Tax Reform Act discarded that rule and substituted a tougher one. It disallows any deductions for losses from activities which the taxpayer is "not engaged in for profit." If a profit is shown in two of five years, IRS would presume that the activity is for profit. If this standard of profitability is not met, the IRS would conclude that the farming enterprise is a hobby and not entitled to the loss privileges given to farmers.

In the case of the breeding, training, showing, or racing of horses, the taxpayer must show profit in two out of seven years to qualify for loss privileges.

There are things you can do to prove that your farm is a farm and not a hobby. You should be able to show that:

• You have substantial receipts from sales and your losses are diminishing.

• You are not using the farm only for vacations and weekends, but are giving it much personal attention.

• Your employes are doing productive work, not domestic duties.

• Your projections of income and outgo indicate a reasonable expectation of profit.

• You have taken steps to cut expenses and consulted the Agriculture Department and other experts to improve productiviity, cut costs, shift from money-losing crops to income-producing lines.

• You have set up a detailed and businesslike system of accounting.

• You have a record of successful farm operation.

Recapture of livestock depreciation. Farmers, as noted, may take depreciation on livestock as if the animals were buildings or machines. But in the case of buildings or machines used in any ordinary business, the Treasury would recover, or "recapture," any excess depreciation when the property was sold and a capital gain reported.

The special rules for farming resulted in unusual tax benefits because depreciation was deducted from ordinary income taxed at regular rates, yet the gain on the sale of livestock was taxed at the lower capital gains rate. In effect, this was a simple way to convert ordinary income into capital gains; the device made livestock a very popular tax shelter.

The 1969 law required that gain on the sale of livestock should be treated as ordinary income up to the amount of the full value of the previous deductions for depreciation.

Conservation expenses. Formerly the law allowed current deductions for some soil and water conservation expenses and land-clearing outlays, and did not provide for the "recapture" of any deductions when the land was sold.

The result was another motivation for the high-income taxpayer to make short-term investments in farming land. He would buy a farm, invest in ponds, grading and terracing to gain current deductions from his nonfarm income, and then get a capital gains tax bargain when the land was sold.

Congress applied the "recapture" technique to this device also. Gains from the sale of farmland are treated as ordinary income, rather than as capital gain, up to the value of deductions allowed for such conservation expenditures made after December 31, 1969.

Citrus groves. Until the 1969 changes, once citrus trees were planted, all expenses of spraying, cultivating, fertilizing and irrigating the groves were deductible when incurred, even though the groves would not come into production for five to seven years.

So groves were widely advertised as tax shelters for nonfarm investors. They could charge off the costs of developing citrus groves as current expenses, then take capital gains treatment on the proceeds when the grove property was sold.

The new law says outlays for buying, planting, cultivating, maintaining or developing a citrus grove must be capitalized if they are incurred within four years after the grove is planted.

Buying a farm

In buying a farm and setting up your accounts, you will want to show how much of the overall cost is attributable to the various types of assets you have acquired.

Try to allocate as much of the purchase price as possible:

First, to assets which you will hold for sale. These include newly purchased crops and livestock. If your receipts from subsequent sales of the crops and animals fall short of the costs shown in acquiring them, you will have immediate losses to write off. The tax savings will help see you through the period of high starting-up costs.

Second, to assets which are depreciable over short useful lives, like fences, sheds, tools and equipment. These will give you rapid write-offs against income.

Third, to depreciable assets of longer useful life, like buildings and barns.

Finally, to the land itself. Since the land can never depreciate in value, it cannot provide depreciation allowances.

The greater the value you can attribute to assets which provide depreciation deductions, the smaller your net profit—and therefore your taxable income—will be.

Development expenses. Your first tax return as a farmer will require you to decide how to treat your development expenses for tax purposes. These expenses include fertilizer, water, land taxes, interest, cultivating and spraying and controlling undergrowth.

You may deduct some, thus writing off the costs in full in the year when the expenses occurred. You may decide to capitalize others, charging off a portion of the cost each year.

Usually the choice is to take current deductions for greater tax savings. But that is not sensible as long as you are running up more expenses than receipts. By choosing to capitalize, taking depreciation over a period of years, you can avoid wasting deductions at a time when there is no income, or not enough to match all your offsetting expenses.

The same choices exist for the costs of clearing trees, dynamiting stumps and removing boulders, and for the expenses of leveling, grading, contouring land and installing drainage ditches.

Accounting methods. The Treasury prescribes no particular form of accounting or record keeping. Its very useful booklet, "Farmer's Tax Guide," IRS Publication 225, available free from the nearest Internal Revenue office, contains examples of record-keeping systems.

But the text emphasizes that the illustrations "should not be looked upon as a recommendation that your records be kept on forms identical to these. They are used only to show the simple form in which farm records can be kept."

You may use any of these accounting methods: cash basis; accrual basis; crop method; or "hybrid" method.

Any other taxpayer engaged in buying or producing merchandise, and therefore dealing with inventories, must use the accrual method. The accrual-basis taxpayer deducts his expenses when he incurs them, not when he pays them; and he reports income when he sends out the bills, not when he receives payment. This requirement does not apply to farmers.

Most farmers use the cash method. It affords greater flexibility, and, of course, it defers the reporting of income until the cash is actually in hand.

Perhaps more importantly, farmers must be on a cash basis in order to deduct currently the costs of raising breeding and dairy livestock. Accrual-basis farmers must capitalize the costs.

Some farmers use the "hybrid" accounting method, a combination of cash and accrual methods. This is acceptable to the Treasury if income is shown clearly and the taxpayer remains consistent in method from year to year.

By applying to the Treasury Department for permission, farmers may elect the "crop method" if they have crops requiring more than twelve months between planting and harvest time. The cost of growing the crop is deducted when the crop is sold. Income and expenses thus are matched.

You may adopt the "crop method" for one crop and not for others. But if you do this, you must keep separate records for each crop, and show how expenses are allocated to each.

If a farmer wants to shift income into the current year, he can take a crop loan from the Commodity Credit Corporation and elect to report the proceeds of the loan as income. (But once he does so, all future CCC loans must be similarly treated, unless IRS consents to a change of method.)

Usually the income is reported when the crop is sold, the CCC loan repaid, and the transaction closed. When the loan is repaid in the same year, it is not reported as income.

Selling a farm

When offering a farm for sale, try to allocate as much of the sales price to capital assets as you can in drawing up the purchase agreement. To the greatest reasonable extent, break down the total sales price of the farm into so much for capital assets like buildings and machinery, so much for land and so much for the value of the farmhouse itself.

The reason for this is that profit from the sale of the capital assets is taxed at the favorable capital gains rate.

If the sales agreement sets forth the value of the farmhouse at a figure which represents a gain over the original purchase price (plus the cost of any capital improvements you put into the farmhouse during your ownership), you get one of the benefits which is available to all householders. You have the right to defer reporting of gain on the sale, to the extent that you reinvest the proceeds in a new residence.

If you are sixty-five or over and take a gain on the sale of the farm residence, you have the additional benefits available to persons sixty-five and over in selling residential property.

If there is an unharvested crop, or fruit on the trees, sell the crop with the land and raise the asking price accordingly. The entire package is treated as a capital gain; the costs of growing the crop are included as part of the cost of the property sold.

If a big and profitable harvest is expected, you may want to consider the advisability of timing the sale to occur just before harvest. Instead of making an ordinary gain on sales of the crops you would take a capital gain, taxable at the much lower rate.

But if it has been a poor crop year, and you are certain to have a loss on the harvest—even though realizing a gain on the overall sale of the farm—this probably would be the advisable course:

Delay the sale until after the harvest. This will give you ordinary loss on the crops and capital gain treatment on the remaining property. Or, as an alternative, sell the land and the crops to two different buyers. In either case you have a winning combination: full deduction on the loss, and taxes to be paid on only half of the gain.

If you expect to buy a larger farm, consider making an exchange of properties. This will avoid tax liability on any gain you would realize on the sale of the old farm.

With all the experts gathered here this evening I doubt that a quarter of them could readily calculate the taxable portion of the pension received by a widow of an employe under a contributory pension plan—and I will include myself among them.

Edwin S. Cohen, Assistant Secretary
of the Treasury for Tax Policy, March 18, 1970

CHAPTER 16

The Retired Taxpayer

The federal income tax laws apply generally to taxpayers regardless of age, but there are a good many concessions to taxpayers sixty-five or over. Family members who support parents and other older persons may also receive special tax privileges, in some cases.

The 1969 Tax Reform Act added substantially to the benefits for older persons. Congress increased the amount of income which can go untaxed and unreported. Millions of lower-income taxpayers aged sixty-five and over no longer need file returns at all.

If both husband and wife are sixty-five or older, a couple is relieved of filing unless their joint income tops $4,300 (or, for 1975 only, $4,900). If their combined income falls short of that total, it does not matter how much either receives. The husband could have all the income and the wife none, for instance.

The higher limits result partly from the low income allowance, defined in the chapter on "Some ABCs of Income Tax," and partly from increased personal exemptions. Every taxpayer automatically gains one more personal exemption of $750 upon reaching age sixty-five. A couple gains two exemptions, for a total of $3,000, plus the low income allowance.

The taxpayer can skip all this arithmetic if his income is under $15,000. He can use the tax tables that come with Form 1040 and Short Form 1040A; the low income allowance, the standard deduction, and the exemptions are built into the tables.

The following table shows the filing requirements for taxpayers sixty-five and older. U.S. citizens and residents in that age group with gross incomes of $750 or more are required to file an income tax return *unless they fall into one of the categories listed.* Persons with incomes below these levels are *not* required to file, but *may do so* if necessary to claim a refund.

Taxpayers who are:	Need not file if income is below:	
	1974, 1976 and after	1975 only
Single, 65 or over	$2,800	$3,100
Married, filing jointly, one spouse 65 or over	3,550	4,150
Married, filing jointly, both 65 or over	4,300	4,900
Single, could be claimed as dependent by another taxpayer, and shows dividend or interest or other types of unearned income on own return	750	750

The Short Form 1040A may be used by any taxpayer, regardless of the amount of his income, if all the income is from wages, salaries, tips, etc., and includes not more than $200 in dividends or $200 in interest income, and if the taxpayer does not itemize his deductions.

Note: For purposes of tax computation, the taxpayer is considered to be sixty-five on the day before his sixty-fifth birthday. Taxpayers whose birthday falls on January 1 can enjoy the benefits of the various sixty-five-and-over rules for the year preceding their sixty-fifth birthday.

Social Security

The planning of most taxpayers for their retirement years begins with Social Security. Social Security benefits are not taxable.

Furthermore, pension payments you receive from a former employer do not alter your right to collect Social Security benefits. Neither does an annuity you bought for yourself, or any holdings of stocks or bonds, or the savings you may have accumulated in the bank.

You have contributed to the Social Security trust fund during your working years; now you are entitled to receive its benefits. But, if you go on working—and earning above certain income limits in self-employment or a job—your Social Security benefits will be reduced, possibly eliminated.

The limits on such earnings have been increased periodically with changes in the Social Security law. They are likely to be changed again.

There is substantial support in Congress for an increase in the amount of income that may be earned without curtailing the Social Security benefits. So it would be well to check with your local Social Security office on the amount of earnings currently permitted.

If you are over seventy-two, your earnings—regardless of amount—do not diminish your Social Security benefits.

Your savings and investments

Some preretirement planning should be done before your sixty-fifth birthday arrives in connection with your debts and investments.

It is a good idea to repay installment loans or other debts before retirement to take advantage of the interest deductions. The deductions may not be needed after retirement when you have a double exemption and other tax advantages.

Paying off a mortgage before retirement may or may not be advantageous. The penalty you may have to pay for closing out the mortgage ahead of schedule is deductible as interest. And the deductions you can claim for monthly interest payments on the mortgage may be less important after retirement.

However, an old mortgage with an interest rate under 5 or 6 percent is not to be abandoned lightly. It can be an attractive feature to an interested buyer when you are ready to sell your home. The cash required to retire it might be more usefully invested in certificates of deposit or other savings paying that much interest, or more.

If you have Series E U.S. Savings Bonds—and if, like most taxpayers, you have not been paying tax year by year on the interest as it accrued —it probably is wise not to cash them before retirement. Your gain will be taxed at a lower rate after you retire.

Or, you might defer the tax liability for another ten years by exchanging them for H bonds, which come in larger denominations and pay interest by check each month. Similarly, stocks and mutual fund holdings can be exchanged for annuities or other types of investment providing a deferral of tax liability, such as the retirement programs set up by many mutual funds.

A good many kinds of income which are typically received in retirement are tax-exempt, in addition to your Social Security or Railroad Retirement payments. The list includes:

• Veterans' pensions and disability payments and other compensation received by a veteran or his family, except retirement pay based on age or service.

• Life insurance proceeds; except that, if paid in installments, the interest portion of the payments is taxable above the widow's or widower's exclusion of $1,000 a year.

• Gifts and inheritances.

• Interest on state, municipal and turnpike authority bonds.

• Death benefits up to an amount of $5,000 paid by an employer to the family or other beneficiaries of a deceased employe.

• Workmen's compensation benefits for sickness or injury, and unemployment insurance benefits.

Your pension

If your pension starts upon retirement, the monthly payments come when your taxable income (and with it your tax rate) is presumably at its lowest level and your personal exemptions at their highest.

But perhaps as you approach the retirement date you realize you will still have too much taxable income for the first few years after retirement. Can some of it be deferred again? Yes, it can.

The conditions that you agreed to in your pension or deferred-income arrangement with your employer probably provided that you begin receiving benefits in the year of retirement. You may now make a "second election" which is recognized by the IRS.

You can wait until just before retirement—when you will know better your actual income and investments—to fix the number of installments, their starting time, and their amounts.

Under a "second election," a company executive or other retiree who finds he has enough income from other sources for his first year of retirement can elect to have his deferred compensation payments start in the second, third or even later years.

A substantial tax-saving opportunity is possible if you can arrange with your company to take a lump-sum payment from the retirement fund instead of the monthly payments usually specified in qualified pension and profit-sharing plans. Most companies will pay the accumulated cash value, up to the time of retirement, in a lump sum if the retiring employe requests it.

The tax advantage, if all the money due you is paid within a single taxable year, is that you can report the entire lump-sum settlement as a capital gain, taxed at the preferential rate. Because of the smaller tax under the capital gains treatment, you will come out wth substantially more cash. It is yours to invest as you choose.

This device is frequently used by retiring corporation executives who feel that they are as well qualified to manage the investment of their accumulated deferred income as the trustees of a pension plan.

Three-year rule. Lesser paid employes, who are likely to have built up less investment in their retirement funds, get a tax break under the "three-year rule."

The law excuses you from all tax on the pension payments you receive under a qualified plan until they equal your own contributions to the plan, under one condition: that your own contributions do not exceed the total benefit payments you would receive in the first three years of the pension program.

This is how it works: Suppose you contributed $1,800 to the cost of a pension annuity, and your employer contributed the rest. Starting July 1, 1971, you received a pension annuity of $60 a month for life. In 1971, 1972 and 1973, you did not report the pension payments as income; to that point, after two and one-half years, they matched your investment annuity, $1,800. But your annuity payments from January 1, 1974, onwards are reported on your return as taxable. If you do not recover all your pension costs within three years after the pension starts, follow the annuity rules given in the chapter, "The Employe."

Retired civil service employes normally recover their costs within three years and do not start paying tax on the pension payments until after the benefits equal their investment. An increase in a civil service pension is not treated as an annuity income; even though it is added to your pension payments it is taxable in full as ordinary income.

If your pension was completely financed by the employer, and if you were not taxed on your employer's contributions as they were made, you report all the pension payments you receive. You have no personal investment in the annuity.

The tax-free portion of annuity payments, when paid to the widow or other beneficiary of a deceased employe, may be increased by all or part of a death benefit paid to the widow.

Death benefit payments up to $5,000 are tax-free. The law provides that this may be treated as part of the employe's cost or investment in the annuity. An equal amount of pension income thereby becomes tax-free to the widow, child or other beneficiary.

This is permitted only if the death benefit was paid solely because of the employe's death and if the employe had no claim on such a payment while he was alive. The provision would not apply, for example, if a widow's death benefit payment was a bonus that was due to her husband when he was alive, or if it represented uncollected salary or unused leave payments that were owing to him.

A special pension break is provided for full-time employes of tax-exempt religious, charitable or educational institutions. It permits you to arrange with your employer for purchase of an annuity, with no tax to you on the premium paid on your behalf. This can be done by reducing your present salary or foregoing a future pay raise.

The allowance can be as much as 20 percent of your pay multiplied by the number of years of employment with the organization. For example: Miss Lillian White, a teacher, receiving $7,500 salary, has been employed two years. The school may buy her an annuity having an annual premium of up to $3,000 with no tax liability to her (20 percent of $7,500 multiplied by two years). On her retirement she will pay tax at the ordinary rate on the annuity income.

If a person is retired because of a disability resulting from active service in the Armed Forces, the U.S. Coast Guard, or the U.S. Public

Health Service, the retirement pay he receives is exempt from taxation.

Disability retirement from a police or fire department or similar uniformed service also carries tax exemption. The retirement income in this case is considered to be equivalent to workmen's compensation, though not so identified.

Under a new provision of the law, a person receiving a pension can request that income taxes be withheld from such payments. He can do so by filing Form W-4P with whomever is paying the pension. This procedure should make it unnecessary to make quarterly lump-sum estimated tax payments.

One-time tax break

A taxpayer who is sixty-five or over may completely escape tax on the profit from selling his home, whether or not he replaces the dwelling.

This is one of the most important of the special tax savings provided for older persons. It helps out financially at a time in life when many homeowners change their mode of living.

With children grown, income reduced, and the exertions of maintaining a household becoming a burden, many couples plan to rent apartments or buy smaller homes.

These taxpayers would not qualify for the homeowner's tax deferment, described in the chapter "The Homeowner and The Investor in Real Estate," because the money they receive from sale of the family home will not be used up in buying a replacement dwelling. Instead, they may use the "sixty-five-or-over exclusion."

Under this rule, if the adjusted sales price is $20,000 or less, the entire gain is tax-free. *It is excluded from gross income, and need not be reported in an income tax return.*

The adjusted sales price, as noted previously, is the sales price minus any selling costs, such as sales commission and fixing-up costs. If it exceeds $20,000, the tax-free portion is figured by the following formula:

Multiply the total gain by $20,000 and divide the result by the adjusted sales price. For example: Wilbur Hawks, sixty-seven, paid $18,000 for his house ten years ago. He added $4,500 in capital improvements and therefore has an adjusted cost of $22,500. He sells it for $30,000.

Hawks' gain is $7,500. To find the tax-free portion he multiplies that by $20,000, with a mathematical result of $150,000,000; this he divides by $30,000, the sales price. The result is $5,000; that much is tax-free. Thus only $2,500 of Hawks' $7,500 gain is taxable.

If the homeowner replaces his dwelling he can enjoy both the break on his sixty-five-or-over exclusion and the postponement of gain under the rules for replacement of residence, described in the chapter on real estate mentioned above. These are his choices:

• He can take the full exemption for the portion of his gain that qualifies under the sixty-five-or-over exclusion, and defer the tax on any excess gain which is postponable under the replacement-of-residence formula.

For example: Jay Jones, sixty-six, sells the house which cost him $24,000 for $30,000. He gains $6,000, but buys a new home for $28,000.

Under the sixty-five-or-over rule he can exclude from any tax $4,000 of his gain ($6,000 multiplied by $20,000 divided by $30,000).

The remainder of his compensation for the old house, $2,000, can be deferred because it is reinvested in a new residence.

• As another option, Jones could decline the sixty-five-or-over exclusion. Instead he could postpone tax on all the gain that qualifies for deferment under the regular replacement rule.

For example: In this case, the adjusted sales price of $30,000 would exceed the cost of the new home by $2,000. The $2,000 would be taxable immediately; the tax on the other $4,000 of gain would be deferred.

Whenever the tax on a gain is deferred, under the replacement-of-residence rules, the adjusted cost basis of the new dwelling is reduced by the amount of gain deferred. In the first example, the $2,000 gain which was invested in a new house reduced the cost basis of that house by $2,000. So, in a subsequent sale, Jones would have to figure its cost as $26,000 instead of $28,000.

In the other example, by deferring $4,000 of gain, he would reduce the adjusted cost basis of the new house by $4,000, to $24,000.

Which option should Jones choose? Usually the first would be preferred. The gain which qualifies under the sixty-five-or-over rule is exempted entirely and permanently. But this rule can be used only once in a lifetime. Though he is sixty-six, Jones may prefer the second option and keep his right to a complete exclusion on a later sale.

But the later sale could not qualify for the sixty-five-or-over exclusion if it took place less than five years from Jones' purchase of the house. The seller must have owned and used the dwelling as his principal residence for five out of the eight years preceding the sale. (Not necessarily for five consecutive years.)

Retirement Income Credit

A boon to many retired persons is the Retirement Income Credit. The fact that Social Security payments are completely untaxed created a tax inequity. Retired persons who relied on some other forms of retirement income—because they never had Social Security coverage, or received inadequate Social Security benefits—usually did not get the same kind of tax break.

To make matters more fair—but more complicated—Congress provided the Retirement Income Credit. It helps many retired persons maintain an adequate standard of retirement living.

If you are retired and if your income is primarily from interest, dividends, pensions or annuities, you may be entitled to a tax credit of 15 percent of your "retirement income." Retirement income may be described as "passive income." It is money that you receive but do not currently work for.

Unfortunately, taxpayers who might otherwise be eligible to use the Short 1040A tax return may not do so if they claim the Retirement Income Credit. The usefulness of the short form thus is denied to many older taxpayers.

The maximum credit you may qualify for is $229. This is based on 15 percent of $1,524; the $1,524 is the maximum amount of retirement income that is eligible for the credit, if you are a single person.

If both husband and wife have retirement income and file a joint return, the maximum amount of combined retirement income eligible for the credit is increased to $2,286. On this amount the credit would be $343.

These amounts—$229 or $343—do not sound like much tax help. But they are more valuable than they seem at first glance because they are credits, not deductions or exemptions.

A deduction or personal exemption merely reduces the amount of income to which a tax percentage is applied. A credit is subtracted in full from the tax which would otherwise have to be paid.

Stated in more impressive terms, the $229 maximum credit means that up to $1,524 of a single person's income may be tax-free; the $343 maximum means that a retired couple may be spared the tax on up to $2,286 of their income.

For persons in lower tax brackets, a credit is worth several times as much as a deduction. But many older taxpayers do not take the Retirement Income Credit because they cannot figure out the formula for computing it.

The former Assistant Secretary of the Treasury for Tax Policy, Edwin S. Cohen, disclosed in a 1970 speech his own dismay that 2 million taxpayers were affected by the Retirement Income Credit but "as many as one-third of those eligible for the credit may not be claiming it because of its complexity."

More than 6 million retired persons now receive pensions and annuities, and the number grows constantly. But the Treasury reviewed the returns of taxpayers receiving federal civil service pensions, and Assistant Secretary Cohen reported the unhappy findings:

"In one study, which included some moderately complicated situations, we found that 75 percent of the tax returns reported these amounts improperly.

"Not only so—and this is the startling aspect—two-thirds of those reporting incorrectly overstated their taxable income and paid too high a tax."

Mr. Cohen challenged his audience of tax professionals: "With all the experts gathered here this evening, I doubt that a quarter of them could readily calculate the taxable portion of the pension received by a widow of an employe under a contributory pension plan—and I will include myself among them."

As this book was published, the search for simplification was still on apparently. Congress in 1972 killed a measure that would have increased the credit and, to some extent, simplified the rules. Tax experts at Treasury and in Congress were sure that, some day, the changes would be made. They will be a boon to retired persons when they come; watch for them.

Until the simpler rules are in effect, however, the retired taxpayer has no choice but to tackle the computation, line by line. It takes an entire page, the Schedule R, which comes with Form 1040.

Your IRS district office will give you free a copy of the pamphlet "Retirement Income and Retirement Income Credit." It includes an explanation, examples, and a sample of the made-out form. Also, the current edition of the annual IRS comprehensive overall guide, "Your Federal Income Tax," devotes pages to an explanation of the credit. (This is a book you must purchase from IRS, not to be confused with the instruction kit accompanying your Tax Forms.) It is as helpful as any of the explanations to be found in currently published "tax guides."

If you run into trouble, use the taxpayers' assistance service operated by IRS. In bigger cities it is listed in the telephone book under Internal Revenue Service as "Income Tax Information and Assistance."

Who is eligible for the credit? You need not be sixty-five to get the credit. Younger persons may use it, if retired with pensions or annuities paid under a government retirement system—federal, state, city, county, or other public civil service system.

For these under-sixty-five retirees, such pensions or annuities are the only kind of "retirement income" to which the credit may be applied.

For those sixty-five or older, a broader definition of retirement income is used. It includes pensions, annuities, interest, rents and dividends.

To qualify you must have had earned income of over $600 in any ten prior years. The ten earning years need not have been consecutive, and a widow can qualify if her husband would have qualified, even if she never had earnings of her own.

If both husband and wife qualify, each gets the credit. If both are over sixty-five and they file joint returns, and if either one of them meets the prior earnings test ($600 in any ten years), their combined retirement income up to $2,286 qualifies for the credit.

However, it should be pointed out that it is possible to have retirement income and yet not be entitled to the credit. This happens usually when the retired person gets a fairly substantial Social Security payment, or receives too much earned income—wages or self-employment income, produced by your own personal services—to qualify for the income credit.

Computing your credit. The credit is 15 percent of the smaller of these two amounts: The retirement income you actually received in the year; or $1,524 minus the total of Social Security and other nontaxable pension or annuity payments you received (and also minus some of the "current earned income" you received).

If you are under sixty-two, you must reduce the $1,524 figure by the amount of wages or other "earned income" you received which is in excess of $900.

If you are over sixty-two but under seventy-two, you subtract from the $1,524 maximum *half* of your earned income between $1,200 and $1,700, and also subtract *all* your earned income above $1,700.

If you are seventy-two or over you need not reduce the $1,524 at all, whatever your earned income.

Also to be subtracted from the $1,524, as mentioned above, is the amount of any Social Security or Railroad Retirement payments you receive; any other pension or annuity payments that are nontaxable (except the portion of such payments that represents a return of your own investment in the pension); and any part of the payments you receive from a matured U.S. government life insurance endowment contract (except the portion that represents a return of your own cost).

When these items are subtracted from the $1,524 maximum, the remainder is what you figure the retirement credit on (assuming it is smaller than your actual retirement income; if the actual retirement income is smaller, it is the figure to be used).

This is how the earned income computation might look for a widower or other single taxpayer.

Samuel Frost is sixty-six. He has a part-time job that pays $2,000, and several other income sources. He computes his credit as follows:

First he adds up the retirement income. It includes $420 from interest; $1,100 from rentals; and $310 from a private annuity (the portion which does not represent a return of his investment). The total is $1,830.

This exceeds the amount of retirement income on which the credit may be taken, $1,524. But his total must be reduced by subtracting some "current earned income" and other excluded income. He must subtract $400 which he receives from a Railroad Retirement pension. Then he must subtract some of his earned income—$300, which is the difference between his $2,000 earned income and the $1,700 limit; and also $250, which is half of the amount of his earned income between $1,200 and $1,700.

The total of the excluded items is $950. Subtracting them from $1,524, Frost finds he has net retirement income of $574. His retirement income credit is 15 percent of that, or $86.10.

Schedule R provides spaces for both husband and wife to report their retirement income and compute the credit. Even when filing a joint return, they may choose to figure the retirement income credit separately. If they prefer to figure it on their combined retirement incomes, the maximum amount is $2,286 instead of $1,524.

In deciding whether to compute the earned income credit individually or jointly, a couple should try out both methods to find out which will provide the largest credit. Here is an example of how one couple uses the combined method:

John and Jane Williams, both sixty-seven, file a joint return. John meets the ten-year test of having prior earned income; Jane does not, but since John does, she is considered to have done so for purposes of making a joint computation of retirement income.

John's income included $4,000 from a taxable pension received from his former employer, in addition to a Social Security pension of $1,100 and wages from part-time work as a watchman, totalling $1,200. His wife had Social Security payments of $800 and wages totalling $1,700.

For a couple filing jointly, the maximum retirement income figure is $2,286. From this must be subtracted John's Social Security, $1,100; Jane's Social Security, $800; and one-half of Jane's wages over $1,200, or $250. The total is $2,150.

Subtract that from the $2,286; the difference is $136. The retirement income credit is 15 percent of that amount, or $20.40.

Now John tries the method of individual computation. In this case his wife has no retirement income credit, and the amount on which the credit may be figured is $1,524. This is his computation:

John's Social Security pension is the only item that must be subtracted from the maximum figure. Taking this $1,100 from $1,524 leaves $424. Fifteen percent of $424 is $63.60, which is the retirement income credit. This is the best method for the Williamses.

Under other sets of circumstances the joint method would have produced a bigger tax credit. (That would have been the case in the above examples if, for instance, Jane's Social Security benefits and wages had been smaller.)

Retired persons who have rented part of their homes or own other rental property may include the rent receipts as retirement income, but with some restrictions.

If their own personal services do not contribute to the rental income, all the rent receipts are retirement income. If they do perform some services—like repairing or maintaining the property—a portion of the rental income (but not more than 30 percent of the net profits from the rental) should be classed as earned income instead of retirement income.

Note that you need not have worked for someone else to establish your right to retirement income credit. You could have met the requirement for "prior earned income" (at least $600 a year in any prior ten years) if you were your own boss in a small business. In businesses which require both capital (inventory, equipment, etc.) and services (your personal effort), you can consider a reasonable amount as earned income for your services, up to 30 percent of the net profits. (A professional man's income is considered to be earned from personal services even if he has a large capital investment, like a doctor or dentist. An independent plumber or painter, with small capital investment, considers his whole gross income as earned income.)

*And it came to pass in those days, that
there went out a decree from Caesar
Augustus, that all the world
should be taxed.*

St. Luke 2:1

CHAPTER 17

Tax Planning for Family Security

The creation of family security is a matter of deep concern to most people. Even after an estate has been built and measures have been taken to protect it from the erosion of income taxes and inflation, the task is far from completed. One must try to insure that it will not be reduced seriously by estate taxes and probate costs.

Extended treatment of estate planning is beyond the scope of this book, but we will discuss three devices which can help shield an estate from the aforementioned threats. They are giving-while-living, trusts, and insurance. They are basic tools of estate planning. Properly employed, each can reduce current income taxes as well as future estate taxes. Each can contribute to long-term security.

Giving-while-living

The practice of making gifts to those who ultimately will inherit your estate—wife, children, grandchildren, beloved friends, church or charity —is growing. If you give while living, your gift remains intact, untouched by estate tax. Also, of course, if you give away income-producing investments, you no longer pay tax on the earnings.

The estate tax is even more steeply graduated than the income tax. It ranges from 3 percent on the first $5,000 of taxable estate—after some substantial exemptions—up to 77 percent on $10 million or more. The tax on gifts is only three-fourths as great. And substantial sums may be given to wife, children or parents without incurring any tax at all— $3,000 to any one person each year and a total gift of $30,000 either in one year or over a lifetime. If a husband and wife join in making the gift, the tax-free amounts are doubled to $6,000 a year up to a total of $60,000 over a period of years.

The gift tax rate on the first $5,000 above the tax-free limit is only 2¼ percent. Over a period of years a very considerable sum could be given away at far less cost than if the money were permitted to pile up until death and then taxed at the steeply progressive estate tax rates.

Since the giver usually is in a higher income tax bracket than the child or other relative who receives the gift, any income earned by investment of the money given is taxable at a lower rate.

If a taxpayer knew he was dying, he could give his money away and protect it all from the estate tax—except that the Treasury has a special rule for gifts made "in contemplation of death." In general, any gift made within three years of death is subject to the estate tax unless the donor had made sure to show that there were other reasons for the gift.

These "other reasons" might be the usual gift-giving occasions such as Christmas, birthday, graduation, marriage, a trip abroad, or an anniversary. If made on these occasions, a gift usually could escape the "contemplation of death" rule.

The gift of securities or other property which has risen in value has some income tax advantage, as well. If you have stock worth $2,500 which cost you $700, and if you sold it to your son at cost, $700, you would in effect have made a gift of $1,800. You had no gain on the sale, so you owe no capital gains tax. Your son in due time may sell the shares at their market value. He would pay the tax on the gain. Since his tax bracket is lower than yours, he pays less tax on the gain than you would have incurred if you had sold the stock to give him the money.

There may or may not be a tax saving in giving gifts to a charity during your lifetime instead of leaving a bequest to the same institution. For a taxpayer with modest current income but a large estate, the saving in taxes would be greater if the donation comes after death. For a taxpayer with high income, the saving might be greater if the gift were made now and the charitable deduction claimed from current income.

While the disparity in rates between the gift tax and the estate tax has given great impetus to lifetime giving, it results in both tax inequity and a loss of Treasury revenues. Predictably, there have been demands for a major overhaul of the estate and gift tax structure.

Such legislation was under Congressional investigation when this book was printed. That fact underscores what would have been an urgent rec-ommendation in any case: Do not undertake to do your own estate plan-ning; get professional help.

Almost certainly, Congress sooner or later will merge the estate tax and the gift tax. They are now separate levies, each with its own rates, rules and exemptions. The taxpayer now can choose between them, to a considerable degree.

He can greatly reduce or completely eliminate his estate tax, for exam-ple, by giving away much of his estate while living. If he starts early and does the giving systematically, he can perhaps eliminate the gift tax too.

But if Congress consolidates the two taxes by applying a single set of rates and exemptions to both—which is the present aim and idea—it won't be possible to do that kind of maneuvering. This leads to a second urgent recommendation: If you have had a family gift program in mind, get moving. Congress could get in ahead of you.

The trust

An increasingly popular way to save for a child's college costs, provide an income for a parent, or safeguard a bequest is to set up a trust. Many persons of comparatively modest means have learned the tax-saving benefits of this device.

In the same sense that a corporation is an artificial person in the eyes of the law, the trust is a legal entity. If you have an income-earning asset, you can entrust it to this artificial being. The trust will conserve it, invest it and make payments (called distributions) out of its income to the beneficiary of your choice.

An individual, called the trustee, administers the trust and sees that it fulfills its aim. He is frequently the trust officer of a bank.

Ordinarily, the assets placed in a trust are stocks, bonds or real prop-erty, but other income-earning assets may be used. Trusts have been cre-ated to hold items like rare coins, though these were income-earning only in the sense that they appreciated in value. There are dozens of kinds of trusts, capable of doing hundreds of different things.

They are most commonly used, however, as a means of transferring a part of the taxpayer's assets to his wife or children or other heirs. If the kind of trust is well chosen, it can reduce the income tax of the per-son who sets up the trust or the estate tax on his estate at death. Or, it can do both.

There are two basic trusts:

First, the "lifetime trust," "living trust," or "inter vivos trust." This is set into operation during the lifetime of the person who creates it.

Second, the "testamentary trust," or "causa mortis trust." It is estab-lished under a will and takes effect only upon the death of the person who drew the will.

Another broad distinction is drawn: The lifetime trust can be revocable or irrevocable.

A revocable trust can be revoked at the wish of the person who set it up. He can elect to end the trust, reclaim the assets he put into it, change the beneficiaries, or specify new terms for the distribution of the trust's income.

An irrevocable trust, once created, must run unchanged for the entire period originally specified.

Generally, current tax benefits come only under an irrevocable trust. When the beneficiary is taxable on the income received from the trust, the creator of the trust is not; he has cut himself off from that income.

And since the beneficiary is usually in a lower tax bracket, such as a child or aged parent, the beneficiary pays a lower tax or none at all.

So, frequently, no income tax at all is paid on the trust's earnings. If the creator of the trust dies, the estate tax is reduced because the property was removed irrevocably from his estate.

Reversionary trust. A type of trust used increasingly in recent years to provide immediate tax savings is the "reversionary" trust. It is irrevocable, but the creator of the trust does not lose control of the property forever. The operation of this trust is limited to a specified period of time; at the end of that time, which must be at least ten years and one day, the property reverts to the trust's creator, unless he dies before the trust expires.

For example: Suppose you are in the 36 percent tax bracket. Your son is eight years old. You wish to build up a fund for his college costs ten years from now. You have bonds that earn $1,600 interest each year, and you can spare that much income from current living expenses. But you would not actually save $1,600 a year because the income tax would take a $576 bite out of each year's interest earnings. You would save only $1,024 a year, or $10,240 in ten years.

You decide instead of simply saving the bond income, to set up a ten-year, irrevocable trust with your son as beneficiary. You put the bonds into it. You pay no tax on the income generated by the trust; it no longer belongs to you. Your son has some tax to pay on it, but not much; his tax bracket is low.

If the trust income is placed each year in the son's savings account, so that these savings also earn interest for him, he might have a fund of about $15,000 when he is eighteen.

For the entire ten years you can continue to claim an exemption for him as a dependent. At the end of the ten years the trust ends and the bonds revert to your ownership and control.

(The trust's income could not have been used simply to support the child; the income from a trust cannot be used to meet a legal obligation of the trust's creator. Support of an under-age child is a legal obligation; a college education is not.)

Until 1972 the income of that trust would have been wholly shielded from tax; your son would have had the benefit of the standard deduction and the low-income allowance, as well as his personal exemption.

But Congress decided to curtail the tax benefits somewhat. It passed what reporters nicknamed "the rich kids' amendment" which decreed that: Any taxpayer for whom another taxpayer could claim a dependency deduction could not shelter any unearned income from tax by use of the low-income allowance or the standard deduction.

So the 15 percent standard deduction and the low-income allowance could be applied, thereafter, only to the amount of the child's income which the child himself earned—not to any "unearned income."

It does not matter that the parent might not claim a dependency deduction for the child; if the parent *can* claim it (even though he doesn't), the child's low-income allowance is limited to his earned income, if any, and his standard deduction is figured solely on the earned income.

For example: A fond uncle has been giving a nephew $3,000 a year; at age fifteen the nephew's bank account totals $18,000. This year it earns $900 in interest. If the child had earned that much money he would have had no return to file or tax to pay. But because he *could* be claimed as a dependent by his father (even though his father did not give him the money and may not even claim him as a dependent), the boy must file a tax return.

The return will show $900 of interest income. It will show no standard deduction or low-income allowance, but the boy can claim his $750 personal exemption. He will pay tax on $150. (If the boy was over nineteen, not in school and not working, the parent could not claim an exemption for him. The youth therefore would not have to file a return or pay a tax. His personal exemption and the standard deduction would eliminate any tax liability, and—since his parent could not claim a dependency deduction for him—the "rich kids' amendment" would not apply.)

If a fifteen-year-old had interest income of $1,400 but also earned $600 a year from a newspaper route, he would figure his tax this way: The 15 percent standard deduction could be applied only to his $600 of earned income. That would amount to only $90, so instead he would take the low income allowance. The $1,300 low-income allowance is limited by the same "rich kids' amendment" to the amount of the earned income, or $600. The boy would claim this $600 plus his $750 personal exemption, a total of $1,350. He would pay tax on $650 ($2,000 less $1,350).

But note well: Despite the "rich kids' amendment," there are still substantial tax savings in the transfer of income to a child or other family member by setting up a trust or making outright gifts of income-producing property. The income is no longer taxable to the parent. The parent and the child can each claim a personal exemption for the child, and the child's income is taxed at low-bracket rates.

Avoiding probate. The fact that a living trust removes the assets put into it from the estate of the person who created the trust has a further advantage. It means that less of the estate is drained off in legal fees and other costs of probating the estate.

Probate is the court procedure of proving that a will is valid and properly executed.

Through the lifetime trust, the bonding fees, commissions, court costs, legal costs and other expenses that go with probate can be saved not only upon the death of the creator of the trust but, in many cases, through two subsequent probate estates. This is because most states permit an individual to provide for the disposition of property to a person now living, plus twenty-one years.

For example: Joseph Baker, after consulting with his accountant and attorney, put $100,000 worth of income-producing stocks into trust. His brother and his attorney were named co-trustees. When he died, they were responsible for collecting the income from the securities and distributing it to Joseph's wife.

Mrs. Baker died soon after her husband. Under the terms of Joseph's will, the trustees transferred the income of the trust to their daughter. She, in turn, was killed in an automobile accident. The trust income—again in compliance with Joseph's will—was paid thereafter to her children, Joseph's grandchildren. Joseph had removed the assets not only from his wife's estate but also from their daughter's.

Often, in a trust of this kind, a "commercial trustee" such as the trust department of a bank would be used. The trustee is obliged to keep the assets invested in income-producing securities. The trust's creator can provide specific investment instructions, however, for the trustee to follow.

Revocable trusts. The tax benefits of a revocable trust—one whose terms give the creator continued control over the assets—are not substantial. What he gains principally is relief from the problem of managing his investments; if he names a commercial trustee to do it, he pays a fee for this professional service. The fee is deductible.

However, there may be a significant estate tax saving in even a revocable trust if the *beneficiary* dies. In the example of Joseph Baker's trust, above, the value of the trust would not be taxed in Mrs. Baker's estate or in their daughter's estate.

But before choosing the greater tax advantages of an irrevocable trust, the taxpayer should seek expert advice—before committing himself to give up all rights to the property. He cannot later change his mind.

For comparison, the tax rules for revocable and irrevocable trusts are given here in capsule:

• Federal income tax: The income from a revocable trust is usually taxed to the creator of the trust. The income from an irrevocable trust is generally taxed to the beneficiaries, to the extent it is distributed to them. If an irrevocable trust is allowed to accumulate income, the trust itself may be taxed on the income, thereby reducing the amount payable to the beneficiary.

 • Federal estate tax: Property placed in an irrevocable trust will generally escape the federal estate tax when the creator of the trust dies. Irrevocable trusts are particularly effective in planning the ultimate disposition of your property to relatives or to charity. The assets in a revocable trust are taxed in the estate of the creator, but if the beneficiary should die also, not in his (the beneficiary's) estate.

The taxpayer who sets up an irrevocable lifetime trust may have to pay a federal gift tax. If so, it is likely to be a much smaller amount than the estate tax which would have been payable if the trust had not been created.

One popular variety of trust was curtailed by Congress in 1969. This is the "accumulation trust." Under its terms the trustee is not required to pay out to the beneficiaries all the trust's income as it is received. He has discretion to pay out certain income or let it accumulate for the benefit of the beneficiaries.

In the past this arrangement has had an important tax advantage. To help out a favored beneficiary, a cooperative trustee could withhold payments until a year when the money would have the least tax impact on the beneficiary—perhaps a year of reduced income, when the tax bracket would be lower, or a year in which he had plenty of losses to offset the trust income.

In the 1969 Tax Reform Act, Congress ordered this loophole closed by stages from 1970 through 1973. After the latter year, Congress said, the beneficiaries are to be taxed on income received from the trust as if the income had been distributed in the year it was earned. The new rule deprives accumulation trusts of most of their tax advantages.

Remainder interest. With still another kind of trust, a taxpayer can make a bequest of property or securities to his church or charity. In so doing, he gives himself an immediate income tax deduction; and can keep for himself the entire income from the property for his lifetime.

The charity receives the property on his death. For this type of giving, the taxpayer sets up a trust and turns the property over to it. He makes himself the beneficiary of the trust for his lifetime, so that he will receive its earnings. The charity gets the "remainder interest"—the property itself—after his death.

The gift of the remainder interest is a charitable deduction from the current year's income. The amount of deduction depends on the value of the property and the taxpayer's life expectancy, as indicated in official Treasury tables.

Life insurance trust. No discussion of trusts, however brief, should fail to mention the life insurance trust.

It requires some affluence to create a lifetime trust of substantial value, but a life insurance trust is within the financial reach of anyone who has built up a substantial amount of life insurance.

A life insurance trust is one created solely to receive the proceeds of a life insurance policy and distribute them as specified by the creator of the trust. If the trust is properly planned, the insurance proceeds are not taxed in the estate.

The trust may be set up in the lifetime of the insured. The trust is made the beneficiary of the policy. The trust goes into operation when it receives the policy proceeds.

While the policyholder lives, he can place income-producing property in the trust with the income earmarked to pay the premiums on the policies.

A further advantage of the trust: It assures that the insurance proceeds go for the intended purposes. They may not be used, for instance, to pay the debts of the deceased.

An alternative way to set up a life insurance trust is by will. This makes your estate the beneficiary; the estate delivers the proceeds of the policy into the trust. But there are some problems. One is that most states levy a tax on the proceeds of life insurance which is made payable to an estate. The other is that the policy proceeds must go through the slow and frequently costly process of probate; the trust must wait until the probate of the will is complete before it can start operating.

If you are considering a life insurance trust, you should consult not only your attorney and accountant but also a Chartered Life Underwriter (C.L.U.) or other qualified professional life insurance adviser.

Insurance

Life insurance is simultaneously an investment, a means of deferring income and a vehicle for tax savings.

The use of annuities or insurance contracts to finance pension and other retirement plans has been described. The money paid into such plans is tax-exempt and the growth of the fund which guarantees the plan is tax-free until the retired worker begins to draw on it.

There are other tax benefits in life insurance. The build-up of cash value in a policy is tax-exempt; when a policy is paid off because of the death of an insured person, the widow or other beneficiary owes no tax on the proceeds.

If the insurance company is of the participating, or mutual, type which pays dividends to its policyholders during their lifetime, the dividends are tax-free.

They are considered a "return of capital" or "return of principal." They represent a return of your own money—in effect, a refund of part of the premiums you paid in.

Whether taken in cash or used to reduce a premium, such dividends are not taxed. They are excluded from gross income and need not be reported on your income tax return. Even if used to buy additional paid-up insurance on your policy, they are exempt from tax.

When dividends are left in the insurance company to earn interest, only the interest they earn is subject to tax. It is taxed as it would be in a savings account, at the ordinary income rate.

Lump-sum payments. Every insurance policy contains a "settlement option." This is the choice, built into the contract, of how the proceeds of the policy are to be paid out to the beneficiary. Generally, settlement options fall into two broad categories—lump-sum payments and installment payments.

Normally the entire amount of a lump-sum payment arising from the death of the insured person is tax-free; it is excluded by the beneficiary from his gross income. This is true whether the beneficiary is an individual, a corporation, a partnership, a trustee or the estate of the insured person.

There are exceptions. All or part of the insurance proceeds may be taxable income if the ownership of the policy has been sold or transferred to someone else for a valuable consideration, or if the proceeds are received as alimony under a court decree.

A variety of other exceptions exist, but only the one mentioned—the payment as alimony—merits discussion in this brief account.

Alimony. If a legally separated or divorced husband or wife receives death benefits as periodic alimony payments under a court's decree of divorce or a separate maintenance agreement, he or she must include the payments in their gross income, subject to tax. The payments cease to be death benefits, in the eyes of IRS, and become alimony payments. Periodic alimony payments are taxable to the husband or wife who receives them.

A lump-sum payment would not be "periodic," and therefore would be tax-free. Installment payments would be periodic if the principal amount was stated in the decree or agreement and if the installments were payable over a period ending more than ten years from the date of the decree.

If the spouse is a wife, for instance, it would be to her advantage, obviously, to avoid any settlement option that would extend the installments more than ten years, if she had the choice.

The periodic payments are taxed to the wife in full if the annual payment does not exceed 10 percent of the total proceeds. She would not be taxed on any payment exceeding the 10 percent.

If the decree specifies that the obligation ends when the husband dies, the insurance proceeds paid to the wife cease to be considered alimony payments on his death. They become tax-free insurance proceeds.

While life insurance proceeds are exempt from the federal *income* tax, they are definitely subject to the *estate* tax—unless the policy is owned by someone else. An individual with a large amount of insurance may arrange to have his wife own the policy or policies on his life. This exempts the proceeds from the federal estate tax upon his death because it is the husband's property which is taxable in the estate. If the insurance policy is his wife's property, the death of the husband does not make it taxable.

When should one assign ownership of an insurance policy to his wife? This technique may be a useful arrangement if the estate is large enough to make it worthwhile. The first $60,000 of an estate is tax-free and, in addition, up to one-half the estate is tax-exempt if left to a husband or wife; this is called the "marital deduction."

But an increasing number of executives and self-employed persons, in estimating their prospective estates, are astonished to find that they may exceed the tax-exempt amounts. The transfer of insurance then makes sense. To establish the exempt status, the wife should buy the policy, or a bona fide gift must be made; all rights and control over the policy must be yielded to the new owner. The benefits of this course become obvious when these two cases are compared:

Morton Brown, fifty-two, buys a $120,000 policy on his own life. He dies unexpectedly two years later, having a net worth of $100,000 plus the proceeds of the policy. His entire estate including the policy proceeds goes to Mrs. Brown, but a federal estate tax of $9,500 must be paid.

Samuel Smart is in the identical situation, except that his wife bought the insurance policy. His estate has no tax to pay because his insurance was not included in it. The result was a saving of $9,500.

Installment payments. If the beneficiary elects to receive the insurance proceeds in installments over a period of time, the portion which is payable as a result of the death of the insured is spread over the period. Part of each installment is a portion of the policy proceeds and part is interest earned on the proceeds which still remain in the insurance company's hands. The part of each installment which represents the policy proceeds is treated as a tax-free "return of investment."

For example, if the beneficiary of a $50,000 policy decided not to take the whole sum in one payment, he might elect to spread it over ten years. Each of the ten annual payments would include $5,000 of the policy proceeds. But each payment also would include an additional amount, representing the interest earnings on the proceeds while they remain in the insurance company's hands.

The beneficiary knows how much of each payment represents a portion of the principal amount of the insurance proceeds—$5,000, in the case cited. On that part of his annual payment he pays no tax. But on the additional amount of each payment (the interest earnings) he must pay tax at his ordinary income tax rate.

However, if the beneficiary is a widow or a surviving husband, taxes are paid only on the amount of interest that exceeds $1,000 a year.

For example: Mrs. Judith Jones received $300 a month from an insurance company in the year following her husband's death. Of the $3,600 a year, $3,200 was a "return of principal" and $400 represented "interest."

The $3,200 paid from the principal was tax-free to Mrs. Jones. The $400 interest was also tax-free because it was less than the $1,000 exclusion for a surviving spouse.

In some cases the proceeds of a policy are left on deposit with the insurance company. The company pays interest only to the beneficiary. (This is usually under a settlement plan which makes the principal payable, at the death of the beneficiary, to a secondary beneficiary.) This interest is taxable in full.

Another option provides the beneficiary with an income for a specified number of years. For example, a widow elects to receive $50,000 of death proceeds over a period of ten years. Her annual installments are $6,140, of which $5,000 may be excluded from income as a "return of principal." The remaining $1,140 represents taxable interest, of which $1,000 is tax-free because she is a surviving spouse.

If the widow dies before the fixed period expires, the secondary beneficiary is entitled to the same "return of principal" exclusion, but is not entitled to the $1,000 "surviving spouse" exclusion. The $1,140 interest payment would be taxed.

A number of other options are in common use, of varying complexity and having various tax consequences. The taxation of insurance proceeds can be diminished greatly by correct planning.

But any taxpayer having substantial amounts of life insurance should consult with his tax and insurance advisers to assure tax savings to himself and his heirs.

Clever little schemes are not admirable when they undermine the foundations of society.

President Franklin D. Roosevelt

CHAPTER 18

If You Are Audited...

Almost every American of above-average income sooner or later will receive the dreaded notice from IRS that his return has been selected for audit. It usually says: "Your Federal tax return for the year specified above, has been assigned to me for examination," and is signed by an Internal Revenue agent.

The verb "audit" means to examine and verify. The notice is not a cause for panic. Most audits turn out to be fairly modest affairs, centering perhaps on a single questioned item and including a general verification of the tax return.

If the problem is merely an error in figures or computation, or a misinterpretation of the law, IRS does not start an audit but takes a simpler course. An IRS notice will advise the taxpayer of the mistake and tell him that his tax is being changed accordingly. There will be no personal contact or further notification. The IRS will send a refund or render a bill for additional payment.

If a taxpayer disagrees with the change he should send a certified letter *immediately* to the IRS office which made the change. The letter should state that the taxpayer disagrees and give the reasons why.

Your reasons might be, for example, that the IRS misread your figures, or misinterpreted your words; or that your return contained a typographical error, or that IRS failed to give you credit for payments on estimated tax which you actually had paid.

Your letter should include your Social Security number, the tax year in question, your full name and address, and the "document locator number" which appears on the notice sent to you.

If possible, enclose a photocopy of the notice and a photocopy of any relevant papers or proofs you wish to submit in support of your position such as canceled checks or typed copies of your computations and itemized lists that substantiate your claim. Usually such incidents are closed without difficulty.

It is unwise to give IRS the original of any document you wish to retain or may require later. It can be lost in the mail, misplaced at the IRS, or otherwise not be available when you need it.

The audit procedures are more formidable matters. There are three main types: mail audits, in which the whole examination usually is begun, conducted and closed by mail; office audits, which are conducted by IRS agents or technicians in the offices of the IRS itself; and "field audits." A field audit is an examination by an IRS agent who makes an appointment and visits you at your home or place of business.

The auditing odds

On a purely numerical basis, your chance of being audited seems small. In 1969, one income tax return in thirty-five was examined; in 1970, one in forty-five; and in 1972, one in fifty-seven. Then audits increased a bit. There is still much less than one chance in fifty, but IRS is trying hard to speed up its audit machinery.

Other factors outweigh the law of averages, however. Your return is more likely to be audited if your income is over $25,000; if your profession or trade is one in which many payments may be made in cash; if you claim an unusually big deduction in proportion to income, for whatever cause; or if you had a casualty loss.

Why does IRS pick on people with casualty losses? For a very simple reason: a lot of people cheat. When there is a theft, or total destruction of property, who is to know what the value really was? This is the reasoning of a good many taxpayers who use the casualty to inflate their itemized deductions. The practice is so common, and IRS is so aware of it, that the honest taxpayer must take extra pains to be ready to prove his loss.

For example, notify the police *immediately* after a theft. (Otherwise IRS could wonder if it was a theft at all.) Do not report a larger loss to IRS than you reported to police; you may need the police record to verify your deduction. And, if the loss was from vandalism, fire, storm or flood, take pictures of the damage and keep them in your tax files.

The happenstances of geography have much to do with your chances of audit. A 1971 Treasury report showed wide variations in the odds from city to city.

Your chance of being audited was one in thirty-one if you lived in Reno, Nev., one in thirty-four if you lived in Manhattan, N.Y., and one out of seventy-seven if you lived in Denver, Colo.

There was great variation also in the settlements approved by various IRS offices when cases reached the Appellate Division. Figures pried out of IRS by a taxpayer involved in a court suit show that a taxpayer in Washington, D.C., or Buffalo, N.Y., could settle for about half as much as a taxpayer in Newark, N.J.

The nationwide average of settlements in tax controversies came to 34 cents on the dollar; that is, the taxpayer ended up paying 34 percent of what the IRS tried to collect. But in Washington the settlement average was 24 cents on the dollar, in Buffalo 25 cents, New York City 31 cents, Philadelphia and Pittsburgh, Pa., 32 cents.

By contrast the settlements averaged 45 cents on the dollar in New Haven, Conn., 46 cents in Richmond, Va., and 50 cents in Newark.

Corporations generally came off better than individuals across the country. But the range of settlements was even wider. A company whose case was argued in Boston, Mass., settled for 23 cents on the dollar, on the average. In Richmond, the average company got off with 30 cents, in Washington, D.C., 34 cents, and in New York City 37 cents. Philadelphia was pretty tough at 44 cents and Baltimore, Md., tougher at 46 cents.

Not fair, you say? True, but unfairness is a simple fact of the income tax laws; and perhaps the publicity given the foregoing figures might inspire IRS efforts to try for greater uniformity.

What else triggers an audit?

• An assertion on the face of a return that looks odd: an unusually large charitable deduction in proportion to the taxpayer's income; a large claim for storm damage on a modest home; or steep expense account claims. The IRS computers are taught to be sensitive to variations from the norm. (The computer is frequently wrong, by the way; 41 percent of all audits in a recent year brought no change in tax liability.)

• A visible inconsistency in the return. An item of $1,212 for "petty cash" outlays might not worry an IRS agent looking at the return of a busy doctor, but it would if the return also showed separate claims for items as small as stamps, stationery, note pads, and pencils. The agent would assume the first category had included these items.

• A return may look perfectly in order but be selected in a sampling check. Such spot-checking of returns formerly was a regular practice to test and encourage accurate reporting. Henceforth, it will be done only in occasional years to provide updated information on taxpayer habits to be fed into the computers.

• The IRS may have information from another source indicating that your return is incorrect. This might be an incorrect Social Security number supplied by you for stocks actually owned by your son; the son's number should have been reported. Or you may have failed to report dividend or interest income for which your broker or bank sent in an information return showing the payment made to you.

• A taxpayer who makes a claim for refund, because of deductions not claimed when he filed his return, or who initiates some other action, may find he has triggered an examination of the return. Do not hestitate to claim what is due you, but be sure you are prepared to back up all the claims made in your return.

The computer technique now in use by IRS for selecting returns for audit is called "DIF," for "discriminate function." It is a method of tagging individual returns in the incoming avalanche of completed Form 1040s. The computer gives each return a score to indicate its probable need for verification. The ranked and sorted forms are sent to local IRS district offices. Then, in each office, the staff sifts through the machine-ranked forms and decides which ones should be assigned to agents for examination.

The DIF technique was used in 1969 only on forms showing gross incomes under $10,000; since 1970, it has been at work on everybody's tax return.

There are other reasons for auditing. If a corporation's return is audited, IRS regulations require that the tax returns of the corporation's principal officers be surveyed to determine the possible need for individual audits.

This pattern applies to partnerships, also. If one partner is audited, the partnership is likely to be audited. If the partnership is audited, and a tax deficiency is found, all the other partners are likely to be audited.

There are situations in which a faulty return in one year will indicate the need to check the prior year or the following year. If one audit showed too much depreciation being claimed, IRS would probably also check the depreciation deduction for the previous year.

Tax informants are occasionally a help to IRS and a headache to a company which has a disgruntled employe "getting even" for his dismissal by reporting real or imagined tax evasion. Wrathful wives have been known to punish straying husbands by reporting their tax misdeeds. An envious clerk may report the tax deductions taken for parties on his boss' yacht.

An informer never has to prove his charges, but the taxpayer has to be ready to prove his honesty if and when the IRS follows up the tip. The Treasury protects the identity of the informer.

The IRS will make an agreement with an informer to pay him up to 10 percent of the taxes recovered as a result of the lead that he provides. The information is cheap at that price. In fiscal year 1968, the IRS collected $11 million as a result of leads furnished by 462 informants. Another estimated 3,300 persons tried to collect for tax evasion information. IRS sifts such information carefully, discards most of it, and pays only for information which actually brings money into the Treasury.

But most of the tax tip-offs are given gratis. There are roughly twenty times as many informants who claim no fee as those who want money for their information.

Records and appeals

It is much easier to face an IRS agent if you know your records are complete and in good order. Some pointers on tax record-keeping are in order at this point. How long should you keep your tax records?

To most taxpayers, the government seems exceedingly vague on this question. Our advice is to keep all records substantiating your income and deductions at least as long as the three-year statute of limitation requires, and longer if you can; and to keep some of your records forever.

Quite aside from tax uses, records can be invaluable assets in your entire economic life. Few taxpayers realize fully, when they start their earning and taxpaying careers, how useful it will be in later years to have the records of their personal finances. They will be used and referred to repeatedly when incomes rise, families grow, houses get too small, wills are written, and the business of living gets more complicated.

For example, keeping a record of every improvement outlay large or small made on your house, right from the day you bought it, may seem a needless bother. But it becomes important when the house is sold, rented or bequeathed.

All capital improvements such as the installation of termite shielding; a new powder room; aluminum siding and storm windows; electrical fixtures and convenience outlets; an added porch; new plantings of shrubs and trees; the pay of the handyman who puts up the fence and builds the trellis are added to the purchase price of your house to give you the "adjusted cost basis."

Every added improvement item builds up your cost, reduces the margin of gain that you report on a sale, and therefore reduces your tax liability. Every item you forgot to record means tax money out of your pocket later on.

In the case of securities, failure to note the date and price of purchase could possibly mean the difference—when you sell them—between realizing a short-term gain on the sale, taxable at full ordinary rates, or a long-term gain, taxable at the low capital gains rate.

It is useful to have old records on hand for other purposes as well—to establish your past earnings for Social Security or private pension records, for instance.

So, unless the records become an intolerable nuisance, why be in a hurry to throw them away?

The key paragraph in the free IRS leaflet No. 552, which describes record-keeping requirements, says:

"Records supporting items on a tax return should be retained until the expiration of the statute of limitations for that return. Ordinarily, the statute of limitations for an income tax return expires three years after the return is due to be filed."

But then the paragraph goes on: "However, there are many cases in which the taxpayer should retain all his records indefinitely." And another paragraph, which advises that your records must be kept available at all times for inspection by IRS officers, says: "The records must be retained as long as their contents may become material in the administration of any Internal Revenue law."

Here are some further good-sense rules:

A business or professional man should keep *all* his canceled checks, paid bills, even cash register tapes, sales slip carbons, and other supporting material for *at least three years.*

Never throw away your copy of your completed Form 1040 for *any* year.

Keep a *permanent* record of some kind of all capital expenditures— that is, the cost, supplier, and date of purchase for all outlays for buildings, furniture, equipment, machinery and other depreciable assets. Without that, you cannot figure your full deductions for depreciation. And you cannot determine the full cost to you of your property; this in turn, when the property is finally sold by you, could make your taxable gain on the sale look bigger than it really is.

If you are in a trade or business, keep *permanent* records substantiating items which must be reported on income tax, employment tax, excise tax and any other returns you are required to file.

The sheer bulk of records can become a burden to a business or professional man. Within limits, the IRS will accept modern-day record-keeping techniques.

Microfilmed records which reproduce general account books (journals, ledgers, registers and the like) are not acceptable, but you can keep your supporting records on microfilm exclusively. The latter records would include payroll records, canceled checks, vouchers and so on. You must provide facilities for preserving the microfilms, for showing them in case of an audit, and for making any transcriptions that may be required.

Computerized records also are acceptable under certain conditions. If you keep your tax records in an automatic data processing (ADP) system, the system must include a method of producing visible and readable records from the tape or punched cards.

The costs of preparing for a tax audit, like the costs of preparing a tax return, are deductible expenses. So are the costs of preparing and storing records for tax purposes, including microfilming, file cabinets, and even transportation costs to your lawyer or the IRS office. Fees paid to a tax lawyer or C.P.A. for assisting a taxpayer in an audit are also deductible.

Though you may find it a nuisance, it is wise to write checks for any and all payments of more than a few dollars. If and when your tax return is audited, the IRS agent *invariably* will ask to see the canceled checks.

There is no handy substitute for a canceled check as proof of a payment, but even the canceled check usually is not enough. A canceled check proves that a payment was made but does not show what the payment was *for*. There should be an invoice, receipted bill or other positive notation describing the outlay.

One good record-keeping idea is to keep vouchers, receipts and canceled checks sorted in separate file folders. A householder can keep these currently in a deep desk drawer, a metal file box, or, in a pinch, a grocer's carton.

The file folders can be labeled "Income," "Contributions," "Interest," "Medical" and other headings used for itemizing deductions. If you incur deductible business expenses, there should be files labeled "Car," "Expense Accounts," "Telephone and Telegraph," "Travel and Transportation" and so on to meet your needs.

When the ordeal of preparing the return is over, the folders can be lifted out bodily, wrapped up or put in a box clearly labeled, and stored in a safe place for use in case of questions from IRS.

Tax filing is easier if the file folders are kept up to date. As you pay each monthly bill, slip the bill stubs or vouchers into the proper file folder. After you have received and verified your monthly bank statement, "spread" the checks in your tax file at once; that is, slip each canceled check into the folder marked for it. Then, when April 15 nears, all the canceled checks will be in the same file folder with the matching receipts.

There is a risk that deductible expenses may be overlooked or forgotten, unless recorded at the time. And a forgotten outlay of $25 during the year will become a loss of $3.50 even to the lowest-bracket taxpayer when he files his return.

Mail audit

The mail audit begins with a letter or questionnaire from the IRS. It will advise you that your return has been selected for examination and will ask you to supply certain information which may be specified on an enclosed questionnaire.

The items most frequently questioned in mail audits are alimony, capital gains and losses, casualty losses, dependency deductions, expenses of a salesman, and itemized deductions for contributions, taxes, interest, medical and miscellaneous expenses. Contributions of securities or property other than cash are often questioned. Deductions claimed for dependents who are not living with the taxpayer, who receive part of their support from others, are also frequently examined.

If you get such a letter:

• Read it carefully; be sure you understand exactly what is being asked for.

• Recheck your return in the light of the information requested, to satisfy yourself that you have made a proper entry.

• Prepare your documentation clearly, concisely, carefully. State why you conclude you are entitled to, let's say, a deduction. In the case of a questioned dependent, for instance, show the total cost of the support of the dependent and the amount supplied by you (or by you and others).

In some cases, the IRS will enclose very detailed questionnaires to be completed by you. Many professional tax advisers hold that you need not complete such questionnaires but may return, instead, a simple written statement of the reasons why you believe you are entitled to the deduction. Send along with it *copies* of the proof which you believe substantiates the claim.

If the substantiating papers are too long or bulky to be photocopied, or if you feel that it would be difficult to set forth your justifications in writing, you may send a letter to the IRS (using the preaddressed envelope sent to you), requesting that your case be assigned to an agent with whom you can have a personal conference.

This letter, or any other correspondence relating to your audit, should be mailed to IRS within the time limit set in its letter to you. It should go by certified mail, return receipt requested. If you find you will need more time to assemble and prepare the information requested, you may request the extra time. If you foresee an extended postponement because of some abnormal situation, such as illness, the aftermath of a fire which has destroyed records, or other such emergency, this should be explained in your letter. In a case of extreme delay, from an illness, let's say, a letter from your physician verifying the incapacity of the patient to take care of his affairs as usual, might be in order. But it is wise to send this request within the time limit set by IRS, and to use certified mail.

Should you fail to answer within the time set, or on some date reasonably close to that time, the IRS will have no choice but to disallow the expense claimed or deduction involved. It will send you a "preliminary notice" of change in your tax. That is the first step in assessing an additional tax against you.

If you have submitted what you consider satisfactory evidence to substantiate your position but the IRS has rejected your contention and sent you a preliminary notice, you can appeal. You may request a "district conference" at the office of the IRS District Director for your area.

The "unallowables"

The IRS has established a new program for correction of returns which it calls the "Unallowable Items Program," or the "Thirty Unallowables." It can save erring taxpayers a trip to the IRS office for an office audit—and spare them a complete examination of the return.

Under the unallowables plan—there are thirty-nine unallowables by now, incidentally, plus ten which affect income earned abroad or earned by aliens—the IRS Service Center identifies tax returns which contain errors *due to improper application of the law.*

The taxpayer, notified by mail, is invited to agree to a correction. The IRS letter contains a one-paragraph explanation of the change. Ninety percent of the taxpayers do accept the adjustment; they pay the deficiency in tax or accept a reduced refund.

If a taxpayer declines to accept the proposed correction, the IRS makes the requested refund but then sends the return to the proper district office for further action—sometimes an office audit. The taxpayer may submit additional information on the questioned item or ask for an interview with a tax auditor.

The entire list of unallowables will be found in the Appendix, with the exact wording of the IRS letters sent to taxpayers in each case. This is a handy checklist of common errors made by taxpayers in applying the tax law.

The IRS says the most frequent "unallowables" brought to light are the omission of the $100 exclusion for each casualty loss; the failure to reduce medical expenses by the 1 percent or 3 percent of adjusted gross income; and the claiming of dividend exclusions greater than $100 on a separate return or $200 on a joint return.

If unallowable items are corrected before April 15, the taxpayer will not be subject to interest charges on his additional payments. Cases in which taxpayers fail to respond are handled under normal audit procedures.

The office audit

Sometimes an IRS letter will ask you to appear at a certain time in the local IRS offices to meet with an agent for examination of specified items in your tax return. Usually the examiner will be named in the letter.

If you cannot keep the date, telephone or write suggesting an alternative date that would be more convenient. Usually you will find the agent quite accommodating, within reason, in postponing or rescheduling the appointment.

Never let a request for a meeting go unanswered, or fail to keep the appointment without notice. If you are unavoidably detained, or miss the meeting because you forgot the date, notify the IRS office at once and request that the appointment be rescheduled.

A failure to respond could start a process in which IRS would be obliged to disallow the deductions or exemptions you have claimed. Then will come notice of adjustments in your tax return. You may find it expensive, difficult, and time-consuming to set about obtaining a reversal or revision of such adjustments at a later time.

If you had professional help in preparing your tax return, you should notify your adviser or his firm before talking to, corresponding with, or negotiating in any way with the IRS.

If you prepared your own return, review it carefully and in detail, so that you are familiar with every item in it.

Do not be afraid of bringing too many records if they relate to the matters questioned. Assemble and bring all the pertinent working papers, canceled checks, vouchers and other source material that you used in preparing your return. Put the papers in good order and logical sequence—perhaps in clearly marked file folders so that you can find readily the ones you want. (For a partial list, see Appendix, "Expense Account Records You Should Keep.")

Carry along the day books, calendars and diaries from which you drew the information on your travel or business expenses, as well as the canceled checks and receipts that support the deductions you have claimed. If an alimony deduction is involved, it is a good idea to take along a copy of the latest court papers on your divorce decree. Be cooperative, prompt and helpful.

Here is some advice on demeanor from a tax specialist in Washington, D.C.:

"Plan to arrive at the IRS office before the appointed time so you'll be ready and unflustered when you meet the tax technician who will review your return with you.

"Be cordial but not overfriendly. Answer questions truthfully and to the point. Do not volunteer extraneous information.

"Do not ask the IRS representative about other areas of your return or of taxation in general, unless these matters could lead directly to bringing you a refund for the years in question, or deductions that you omitted when you filed your return.

"Keep your composure. Remember that if you feel the person you are dealing with is in error or is unduly harsh, you have a right of appeal from his decisions and are not necessarily bound by them.

"Emotions have no place in this discussion. It is not what is fair, logical or reasonable that counts, but rather what is in the tax law.

"The burden of proof of supporting your claimed exemptions and deductions lies with you. The better you present the facts, and the more conclusive your documentation, the easier it is to support your claims."

Office audits cover generally the same types of questioned deductions and exemptions as were listed for the mail audit. They may also include examinations of items like property rentals and income from business or profession.

Field audit

A "field examination" is an audit conducted in your home, office or place of business. The agents who make them usually are assigned to the more complex tax returns, including those showing income from a trade, business or profession, partnership or corporation.

A request by letter or telephone for an appointment, suggesting the place and date, is the usual opening. In the field audit, the agent will usually wish to review all the income and deduction items on your return, not just one item or a few.

Again, if your return was prepared with professional assistance, notify your adviser. Usually he is in a better position to discuss the return with the IRS agent. He may request that you sign a form giving him the power of attorney to act in your behalf in dealing with IRS. If you have confidence in him you should not hestitate to sign the authorization.

It is perfectly proper, however, for you to request that he not agree to any proposed changes without first discussing them with you.

The guidelines for your conduct suggested earlier are appropriate also for a field audit. Usually, field agents are considerably more sophisticated and better trained than the technicians who conduct office audits. They are generally better informed on the customs, methods and practical problems of various businesses and professions, and are less interested in minor changes involving only a few dollars. For the field audit, the Washington, D.C., tax specialist offers this advice:

"Do not be disarmed by the friendly manner of an agent; some use the technique in hope you will confide in them to your own disadvantage.

"Do keep in mind that the revenue agent is a representative of the United States government and is entitled to the courtesy that you would extend a banker, your broker, or other person with whom you have business.

"Do not be oversolicitous, and never—under any circumstances whatever—make any gesture that could be construed as seeking to influence the agent—whether by mentioning 'my Uncle Ben, the Senator,' or by offering a pair of football tickets or a bottle of bourbon. It is all right to offer a cup of coffee, if you are having one, but do not be surprised if the agent declines."

A contact by a *special agent* of the IRS is a more serious matter. He will identify himself as a special agent when he requests an appointment with you, by telephone or letter. When he meets you, he will advise you that he is examining your return to determine whether or not a fraud has been committed. He will read a statement telling you of your right to counsel, and advising you that anything you say may be used by him in preparing a criminal tax fraud proceeding against you. He may ask you to initial a copy of this statement after he has read it aloud to you.

Without fail, in such a case, the taxpayer should state that he wishes to consult with his attorney or tax adviser, or both, before discussing any matters with the agent. He should immediately get in touch with his lawyer and with the person who prepared his return and discuss the problem with them in detail.

Fraud investigations sometimes result from similarity of names, a coincidence of circumstances, or even a poison-pen letter from someone who bears a grudge against you. Whatever the cause, and however clear your record may be, you should never engage in an interview with a special agent without professional assistance.

Somebody else's tax troubles may also bring an agent to your door seeking help. You may face a difficult moment when, as sometimes happens, a special agent of IRS asks you for information concerning his examination of another person's tax return. The other taxpayer may be one of your customers or suppliers.

You should cooperate, fully. Your failure to supply canceled checks, invoices or other papers as requested could lead the agent to believe that you might be involved in some way in a tax conspiracy. That could start a special investigation of your own return, with attendant expense and difficulty. And it could not possibly help the taxpayer the agent was originally examining.

In addition, the agent has the right of subpoena, and could serve you with a legal order to produce the requested records, at a time and place of his own choosing, if your information were necessary.

How to appeal

If the office audit or the agent's decision goes against you, you can appeal. The methods of initiating an appeal differ somewhat at the start but become basically the same after the first stages.

To appeal the decision from a mail audit, write a letter advising IRS that you do not concur in the preliminary report sent to you. Request a conference at the office of the District Director of IRS.

At the close of an office audit, if you do not agree to the tax changes proposed, you will be advised that you are entitled to an Audit Division conference; frequently this can be arranged almost immediately, while you are still at the IRS office.

In the case of a field examination, if you disagree with the agent who has audited your return, you will receive a "thirty-day letter." It will contain a copy of the agent's report, an explanation of the appeals procedures, and a request that you inform IRS within thirty days of your choice of action. In cases involving more than $2,500 in additional tax, you will be asked to file any protest in writing, setting forth the reasons why you feel no change should be made.

The first level of appeal, as in the case of an office audit, is the Audit

Division Conference. If the decision goes against you, the next level of appeal procedure is the District Conference. In a fairly recent change of procedure, the IRS District Conferee has been granted new and broader powers to make compromises in tax settlements. Formerly, the District Conferee could make settlements only on factual questions, not in the spirit of compromise. If, however, the District Conference produces no agreement, the taxpayer may request that his case be considered by the Appellate Division of the Office of the Regional Commissioner. This is the last step before taking the case to court; it is highly recommended, though not mandatory, that the taxpayer be represented by a professional at this point.

If you are still unable to reach a settlement, you will receive a statutory notification of your tax deficiency—called the "ninety-day letter"—advising you that if you wish to carry the case further you make take an appeal to the Tax Court of the United States within ninety days.

At this point, there are other options. If he wishes to bypass the Tax Court, the taxpayer can pay the additional tax that he feels was improperly assessed, then file a claim for refund of the money. When that is rejected, the rejection can become the basis of a law suit against the government in the U.S. District Court or the U.S. Court of Claims.

Appeals from a Tax Court or U.S. District Court decision can be made to the United States Court of Appeals. Appeals from the Court of Claims or the Court of Appeals may be taken to the Supreme Court of the United States.

Once the case goes beyond the IRS Appellate Division, the court appearances are time-consuming and costly. Every effort should be made to reach a fair and reasonable settlement before moving higher into the judicial machinery.

An opportunity for pretrial settlement will arise before a case is called to trial in the Tax Court; conferences called for that purpose frequently result in settlements.

It is a fact of life to be considered that the government scores a very high percentage of victories in its court contests. And its lawyers usually try to reach a reasonable settlement before letting a case be taken to the Tax Court.

Taxpayers with relatively small amounts at stake often have found it too costly to appeal an IRS decision to the Tax Court. They felt they had no impartial tribunal for appeal, until Congress in 1969 authorized a new Small Tax Case Division in the Tax Court, for cases involving less than $1,000.

The taxpayer, if he chooses, can appeal to the division. The procedures are simple, informal, rapid and inexpensive. The taxpayer can be his own lawyer. But there is no further appeal. The rulings are final.

Appendix I

THE UNALLOWABLES

Following are the "unallowable items" under the new IRS program for correction of returns without audit. The one-paragraph explanation is quoted in each case from the IRS letter which a taxpayer will receive if IRS finds an error due to misapplication of the law. The taxpayer is invited to accept the adjustment by paying the tax deficiency or taking a reduced refund. This frequently saves an "office audit" involving examination of the whole return.

Automobile Expenses—Donated Services

Your deduction for automobile expenses incurred in donating your services to a qualified charitable organization, reported on Schedule A, has been adjusted because you used an unallowable mileage rate to compute your automobile expenses. When using a mileage rate to determine automobile expenses for donated services, you are limited to seven cents a mile, which is the rate we used in determining your deduction.

Automobile Expenses—Medical Care

Your medical expense deduction, reported on Schedule A, has been adjusted because you used an unallowable mileage rate to compute your automobile expenses. When using a mileage rate to determine automobile expenses for medical care, you are limited to seven cents a mile, which is the rate we used in determining your deduction.

Automobile Expenses—Trade or Business

Your deduction for automobile expenses incurred in your trade or business or for the production of income has been adjusted because you used an unallowable mileage rate to compute your automobile expenses. When using a mileage rate to determine automobile expenses incurred in trade or business or the production of income, you are limited to fifteen cents a mile for the first 15,000 miles and ten cents a mile for each additional mile, which are the rates we used in determining your deduction.

Automobile License, Registration, and Tag Fees or Taxes

Your deduction for automobile license, registration, tag fees, or taxes, reported on Schedule A, has been adjusted. The law provides that such amounts may be deductible as personal property taxes only if they are imposed by your state annually, and in an amount based on the value of your automobile. Because your state does not impose the fees and taxes in this manner, they do not qualify as personal property taxes, and are therefore not deductible.

Capital Gain Distribution

The amount of income reported on your return has been adjusted to include a capital gain distribution as required by law.

Casualty or Theft Loss

Your casualty or theft loss deduction, reported on Schedule A, has been adjusted because each such loss of property used solely for personal purposes is deductible only to the extent it exceeds $100. Your deduction has been reduced by $100 for each loss, as required by law.

Contributions—Non-Qualifying

Your charitable contributions deduction, reported on Schedule A, has been adjusted because contributions to individuals or to other non-qualifying recipients, such as lobbying organizations and foreign charities (except Canadian charities) are not deductible by law.

Credit for Contributions to Candidates for Public Office

Your tax credit for contributions to candidates for public office has been adjusted because the law limits this credit to $12.50 ($25 on a joint return).

Deceased Husband (Wife)

We regret that the exemption you claimed for your deceased husband (wife) on Form 1040 must be disallowed. The law does not allow an exemption for a husband (wife) who died before the start of the tax year.

Deduction for Contributions to Candidates for Public Office

Your deduction on Schedule A for contributions to candidates for public office has been adjusted. The law limits this deduction to $50 ($100 on a joint return) and prohibits any deduction when you elect a credit against the tax on Form 1040.

Dividend Exclusion—Joint Return

Your dividend exclusion, reported on Form 1040 or 1040A, has been adjusted because an exclusion of more than $200 on a joint return is not allowable. Under the law, a husband and wife may exclude up to $100 each, whether filing jointly or separately.

Dividend Exclusion—Separate Return

Your dividend exclusion, reported on Form 1040 or 1040A has been adjusted because an exclusion of more than $100 is not allowable. The law allows you to exclude only the first $100 of dividends you received from qualifying domestic corporations during the tax year.

Duplicate Deduction

Your return has been adjusted because you claimed the same deduction on more than one schedule.

Educational Expenses for Other Than Taxpayer or Husband (Wife)

Your deduction of educational expenses for someone other than yourself or your husband (wife), reported on Schedule A, has been disallowed. Deductions for personal, living, or family expenses are allowable only if expressly provided for in the law. Educational expenses for someone other than yourself or your husband (wife) are not provided for, and are therefore not deductible.

Exemption for Husband or Wife Disallowed

When husband and wife file separate returns, the law does not allow either of them to claim an exemption for the other. Therefore, we have adjusted your taxable income for the unallowable exemption and recomputed your tax accordingly.

Expenses for Household Services and Dependent Care Deduction Limitation

Your deduction of expenses for household services and dependent care, reported on Schedule A, has been adjusted because the law limits the deduction to $400 a month. The law also requires that the deductible expenses be reduced by one-half the amount your adjusted gross income exceeds $18,000 for the year.

Expenses for Household Services and Dependent Care—Qualified Dependents

Your deduction of the expenses for household services and dependent care, reported on Schedule A, has been disallowed. The law allows a deduction for such expenses only if you are entitled to claim the children or dependents as exemptions.

Expenses for Household Services and Dependent Care—Separate Return

Your deduction of expenses for household services and dependent care, reported on Schedule A, has been disallowed. The deduction for such expenses is not allowable by law because you and your husband (wife) did not file a joint return.

Expenses for Support of Children or Other Dependents

Your deduction of expenses for support of children or dependents, reported on Schedule A, has been disallowed. Deductions for personal living, or family expenses are allowable only if expressly provided for in the law. The deduction you claimed is not provided for, and therefore is not deductible.

Federal Taxes

The deductions you claimed on Schedule A for federal taxes have been disallowed. The law denies a deduction for federal income tax; Social Security and Railroad Retirement taxes; Social Security tax you paid for a personal or domestic employe; federal excise taxes on automobiles, tires, telephone service, and air transportation; custom duties; and federal estate and gift taxes.

Form 1099 Income

The amount of income reported on your Form 1040 or 1040A must include all income reported on Form 1099 issued to you for interest, dividends, rents, royalties, etc. Any amount excludable from your gross income should be deducted, adjusted, or otherwise explained.

Fractional Exemption

The partial exemption you claimed on your return has been disallowed because the law does not provide for fractional or partial exemptions.

Gambling Losses

Your deduction for gambling or wagering losses, reported on Schedule A, has been adjusted because the law does not allow any deduction for such losses that exceed the amount of gambling or wagering winnings.

Job-Seeking Expenses

Your deduction of expenses incurred seeking employment, reported on Schedule A, has been disallowed. Deductions for personal, living, or family expenses are allowable only if expressly provided for in the law. Expenses for seeking or securing employment (other than employment agency fees) are not provided for, and are therefore not deductible.

Joint Tax Rates—Widow (Widower)

Your tax shown on Form 1040 or 1040A has been adjusted because you used the joint or widow (widower) tax rate. The law allows you to use this rate only if your husband (wife) died during the two-year period preceding the tax year for which the return is filed and you are also entitled to an exemption for your son, daughter, or stepchild who lived with you during the entire tax year in a household you maintained. Because you do not meet all these conditions, your tax has been recomputed using the appropriate tax rate.

Life and Other Personal Insurance Premiums

Your deduction of personal insurance premiums, reported on Schedule A, has been disallowed. Deductions for personal, living, or family expenses are allowable only if expressly provided for in the law. Personal insurance premiums (other than for medical care) are not provided for, and are therefore not deductible.

Loss on Sale of Personal Residence or Other Personal Property

The loss on the sale of your personal residence or other personal property has been disallowed. The law does not permit a deduction for a loss on the sale of property used for personal purposes, such as your personal residence, your automobile, furniture, jewelry, etc.

Medicine, Drug, Medical, and Dental Expenses

Your medical expense deduction, reported on Schedule A, has been adjusted because the law allows you to include in medical expenses only that part of medicine and drug expenses exceeding one percent of your adjusted gross income, regardless of your age, and only that part of medical and dental expense exceeding three percent of your adjusted gross income. You may deduct one-half of your medical insurance premium without regard to the three percent rule, but this deduction may not exceed $150. You may add the remainder of your premium to your other medical and dental expenses to determine how much you may deduct under the three percent rule.

Personal Legal Expenses

Your deduction of legal expenses, reported on Schedule A, has been disallowed. Deductions for personal, living, or family expenses are allowable only if expressly provided for in the law. Personal legal expenses for wills, trusts, adoption, divorce, and other items not connected with the production of income are not provided for, and are therefore not deductible.

Personal Living Expenses

Your deduction of personal expenses, reported on Schedule A, has been disallowed. Deductions for personal, living, or family expenses are allowable only if expressly provided for in the law. Expenses for items such as commuting to work, household costs, and maintenance of your personal residence or auto are not provided for, and are therefore not deductible.

Personal or Living Expenses—Medical Care

Your medical expense deduction, reported on Schedule A, has been adjusted because deductions for personal, living, or family expenses are not allowable unless expressly provided for in the law. Expenses for items such as meals and lodging, not furnished by a hospital or similar institution as a necessary incident to medical care, are not provided for, and are therefore not deductible.

Retirement Income Credit

The retirement income credit you claimed on your return has been disallowed. The law does not provide credit if the total of Social Security and railroad retirement benefits is $1,524 or more.

Sale or Purchase of Personal Residence

Your deduction of expenses incurred in the sale or purchase of your residence, reported on Schedule A, has been disallowed. Deductions for personal, living, or family expenses are allowable only if expressly provided for in the law. Closing expenses, settlement fees, legal fees, or realtor commissions are not provided for, and are therefore not deductible.

Schedule D Loss

The capital loss claimed on Schedule D of your return has been adjusted. The maximum loss allowable on a return is $1,000 ($500 on a return of a married person filing separately).

Self-Employment Tax

Your return has been adjusted because you reported $400 or more income from self-employment on your return, making you liable for self-employment tax under the law. Your tax liability has been computed accordingly.

State and Local Taxes

Your deduction for taxes, reported on Schedule A, has been adjusted. To be deductible, the tax you paid must have been imposed on the specific items at the general sales tax rate. State and local taxes, such as those for hotel, air fare, inheritance, stamp, poll, and mortgage transfer are not so imposed, and are therefore not deductible by law.

Utility Taxes

Your deduction for taxes, reported on Schedule A, has been adjusted. To be deductible, the tax you paid must have been imposed on the specific items at the general sales tax rate. Utility taxes with respect to sewers, water, phones, and garbage collection are not so imposed and are therefore not deductible by law.

Wages

The wages reported on your Form 1040 or 1040A do not agree in total with the Forms W-2 attached to the return. We have increased the amount of wages to agree with the amounts shown on the Forms W-2.

War or Other Protest

A deduction, credit, omission of income, or other adjustment on a federal tax return as an expression of war or other protest is not provided for in the law. We have corrected your tax for the adjustment you made.

The following "unallowables" refer to income earned by aliens, or earned abroad, or to other international aspects of the income tax.

Exclusion of Income Disallowed—U.S. Government Employe

Income received from the U.S. Government or any of its agencies as compensation for services, regardless of where the services are performed, cannot be excluded under Section 911 of the Internal Revenue Code. We have increased the amount of wages on line 11, Form 1040, by the amounts of income from the U.S. Government or any of its agencies.

Exclusion of Income From Sources Within a Possession of the United States—Only One Exemption Allowed

Citizens of the United States entitled to the benefits of Section 931 of the Internal Revenue Code may claim only one personal exemption, regardless of whether a joint or separate return is filed. We have corrected the amount claimed for exemptions on your Form 1040.

Exemptions

A non-resident alien may claim only one personal exemption unless he is a resident of Mexico, Canada, or Japan.

Failure to Qualify for Bona Fide Residence or Physical Presence in a Foreign Country

Income earned outside the United States is not excludable under Section 911 of the Internal Revenue Code since you were not a bona fide resident of a foreign country or countries for the entire taxable year or were not physically present in a foreign country or countries for at least 510 full days during a period of 18 consecutive months. We have increased your income from wages and salaries on line 11, Form 1040, or appropriate schedules, by the amounts you previously reported as excludable on Form 2555.

Foreign Tax Claimed as Both Credit and Itemized Deduction

Under Section 275 of the Internal Revenue Code, an itemized deduction is not allowed for foreign tax if you have also claimed a foreign tax credit for income tax paid or accrued to a foreign country.

Income Earned While in U.S. on Business

Compensation for services performed while in the United States on business is not excludable under Section 911 of the Internal Revenue Code. It must be included in income even though the business you transacted in the United States is directly related to your business abroad. We have included compensation for services performed in the United States, which you reported in Part I or II of Form 2555, in taxable income on your Form 1040.

Itemized Deduction

A non-resident alien may not claim deductions for medical expenses, interest, or taxes unless they are connected with the conduct of a trade or business within the United States.

Unearned Income Not Excludable Under Section 911

Unearned income, such as dividends, interest, capital gains, alimony, and other non-wage income, is not excludable under Section 911 of the Internal Revenue Code. We have included unearned income, which you reported in Part III of Form 2555, in taxable income on your Form 1040.

Unreported Income

Taxable income from your occupation was not reported on your Form 1040 or appropriate schedules. We have increased the amount of income on line 11, page 1, Form 1040 or appropriate schedules, by the amount of income you reported in your letter.

Unreported Income Earned in the United States

Taxable income earned in the United States either before your departure to go abroad or following your return was not reported on your Form 1040. We have increased your taxable income by the amount you reported in your letter.

Appendix II

A facsimile of Form 1040, front and back, is shown on the following two pages for purposes of general reference only. Major categories usually do not change from year to year, but some revisions are made from time to time. Thus, a tax form for one year is not to be used for subsequent years.

Form 1040 is mailed to the taxpayer each new year as part of a package containing certain commonly used supplemental forms. The package usually contains, in addition to Form 1040, the following: Schedules A&B, "Itemized Deductions and Dividend and Interest Income"; Schedule C, "Profit (or Loss) from Business or Profession"; Schedule D, "Capital Gains and Losses"; Schedules E&R, "Supplemental Income Schedule and Retirement Income Credit Computation"; and Schedule SE, "Computation of Social Security Self-Employment Tax."

Additional copies of any of these may be ordered from your nearest IRS District Director's Office, or found at many banks and post offices. Some specialized forms for a variety of specific needs are available *only* at IRS offices.

Form **1040**

US Department of the Treasury—Internal Revenue Service
Individual Income Tax Return **19**

For the year January 1–December 31, 19 ____ or other taxable year beginning _____, 19 ____ ending _____, 19 ____

Name (If joint return, give first names and initials of both)	Last name

Please print or type

COUNTY OF RESIDENCE	Your social security number

Present home address (Number and street, including apartment number, or rural route)

| | Spouse's social security no. |

City, town or post office, State and ZIP code

| Occu- | Yours ▶ |
| pation | Spouse's ▶ |

Filing Status—check only one:

1 ☐ Single
2 ☐ Married filing joint return (even if only one had income)
3 ☐ Married filing separately. If spouse is also filing gife spouse's social security number in designated space above and enter full name here ▶ _____
4 ☐ Unmarried Head of Household (See instructions on page 5) ▶ _____
5 ☐ Widow(er) with dependent child (Year spouse died ▶ 19 ____)

Exemptions   Regular / 65 or over / Blind

6a Yourself . . . ☐ ☐ ☐
 b Spouse . . . ☐ ☐ ☐

  Enter number of boxes checked ▶

 c First names of your dependent children who lived with you _____

  Enter number ▶

 d Number of other dependents (from line 27) . . . ▶
7 Total exemptions claimed . . . . ▶

8 Presidential Election Campaign Fund . . ▶
Do you wish to designate $1 of your taxes for this fund? . . . . | Yes | | No |
If joint return, does your spouse wish to designate $1? . . . . | Yes | | No |

Please attach Copy B of Forms W-2 here

Income

9 Wages, salaries, tips, and other employee compensation . . . . | 9 |
 (Attach Forms W-2. If unavailable, see instructions on page 3.)

10a Dividends (See instructions on pages 6 and 13)$ ...., 10b Less exclusion $............., **Balance** ▶ | 10c |
 (If gross dividends and other distributions are over $400, list in Part I of Schedule B.)

11 Interest income. [If $400 or less, enter total without listing in Schedule B / If over $400, enter total and list in Part II of Schedule B.] | 11 |

12 Income other than wages, dividends, and interest (from line 38) . . . . . | 12 |

13 Total (add lines 9, 10c, 11, and 12) . . . . | 13 |

14 Adjustments to income (such as "sick pay," moving expenses, etc. from line 43) . | 14 |

15 Subtract line 14 from line 13 (adjusted gross income) . . . . | 15 |

● If you do not itemize deductions and line 15 is under $10,000, find tax in Tables and enter on line 16.
● If you itemize deductions or line 15 is $10,000 or more, go to line 44 to figure tax.
● CAUTION. If you have unearned income and can be claimed as a dependent on your parent's return, check here ▶ ☐ and see instructions on page 7.

Tax, Payments and Credits

16 Tax, check if from: | Tax Tables 1–12 | Tax Rate Schedule X, Y, or Z |
 ☐ Schedule D | ☐ Schedule G | ☐ Form 4726 **OR** ☐ Form 4972 | 16 |

17 Total credits (from line 54) . . . . | 17 |
18 Income tax (subtract line 17 from line 16) . . . . | 18 |
19 Other taxes (from line 61) . . . . | 19 |
20 Total (add lines 18 and 19) . . . . | 20 |

21a Total Federal income tax withheld (attach Forms W–2 or W–2P to front) . . . . | 21a |
 b 19 ____ estimated tax payments (include amount allowed as credit from 19 ____ return) . . | b |
 c Amount paid with Form 4868, Application for Automatic Extension of Time to File U.S. Individual Income Tax Return | c |
 d Other payments (from line 65) . . . . | d |
22 Total (add lines 21a, b, c, and d) . . . . | 22 |

Pay amount on line 23 in full with this return. Write social security number on check or money order and make payable to Internal Revenue Service.

Balance Due or Refund

23 If line 20 is larger than line 22, enter **BALANCE DUE IRS** . . . . . . ▶ | 23 |
 (Check here ▶ ☐, if Form 2210, Form 2210F, or statement is attached. See instructions on page 8.)
24 If line 22 is larger than line 20, enter amount **OVERPAID** . . . . . . ▶ | 24 |
25 Amount of line 24 to be **REFUNDED TO YOU** . . . . ▶ | 25 |
26 Amount of line 24 to be credited on 19 ____ estimated tax. ▶ | 26 |

Please attach Check or Money Order here

Sign here

Under penalties of perjury, I declare that I have examined this return, including accompanying schedules and statements, and to the best of my knowledge and belief it is true, correct, and complete. Declaration of preparer (other than taxpayer) is based on all information of which he has any knowledge.

▶ Your signature _____ Date _____ | Preparer's signature (other than taxpayer) _____ Date _____

▶ Spouse's signature (if filing jointly, BOTH must sign even if only one had income) | Address (and ZIP Code) _____ Preparer's Emp. Ident. or Soc. Sec. No.

16—■■■—1

Form 1040 (19)

	(a) NAME	(b) Relationship	(c) Months lived in your home. If born or died during year, write B or D.	(d) Did dependent have income of $750 or more?	(e) Amount YOU furnished for dependent's support. If 100% write ALL.	(f) Amount furnished by OTHERS including dependent.
Other Dependents					$_____	$_____

27 Total number of dependents listed in column (a). Enter here and on line 6d . . . . ▶ |

Part I Income other than Wages, Dividends, and Interest

28 Business income or (loss) (attach Schedule C)	28	
29 Net gain or (loss) from sale or exchange of capital assets (attach Schedule D)	29	
30 Net gain or (loss) from Supplemental Schedule of Gains and Losses (attach Form 4797) . .	30	
31 Pensions, annuities, rents, royalties, partnerships, estates or trusts, etc. (attach Schedule E) . .	31	
32 Farm income or (loss) (attach Schedule F)	32	
33 Fully taxable pensions and annuities (not reported on Schedule E—see instructions on page 8)	33	
34 50% of capital gain distributions (not reported on Schedule D—see instructions on page 8) .	34	
35 State income tax refunds (does not apply if refund is for year in which you took the standard deduction—others see instructions on page 8).	35	
36 Alimony received . . . . . . (Caution: Do not report self-employment income here. Use	36	
37 Other (state nature and source) (Schedule C or Schedule F and Schedule SE, if applicable)	37	
▶		
38 Total (add lines 28, 29, 30, 31, 32, 33, 34, 35, 36, and 37). Enter here and on line 12 . ▶	38	

Part II Adjustments to Income

39 "Sick pay." (From Forms W-2 and W-2P. If not shown on Forms W-2 or W-2P, attach Form 2440 or statement.)	39	
40 Moving expense (attach Form 3903)	40	
41 Employee business expense (attach Form 2106 or statement)	41	
42 Payments as a self-employed person to a retirement plan, etc. (see Form 4848) . . . ▶	42	
43 Total adjustments (add lines 39, 40, 41, and 42). Enter here and on line 14 . . . . ▶	43	

Part III Tax Computation (Do not use this part if you use Tax Tables 1–12 to find your tax.)

44 Adjusted gross income (from line 15)	44	
45 (a) If you itemize deductions, check here ▶ ☐ and enter total from Schedule A, line 41 and attach Schedule A	45	
(b) If you do not itemize deductions, check here ▶ ☐ and enter 15% of line 44, but do NOT enter more than $2,000. ($1,000 if line 3 checked)		
46 Subtract line 45 from line 44	46	
47 Multiply total number of exemptions claimed on line 7, by $750	47	
48 Taxable income. Subtract line 47 from line 46	48	

(Figure your tax on the amount on line 48 by using Tax Rate Schedule X, Y, or Z, or if applicable, the alternative tax from Schedule D, income averaging from Schedule G, maximum tax from Form 4726, or special averaging from Form 4972.) Enter tax on line 16.

Part IV Credits

49 Retirement income credit (attach Schedule R)	49	
50 Investment credit (attach Form 3468)	50	
51 Foreign tax credit (attach Form 1116)	51	
52 Credit for contributions to candidates for public office—see instructions on page 9 . . .	52	
53 Work Incentive (WIN) credit (attach Form 4874)	53	
54 Total credits (add lines 49, 50, 51, 52, and 53). Enter here and on line 17 . . . . . ▶	54	

Part V Other Taxes

55 Self-employment tax (attach Schedule SE)	55	
56 Tax from recomputing prior-year investment credit (attach Form 4255)	56	
57 Tax from recomputing prior-year Work Incentive (WIN) credit (attach schedule)	57	
58 Minimum tax. Check here ▶ ☐, if Form 4625 is attached	58	
59 Social security tax on tip income not reported to employer (attach Form 4137)	59	
60 Uncollected employee social security tax on tips (from Forms W-2)	60	
61 Total (add lines 55, 56, 57, 58, 59, and 60). Enter here and on line 19 . . . . . . ▶	61	

Part VI Other Payments

62 Excess FICA tax withheld (two or more employers—see instructions on page 9)	62	
63 Credit for Federal tax on special fuels, nonhighway gasoline and lubricating oil (attach Form 4136)	63	
64 Credit from a Regulated Investment Company (attach Form 2439) . . . . ▶	64	
65 Total (add lines 62, 63, and 64). Enter here and on line 21d	65	

Foreign Accounts Did you, at any time during the taxable year, have any interest in or signature or other authority over a bank, securities, or other financial account in a foreign country (except in a U.S. military banking facility operated by a U.S. financial institution)? . . . . ▶ ☐ Yes ☐ No
If "Yes" attach Form 4683. (For definitions, see Form 4683.)

Appendix III

Federal Income Tax Rate Schedules*								
	Married Filing Joint Return		Married Filing Separate Return		Head of Household		Unmarried Individuals	
Taxable Income over	Taxes Due: amt. in col. 2 plus % in col. 3 on excess over amt. in col. 1		Taxes Due: amt. in col. 2 plus % in col. 3 on excess over amt. in col. 1		Taxes Due: amt. in col. 2 plus % in col. 3 on excess over amt. in col. 1		Taxes Due: amt. in col. 2 plus % in col. 3 on excess over amt. in col. 1	
1	2	3	2	3	2	3	2	3
$	$	14%	$	14%	$	14%	$	14%
500	70	14	70	15	70	14	70	15
1,000	140	15	145	16	140	16	145	16
1,500	215	15	225	17	220	16	225	17
2,000	290	16	310	19	300	18	310	19
3,000	450	17	500	19	480	18	500	19
4,000	620	19	690	22	660	19	690	21
6,000	1,000	19	1,130	25	1,040	22	1,110	24
8,000	1,380	22	1,630	28	1,480	23	1,590	25
10,000	1,820	22	2,190	32	1,940	25	2,090	27
12,000	2,260	25	2,830	36	2,440	27	2,630	29
14,000	2,760	25	3,550	39	2,980	28	3,210	31
16,000	3,260	28	4,330	42	3,540	31	3,830	34
18,000	3,820	28	5,170	45	4,160	32	4,510	36
20,000	4,380	32	6,070	48	4,800	35	5,230	38
22,000	5,020	32	7,030	50	5,500	36	5,990	40
24,000	5,660	36	8,030	50	6,220	38	6,790	40
26,000	6,380	36	9,030	53	6,980	41	7,590	45
28,000	7,100	39	10,090	53	7,800	42	8,490	45
32,000	8,660	42	12,210	55	9,480	45	10,290	50
36,000	10,340	45	14,410	55	11,280	48	12,290	50
38,000	11,240	45	15,510	58	12,240	51	13,290	55
40,000	12,140	48	16,670	58	13,260	52	14,390	55
44,000	14,060	50	18,990	60	15,340	55	16,590	60
50,000	17,060	50	22,590	62	18,640	56	20,190	62
52,000	18,060	53	23,830	62	19,760	58	21,430	62
60,000	22,300	53	28,790	64	24,400	58	26,390	64
64,000	24,420	55	31,350	64	26,720	59	28,950	64
70,000	27,720	55	35,190	66	30,260	61	32,790	66
76,000	31,020	58	39,150	66	33,920	62	36,750	66
80,000	33,340	58	41,790	68	36,400	63	39,390	68
88,000	37,980	60	47,230	68	41,440	64	44,830	68
90,000	39,180	60	48,590	69	42,720	64	46,190	69
100,000	45,180	62	55,490	70	49,120	66	53,090	70
120,000	57,580	64	69,490	70	62,320	67	67,090	70
140,000	70,380	66	83,490	70	75,720	68	81,090	70
160,000	83,580	68	97,490	70	89,320	69	95,090	70
180,000	97,180	69	111,490	70	103,120	70	109,090	70
200,000	110,980	70	125,490	70	117,120	70	123,090	70

* Note: While federal tax rates have remained stable in recent years, the above rates, as of 1974, may or may not change in the future. It is necessary to check current schedules.

Appendix IV

Expense Account Records You Should Keep

To qualify your travel and entertainment expenses for tax deductions, you should be able to supply the following information:

Entertainment expenses generally

Cost: time, including the date, name of the place or places, including the address of restaurant, theater or entertainment place, if the location is not generally known.

Business relationship of those entertained for whose costs a deduction is claimed, including the title or occupation which shows the business relationship to you.

(Note that for "quiet business meals" it is not necessary to record the nature of the business discussion.)

Entertainment expenses directly preceding or following a business discussion; additional information is required, as follows:

Length of the business discussion, as well as date and time.

Place of the business discussion (as well as the place of the entertainment).

Business purpose, including nature of the discussion and business reason for the entertainment, or nature of the business derived or expected.

Business relationship of those participating, including identifications or titles.

Traveling expenses

Costs, including meals, lodging, transportation, telephone and telegraph.

Place or places visited by names of cities or localities.

Business reason for the travel, or nature of the business benefit derived or expected as a result of the visit to each place.

Other deductible travel expenses

The following are deductible as travel costs away from home:

Plane, railroad, taxi, bus and other transportation fares
Meals, hotel and motel expenses
Auto expenses for business purposes, including cost of commuting from
   hotel to point where you are working while on a business trip
Attendance and registration costs at business convention
Display expenses such as hotel and sample room costs
Baggage charges and porters' charges
Public stenographers' costs
Costs of copying, mimeographing or duplicating
Laundry or cleaning expenses
Telephone and telegraph costs
Tips

Appendix V
_____

Deductions for All Taxpayers

Individual taxpayers, regardless of source of income, can deduct the following items. Business and professional men and investors may deduct all the ordinary and necessary expenses connected with their businesses, professions and investment activities. Medical expenses and many others listed are subject to limitation.

Alimony and separate maintenance (periodic payments)
Appraisal fees, for contributions of charitable property and for casualty
   loss determination
Artificial teeth, limbs, etc.
Automobile accidents, damage, over $100
Automobile registration (if personal property tax)
Bad debts
Bonds, worthless
Casualty losses (see Losses), over $100
Charitable contributions
Child care expense
Chiropodists' fees
Chiropractors' fees
Church contributions
Damages, uninsured, resulting from casualty, over $100
Debts, uncollectable
Dental expenses
Doctors' fees
Drought losses
Drugs and medicines
Excise taxes, state and local
Eye glasses, examination fees
FHA loans, discount on
Fire losses, over $100
Flood losses, over $100
Fraternal organizations, contributions to
Gambling losses (to extent of gambling gains)
Gasoline tax, state
Health and accident insurance premiums
Hurricane damage, over $100
Income tax, state or local

Interest paid, including
  carrying charge on installment purchase
  discount on mortgage or other borrowing
  "points" on mortgage or other loan
  "unstated interest" on certain deferred-payment purchases
Investment counseling
Loans, uncollectable
Losses, not insured, over $100
  automobile accidents

bad debts	hurricane
burglary	ice jams
casualty	shipwreck
embezzlement	storm
fire	theft
flood	vandalism
frozen pipes	worthless securities

Medical expenses
Personal property taxes, state or local
Psychiatrists' and psychologists' fees
Real estate taxes, state or local
Red Cross workers, volunteer, expenses
Safety equipment for job
Sales taxes, state or local
Separation payments (periodic) to wife
Sublease of apartment, loss on
Tax counseling, cost of
Tax litigation expenses
Tax returns, cost of preparing
Taxes, state or local

auto registration	motor fuel
(if personal property tax)	personal property
excise	real estate
gasoline	sales
income	

Taxes paid in connection with business or in producing income

admission taxes	liquor taxes
auto registration	mortgage taxes
beverage taxes	occupancy
cigarette taxes	stock transfer taxes
driver's license fees	tobacco taxes
excise taxes	

Union dues and assessments

Appendix VI

Income Free of Tax

The following types of income are nontaxable and need not be reported on your income tax return:

Accident and health insurance premiums paid by employer
Accident insurance proceeds
Alimony (if lump-sum)
Allowances received from husband, parent or guardian
Annuity, portion representing a return of your cost
Bad debts, recovery of (if not previously used to offset income)
Board and lodging furnished by employer for his convenience
Cancellation of debt under bankruptcy proceeding
Capital, payments representing a return of
Child support payments
Combat pay of servicemen
Compensation earned by another but assigned to you
Damages for
    alienation of affections
    breach of promise
    libel or slander
    personal injuries
Death benefit from employer, up to $5,000
Disability payments and other benefits from Veterans Administration
Distributions from trust, certain
Dividends on unmatured life insurance policies
Employer's payment on employe's health and accident insurance
Employe's expense, reimbursement of
Foreign earnings of nonresident U.S. citizens, in some cases
Gifts
Group accident and health insurance premiums, paid by employer
Group life insurance premiums, paid by employer, up to $50,000 coverage
Health and accident benefits, employe's (restricted)
Health and accident plans for employes, employer contributions to
Household allowance to wife or family member
Housing furnished by employer for his convenience
Increase in value of property, not realized by sale
Inheritances
Insurance proceeds
Interest on state or municipal bonds
Juror's commuting allowance

Life insurance
    dividends on unmatured policies
    proceeds on death of insured
Literary prizes and similar awards
Loans, principal of, repaid
Loss of limb or eye, employer's payment for
Marriage settlements, lump-sum payments
Military personnel (see Servicemen)
Minister's dwelling or rental allowance
Moving expenses, reimbursement by employer
Parents' allowances to children
Pensions, war veterans and families
Railroad passes to employes and families
Railroad Retirement annuities and pensions
Refunds of tax not previously deducted
Reimbursed employe expenses (if "accounted for" to employer)
Reimbursement for loss
Residence, gain on sale of, by person sixty-five or over
Returns of capital
Scholarships and fellowships (if not given as compensation)
Servicemen
    allowances for quarters, subsistence, and uniforms
    combat pay
    disability pay
    family allowances paid by government
    mustering out pay
    terminal leave pay, certain
Social security benefits
Supper money received from employer
Uncollectable income
Unemployment compensation benefits
Veterans
    autos received by disabled veterans
    disability allowances and pensions
    family allowances paid by government
    GI loans, government payments of
    government insurance proceeds and dividends
    pensions (retirement pay is taxable, however)
    readjustment benefits
    specially designed homes and cars granted to paraplegic veterans
Workmen's compensation payments

Appendix VII

Deductible Medical Expenses

Abortion, legal
Ambulance hire
Artificial limbs and teeth
Birth control pills, prescribed
Braces
Chiropodists' fees
Chiropractors' fees
Christian Science practitioners' fees
Crutches
Dental bills
Dentures
Drugs and medicines
Elastic stockings
Eyeglasses, contact lenses
Health insurance
Hearing aids
Hospital costs
Hospitalization insurance
Institution for physically or mentally handicapped
Laboratory fees
Nursing fees, including nurse's board paid by you
Obstetrical expenses
Psychiatric care
Psychologists' fees
Physicians' fees
Seeing-eye dog and upkeep
Surgical fees
Teeth straightening
Therapy
Transportation to doctor or hospital and return
Vasectomy, legal
Vitamins and mineral supplements prescribed for medical
  (not nutritional) reasons
Wheelchairs
X-rays

Appendix VIII
_____

Nondeductible Medical Expenses

Cosmetics
Dancing or swimming lessons
Diets, if substituting for normal diet
Disability insurance
Domestic help
Feminine hygiene supplies
Funeral expenses and plots
Health Club dues
Illegal operation
Life insurance premiums
Maternity clothing
Soap
Toothpaste, toothbrush
Trips, for general health improvement
Vitamins, for nutritional purposes

Appendix IX
_____

Deductions for the Outside Salesman

Following are business expenses which an outside salesman can deduct as "adjustments" to gross income:

Advertising and business cards
Auto operating expenses
Baggage and transfer charges
Cleaning and laundry bills while away from home
Cost of meals while away from home overnight on business
Dues paid to business associations, unions, professional societies
Educational expenses
Entertainment and business gifts
Gifts to customers (limited to $25 per customer per year)
Hotel expenses
Local transportation costs
Loss on sale of a business auto
Loss on sale of any other business-used asset
Miscellaneous auto expenses, including depreciation, garage rent, parking
    and storage charges, insurance, inspection fees, auto and driver's licen-
    ses, highway tolls and towing charges
Moving expenses
Record-keeping and accounting costs, and preparation of tax returns
Samples and sample room displays, including room rent for the displays
"Split commissions" shared with another
Stenographic expenses
Subscriptions to publications used in his work
Taxi fares
Telephone and telegraph charges
Tips
Travel expenses, including airplane, railroad, bus and steamship fares

Note: The outside salesman who maintains an office in his home may charge as a deduction against gross income the costs of cleaning, decorating, depreciation, heat, insurance, interest on mortgage, light, rent, repairs and taxes. The charges are claimed in proportion to the space devoted to the office: for example one room used as an office in a seven-room home would permit the deduction of one-seventh of all the above expenses.

Appendix X

Employe's Business Deductions

Salesmen and other employes can deduct the ordinary and necessary expenses incurred in connection with their jobs. The following are typical deductible costs. (Note: Many are not deductible by employes who use the Tax Table method of computing tax, or who take the standard deduction.)

Automobile expenses (portion allocated to business)
   depreciation
   garage rent
   gasoline and oil
   inspection and registration fees
   insurance
   parking charges, meters
   repairs
   tolls
Christmas gifts to customers (limited)
Conventions, costs of attending
Dues paid to:
   business associations
   labor unions
   professional societies
   social or athletic clubs used primarily for business purposes
Educational expenses, certain
Employment agency fees for obtaining employment
Entertainment expenses
Fidelity bonds, cost of
Gifts to customers and prospects (limited)
Home expenses chargeable to business use
   cleaning
   depreciation
   heat
   insurance
   interest
   light
   repairs
   taxes
   telephone

Insurance premiums
  automobile (to extent of business use)
  bonds (fidelity, etc.)
"Kickbacks" paid, if legal
Laundry, dry cleaning and valet service
Meals and lodging (while traveling)
Moving expenses, certain
Parking meter fees, garage charges
Passport fees for business travel
Reimbursed expenses (if reimbursement is included in income)
Repairs to auto, if used in business
Safety equipment
Subscriptions to professional journals and magazines
Tax return, cost of preparing
Teachers, summer school expenses (if necessary to keep position)
Technical periodicals
Telephone and telegraph expenses (including necessary phones in home)
Tips
Tools, cost of
Transportation expenses
Traveling expenses
  baggage charges
  fares
  laundry and cleaning costs away from home
  meals and lodging away from home
  passports
  sample rooms
  taxis
  telephone and telegraph
  tips
  wife's expenses, when employer requires that she accompany you
Tuition fees, certain
Uniforms
Union initiation fees, dues, assessments
Work clothes

Appendix XI

Expense Deductions for the Businessman and the Professional Man

The following are deductible without limit as "ordinary and necessary" expenses:

Accounting fees
Advertising expenses
Appraisal costs
Attorney's fees, related to the business, or services rendered in connection with the business
Automobile upkeep and maintenance
Conventions related to business, and costs of attending
Depreciation on business assets
Dues, professional or business organizations
Gifts or contributions to a political party or for the benefit of a political candidate (limited)
Gifts to customers ($25 limit per individual)
Insurance

burglary	hospitalization insurance for employes
business interruption	plate glass
business "package" policies	public liability
employes' group life	storm
fire	theft
holdup	workmen's compensation
hospitalization	

Interest
License fees
Light bills
Machinery repairs
Mortgage prepayment policies
Painting
Picnics, parties and dances for employes
Postage
Refuse removal
Rent
Repairs to business property
Salaries, bonuses, commissions paid
Sales commissions
Stationery
Subscriptions, professional and trade publications
Supplies

Taxes on your business
Telephone
Theft, business losses not compensated by insurance

Not deductible:
A fine or penalty paid for violation of federal or state laws, or other payments which would "frustrate public policy." (Example—a bribe or illegal kickback.)

Appendix XII

Deductions for the Farmer

As in every business, all ordinary and necessary costs are deductible. Costs of farm buildings and major equipment are capitalized (depreciated over useful life), not deducted currently. Costs of crops or livestock which are lost by death, storm, freezing, water damage or shrinkage ordinarily cannot be deducted if the taxpayer already has deducted the costs of growing them. Food grown on the farm and provided to farm hands is not deductible if growing costs have been deducted. The following are deductible:

Automobile expenses and depreciation, farm share
Board for farm help
Breeding fees
Casualty, storm, theft losses
Depreciation of draft, breeding or dairy livestock and farm buildings
    and equipment
Dues to farmers' and growers' organizations
Erosion prevention costs
Feed
Fertilizer and lime
Gasoline, fuel and oil for farm use; federal tax is refundable
Ginning
Insecticide sprays and dusts
Insurance premiums on farm property
Land clearing costs
Legal and accounting fees
Losses on purchased animals sold or lost by death
Marketing quota penalties
Plants
Publications, farm journals
Rent (of equipment, land, machinery, pasture, water)
Repairs on farm buildings and vehicles
Sacks, twine, wire, containers
Seed
Soil and water conservation
Tools with useful life of one year or less (otherwise depreciate)
Travel for farm business
Tying material and containers
Veterinary fees
Veterinary medicine
Wages of help, including reasonable pay to children

Appendix XIII

Casualty Loss Deductions

Here is a checklist of causes or sources of uninsured losses which qualify for casualty deductions, after reducing the loss by $100:

Automobile accidents (unless caused by your gross negligence)
Blasting nearby
Boat wrecked by storm
Boiler bursting
Clean-up and repairs after casualty
Earthquake
Embezzlement
Explosion, accidental
Fire
Flood, heavy rains
Freezing of pipes, etc.
Hurricane or wind storm
Ice damage
Mine cave-in damage
Orchards, damaged by storm or drought
Riots
Sonic boom damage
Theft, robbery
Tornado
Vandalism

Losses from these causes are not deductible

Baggage lost in transit
Breakage of china, glassware, etc., by yourself or pets
Cave-in of partly completed well or cellar
Confiscation of property by foreign government
Erosion
Moth and carpet beetle damage
Rat damage
Rental, fuel, moving costs if temporary quarters needed
Termite damage
Trees lost by disease, fungus, insects and worms
Well drying up because of heat or drought

Index

A

ADR. *See* asset depreciation range
AGI. *See* adjusted gross income
abortion, 23
accelerated depreciation:
    LTP, 153
    rapid write-off, 22-23
    rental property, 198-199
    selling rental property, 211-212
accidents, casualty losses, 111
accounting methods:
    business and professional men,
        237-242
    farmers, 282
accrual method (accounting),
    240, 282
accumulation trust, 305
adjusted basis, casualty losses, 114
adjusted cost basis, sale of house,
    200, 315
adjusted gross income, 51-55:
    child care deduction and, 171

adjusted gross income *(continued)*
    deductions and, 57
    definition, 48
    medical expense, 108-109
    office-at-home, 134-135
    state sales tax, tables, 95
adjusted sales price (house),
    200, 290
adjustment from gross income:
    business transfer taxes, 97
    outside salesmen, 175
adjustments to gross income:
    employes' business expenses, 121
    itemized deductions, 74
    self-employed, 110
"against the box," 186
aged. *See* older persons
alimony, 117-118, 307
alternating deductions, 17, 60-61,
    94, 97, 179
"alternative tax" method, capital
    gains, 67

amended returns, disaster losses,
115-116
American Bar Association, 37
American Medical Association
(AMA), 269
annuity:
employe's benefit, 123
executives, 154
Keogh plan, 250
tax withholding, 75
your pension, 125
anti-pollution bonds, 193
apartment projects, 22-23
appeals:
mail audit, 318
tax audits, 322-323
tax counsel and, 38-40
appraisals:
casualty losses, 114
fee, 109
appreciated property, 104
appreciated stocks, 101
armed forces, disability retirement,
123, 289
Articles of Incorporation
(document), 264
art objects, charitable deduction, 24
asset depreciation range, 232
"associated" rule, expense account
deductions, 156
"at the top" deductions, 56, 134
attorneys, 22, 38:
incorporation and, 254
professional incorporation and,
264
public-interest law firms, 108
tax audits and, 317, 322
audits, 36:
alimony payments, 118
average deductions and, 94
if you are audited, 311-323
automobiles:
as business deduction, 129
casualty losses, 112
charitable use, 102
collision insurance, 109
depreciation, 23
employes' business expenses, 111
expense account deduction,
157-158
sales tax, 96
used in business, 18, 21
averageable income, 17
averaging. See income averaging
avoiding probate, 304

B
bad debts, 116, 153
banks:
constructively received income, 50
credit card charges, 98
establishing a business, 238
mortgage interest, 99
bargain sales (stocks), 101, 105-106,
153
before-tax dollars, insuring with,
268-269
beneficiaries, trusts, 302, 306
Bennett, Wallace, 35
bequest vs. giving while living, 300
Big Brothers of America, 104
binding contract rule, capital gains,
69
birth-control pills, 23, 109
blind:
exemptions for, 62
medical deductions, 110
blood donations, 102
boats, sales tax, 96
bonds:
bond-purchase plans, 125
Series E, 287
Series H, 287
tax savings, 189
bonus grants:
employe benefits, 124
executives, 149, 154
"brackets" (tax brackets), 33, 43-44
brokers' commissions, 186
Brookings Institution, 31
business bad debt, 116
business expenses deductions, 22,
55, 236-237:
employes' deduction, 110-111
expense account deductions, 155
wage-price controls, 257
business gifts, 157
business travel, 25, 130
businessman, tax savings for,
235-257, 316

C
C.P.A. See Certified Public
Accountant
calendar year, 242, 266
capital assets, farms, 281, 283
capital expenditures, 239
capital gains and losses, 20, 182-186:
bonds and, 190
corporate shares, 254
definition, 65

capital gains and losses *(continued)*
depreciation and, 222
dividends, 189
farm resale, 273
giving appreciated property, 105
income average and, 204
investment interest, 100
land investment, 216-217
livestock, 275, 279
LTP and, 153
overpayment and, 30
partnership, 248
pensions, 127-128
professional corporations, 260
real estate equity, 93
recapture problem and, 227-228
retirement fund pay, 288
sale of real property, 200, 283, 290
stock options, 147
capital improvements:
adjusted basis and, 114
land investment, 217
real property, 203, 206
records of, 315
carrying charges. *See* interest
charges
cash method (accounting), 50, 239,
282
cash value (life insurance), 306
casualty losses, 111-116:
auditing, 312
auto, 21, 131
cattle, 275
ceiling rate on earned income, 150
Certified Public Accountant, 38:
business records and, 237
tax audits and, 317
charitable remainder trust, 187, 305
charities:
giving while living, 300
remainder interest, 305
stock donations to, 187
travel for, 24
Chartered Life Underwriters, 306
"check-off" plans, political
contributions, 108
checks, as tax records, 238, 317
child care deduction, 118, 166,
170-171
children:
alimony payments and, 118
child support, exemptions and, 62
medical expenses, 110
reversionary trusts, 302

children *(continued)*
splitting income, 81
what is a dependent, 62-63
chiropractors, 108-109
Christian Science practitioners,
108-109
churches:
contributions to, 104
stock donations to, 186-187
travel for, 24
citrus groves, 281
civil service, retirement system, 127
clergymen, 46
"closely connected" person, 156
clothing, used, donation to charity,
104
clubs and facilities, expense account
deductions, 158
coal royalties, 219
Coast Guard, 123, 289
"Cohan rule," 162-163
Cohen, Edwin S., 284, 292-294
collision insurance, 109
combat pay, 49
commercial trustee, definition, 304
commissions, outside salesmen, 178
common-law marriage, 83
community property system, 82,
85-86
commuting, auto deduction, 129, 131
company car, fringe benefit, 18
computers, tax audits, 36, 316
condominium, tax savings, 206, 207
conference (Audit Division),
322-323
conservation expenses, 280
"constructively received" money,
50, 148, 240, 267
continuity of corporate life, 268
contraceptive pills, deduction, 23,
109
contributions (charitable,
educational, etc.), 101-108:
auto driving, 131
pension plans, 125-126
securities, 186-187
convertible bonds, 191
corporate bonds, 190
corporation, 26, 251-256:
definition, 245
farm losses, 279
incorporation, fiscal savings, 243
officers, audits, 314
professional men, 259, 271
tax settlements, 313

corporation *(continued)*
    tax shelter, 19
corporation taxes, 252
cost basis, ("bargain sales"),
    105-106
cost depletion, oil and mining, 217
cost of living:
    inflation and taxes, 15-16
    living costs at new location, 52
credit transactions, interest
    payments, 98
crop method (accounting), farms,
    282

D
DIF. *See* discriminate function
DISC. *See* Domestic International
    Sales Corporation
dairy cattle, 275
day-care centers, 173
deadlines:
    establishing a stock tax loss, 185
    estimated tax declarations, 75-76
    filing tax return, 77
    mail audits, 318
    "second homes" deductions, 209
    the "Unallowables," 319
deaf, medical deductions for, 110
death:
    gifts in contemplation of, 300
    joint returns and, 83
    recapture of depreciation, 228
death benefits:
    alimony and, 307
    annuity and, 289
    professional incorporation, 267
    retirement and, 287-288
death bonds. *See* flower bonds
death taxes. *See* estate taxes
debentures, 191
debit managers, 176
debts, bad debts, 116, 153
declining balance depreciation
    method, 158, 223-224
deductions. *See also* itemized
        deductions, miscellaneous
        deductions, standard deductions
    "average" deductions, 93
    businessmen, 55, 236
    capital losses, 68
    child care, 166
    condominiums, 207
    depletion allowances, 217-218
    depreciation methods, 224-225
    executive's insurance, 143-144

deductions *(continued)*
    farm expenses, 280-282
    farm losses, 278
    farm owner's outlays, 274
    fiscal savings, 243
    "hobby farms," 279-280
    itemized deductions, 91-119
    itemizing and "alternating," 60
    land investment, 216
    partnerships, 248
    real estate investment, 216
    rental properties, 206
    retirement and debt, 287
    sale of rental property, 229
    sales of stock, 254
    second homes, 209
    securities investors, 186
    selling rental property, 212
    standard deduction, 57
    tax audits and, 316-317
    timing and, 16
deep-discount bonds, 194
"defense tax," 34
deferred income. *See* income
    deferral
dental expense deductions,
    108-110
dentists, office-at-home, 135
dependents:
    care of, 170-172
    exemptions, 21
    what is a dependent, 62
depletion allowances, oil and
    mining, 217-218
depreciation:
    auto, 23
    business auto, 130
    buying a farm, 281
    exchange of property, 204
    farm outlays, 274
    income-producing property, 22
    livestock, 280
    real estate, 215
    REITs, 214
    rental property, 197-199,
        205-206, 211-212
    tax savings, 221-233
development expenses, farms, 281
direct taxes, 32-33
"directly related" rule,
    expense account deductions,
    156, 158-159
disability insurance, Keogh
    plan and, 250
disability retirement, 123

disaster, casualty losses,
112-114, 115
disclosure of information,
tax preparers, 40
discriminate function (DIF),
314
distance, moving expenses, 53
distortion of income, 101
distributions (trusts),
definition, 301
dividend exclusion, 20, 63, 181, 268
dividends:
executive loans, 145
gross income, 50
insurance, 306-307
loans and, 253
real estate corporations, 213
wage-price controls, 257
divorce, 63, 83
doctors. *See* physicians
document locator number, 312
Domestic International Sales
Corporation (DISC), 256-257
drugs, deductions, 109
dues and memberships, outside
salesmen, 178

E
EDA. *See* Excess Deductions
Account
earned income ceiling, 88
earned income credit, 65, 71
Economic Stabilization Act of
1971, 257
education expenses, 118-119
"elections" (tax law), definition,
237
employes:
business expenses, 54,
110-111, 121-122
incorporation and, 251-252
Keogh plan, 250
moving expenses, 25
outside salesman, 175-179
tax savings, 121-139
three-year rule, 288-289
who is self-employed, 236
woman who works, 165-173
engineer, education expenses,
119
entertainment, expense account
deductions, 156, 158
equipment:
depreciation, 223-233
investment credit, 70
tax credit, 26

equity:
condominiums, 208
pension plans, 125
errors on tax returns, 311
estate tax, 305, 307:
giving while living, 299-301
incorporation and, 267
pension funds and, 263-264
estimated tax declaration,
75-76, 80
ethics, evasion and avoidance, 35
Excess Deductions Account (EDA),
278
excess investment interest, 216:
definition, 100-101
tax preference and, 154
excess percentage depletion, 153
excess profits tax, 34
exchange of property, 204-205, 283
exclusions from income. *See*
income exclusions
executives, tax savings, 141-163
exemptions. *See* personal
exemptions
expense account deductions, 155
"expensed" outlays, 274
export goods, DISC, 257
extension of time, tax returns, 77

F
"faculty tax," 32
"fair market value," 104, 206
family. *See also* married couples
dividend exclusion and, 20
income diversion, 24
planning for security, 299-309
splitting income, 81
farm loss, 275
farmers, tax savings, 273-283
fees:
attorney, 38
professional incorporation, 266
feminism, women's groups and
taxes, 172-173
field audit, 321-322
field audits, definition, 312
filing, who files, 45
finance charges. *See* interest
payments
fire, losses, 111
firemen, disability retirement, 123
first year depreciation allowance,
232
fiscal year, 242, 266, 268
fix-up costs, house sales and, 200
flower bonds, 194

foreign income, 47, 70
foreign taxes, 95, 97
foreign travel, per diem, 132-133
forms:
    Form 1040, 31, 37, 44, 46, 51,
        64, 73-89, 246, 316
    Form 1040A, 31, 40, 46, 73-74,
        286, 292
    Form 1040-ES, 76
    Form 1040-X, 94, 116
    Form 1065, 187, 246
    Form 1116, 79
    Form 1120X, 116
    Form 2106, 176
    Form 2120, 64
    Form 2440, 79
    Form 2555, 47
    Form 2688, 77
    Form 2950SE, 55
    Form 3468, 79
    Form 3903, 54, 79
    Form 4136, 133
    Form 4255, 79
    Form 4506, 89
    Form 4625, 79
    Form 4683, 70
    Form 4782, 53-54
    Form 4832, 232
    Form 4868, 77, 79
    Form 4875, 108
    Form W-2, 48, 49, 50, 54, 74
    Form W-4, 75, 170
    Form W-4E, 46, 76
    Form W-4P, 75, 290
    what forms to use, table, 78-79
foster child, 63
foundations (tax exempt), 146
fraud, field audit and, 321-322
fringe benefits, 18-19:
    business and professional men,
        254
    employes' deductions, 122-125
    executives, 141-163
    gross income and, 50
    outside salesmen, 176-178
"fruit of the tree" principle, 50
furniture:
    depreciation, 226
    used, donation to charity, 104

G
gainfully employed, definition,
    170
gasoline taxes, 23, 96, 133
general sales tax, 96
"gentleman farmer," 273

gift tax, giving while living,
    300, 305
gifts:
    appreciated property, 104, 106
    business gifts, 157
    deductions for charitable
        giving, 101-108
    dependent parents and, 63
    merchandise to charity, 106
    retirement and, 287
"give-up deduction," 57
"giving while living," 299-306
goodwill entertainment, 159
goodwill payments, 248, 270
graduated income tax theory, 29
gross income, 45-46, 48, 49
guidance for tax questions, 37-41

H
Hand, Learned, 37
handicapped children, 110
harvests, selling a farm, 283
head of household, 82, 84:
    separated, married persons, 85
    sin tax and, 168
    woman who works, 166
health and hospitalization
        insurance, 109:
    accident insurance, 109
    fringe benefit, 18
    outside salesmen, 176-178
    professional incorporation
        and, 268
    sick pay exclusion, 51-52
"hobby farmer," 273, 279
homeowners:
    owning vs. renting, 92-93
    sale of home, over 65s, 290
    tax savings, 197-205
hospitalization insurance.
    See health and
    hospitalization insurance
house-hunting trips, 22, 52
house sale. See sale of house
housekeeping, dependent care
    deduction, 171
housing:
    owning vs. renting, 92
    selling a farm, 283
    tax savings, 197-211
    used, 225
housing tax credit, 201
husband and wife. See
    married couples
hybrid method (accounting),
    241-242, 282

I
IRS. *See* U.S. Internal
    Revenue Service
income:
    ceiling tax rate, 150
    splitting income, 81, 117, 145
    tax credits and, 25
    tax-exempt, 287
    timing and, 16
    what is taxed, 48
income averaging, 17, 18, 86-88:
    capital gains and, 187, 204
    outside salesmen, 178
    pension plans, 128
    ten-year forward, 127
income deferral, 18, 147, 266:
    outside salesmen, 178
    professional incorporation, 267
    professional men, 243
    retirement and, 288
    stock options, 146-147
income diversion, 24
income exclusions, 25, 95, 290
income-producing property, 22, 24
income tax, ABCs of, 43-71
incorporated talent, 262
incorporation. *See* corporations
indirect tax, 33
industrial development bonds,
    193-194
inflation:
    investment credit and, 70
    taxes and, 15-16
    tax-exempt bonds and, 192
informants, 314-315
information:
    disclosure of, 40
    investment publications, 186
    tax audits, 322
in-laws, 62
installment method (accounting),
    241
installment payments, insurance,
    308
installment sales, 17, 203
insurance. *See also* health and
        hospitalization insurance,
        life insurance
    cash from corporation, 145
    casualty loss and, 112
    employe fringe benefits, 122
    executive, 144
inter vivos trust. *See* lifetime trust
interest payments:
    auto purchase, 131
    deductions for, 92, 97

interest payments *(continued)*
    investment, 100, 215-216
    LTP and, 154
    margin accounts, 186
    mortgage interest, 92, 98
    municipals, 193
    net return of capital, 48-49
    real estate investments, 215
    retirement and, 287
    service charge, 98
    U.S. bonds, 191
Internal Revenue Code, how it
    grew, 32
Internal Revenue Service. *See*
    U.S. Internal Revenue Service
inventory, 239, 240
investment:
    investor in securities, 181-195
    professional incorporation, 270
    retirement and, 287
investment clubs, 187, 248
investment credits, 25, 70, 112
investment interest, 100, 215
invisible tax process, 16
irrevocable trust, 302, 304
itemized deductions, 91-119:
    definition, 55
    Form 1040 and, 74
    itemizing and alternating, 60-61
    office at home, 136-139
    vs. standardized deduction, 17

J
Job Development Investment
    Credit, 25, 70
job hunting, women who work, 167
joint returns, 83

K
Kennedy, John F., 37, 234
Keogh Act, 21, 138, 249-251, 255, 260
key man insurance, 253

L
LIA. *See* Low Income Allowance
LTP. *See* limitation on tax
    preferences
land-clearing outlay, 274
land investment, 216-217
landscaping, 22
law:
    legal guidance, tax advice and, 37
    tax evasion and avoidance, 35
lawyers. *See* attorneys
liability, personal, 261, 268
life expectancy, pensions, 126

life insurance:
    executive fringe, 143
    family security and, 306-309
    fringe benefit, 18
    Keogh plan, 250
    key man, 253
    life insurance trust, 305
    outside salesmen, 178
    partnerships and, 248
    professional incorporation, 268
    retirement and, 287
    U.S. government life
        insurance, 295
lifetime trust, 301, 304
limitation on tax preferences,
    69, 150, 152, 193
limited liability, 268
limited partnership. See
    syndicate (real estate)
livestock, tax shelter, 275, 279
living costs. See cost of living
loans:
    bad debts and, 117
    corporation officers, 145, 253
    DISC, 257
    farms, 282-283
    mortgage interest, 99
local taxes, deductions, 92, 95, 130
long-term capital gain, 65, 182
"loopholes" for little taxpayer, 30
losses:
    capital losses, 69
    casualty losses, 111-116
    establishing a loss, 184
    "hobby farms," 279
    livestock, 275
    selling your house, 20
    sole proprietorship, 246
    tax loss time, 183
lots, land investment, 217
low income allowance, 64:
    reversionary trusts, 303
    underwithholding and, 169
low-income persons, 44
lump-sum payments:
    alimony, 307
    insurance, 307
    pension, 127-129
    retirement, 288

M
machinery, tax credit, 26
mail audits, 312, 317-318
management personnel. See
    executives
"managing executive," 161

market value, casualty losses, 115
married couples:
    assigning insurance policy, 308
    child care deduction, 171
    giving while living, 300
    incapacitated spouse, 118
    older persons, 285
    separated married persons, 85
    sin tax, 167
    tax planning, 14-15
    tax returns, 83
    tax traps, 168-169
    women who work, 167
material distortion of income, 101
"maxitax," 151
McGrath, Kathryn B., 167
meals, deductions, 156
medical expense:
    AGI and, 56
    deductions, 23-24, 108-110
    executive fringes, 144
    insurance payments, 91-92
    itemized deductions, 92
    travel, 131
medical expense reimbursement
    plan, 268
Medicare, 109
medicines, deductions, 109
merchandise, gifts of, 106
Merrill, Lynch, Pierce, Fenner
    and Smith, 187
microfilmed records, 316
middle-income families, 30
mileage deductions, 130, 132, 158
mineral depletion, 153
miscellaneous deductions:
    bond premium, 190
    education expenses, 119
    investment clubs, 188
Money (magazine), 166
money-purchase pension plan,
    265
"moonlighting" (second jobs),
    22, 111
mortgage bonds, 191
mortgages:
    real estate investment, 199
    retirement and, 287
    vacation and principal
        residence, 211
mortis trust. See testamentary
    trust
mothers, child care costs, 170
moving expense deductions, 22, 52
municipals, 19, 63, 192-193, 194, 288
mutual fund rule, 195

mutual insurance, 306

N
negative income tax, 65
net cost (pensions), 126
net long-term capital gain, 67
nonbusiness bad debt, 116
noncitizens, tax liabilities, 47
notes, tax-free, 194
nursing care, 109

O
office at home, 21, 111, 133-138
office audits, 312, 319-320
oil depletion, 153
older persons:
    exemptions, 62
    farm sales and, 283
    house sales and, 20, 200
    medical expense, 110
    tax savings, 285-297
150% declining balance
    depreciation method, 224
125% declining balance
    depreciation method, 224
optional state sales tax tables, 95
ordinary and necessary expenses,
    51, 121, 237, 239
osteopaths, 108-109
out-of-country, filing, 80
out-of-pocket expenses, 102, 110
overpaying taxes, 29-41:
    itemized deductions, 95
    tax avoidance, 35
    tax refunds, 80
overseas Americans, per diem
    rates, 132-133
overwithholding, married couples,
    168-169
owner-employe, 250
owning vs. renting, 92

P
painting, office-at-home, 133
parents, 63
parsonage allowance, 46
participating insurance, 306
partnership, 26, 246-249:
    attorneys and, 269
    audits and, 314
    definition, 245
    investment clubs as, 187
    real estate investment, 212
    Subchapter S corporations, 254
    vs. corporation, 252, 261
part-time employment, 111

penalty charge, (loans), 21
penalty for prepayment
    (mortgages), 99
penalty interest, late filing, 77, 80
pensions, 124:
    capital gains from, 127
    elections, 288
    employes', 125-129
    executives, 154
    professional corporations,
        260, 265-266, 270
    reforms of 1974, 124, 127-129
    Social Security and, 286
    tax withholding, 75
    voluntary contributions, 268
percentage depletion, oil and
    mining, 218
percentage standard deduction, 93
per diem rate, 132-133
"periodic" payment (alimony), 117
personal exemption, 20, 33:
    adjusted gross income and, 57
    alimony payments and, 118
    increases, 62
    older persons, 285-286
    trusts and gifts, 303
personal holding company, 262,
    265, 270
photographs, casualty losses, 111
physicians, 22, 26:
    education expenses, 119
    medical deductions, 109
    office-at-home, 135
    professional corporations and,
        259, 269
pledges to charity, 104
"points" (home loans), 21, 54, 99
police:
    disability retirement, 123
    notifying of loss, 312
political contributions, 107
pollution, anti-pollution bonds, 193
pooling investments (real
    estate), 212
postponing income, 19
poverty level, 30
preliminary notice (tax
    assessment), 318
principal residence, 202
private foundations
    (tax-exempt), 146
prizes in a sales contest, 50
probate, avoiding probate, 304
professional corporation, 26,
    259-271
professional men, 235-257, 316

professional tax helpers, 38
profit, farms showing, 280
profit-sharing plans, 124, 147, 260
progressive taxes, 33
property:
    adjusted basis cost, 114
    ceiling tax rate, 151
    depreciation, 221-233
    use, 106
proprietorship, 26
pseudo-corporation, 254
"public accountants," 38
public-interest law firms, 108
publications:
    employes' business expenses,
      110-111
    investment information, 186

Q

qualified pension and
    profit-sharing plans, 123
qualified stock options, 153
questionnaires, mail audits, 318
"quiet meals," expense account
    deductions, 156, 158

R

raffles, 104, 107
rapid write-off. *See*
    accelerated depreciation
rare books, coins, etc.,
    charitable deduction, 24
real estate, 197-219:
    depreciation, 225
    income averaging, 89
    real estate corporations, 213
    tax savings, 205-216
Real Estate Investment Trust
    (REIT), 214
real property, write-off
    percentages for, table, 225
rebates, tax, 71
recapture procedure, 212, 227, 280
reciprocal ("quiet lunch"), 157
records:
    business and professional
      men, 237
    casualty losses, 111-114, 312
    errors on tax returns, 312
    expense account deductions, 161
    office audit, 320
    outside salesmen, 179
    records for audit, 315
    tax sales of stock, 185
recreational facilities, 158

relatives:
    bad debts and, 117
    child care deductions, 172
    "wash sales" and, 184
    what is a dependent, 62-63
relocation expenses. *See*
    moving expenses
remainder interest (trust), 305
rental property:
    condominium *vs.* apartment, 207
    house, 54
    land investment, 216
    owning *vs.* renting, 92
    real estate, 205, 211-212
    recapture problem, 227
    second homes, 208-209
rent-free use of property, 102
repair charges:
    business auto, 130
    rental property, 206
reserves, bad debts, 153
residence:
    capital improvement of, 217
    principal residence, 202
    revenue sharing, 74
resident aliens, 47
residential real property,
    depreciation, 226-227
resort property:
    condominiums, 206
    sale of, 200
restricted stock bonus plans,
    124, 146, 153
retained earnings, accumulation
    of, 269
retirement:
    clergymen, 46-47
    executives, 154
    incorporation and, 20
    Keogh plan, 249-251
    pension plans, 125-129
    postponing tax, 19
    professional corporation and,
      26, 263
    self-employed, 54
    Subchapter S corporations, 255
    tax savings, 285-297
retirement bonds (U.S. securities),
    250
Retirement Income Credit, 25,
    291-297
return of capital:
    definition, 48
    depreciation basis, 221
    house installment sale, 203

reversionary trusts, 302-303
revocable trust, 302, 304
revolving credit account, 98
"rich kids' amendment," 303
Rogers, Will, 216
Roosevelt, Franklin D., 262, 310
royalties, oil and mining, 218
Ruml, Beardsley, 34

S

salary payments, corporations,
    252-253
sale of business, 256-257
sale of farm, 283
sale of house, 199-204:
    age and, 20
    income-averaging, 89
    itemized deductions, 95
    moving expenses exclusion, 54
    older persons, 290
    "points," 99
    records and, 315
sale of rental property, 211-212, 228
sales tax, 23, 95-97
salesmen:
    education expenses, 119
    outside salesman, 54, 175-179
salvage value, depreciation
    methods, 223-224
savings:
    not basic item of support, 21
    overwithholding as, 169
    planning for tax savings, 13-27
    retirement and, 287
    Social Security and, 286
schedules:
    A, 78, 121
    B, 78
    C, 78, 116, 119, 121-122, 135
    D, 78, 116, 182
    E, 78, 210
    F, 78
    G, 79, 87-88
    R, 79, 294
    SE, 79
scholarships, 62
"second election," (retirement
    income), 288
"second homes," 208-209
second job, travel deductions, 132
secrecy, 108
securities, investor in
    securities, 181-195, 315
"self-dealing" loans, 146
self-employed:
    businessmen, fringe benefits, 123

self-employed (continued)
    education expenses, 119
    moving expenses, 22, 52, 53
    outside salesman, 175-179
    retirement programs, 19, 25,
        54, 138, 194
    Social Security and, 16
    timing income, 18
    who is self-employed, 236
Self-Employed Individual
    Retirement Act of 1962, 249
"sell short against the box," 186
separate maintenance payments,
    117-118
separated couples, 83, 85
service and delivery personnel, 176
service charges. See interest
    charges
service industry, undistributed
    profits, 252
services, donation of, 102
settlement options (insurance),
    307
settlements. See tax settlements
"seven-year forward" averaging
    formula, 128
short form 1040A, 31, 74
"short-term" capital gain, 65
short-term sale (securities), 182
sick pay, 25, 51, 267
side businesses, executives, 145
signature, tax returns, 40, 83
"sin tax," 84, 167
single persons, 82, 84, 167-168
"sixty-five or over exclusions," 290
small business, incorporation
    and, 20, 254
small cash contributions to
    charity, 24
Small Tax Case Division (Tax
    Court), 323
Social Security, 167, 237, 286,
    291, 294, 296, 314
Social Security tax, 16, 109:
    F.I.C.A. employee tax, 75
    W-2 forms and, 75
soil conservation, 274
sole proprietorship, 246:
    definition, 245
    vs. corporation, 252
special agent (IRS), 321
splitting income. See income
spot-checking of tax returns, 313
Springer, John L., 37
standard deduction:
    definition, 55

standard deduction *(continued)*
    office at home, 136-139
    reversionary trusts, 303
    sin tax, 168
    vs. itemized deduction, 17, 93
state and municipal bonds, tax
    shelter, 30
state gasoline taxes, 23, 96
state income tax, 84
state sales tax, 23, 95-97
state taxes:
    business autos, 130
    itemized deduction, 92, 95
state transfer taxes, 97
states:
    local governments, 95
    professional corporations
        and, 260-261, 264, 267
statute of limitations, 70, 316
stock bonus plan, 124
stock dividends, 188
stock (securities), gain and
    loss on, 182-183, 254
stockholders agreement
    (document), 264-265
stockholders meetings, professional
    corporations, 262
stock-option plans, 125, 146-147, 153
storm losses, 111
straight-line rate (depreciation),
    158, 198-199, 222, 223
students:
    avoiding withholding, 76
    charity sponsored, 102-104
    tuition contract, 98
    who files, 46
Subchapter S corporation,
    definition, 245, 254-256, 261, 279
substantial improvement,
    definition, 217
"substituted basis," exchange of
    property, 205
sum-of-the-years-digits
    depreciation method, 224-225
support of dependents, 21, 63, 84
"surtax," 33
syndicate (real estate), 212

T
take-home pay, working wives,
    table, 15
tariff system, 32
tax avoidance, 34
tax counselors, 31:
    field audits and, 321
    office audit and, 320

tax credits:
    gasoline tax, 133
    political contributions, 107
    Retirement Income Credit,
        291-294
tax evasion, 35, 36
"tax farming," 276
tax preferences, 34, 36, 153:
    capital gains, 182
    LTP and, 152
    1969 Tax Reform Act, 150, 151
tax preparation firms, 40
Tax Reduction Act of 1975, 71
Tax Reform Act of 1969, 34-35:
    charitable giving, 101, 105
    deferred-income, 150
    depletion allowances, 218
    depreciation rules, 226
    farmers and, 276-281
    head of household, 82, 84
    municipals, 193
    older persons, 285
    pension plans, 127
    private foundations, 146
    professional corporations, 263
    property depreciation, 225
    real estate sales, 204
    stock distribution, 188-189
    Subchapter S corporations, 254
tax returns:
    errors on, 311
    filing, 77
    retention of, 238
    separate returns, 83
    who files, 44
tax settlements, 313
tax shelters:
    farming, 274-275
    Keogh plan, 249-251
    LTP and, 152
    "second homes," 208-209
    securities, 194
    self-employed retirement, 138-139
    Subchapter S corporations, 255
    Tax Reform Act of 1969, 106-107
taxable income definition, 48
tax-exempt bonds. *See* municipals
tax-exempt foundation, 146
tax-exempt religious, charitable,
    or educational organizations,
    123, 173
tax-exempt stocks, 189
tax-option corporation, 254
"taxpayers' revolt," 34
teachers, education expenses, 119

telephone, business expenses,
    111, 133, 135
testamentary trust, 301
theft, casualty losses, 112
"Thirty Unallowables," 319
"thirty-day letter," 322
three-year rule, 127, 288
thrift plan, executives, 154
timber lands, 219
time and timing. *See also* deadlines
    accumulation trust, 305
    alimony payments, 117
    audit records, 315
    avoiding probate, 304
    capital losses, 183
    deferring income, 147
    depreciation allowances,
        221-233
    expense account deductions, 156
    filing your return, 77
    fiscal or calendar year, 242
    income and deductions, 16
    insurance payments, 308
    itemizing and alternating, 60
    livestock holding period, 279
    moving expenses exclusions, 53
    mutual fund rule, 195
    outside salesmen, 178
    pension plan, 126
    prepayment of interest
        charges, 101
    real estate depreciation, 215
    recapture problems, 227
    reinvesting in home, 200
    reversionary trusts, 302
    selling your house, 199
    seven-year averaging, 128
    tax preferences, 153
    thinking in tax terms, 13-14
    three-year rule, 127
    trust's existence, 25
    widows, joint returns, 83
tolls, business travel, 23
training, new business, 237
transfer of assets, trusts, 301
transfer taxes, 97
transportation:
    blood donations, 102
    business deduction, 129
    medical treatment, 131
travel:
    business travel, 23
    church or charity, 24
    education expenses, 119
    employes' business expenses, 54

travel *(continued)*
    expense account deductions,
        156, 159-161
    for health reasons, 109-110
    moving expenses exclusion, 53
    to work, 129
trees and shrubs, 114
trusts:
    farm losses and, 279
    income diversion, 24-25
    pension plans, 124
    planning for family
        security, 301
    professional incorporation, 264
    splitting income, 81-82
    vs. tax-exempts, 193
tuition contracts, 98
turnpike authority bonds, 288
200% declining balance
    depreciation method, 222
two-year trusts, 106

U
Unallowable Items Program, 318
underpayment of taxes, 80
underwithholding, married
    couples, 168, 169-170
undistributed profits, 252-253, 263
U.S. Agriculture Department, 280
U.S. bonds, 191
U.S. Commodity Credit
    Corporation, 282
U.S. Congress:
    depreciation and, 199
    estates and gifts, 301
    private foundations, 146
    professional corporations, 263
    self-employed retirement plans, 55
    sin tax and, 167-168
    Social Security and, 286-287
    tax changes and, 17
    tax evasion and, 36
    "tax farming," 276
    tax policy and, 34, 35
    women's groups and, 172
U.S. Constitution, 16th
    Amendment, 32-33
U.S. Federal Trade Commission, 40
U.S. government life insurance,
    295
U.S. Internal Revenue Service,
    32, 36, 38, 40-41:
    farm tax shelters, 275
    free tax service, 74
    if you are audited, 311-323
    interest *vs.* service charge, 98

U.S. Internal
  Revenue Service *(continued)*
  partnerships, 248
  professional corporations,
    260, 262, 266, 270
  qualified pension plans, 123
  tax informants, 314-315
  tax records and, 316
U.S. President, tax policy and,
    34, 115, 139
U.S. Public Health Service, 289
U.S. Retirement Plan Bonds, 125
U.S. Savings Bonds, 287
U.S. Supreme Court, 33, 82, 162, 222
U.S. Tax Court, 32, 323
U.S. Treasury Department, 169,
    230-231, 276-277, 292-294
unlimited contributions, 106
unrealized appreciation, 49, 105
upper-income persons:
  charitable contributions, 101-102
  farm investments, 273
  fringe benefits, 122
  if you are audited, 311
  pension funds, 263-264
  tax avoidance, 34
  tax behavior of, 31-32
used clothing, furniture, etc.,
  donations, 104
useful life, 222, 231

V

vacation, expense account
  deduction, 159-161
vacation property ventures,
  208-211
vandalism, casualty losses, 21, 112
veterans' pensions, 287

Victory Tax, 34
Vietnam War, 34, 49

W

WIN. *See* Work Incentive Program
wage earners. *See* employes
wage-price controls, 257, 270
Walters, Johnnie M., 40-41, 164
"wash sale," 184
water and sewer assessments, 95
water conservation, 274
western states, 82, 85-86
White, Forrest P., 244
widows and widowers, 82, 289
wigs, 23
will:
  avoiding probate, 304
  life insurance trusts, 306
withholding system, 34, 75, 290
wives. *See also* married couples
  abandoned, 85
  expense account deductions, 156
  job hunting, 167
  working, table, 15
women:
  child care deductions, 118
  tax savings for working women,
    165-173
  women's groups, taxes and,
    172-173
Work Incentive Program, 70
work, Social Security and, 286
working wives, table, 15
workmen's compensation, 288
write-off percentages for real
  property, tables, 225

Y

young people, income averaging, 88